THE SYRIAN WAR

Starting in March 2011 as a civil uprising calling for liberal reforms, the unrest in Syria rapidly deteriorated into a proxy-led armed conflict involving multiple state-sponsored and non-state actors, including foreign militias and local armed groups. The current state of affairs in Syria and the uncertainty regarding its future raise numerous questions for scholars and practitioners of both international law and politics about justice within the context of a changing political reality in Syria.

This book contributes uniquely to the scholarship on the Syrian war, raising voices from the Middle East and beyond not often heard within this research context. The volume is divided into three sections: Part I sets the factual and legal framework for the Syrian conflict; Part II focuses on the implications of the conflict for the Syrian neighbourhood; and Part III analyses possible post-conflict scenarios. Together, they address the key themes and questions of the conflicts.

HILLY MOODRICK-EVEN KHEN is Senior Lecturer at the Academic College for Law and Science and Lecturer at Ariel University. She is author of *National Identities and the Right to Self-Determination of Peoples: 'Civic-Nationalism-Plus' in Israel and Other Multinational States* (2016); *Terrorism and International Law: Combatants and Civilians in Modern Battlefields* (2010, Hebrew); and articles in scientific journals in the fields of international humanitarian law, international criminal law, and philosophical-juridical interdisciplinary scholarship.

NIR T. BOMS is Research Fellow at the Moshe Dayan Center, Tel Aviv University, and at the International Institute for Counter-Terrorism (ICT) in Hertzliya. He is a member of the board of the Israeli Council of Foreign Relations and co-founder of CyberDissidents and the Tiyul-Rihla project. He is co-author of *Expact-ing Democracy* (with Peter Lang, 2016), and has written over 300 articles.

SARETA ASHRAPH is a Barrister specialising in International Criminal and Humanitarian Law. She served as Chief Legal Analyst on the International Independent Commission of Inquiry on the Syrian Arab Republic, documenting violations of international law in the context of the ongoing conflict in Syria. In 2017, she consulted on the establishment of the International Impartial and Independent Mechanism to Assist in the Investigation and Prosecution of Persons Responsible for the Most Serious Crimes under International Law Committed in the Syrian Arab Republic since March 2011, more commonly known as the Syria IIIM.

THE SYRIAN WAR

Between Justice and Political Reality

Edited by

HILLY MOODRICK-EVEN KHEN

The Academic College for Law and Science

NIR T. BOMS

Tel-Aviv University

SARETA ASHRAPH

Garden Court Chambers

CAMBRIDGE
UNIVERSITY PRESS

CAMBRIDGE
UNIVERSITY PRESS

University Printing House, Cambridge CB2 8BS, United Kingdom

One Liberty Plaza, 20th Floor, New York, NY 10006, USA

477 Williamstown Road, Port Melbourne, VIC 3207, Australia

314–321, 3rd Floor, Plot 3, Splendor Forum, Jasola District Centre, New Delhi – 110025, India

79 Anson Road, #06–04/06, Singapore 079906

Cambridge University Press is part of the University of Cambridge.

It furthers the University's mission by disseminating knowledge in the pursuit of education, learning, and research at the highest international levels of excellence.

www.cambridge.org
Information on this title: www.cambridge.org/9781108487801
DOI: 10.1017/9781108768016

First published 2020

Printed in the United Kingdom by TJ International Ltd. Padstow Cornwall

A catalogue record for this publication is available from the British Library.

ISBN 978-1-108-48780-1 Hardback

To my children, Itamar and Yael, who were privileged to live a peaceful life – but whose hearts and minds are with those who were not – and to all those who suffered from the miseries of war

Hilly Moodrick-Even Khen

To my Israeli and Syrian partners who together were able to save lives during a bleeding period of horror

Nir T. Boms

For my parents, Azad and Sarah Ashraph

Sareta Ashraph

CONTENTS

CONTRIBUTORS

KAMAL ALABWANI, MD, is a Syrian human rights activist and a prominent member of the Syrian opposition movement. He became an opponent of the Baathist rule in 1981 (when Hafez al-Assad was ruling Syria), having witnessed the Hama massacre, during his compulsory military service as an MD. After Bashar al-Assad became President, Dr. Allabwani took part in meetings of activists who called for political reforms and the strengthening of civil society and institutions – later known as the "Damascus Spring" events of 2000–2001 – and founded the Syrian Liberal Democratic Union. Dr. Allabwani was arrested twice for those actions and spent nine years in prison (2001–2004; 2005–2011), three of which were in solitary confinement. He continues his activism in exile and lectures on his views of the Syrian war worldwide.

SARETA ASHRAPH is a barrister specialising in international criminal and international humanitarian law. In 2017, she worked with the International, Impartial and Independent Mechanism for Syria, established by the General Assembly. From May 2012 to November 2016, she was Chief Legal Analyst on the UN Commission of Inquiry on Syria. She continues to work as a senior consultant on projects dedicated to pursuing criminal accountability for crimes committed in Syria and for the empowerment of Syrian civil society.

LINA BISCAIA is the coordinator of the Reporting Unit of the Human Rights Section of the UN Mission on Justice Support in Haiti. She is a lawyer specialising in international criminal law, international humanitarian law, and international human rights law. Her vast experience includes working with the Investigations Division of the Office of the Prosecutor of the International Criminal Court, the Office of the Prosecutor of the UN International Criminal Tribunal for the former Yugoslavia, and, more recently, the UN Commission of Inquiry on the 2014 Gaza conflict and the UN Commission of Inquiry on the

Syrian Arab Republic. She holds a degree in law from the University of Coimbra, Portugal, and a master's degree in human rights from the European Inter-University Centre for Human Rights, Venice.

NIR T. BOMS is a Professor of Political Science, Research Fellow, and Director of Special Programs at Dayan Center for Middle Eastern and African Studies as well as coordinator of TAU workshop on Israel and the Middle East. Dr. Boms is also a social activist, and in 2009 he co-founded CyberDissidents (www.movements.org), NYC/Israel, an international non-profit organization dedicated to supporting dissidents and democracy activists in the Middle East by providing a cyberspace and physical platform for the dissemination of messages.

AMICHAI COHEN is Professor of International Law at Ono Academic College and a Senior Fellow at the Israel Democracy Institute where he is Director of the National Security and Democracy program. His research areas are international law of the use of force, international humanitarian law, and national security law. He is a graduate of Hebrew University (LLB) and Yale Law School (LLM, JSD).

FRANCESCO FARINELLI is Programme Manager of the European Foundation for Democracy. His work focuses on the role of ideology, propaganda, and fake news in radicalisation processes. Farinelli earned a bachelor's degree in Performing Arts and a master's degree from the University of Bologna, Italy. In 2013 he completed his doctorate in History in the framework of the joint international programme on 'Humanism, Neo-Humanism and Post-Humanism in the Age of Media', at the University of Bologna and Brown University (USA).

TOM GAL is a research and teaching assistant at the Geneva Academy of Humanitarian Law and Human Rights. She is a PhD candidate at the University of Geneva and a grantee of the Swiss National Science Foundation's Marie Heim-Vögtlin grant. She is also the co-founder and vice-chair of ALMA – the Association for the Promotion of International Humanitarian Law. Her research focuses on the territorial control of non-state armed groups and its implications in international law.

SIRWAN KAJJO is a Syrian Kurdish affairs analyst and journalist based in Washington DC. He previously worked for Voice of America (VOA), where he focused on violent extremism in the Middle East. Prior to VOA, he worked at Caerus Associates, a research company through which he conducted research on local governance and security in Syria.

MORAN LEVANONI is a PhD candidate at the Zvi Yavetz School of Historical Studies in Tel Aviv University and a research assistant at the Dayan Center for Middle Eastern and African Studies, specialising in contemporary Syria and Lebanon. The subject of his doctoral dissertation is the Shiʾite community in *Bilad al-Sham* and Mandatory Lebanon and the construction of modern Lebanon (1918–1946).

HILLY MOODRICK-EVEN KHEN (LLD, Hebrew University of Jerusalem) is Senior Lecturer at the Academic College for Law and Science and Lecturer at Ariel University. Her research and teaching focus on international humanitarian law, international criminal law, and philosophical-juridical interdisciplinary scholarship. Among her publications are *National Identities and the Right to Self-Determination of Peoples: 'Civic-Nationalism-Plus' in Israel and Other Multinational States* (Brill/Nijhoff, 2016) and *Terrorism and International Law: Combatants and Civilians in Modern Battlefields* (Hebrew University of Jerusalem, 2010).

JOEL PARKER (PhD, Tel Aviv University) is the internship and visiting scholars manager at the Moshe Dayan Center and the deputy managing editor of *Bustan: The Middle East Book Review* (PSU Press). His research often utilises a biographical framework to analyse politics and society in contemporary Syria and Lebanon.

BETH VAN SCHAACK is Leah Kaplan Visiting Professor in Human Rights at Stanford Law School and a faculty fellow with the Handa Center for Human Rights and International Justice at Stanford University. She was a fellow at the Center for Advanced Study in the Behavioral Sciences at Stanford University for the 2017–2018 academic year. Prior to returning to academia, she served as Deputy to the Ambassador-at-Large for War Crimes Issues in the Office of Global Criminal Justice of the US Department of State.

YAEL SIMAN (Doctor of Political Science, University of Chicago) holds the A. G. Leventis Chair on Cyprus Studies, Anáhuac University, and teaches at Iberoamericana University and Instituto Tecnológico Autónomo de México. Her research interests concern the experiences and narratives of victims of genocide and mass violence.

EYAL ZISSER is Vice Rector of Tel Aviv University and the holder of the Yona and Dina Ettinger Chair in Contemporary History of the Middle East. He was Director of the Moshe Dayan Center for Middle Eastern and African Studies 2007–2010 and head of the Department of Middle Eastern and African History. He wrote extensively on the history and the modern politics of Syria and Lebanon and the Arab–Israeli conflict.

ABBREVIATIONS

CoI Syria	Independent Impartial Commission of Inquiry on the Syrian Arab Republic
ECHR	European Convention for the Protection of Human Rights and Fundamental Freedoms
ECtHR	European Court of Human Rights
FSA	Free Syrian Army
IAC	International Armed Conflict
IDF	Israel Defence Forces
IDPs	Internally Displaced Persons
ICC	International Criminal Court
ICRC	International Committee of the Red Cross
ICTR	International Criminal Tribunal for Rwanda
ICTY	International Criminal Tribunal for the former Yugoslavia
IHL	International Humanitarian Law
ILC	International Law Commission
ISIS	Islamic State of Iraq and Syria
NIAC	Non-International Armed Conflict
KDP	Kurdistan Democratic Party
KDP-S	Kurdistan Democratic Party of Syria
KNC	Kurdish National Council
KRG	Kurdistan Regional Government of Iraq
NGOs	Non-Governmental Organisations
OPCW-UN	Organisation for the Prohibition of Chemical Weapons – United Nations Joint Mission
PDKS	Kurdish Progressive Democratic Party in Syria
PKK	Kurdistan Workers' Party
PUK	Patriotic Union of Kurdistan
PYD	Democratic Union Party
SDP	Syrian Democratic Forces
TEV-DEM	Democratic Society Movement
TFEU	Treaty on the Functioning of the European Union

UDHR	Universal Declaration of Human Rights
UNHCR	United Nations High Commissioner for Refugees
UNSC	United Nations Security Council
USHMM	United States Holocaust Memorial Museum
YPG	People's Protection Unit

TABLE OF TREATIES

TABLE OF CASES

ICJ Cases

ICC Cases

EctHR Cases

ICTY Cases

Prosecutor *v.* Blaskić, Case No. IT-95-14-A, Appeals Judgment/Appeals Chamber Judgment, 29 July 2004. p. 111, 112, 114
Prosecutor *v.* Jelisić, Case No. IT-95-10-T, Trial Judgment, 14 December 1999. p. 112
Prosecutor *v.* Jelisić, Case No. IT-95-10-A, Appeals Judgment, 5 July 2001. p. 127
Prosecutor *v.* Haradinaj, Case No. IT-04-84, Trial Chamber Judgment, 3 April 2008. p. 31, 44, 46.
Prosecutor *v.* Kordić and Cerkez, Case No. IT-95-14-2-A, Trial Judgment, Appeals Judgement, 17 December 1994. p. 111
Prosecutor *v.* Kordić and Cerkez, Case No. IT-95-14-2-T, Trial Judgment, 26 February 2001. p. 112
Prosecutor *v.* Krstić, Case No. IT-98-33-T, Judgment, 2 August 2001. p. 128, 130, 131
Prosecutor *v.* Naletilić and Martinovic, Case No. IT-98-34-T, Trial Chamber Judgment, 31 March 2003. p. 38, 39, 112
Prosecutor *v.* Prlić, Case No. IT-04-74-74-T, Trial Chamber Judgment, 29 May 2013. p. 40
Prosecutor *v.* Stakić, Case No. IT-97-24-T, Trial Chamber Judgment, 31 July 2003. p. 130
Prosecutor *v.* Tadić, Case No. IT-94-1-AR72, Decision on the Defence Motion for Interlocutory Appeal on Jurisdiction, 2 October 1995. p. 30, 31, 34, 46, 83
Prosecutor *v.* Tadić, Case No. IT-94-1-T, Opinion and Judgment, 7 May 1997. p. 111
Prosecutor *v.* Tadić, Case No. IT-94-1-A, Appeals Chamber Judgment, 15 July 1999. p. 42

ICTR Cases

Prosecutor *v.* Akayesu, Case No. ICTR-96-4-T, Trial Chamber Judgment, 2 September 1998. p. 127, 135, 137
Prosecutor *v.* Kayishema, ICTR-95-1, Trial Chamber Judgment, 21 May 1999. p. 136
Prosecutor *v.* Muvunyi, Case No. ICTR-00-55A-T, Trial Chamber Judgment, 12 September 2006. p. 111

Other courts

Israel, Military Court sitting in Ramallah, Military Prosecutor *v.* Omar Mahmud Kassem and Others, Judgment, 13 April 1969. p. 93

1

Introduction

An Overview of Stakeholders and Interests

HILLY MOODRICK-EVEN KHEN, NIR T. BOMS, AND SARETA ASHRAPH

In March 2011, inspired in part by the 'Arab Spring', protests erupted on the streets of the Syrian Arab Republic (referred to as 'Syria' throughout this volume). The Syrian government's harsh reaction turned the protests into a rebellion which quickly descended into one of the bloodiest and most brutal armed conflicts in the modern history of the Middle East. After eight years of death and destruction, the Syrian conflict appears to be coming to an end, with the government, still led by President Bashar al-Assad, regaining effective control of much of the territory of Syria.

Throughout the combat years, the conflict evolved and changed shape and form at an unimaginable pace. In 2011, the protests spread from the southern city of Daraa and moved north to Aleppo and the north-east. When the protests acquired a militant nature, shedding their previously civil character, the Free Syrian Army (FSA), a militia composed of officers who defected from the Syrian military, took the lead, though ultimately without ability to maintain a unified command structure. The quick pace of events and the dissipation of the Syrian military attracted other players to the Syrian arena, including Islamist-jihadist groups such as the al-Nusra Front, Jeish al Islam, and the Islamic State of Iraq and Syria (ISIS). Kurdish forces in the north and north-east of the country, who have had an opportunity to renew their historical interest in gaining independence, also entered the battlefield.

By 2013, the war was marked by armed militias and proxy groups such as Hezbollah and Ahrar al-Sham supported by a growing list of foreign stakeholders from the region and beyond. The conflict thus obtained an international dimension with the involvement of foreign powers such as Russia, Iran, Turkey, and the United States, each aiming to secure their differing interests. It then took on additional complexity with the use of chemical weapons in early March 2013 and again with the rise of ISIS, which quickly captured close to 50 per cent of Syrian territory and established a capital in the city of Raqqa in January of 2014.

The turning point of the war began in September 2015, when Russia became actively involved in the conflict and utilised its air force to carry out relentless bombing attacks against the Syrian government's opponents. The Russian effort on the one hand and those of Western-led coalitions against ISIS on the other significantly weakened the remaining opposition to the Syrian government, and in 2017 the Syrian army – now significantly strengthened by Shiʾa militias – was able to retake control over most of territories previously lost. In 2018, the Syrian military, supported by Russia and Iran, was able to crush most of the remaining pockets of resistance.

Peace, however, or at least the absence of violence, is still some ways off. As of this writing, small pockets of the country – especially Idlib province in the northwest – are still held by anti-government armed groups as well as groups espousing jihadist ideologies; ISIS, despite having been driven from nearly all its territory in Syria and Iraq, remains a threat; and the Syrian and Turkish governments' responses to de facto control of areas to the north and north-east of the country by Syrian Kurdish forces are yet to fully unfold.

Nevertheless, despite the irresolute situation, it is also a vantage point that allows us to cast an eye back over the Syrian conflagration and analyse the events that have shaped the unrest and war. The Syrian conflict has been characterised by the complete disregard for international law shown by the warring parties. It is estimated to have taken the lives of over 600,000 Syrian women, men, and children; many more have been maimed, injured, and/or disappeared.[1] The war has led to the biggest humanitarian crisis of the twenty-first century, with over half of the Syrian population displaced from their homes and many suffering multiple subsequent displacements. According to the United Nations High Commissioner for Refugees, as of October 2018, over 5.6 million Syrians have registered as refugees, with the majority living in neighbouring countries. A further 6.5 million people, including 2.8 million children, are internally displaced.

[1] See the discussion in the final paragraph of Section 1.1 regarding the use of figures and measures in the volume.

The conflict quickly attracted a growing cast of players and stakeholders and, with them, a variety of agendas, priorities, and alliances. The result: the original war being fought between the Syrian government and anti-government armed groups metastasised, becoming a myriad of conflicts and sub-conflicts, a minor constellation of civil, regional, and internationalised wars. As the conflict spread and spiralled, conflicting narratives arose: Who were the aggressors? Who can be considered a 'rebel'? Who is defending Syria, and who represents its people? The debates extended to the arena of international law: Who intervened and under which justification? Was there a 'Responsibility to Protect'? Who should be accountable for the war crimes, crimes against humanity, and genocide committed during the conflict? And are there realistic options for transitional justice?

These and other complex questions are addressed in this volume through prisms of post-conflict justice and its regional implications. Despite the fact that all of the warring parties have committed significant violations of international law, by and large we focused on those committed by the Syrian government. The crimes of the Syrian government – as a chief accountable party and an organ which had significantly more resources at hand – were greater in scale and better documented and investigated by the UN and NGOs. Yet, we have also addressed one of the crimes committed by ISIS – the Yazidi genocide – due to its gravity and the evidence that was collected to support the allegations against ISIS.

The volume's multidisciplinary analytical approach sets the stage for the research and conclusions of scholars, experts, and practitioners on how the Syrian conflict fluctuated between justice and political reality. The intersection of the legal and political aspects of the Syrian conflict stands at the core of this volume's analysis and seeks to provide broader insights for understanding the conflict in all its iterations.

1.1 Use of Terms and References

The complexity of the issues discussed in the volume, itself an assembly of different perspectives and scholarships, raised editorial dilemmas regarding choice of words and terms of reference. These dilemmas were fortified by the dominant role that terms and definitions play in the representation of the conflict and its narratives.

As Syria is not a democracy, its government is often referred to as a 'regime'. In the context of the Syrian conflict, this term has nonetheless regained pejorative connotations, as it was mainly used by the Syrian government's opponents within and outside Syria to criticise the government. The word 'rebels' became fraught with interpretations as well, as for some it represented the 'Free Syrian Army' (FSA), a more moderate, Western-supported umbrella group of opposition, while for others it meant any group that sought to replace Bashar al-Assad and included those groups with Islamist-Jihadist orientations. The various belligerents and their supporters quickly tagged their opponents as 'aggressors' and 'terrorists'. The editorial task was to find a way to reflect some of those authentic voices while upholding academic standards of accuracy and research.

We have decided to use the more neutral term of 'Syrian government' instead of 'Syrian regime' in order to avoid the perception of bias and to focus the reader's attention on the description of actions attributed to the Syrian military and other organs of its administration. However, some writers preferred the term 'Syrian regime' and even 'Assad regime' when it better served their views of the conflict and its representation.

The word 'rebels' was used to address a broad set of groups intending to undermine the sovereignty of the Syrian government in any capacity. The interests, tactics, orientations, and ideologies of the rebel groups were, however, quite different and even contrasting. For example, while the FSA broadly sought a democratic alternative to the Syrian Republic, the objective of ISIS was to absorb Syria into the Islamic Caliphate they intended to establish in Iraq and the Levant. Moreover, as the war progressed, the different rebel groups (often with the encouragement of their proxy supporters) have opened new fronts against each other. Nevertheless, at times there was a need to use the term 'rebels' as a generalisation, though we have sought to qualify which segments are referred to throughout the volume.

'Islamists' is another term fraught with meanings and interpretations, as the religious dimension of the conflict was often incorporated by various groups having different perspectives and interpretations of Islam. The term 'Islamists' was largely used to differentiate between the group of protesters who formed the FSA (which was led, mainly, by defectors from the Syrian military) and the more radical groups who joined the conflict in a latter phase with agendas emanating from pan-Islamic ideology, such as al-Qaeda affiliates and ISIS. Another important distinction between the Islamist groups relates to their origin and local orientation. The Syrian Front (Jabhat al Nusra, later known as Jabhat Fath al Sham – standardised in this book as the al-Nusra Front) was a group of local rebels broadly focused on the original objective of 'regime change' while, as already stated, ISIS was not. There were also other Islamists who came from outside Syria to join the ranks of ISIS and other rebel groups.

Lastly, the use of figures and measures was likewise complex, since these were often contested, mainly due to the difficulties in conducting authoritative data collection as the war was raging. Numbers are often used as a primary means for measuring some aspects of the conflict, such as deaths and casualties, refugees and internally displaced persons (IDPs), and the number and quantity of foreign forces in Syrian territory. We are aware that measurements may sometimes be manoeuvred by the measuring source's agenda and affiliations. Therefore, we often used United Nations (UN) statistics, but at times we also used other sources which we considered credible to present readers with the most pluralistic picture possible. Naturally, as a result of the rapidly changing reality in Syria, numbers mentioned throughout the book apply to the time statistics were made.

1.2 Overview of the Chapters

This volume has twelve chapters in three sections, bookended by this introduction and a conclusion. It also contains an epilogue written by a participant in the events, a Syrian now in exile under political asylum in Sweden, who took part in the June 2000 'Damascus Spring' and later in the protests of March 2011.

Part I surveys and analyses issues forming the legal and political framework of the conflict, beginning with an analysis of the legal framework of the conflict. Following this Introduction, Chapter 2 by Amichai Cohen, addresses *jus ad bellum* issues within the conflict. Cohen discusses the legality of the use of force which occurred in the framework of the Syrian conflict, including the right to humanitarian intervention and the responsibility to protect. He also discusses a less-researched theme – the role of *jus ad bellum* in armed conflicts that are intra-state and transnational (i.e. between a state and a non-state actor in another country) in the context of the Syrian conflict.

Chapter 3, by Tom Gal, addresses *jus in bello* issues and delves into a legal classification of the types of conflicts created by the myriad of stakeholders in the war in Syria. The classification serves to enable understanding and analysis of the different legal obligations of the belligerents in the conflict and the implications of the classification for peace and justice in post-conflict Syria.

Chapter 4, by Eyal Zisser, is a portrayal of Syria's descent into conflict containing a description and analysis of the Syrian government's strategies in the conflict and the commission of international law violations. The chapter focuses on the Syrian government's leading role and, more specifically, President Assad's personal role in the conflagration. Zisser provides a survey of the development of the conflict through a prism that sees the conflict as President Assad's strategy of a 'total war' against his own people.

The last three chapters of Part I – Chapters 5, 6, and 7 – address the atrocities of the conflict – that is, war crimes, crimes against humanity, and genocide committed by the Syrian government and some armed groups. In Chapter 5, Sareta Ashraph focuses on violations of international humanitarian law which quickly became hallmarks of the Syrian war, in particular indiscriminate attacks, including attacks by governments and armed groups, and the use of chemical weapons on the battlefield. She asks whether the Syrian conflict represents a nadir in the international community's response to a war where international humanitarian law is breached with impunity and, if so, whether the value of the laws of war has been eroded.

In Chapter 6, Hilly Moodrick-Even Khen and Yael Siman survey crimes against humanity and genocide in the conflict. The authors provide a legal conceptual analysis of the two different international crimes – which share common features distinguishing them from ordinary crimes and yet are also legally distinguished from each other. Moodrick-Even Khen and Siman focus on specific conducts that form two of the most documented crimes in the Syrian conflict: the crimes against humanity of torture and extermination of prisoners in detention facilities of the Syrian government; and the genocide of the Yazidis committed by ISIS. The legal analysis is used to explain who, among the various parties to the conflict in Syria, is responsible for each crime and the justifications for the allegations against each party.

Chapter 7, by Lina Biscaia, is an analysis of gendered perspectives of sexual violence committed against women and men by the Syrian government throughout the conflict. Biscaia analyses the reasons why sexual violence was used, its consequences (which are closely linked to its reasons), and the extent to which government forces achieved their goals by using violence of a sexual nature. Biscaia also provides a perspective on the status and roles of Syrian women before and within the Syrian conflict.

Part II of this volume examines aspects of the conflict that go beyond Syria's sovereign territory, focusing on the spillover within Syria's neighbourhood. The first two chapters relate to non-Syrian stakeholders involved in the conflict. In Chapter 8, Moran Levanoni explores the involvement of two external entities – Hezbollah, a Lebanese militia, and Hamas, a Palestinian militia – in the Syrian conflict and their different interests within the Syrian conflict. Levanoni suggests that this involvement was facilitated by the political vacuum created by the conflict that quickly drew external powers into the Syrian arena. In Chapter 9, Nir T. Boms explores the relationship between Syria and Israel, close neighbours and yet formal foes. Boms analyses Israel's policy towards the conflict as it shifted from being a passive onlooker to a 'good neighbour', launching humanitarian operations while simultaneously being an active military rival against the Iranian presence in Syria.

The last two chapters in Part II address the Syrian refugees. In Chapter 10, Joel D. Parker examines the situation of the almost 6 million Syrians who live as refugees, predominantly in neighbouring states. Parker surveys some of what is known about the condition of those refugees. He argues that the international community should take a proactive and pragmatic approach that encourages host countries to absorb Syrians into their sociopolitical systems as much as possible to avoid leaving them in limbo for the undetermined future. In Chapter 11, Francesco Farinelli analyses the condition of Syrian refugees who sought safe haven in Europe. Farinelli offers a snapshot of the main issues related to the integration process of Syrian refugees in Europe, as well as of the good practices and policies implemented thus far, providing the reader with both statistical data and concrete examples in the form of testimonies from a qualitative research on Syrian refugees' integration in Europe conducted in 2017 by the European Foundation for Democracy (EFD).

Part III, the final part of the volume, contains two chapters that address the legal and political implications of a post-conflict Syria as it relates to the framework of the volume of justice and political reality. In Chapter 12, Beth Van Schaack examines the role of the international community in fostering pre-transition transitional justice in Syria. Van Schaack explores the origins and internationalisation of the field of transitional justice and ponders the future of, and possibilities for, transitional justice in a Syrian state still ruled by President Assad. In Chapter 13, Sirwan Kajjo offers a survey of the Kurdish community in Syria, which has expressed autonomous ambitions for a long time, partly as a result of the regional Kurdish movement for independence in Turkey and Iraq.

Kajjo's chapter provides a historical perspective and an assessment of possible post-war scenarios, suggesting that political fragmentation within the Syrian Kurdish community and their respective regional and political patrons may undermine their chance for autonomy.

Lastly, in Chapter 14, the volume presents an epilogue by Kamal Allabwani, a Syrian medical doctor, human rights activist, and political dissident. Dr. Allabwani became an opponent of the Baathist rule in 1981 (during Hafez al-Assad's presidency), having witnessed the Hama massacre during his compulsory military service as a medical doctor. In 2000, when Bashar al-Assad became president, Dr. Allabwani called for political reforms and the strengthening of civil society and institutions, later known as the 'Damascus Spring'. Dr. Allabwani was arrested for his involvement and served an overall period of nine years' imprisonment, during three of which he was held in solitary confinement. In this epilogue, Dr. Allabwani describes his perspective of the Syrian conflict and his vision for Syria – for the state he hopes one day his country will become but which, at this juncture, seems as remote as ever.

PART I

The Syrian War

Factual and Legal Framework

2

Syria: International Use of Force and Humanitarian Intervention

AMICHAI COHEN*

2.1 Introduction

The armed conflict in Syria is one of the gravest conflicts occurring in the world today. Since violence erupted in 2011, nearly half a million people, some of them soldiers and many more civilians, have been killed, and more than 11 million, almost half of the total Syrian pre-war population, have been displaced. Parties to the conflict include, in addition to the Syrian army loyal to President Assad, non-governmental armed groups, some of them supported by Western countries and Saudi Arabia; external non-state actors such as ISIS and Hezbollah; Syrian Kurdish forces; and armed forces of states such as the USA,[1] Iran, and Russia.[2]

* I would like to thank Stuart A. Cohen and the editors of this volume for comments on earlier drafts and Lee Tel-Ari for excellent research assistance.

[1] The Pentagon has estimated that there are about 2,000 US troops operating inside Syria, many of whom are engaged in active combat. See Charlie Savage, 'US Says Troops Can Stay in Syria Without New Authorization', *The New York Times*, 22 February 2018, www.nytimes.com/2018/02/22/us/politics/isis-syria-american-troops.html.

[2] For a map of troop distribution, see Thomas Gibbons-Neff, Jeremy White, and David Botti, 'The US Has Troops in Syria. So Do the Russians and Iranians. Here's Where', *The New York Times*, 11 April 2018, www.nytimes.com/interactive/2018/04/11/world/middleeast/syria-military-us-russia-iran.html; Talal Nizameddin, 'Squaring the Middle East Triangle in Lebanon: Russia and the Iran-Syria-Hezbollah Nexus', *The Slavonic and East European Review* 86 (July 2008): 475; CNN Middle East desk, 'Hezbollah condemned for "attack on Syrian villages"', *CNN*, 18 February 2013, www.bbc.com/news/world-middle-east-21496735; 'Russia proposes UN resolution on Syria; U.S. hopes to work with Moscow on draft', *Al Arabiya*, 15 December 2011, www.alarabiya.net/articles/2011/12/15/182807.html; BBC Middle East desk, 'Syria Iraq: The Islamic State militant group', *BBC*, 2 August 2014, www.bbc.com/news/world-middle-east-24179084.

In view of the immense casualties, as well as the involvement of the international community, it is not surprising that various issues have been raised regarding the international law of the use of force (*jus ad bellum*) in connection with the Syrian conflict. One of the most intriguing facets of the Syrian conflict, and perhaps the fact that drew the most public attention, is the lack of intervention by the United Nations Security Council (UNSC). As a formal legal matter, the issue is simple enough. The willingness of the Russian Federation to use its veto power over this issue means that the UNSC cannot reach any decision that would create obligations on other states to intervene.[3] Notwithstanding this formal legal explanation, the failure of the UNSC to intervene in the Syrian conflict is disastrous to the legitimacy of international law in general and the Council in particular. In response, some have renewed the calls to limit the use of veto power in the UNSC[4] or to reform it altogether.[5]

This chapter will not survey these discussions, which focus on what should have happened. Instead, the chapter will focus on the discussions regarding the legality of the use of force which did occur in the framework of the Syrian conflict. Particularly exhaustive are discussions regarding two issues. First is the right of State A to use force in self-defence against non-state actors (NSAs) who are operating in State B without State B's consent (such as in the context of US actions against ISIS in Syria). The second issue widely discussed is the right of humanitarian intervention or, as it is sometimes called, the responsibility to protect.[6]

This chapter will critically review current literature on these two subjects and apply them to the Syrian case. Additionally, the chapter will cover the less frequently discussed subject of the exclusive right of the

[3] Surya P. Subedi, *The Effectiveness of the UN Human Rights System* (New York: Routledge, 2017), 230.

[4] See statements by various state leaders on this matter: "References on the need for veto restraint by the UN Security Council in mass atrocity situations," Global Center for the Responsibility to Protect, 31 January 2015, www.globalr2p.org/media/files/veto-restraint-references-1.pdf.

[5] Nadia Banteka, 'Dangerous Liaisons: The Responsibility to Protect and a Reform of the UN Security Council', *Columbia Journal of Transnational Law* 54 (May 2015): 382.

[6] See, e.g., Chris Ford, 'Syria: A Case Study in International Law', *University of Cincinnati Law Review* 85 (April 2017): 185; Milena Sterio, 'Humanitarian Intervention Post-Syria: Legitimate or Legal?', *Brooklyn Journal of International Law* 40, no. 1 (February 2014): 109; Patrick B. Grant, 'Islamic Law, International Law, and Non-International Armed Conflict in Syria', *Boston University International Law Journal* 35 (February 2017): 1; Banteka, 'Dangerous Liaisons'.

recognised government to ask for international support.[7] Specifically, I suggest that current discussions of these issues are deficient because we lack a full understanding of the role of *jus ad bellum* in armed conflicts that are intra-state and transnational (i.e. between a state and a non-state actor in another country). Recent conflicts have raised awareness of this deficiency. This chapter will delineate the emerging general principles regarding the role of *jus ad bellum* in intra-state conflicts.

2.2 *Jus ad Bellum* Controversies

2.2.1 The American Role in Syria – The Fight Against ISIS

As of this writing, the United States, along with other countries, has troops on the ground in Syria. Their official role is to participate in the fight against ISIS.[8] As traditionally understood, international law permits one state to use force against another (including in the territory of a third party) only in two cases. The first is when authorisation has been issued by the UNSC under Chapter VII of the UN charter.[9] The second is in self-defence against an armed attack directed at the state. Article 51 of the UN Charter, which deals with the right of self-defence, expressly permits 'collective self-defence'.[10] Later developments in law crystallised the conditions for the use of the right of self-defence.[11]

However, there is an ongoing debate regarding the legality of the use of force in self-defence by a state against an armed attack directed at it by a non-state actor (NSA) acting from the territory of another state. Various decisions by the UNSC, especially after the 9/11 attack on the USA,[12] seemed to suggest that attacks by an NSA trigger the right of self-defence and trump the sovereignty of the state from which the NSA is

[7] Mohamad G. Janaby, 'The Legal Status of Hezbollah in the Syrian Conflict: An International Humanitarian Law Perspective', *Arizona Journal of International & Comparative Law* 33, no. 2 (November 2016): 383.

[8] See, e.g., 'U.S. Marines Join Local Forces Fighting in Raqqa', *CNN*, 7 March 2017, https://edition.cnn.com/2017/03/08/politics/marines-raqqa-assault-syria/.

[9] *Charter of the United Nations*, 24 October 1945, 1 UNTS XVI, Arts. 2(7), 24, 25 (UN Charter).

[10] UN Charter, Art. 51.

[11] Military Aid and Paramilitary Activities In and Against Nicaragua (*Nicaragua* v. *U.S.*) (Merits) 1986 I.C.J. 14, para 176, 191, 193, 195, 248–9. Compare dissenting Opinion of Judge Schwebel, para 165–7.

[12] United Nations Security Council resolution 1373, 28 September 2001 (regarding the 9/11 terror attacks); United Nations Security Council resolution 2249, 20 November 2015 (regarding ISIS).

operating. On the other hand, the Advisory Opinion of the International Court of Justice (ICJ) in the Wall Advisory Opinion[13] and its Judgment in the Armed Activities in the DRC (*DRC* v. *Uganda*) case[14] suggest otherwise. In these cases, the ICJ held that the only armed attack that triggers the right of self-defence is one launched either by a state or by an NSA that is effectively controlled by a state.[15]

Michael Scharf has suggested that the Syrian crisis contributed to the crystallisation of customary international law in support of a state's right to self-defence against NSAs operating from another country if that country is itself 'unwilling or unable' to operate against the offending NSA.[16] Scharf finds proof of what he calls 'a Grotian moment' in, inter alia, UNSC Resolution 2249 (2015), which approves the actions against ISIS in Syria and even calls for the intensification of the operation. Scharf claims that, in the light of the terrorist attacks perpetrated by ISIS in 2015 in France, Egypt, Turkey, and Russia, there exists universal agreement that the use of force in this case and in similar cases is allowed under Article 51's self-defence clause.[17]

2.2.2 Humanitarian Intervention and the Responsibility to Protect

Another problematic aspect of the armed conflict in Syria is the discussion of the controversial 'responsibility to protect' or the case for humanitarian intervention. The issue arose specifically around the response to the alleged use of chemical weapons by the government against the Syrian rebels. In 2015, US President Obama threatened to bomb Syria in response to the use of chemical weapons, a response that was avoided when President Assad committed to dismantling the Syrian chemical weapons arsenal under Russian supervision.[18] In 2017, and again in 2018, the United States fired missiles directly at several Syrian government

[13] Legal Consequences of the Construction of a Wall in the Occupied Palestinian Territory, Advisory Opinion, 2004 I.C.J. 136, 9 July 2004, para 138–9.

[14] Case Concerning Armed Activities on the Territory of The Congo (*Democratic Republic of the Congo* v. *Uganda*) 2005, para 128, 148.

[15] Legal Consequences of the Construction of a Wall; Legal Consequences of the Construction of a Wall, Separate Opinion of Judge Higgins, para 33–5.

[16] Michael P. Scharf, 'How the War Against ISIS Changed International Law', *Case Western Reserve Journal of International Law* 48, no. 1 (March 2016): 16, 30–38.

[17] Ibid., 37–41, 50–1.

[18] Eyal Benvenisti, 'After Aleppo: Humanity's Right of Self-Defence', *Global Trust Blog*, 27 December 2016.

installations in response to a reported use of chemical weapons.[19] The declared goal of those missile attacks was to deter the Syrian government from using chemical weapons.[20] True, the US intervention was limited, and one could say that, in comparison to the humanitarian crisis taking place in Syria, the US intervention was insufficient. Yet, even regarding this limited intervention, the legality of the use of force by the United States is debatable.

The position of the USA seems to be connected to a wider discussion in current international law regarding the right to 'humanitarian intervention', i.e. the rights of states to use force in the territory of another state in order to protect the citizens of the latter state from their own government.[21]

The legality of the humanitarian intervention is doubted because it does not satisfy the formal requirements of international law. According to the traditional view of international law, in civil wars only the recognised government can ask external powers to intervene, unless those powers can claim an independent right of self-defence.[22] Hence, there is no formal basis for the intervention of other states in an intrastate conflict. The only option for international intervention in a domestic conflict, if that conflict does not pose a threat to any other country, is the authorisation of the use of force by the UNSC.[23]

This interpretation has come under heavy criticism.[24] The result of this position is that – should the UNSC not authorise the use of force, usually

[19] 'Syria Missile Strikes: US Launches First Direct Military Action Against Assad', *The Guardian*, 7 April 2017, www.theguardian.com/world/2017/apr/06/trump-syria-missiles-assad-chemical-weapons; Harold H. Koh, 'Humanitarian Intervention: Time for Better Law', *AJIL Unbound* 111 (October 2017): 287; 'Syria Air Strikes: US and Allies Attack "Chemical Weapons Sites"', *BBC News*, 14 April 2018, www.bbc.com/news/world-middle-east-43762251.

[20] Ibid.

[21] Daniel Franchini and Antonios Tzanakopolous, 'The Kosovo Crisis – 1999', in *The Use of Force in International Law: A Case-Based Approach*, eds. T. Corten, O. Ruys, and A. Hofer (Oxford: Oxford University Press, forthcoming), 1, 13, 15–25, 27–30; Koh, 'Humanitarian Intervention'; J. L. Holzgrefe, 'The Humanitarian Intervention Debate', in *Humanitarian Intervention: Ethical, Legal And Political Dilemmas*, eds. J. L. Holzgrefe and Robert O. Keohan (Cambridge: Cambridge University Press, 2003), 15.

[22] Mary Ellen O'Connell, 'Continuing Limits on UN Intervention in Civil War', *Indian University School of Law* 67, no. 4 (1992): 903–4.

[23] UN Charter, Arts. 2(7), 24, 25.

[24] Daniel Bethleham, 'Stepping Back a Moment – The Legal Basis in Favor of a Principle of Humanitarian Intervention', *EJIL: Talk!*, 12 September 2013, www.ejiltalk.org/stepping-back-a-moment-the-legal-basis-in-favour-of-a-principle-of-humanitarian-intervention/; Sterio, 'Humanitarian Intervntion Post-Syria', 111; Koh, 'Humanitarian Intervention'; Banteka, 'Dangerous Liaisons'.

because one or more of the permanent members of the UNSC exercises its veto power – there exists no legal way to assist people even against severe crimes committed by their states. Many believe that such an approach runs counter to the basic values and goals of the international community, namely to protect people against wrongs committed by their governments.[25]

An alternative approach arose after the 1999 international intervention in the war in Kosovo. An attempt by the government of Serbia to carry out ethnic cleansing against the Kosovar population was halted by an international coalition led by the United States, which acted without approval by the UNSC due to a Russian veto.[26]

That operation – together with lesser-known interventions of the Economic Community of West African States in Liberia (1999) and Sierra Leone (1997)[27] – gave rise to the proposition that humanitarian intervention is allowed under international law in some specific circumstances.[28] The claim was that a new customary exception to the prohibition of the use of force is emerging. In a famous article, Daniel Bethlehem defined the position of the United Kingdom – the prime supporter of this position – and argued that humanitarian intervention by a state, even if the UNSC blocks the action, is allowed when three conditions are met:[29]

(1) That there exists convincing evidence, accepted by the international community, 'of extreme humanitarian distress on a large scale, requiring immediate and urgent relief'.
(2) That there is no practical alternative to intervention.
(3) That such intervention would be proportional, and that force would be used only for humanitarian relief.[30]

[25] Jordan Paust, 'US Use of Limited Force in Syria Can Be Lawful Under the UN Charter', *JURIST*, 10 September 2013, www.jurist.org/forum/2013/09/jordan-paust-force-syria.php; Sterio, 'Humanitarian Intervntion Post-Syria', 148–50.

[26] Franchini and Tzanakopolous, 'The Kosovo Crisis'.

[27] Danny Hoffman, 'The Civilian Target in Sierra Leone and Liberia: Political Power, Military Strategy, and Humanitarian Intervention', *African Affairs* (2004): 211.

[28] Christine M. Chinkin, 'Kosovo: A "Good" or "Bad" War?' *American Journal of International Law* 93, no. 4 (October 1999): 841–7; Sterio, 'Humanitarian Intervention Post-Syria'; Koh, 'Humanitarian Intervention'.

[29] Bethleham, 'Stepping Back a Moment'. After the April 2018 attack the UK issued a legal statement essentially reiterating the earlier UK position. 'Syria Action – UK Government Legal Position', *Policy Paper*, 14 April 2018, www.gov.uk/government/publications/syria-action-uk-government-legal-position/syria-action-uk-government-legal-position.

[30] 'Policy Paper: Chemical Weapon Use by Syrian Regime: UK Government Legal Position', 29 August 2013, www.gov.uk/government/publications/chemical-weapon-use-by-syrian-regime-uk-government-legal-position/chemical-weapon-use-by-syrian-regime-uk-government-legal-position-html-version.

However, it seems that there is no widespread support for the United Kingdom's position that such a customary exception to the prohibition of the use of force actually exists.[31] Most states would still want to see some kind of UNSC authorisation, even if only implicit, before using force in the territory of another state, even where that state is committing atrocities. As will be discussed in Section 2.2.3, a humanitarian intervention claim might be a cover for intervention in the self-interest of the intervening state. Hence, the Responsibility to Protect is interpreted by many as merely the ability of the UNSC to intervene in domestic conflicts, even if there exists no danger that these conflicts would trigger some threat to any other state. In view of the seeming inability of the UNSC to act in many cases, suggestions for reforms in the UNSC have surfaced.[32] Most of these deal with the elimination, total or partial, of the veto power of all permanent members of that body.

2.2.3 Russian and Iranian Intervention and US Support of Rebels

Conversely, perhaps even counter-intuitively, one aspect of the Syrian conflict seems to generate fewer controversies in international law: the intervention of the Russian and Iranian forces (and Iranian proxy Hezbollah) in the Syrian conflict.[33] The reason for this apparent lack of legal interest seems clear – it was the recognised government of Syria, the Assad government, which asked for intervention by external forces. In such instances, if the state itself, by means of its recognised government, requested international assistance, this assistance raises no concern in international law. The recognised government may 'consent' to international intervention, which would therefore not be classified as external intervention in the internal affairs of the state and hence would not be prohibited.[34] On the other hand, international support for the rebels would be considered illegal.[35] As such, while the US-led coalition justifies its intervention in Syria as self-defence against ISIS or as humanitarian

[31] See discussion regarding the UK statement in the United States, Dapo Akande, 'US Debates Regarding the Legality of Intervention in Syria', *EJIL: Talk!*, 30 August 2013, www.ejiltalk.org/us-debates-regarding-the-legality-of-intervention-in-syria/.

[32] Banteka, 'Dangerous Liaisons'; Koh, 'Humanitarian Intervention'.

[33] Nizameddin, 'Squaring the Middle East Triangle'.

[34] Yoram Dinstein, *War, Aggression and Self Defense*, 4th ed (Cambridge: Cambridge University Press, 2005), 113.

[35] Nicaragua case, para 115.

intervention in response to the use of chemical weapons, any military activity and intervention for the support of the rebels is illegal. The exception to this is limited to the provision of logistical support, which does not violate the prohibition on intervention in the matters of another state.

However, the legal rule is not so clear. Legal scholars differ as to the legality of intervention by external forces in civil wars, even when the intervention was consented to by the government. On practical grounds, it is not always possible to identify the effective government, such as when the government lacks control over the entire area of the state.[36] On normative grounds, Lauterpacht views intervention in civil wars as a violation of the right of self-defence.[37] Some governments commit violations of international law during civil wars, and it is unclear whether international law should continue to recognise the rights of these governments to receive foreign assistance while states are forbidden from assisting the insurgents, who might be the just party in the conflict.[38]

2.3 *Jus ad Bellum* and the Problem of Failed States

The discussions – namely, collective self-defence against NSAs, the right of humanitarian intervention against a government, and the exclusive authority of the government to consent to foreign intervention – are usually thought of as distinct discourses. However, there is a connection between these questions. At the core of all these issues is the role of *jus ad bellum* in current armed conflicts in failed states, as explained in Section 2.3.1.

2.3.1 *Current Armed Conflicts and* Jus ad Bellum

Jus ad bellum was formulated in an era dominated by armed conflicts between states.[39] In such conflicts, the damage caused to the fighting parties, and to other parties, was so great that limiting the outbreak of war was of paramount importance. Current armed conflicts are very different: they 'comprise . . . volatile mixes of both conventional warfare and

[36] Antonio Cassese, *International Law* (Oxford: Oxford University Press, 2005), 371.

[37] Hersch Lauterpacht, *Recognition in International Law* (New York: AMS Press, 1947), 233.

[38] Eliav Lieblich, *Intervention in Civil Wars: Intervention and Consent* (Abingdon: Routledge, 2013), 136.

[39] Oona A. Hathaway and Scott J. Shapiro, *The Internationalists: How a Radical Plan to Outlaw War Remade the World* (New York: Simon and Schuster, 2017).

insurgency, the use of both regular and irregular forces, the blurring of "front" and "rear" in battle'.[40]

Legally speaking, an important characteristic of such conflicts is that *jus ad bellum* has become nearly irrelevant. It is difficult to differentiate between the aggressive party and the one acting in self-defence. There is no clear starting point at which to decide whether the use of force is justified or legal.[41] In many cases, victory in these conflicts is very hard to define,[42] and the goals of the parties are unclear, making the application of the proportionality and necessity requirements of the legality of the use of force irrelevant.[43] In short, there is very little that is left of the rules of *jus ad bellum* in these conflicts.

Yet, even without clear application of *jus ad bellum*, international law does provide some framework for these internal conflicts. Owing to its traditional preference for stability,[44] international law gives a higher degree of legal protection and operational options to the formal government than to the NSAs fighting against the government.[45] For example, only a government may ask other states for assistance,[46] and only combatants fighting for the government enjoy the full protection of International Humanitarian Law (IHL).[47]

Furthermore, the respect international law has for the principle of sovereignty protects the state, even when in a situation of internal

[40] Eyal Ben Ari and Amichai Cohen, 'Legal Advisors in the Armed Forces', *Political and Military Sociology* 42 (January 2014): 125, 126; Rupert Smith, *The Utility of Force* (New York: Penguin Books, 2008).

[41] See Yael Ronen's attempt to apply the *jus ad bellum* test to the Second Lebanon War, Yael Ronen, 'Israel, Hezbollah and the Second Lebanon War', *Yearbook of International Humanitarian Law* 9 (October 2006): 388–92. Israel and Hezbollah were in constant conflict, and the major Israeli claim was that unless full force would be used, Hezbollah would simply go on threatening Israel. In non-legal terms this means that there is no sense in trying to point to the exact beginning of the specific conflict.

[42] Israel and the USA speak of 'exit strategy' from the recent conflicts.

[43] William C. Banks and Evan J. Criddle, 'Customary Constraints on the Use of Force: Article 51 with an American Accent', *Leiden Journal of International Law* 29, no. 1 (February 2016): 67–77.

[44] As the UN Charter stipulates, 'With a view to the creation of conditions of stability and well-being which are necessary for peaceful and friendly relations among nations', UN Charter, Art. 55.

[45] Lieblich, *Intervention in Civil Wars.*

[46] The identity of the legitimate government that can give its consent may prove to be difficult in complex long-term civil wars. Some approaches look to a formal test, whereas others look to an effective control or civilian protection test. Lieblich, *Intervention in Civil Wars*, 274–356.

[47] ICRC, Interpretive Guidance on the Notion of Direct Participation in Hostilities under IHL 9, 15–16 (2009).

armed conflict.[48] It is rare that the international community actually intervenes in the actions of the state against its internal foes.[49] As we have seen, even when NSAs act from within one state against another, and do so against the wishes of the former, the responsibility for halting these attacks usually lies with the state from which these NSAs act.[50] The same attitude is reflected in the reluctance of the UNSC to use its Chapter VII powers to intervene in internal conflicts.[51]

2.3.2 *The Problem of Failed and Fragile States*

The term 'failed' or 'fragile' states is used quite liberally by states, scholars, and NGOs.[52] An exact definition of the term will not be offered in this chapter;[53] it is noteworthy, however, that modern armed conflicts are accompanied by (or perhaps caused by) internal conflicts which cause the disintegration of central governments.[54] This trend usually goes hand in

48 Nicaragua case, para 202; Protocol Additional to the Geneva Conventions of 12 August 1949, and Relating to the Protection of Victims of Non-International Armed Conflicts (Protocol II), (1977), Art. 1(2).

49 The extreme case of such non-intervention is the UN failure to prevent the 1994 Rwanda genocide. On the UN apology, 'UN Admits Rwanda Genocide Failure', *BBC*, 15 April 2000, http://news.bbc.co.uk/2/hi/africa/714025.stm.

50 Robert P. Barnidge, *Non-State Actors and Terrorism* (Cambridge: Cambridge University Press, 2007); Quan Li, 'Does Democracy Promote or Reduce Transnational Terrorist Incidents?', *Journal of Conflict Resolution* 49 (April 2005): 278.

51 David Schweigman, *The Authority of the Security Council Under Chapter VII of the UN Charter* (Alphen aan den Rijn: Kluwer Law International, 2001), 178; Paul C. Szasz, 'Role of the United Nations in Internal Conflicts', *Georgia Journal of International and Comparative Law* 13, no. 4 (January 1983): 345.

52 E.g. Stewart Patrick, '"Failed" States and Global Security: Empirical Questions and Policy Dilemmas', *International Studies Review* 9, no. 4 (December 2007): 644, claiming that 'the concept of the "failed state" has suffered from several analytical shortcomings. These include the absence of clear criteria to define "failure"; a cavalier tendency to apply this single label to a heterogeneous group of countries; and inattention to the specific histories, trajectories, and regimes of the countries so designated.'

53 One extreme view: 'A failed-state can be identified as one in which there is a total or near total breakdown of the institutions guaranteeing law and order, even *within* territories controlled by different factions; moreover, a failed state does not have a body capable of representing it internationally in terms of *any* form of legitimacy, be it based on territorial effectiveness, democratic representation or otherwise.' Lieblich, *Intervention in Civil Wars*, 163 (emphasis in original).

54 Daron Acemoglu and James A. Robinson, *Why Nations Fail: The Origins of Power, Prosperity and Poverty* (New York: Crown, 2012); for an article summarising the main argument of the book, see Daron Acemoglu and James A. Robinson, '10 Reasons Countries Fall Apart', *Foreign Policy*, 18 January 2012, http://foreignpolicy.com/2012/06/18/10-reasons-countries-fall-apart/.

hand with the deterioration in the state's ability to provide security and basic services to its citizens, as well as with violations of human rights, domestic conflicts, and a diminishing sense of security. For the purposes of this chapter, the term 'fragile state' or 'failed states' will describe the situation when this process of weakening of the state has already significantly reduced the ability of the state to provide protection to its citizens. Usually, such states are also characterised by weak social and economic conditions.[55]

Armed conflicts in these fragile or failed states seem to raise different considerations on the part of external states. On the one hand, the claims of sovereignty and stability are less relevant in such cases. The existence of these states does not provide stability, either regionally or globally. Armed conflicts in these states can easily get out of hand and endanger the stability of neighbouring countries.[56] Additionally, these states do not perform their duties as sovereigns towards their own citizens.[57] The idea that sovereignty provides stability is clearly not relevant in a fragile or failed state. The formal understanding of the sovereignty of a state, and the desired result of stability and responsibility in international law, seem to be at odds.

Hence, it seems that many of the limitations which are usually associated with the reluctance of states to intervene in internal conflicts are lacking in the case of a failed or fragile state. This drives states, especially those involved in the conflict, to adopt a more flexible attitude towards the interpretation of international law. Usually, international law is interpreted in a way that invariably prohibits intervention by external forces.[58] In cases of failed or fragile states, interested states – and those that feel threatened by the domestic conflict in the failed state – seem to adopt a flexible interpretation allowing them to intervene.[59]

On the other hand, for other states, intervention raises a new kind of anxiety – the possibility of manipulation. Failed or fragile states constitute

[55] See the 'Fragile State Index 2017' of the Fund for Peace, which tracks many of the factors which are usually connected with the 'failed state' phenomenon: http://fundforpeace.org/fsi/2017/05/14/fragile-states-index-2017-annual-report/.

[56] James Piazza, 'Incubators of Terror: Do Failed and Failing States Promote Transnational Terrorism?' *International Studies Quarterly* 52, no. 3 (September 2008); Stephen D. Krasner and Carlos Pascual, 'Addressing State Failure', *Foreign Affairs* 84, no. 4 (July 2005).

[57] Barnidge, *Non-State Actors and Terrorism*; Li, 'Does Democracy Promote'.

[58] Lieblich, *Intervention in Civil Wars*.

[59] Ben N. Dunlap, 'State Failure and the Use Of Force in the Age of Global Terror', *Boston College International and Comparative Law Review* 27 (May 2004): 464.

easy prey for external forces. Their fragility is exactly the reason why states would want to intervene – and profit. Hence, the reason the international community would be wary of a rule allowing other states to intervene in fragile states is that these rules could be wide open to abuse.[60]

The major reason states refrain from fighting over their disagreements is not because of legal prohibitions but rather because of their cost-benefit analysis. Bargaining theory in international relations notes that war creates deadweight losses. In most cases, economic consideration would lead states to bargain over their differences rather than go to war. According to this theory, wars and armed conflicts occur when there is some 'market failure' which causes states to go to war instead of bargain over the difference.[61]

Regarding failed or fragile states, however, the situation is different. If in 'regular' wars states assume that other states, which have no direct connection to the conflict, would refrain from participating in the fray because of the costs they are liable to incur, a different assumption can be made regarding failed or fragile states. Here, the chances of external actors gaining from intervention might be higher. Because the state under attack is fragile and collapsing, other states might consider the possibility of sending troops or otherwise intervening in its affairs in order to achieve gains of their own.

The Syrian conflicts presents a good example of this phenomenon. It is widely assumed that Iran's intervention in the Syrian conflict was driven by its desire to achieve some greater degree of influence in Syria, as well as a direct land connection between Iran and Lebanon and access to the Mediterranean Sea.[62] A similar analysis has been offered concerning the Russian intervention in the Syrian conflict.[63] Russian interests in the region include the Russian naval facility in Tartus, as well as Russia's reputations as a reliable protector of its allies.[64]

[60] An example can be the conflict surrounding United Nations Security Resolution 1973 (2011) regarding Libya. Russia and China claim NATO countries infringed the right given by the resolution due to the fact that their attacks in Libya targeted the Gaddafi regime only and de facto assisted the rebels until the fall of the Gaddafi regime. That is a strong conflict regarding the content and use of an authorisation to act.

[61] E.g. James D. Fearon, 'Rationalist Explanations for War', *International Organization* 49, no. 3 (June 1995); Jack Levy, 'Theories and Causes of War', in *The Handbook of the Political Economy of War* (Edward Elgar Publishing, 2011).

[62] Nizameddin, 'Squaring the Middle East Triangle'; Zvi Magen, Udi Dekel, and Sima Shine, 'Russia in Syria: Between Iran and Israel', *INSS Insight no.* 970 (3 September 2017).

[63] Ibid.

[64] Simon Saradzhyan, 'Russia's Interest in Syria Is Not Assad', Belfer Center for Science and International Affairs, 21 October 2015, www.belfercenter.org/publication/russias-interest-syria-not-assad.

2.4 Adapting *Jus ad Bellum* to Current Conflicts in Failed States

The first sections of this chapter briefly surveyed three *jus ad bellum* issues that the war in Syria raises. The next sections discussed the phenomenon of the failed or fragile state and the problems that international law faces when dealing with failed or fragile states. Section 2.4 shall connect these threads, showing that discussions over *jus ad bellum* issues are actually an attempt to adapt international law to the problem of failed or fragile states and reflect the anxieties of states over the situation of failed or fragile states. As internal conflicts become more frequent, so will international law adapt more easily to the concepts suggested here.

2.4.1 Humanitarian Intervention

Humanitarian interventions seem to be an area of international law in which some thought has been given to the problem of *jus ad bellum* and failed states. The developments in *jus ad bellum* that are seen in the Syrian case reflect the realisation that a balance needs to be struck between competing interests. On the one hand, in failing or fragile states it is the interest and duty of the international community to protect the interests of other states and of civilians, more than in the case of stable states. On the other hand, a free hand that would allow states to intervene in failed states is also a possible consequence, which the international community wishes to avoid.[65]

In effect, states are concerned that the real motive behind foreign intervention is not the protection of the populace but rather the desire to bring about regime change, to achieve political gains domestically, or to weaken the position of a foe.[66] Due to the weakness of the attacked state, these goals could be attained without the costs usually attached to war.[67] As the attacked state is involved in domestic conflicts, the option of bargaining is unrealistic. Thus, the international norm should differentiate between 'legitimate' claims – those which are intended to protect

[65] Scharf, 'How the War Against ISIS Changed International Law'; Paust, 'US Use of Limited Force in Syria'; Bethleham, 'Stepping Back a Moment'; 'Policy Paper: Chemical Weapon Use by Syrian Regime', United Kingdom's three conditions.

[66] As in the example discussed in Note 55: Micha Zenko, 'The Big Lie About Libyan War', *Foreign Policy*, 22 March 2016, http://foreignpolicy.com/2016/03/22/libya-and-the-myth-of-humanitarian-intervention/. Nizameddin, 'Squaring the Middle East Triangle'; Magen, Dekel, and Shine, 'Russia in Syria'.

[67] See discussion in Section 2.3.2 of the problem of failed states.

persons from severe violations of their basic rights – and illegitimate claims, those based on the interests of the intervening state.

Consequently, in order to discover whether it is in the interest of the international community that force be used, international law should differentiate between the gains of the specific state and the gains and costs of the entire international community. Indeed, rules that were suggested and discussed earlier to limit occasions of humanitarian intervention seem to have exactly the desired effect of limiting such interventions only to those cases beneficial to the entire international community.

For example, the idea that humanitarian intervention should be limited solely to cases in which massive atrocities have occurred attempts to assure that the situation is serious enough to mandate international intervention.[68] The suggested rule that requires the formation of an international or regional coalition prior to intervention aims to ensure that the real motive for intervention is not the self-interested political gain of one state but rather the attainment of regional or global stability.[69] In addition, this rule significantly decreases the chance that a nation would intervene in order to further its own reputation as a powerful nation and deter its enemies. If other states join in the action, then the reputational gains resulting from the operation are shared among several states. The suggested rules regarding humanitarian intervention are therefore designed to take into account that the interest of the international community should be paramount, and the ability to intervene is limited in ways that prevent states from manipulating the rule.

In the Syrian case, there is a widespread unwillingness by the international community to intervene and protect civilians. It seems clear that all powers with a potential to intervene seem to want to gain some concrete advantage from the conflict in Syria.[70] In these circumstances, it seems that any external intervention would be suspected as an attempt to use humanitarian intervention as an excuse. Paradoxically, the fact that the new US administration shows very little interest in the Syrian conflict[71]

[68] The United Kingdom's first condition; see Note 30.

[69] Koh, 'Humanitarian Intervention', fourth condition; Also see Economic Community of West African States (ECOWAS), Protocol Relating to the Mechanism for Conflict Prevention, Management, Resolution, Peace-Keeping and Security (1999), Art. 1, 3(a), 3(h), 10(d), 21–2, 25–6, 52.

[70] Nizameddin, 'Squaring the Middle East Triangle'; Magen, Dekel, and Shine, 'Russia in Syria'; Julien Barnes-Dacey, 'To End the War: Europe's Role in Bringing Peace to Syria', *European Council on Foreign Relations – Policy Brief* (September 2017).

[71] Elliott Abrams, 'Trump the Traditionalist: A Surprisingly Standard Foreign Policy', *Foreign Affairs* 96 (July 2017): 14.

gives it more credibility to use the claim of humanitarian intervention in the Syrian case.

2.4.2 Self-Defence and NSAs

As detailed in Section 2.3.2, some scholars claim that international law recognises the right of self-defence against NSAs acting from the territory of a failed or fragile state.[72] This seems to suggest that international law acknowledges the need to develop tools by which respond to the fact that failed states require a different approach.

The concept of self-defence is notoriously opaque and open to manipulation. It is, and has always been, difficult to discern which party is the aggressor and which is acting in self-defence.[73] In fact, even agreeing on a definition for an act of aggression is still arguably under discussion in international law.[74] In many cases throughout history, it has been very hard to determine which party to a specific conflict was the aggressor.[75] Acting against NSAs only adds to this inherent ambiguity. It is difficult to identify specifically which NSA committed which acts, since membership and chain of command in these organisations are typically difficult to identify.[76] Furthermore, identifying the whereabouts of the NSA is also complicated, since these organisations move between sites and act from within civilian populations.[77] This ambiguity means that there is much room for manipulation. Once permitted to intervene in other countries for reasons of self-defence against NSAs acting from within that country, states could well exploit this ambiguity for their own ends.

Therefore, there exists a need to develop tools which would counter this possibility. Even if states are allowed to use force against NSAs attacking them from a failed state, this use of self-defence should be limited. One

72 See the Nicaragua case and the text before Note 11; Schweigman, *The Authority of the Security Council*; Szasz, 'Role of the United Nations'.

73 Lauterpacht, *Recognition in International Law*.

74 Yoram Dinstein, *War Aggression and Self Defense*, 5th ed. (Cambridge: Cambridge University Press, 2011), 124–134; Christine Gray, *International Law and the Use of Force* (Oxford: Oxford University Press, 2000), 179–82.

75 The United Nation, *Historical Review of Developments Relating to Aggression* (2003), http://legal.un.org/cod/books/HistoricalReview-Aggression.pdf; Lauterpacht, *Recognition in International Law*; Nizameddin, 'Squaring the Middle East Triangle'; Magen, Dekel, and Shine, 'Russia in Syria'; Zenko, 'The Big Lie About Libyan War'.

76 Heike Krieger, 'A Turn to Non-State Actors: Inducing Compliance with International Humanitarian Law in War-Torn Areas of Limited Statehood', SFB-Governance Working Paper Series, No. 62, C*ollaborative Research Center* (SFB) 700, October 2013, 8.

77 State Of Israel, *The 2014 Gaza Conflict: Factual And Legal* Aspects, May 2016, 73–97.

example for the limitation is the decisions of the International Court of Justice in the *DRC* v. *Uganda* case in 2005, in which the ICJ determined that Uganda responded in a disproportionate manner to the attacks on it from the DRC.[78] Another possibility is to allow states to respond only to NSA acts that can be classified as 'very severe', for example on the scale of the 9/11 terrorist acts in the United States.[79]

International law has not yet developed such tools. Scharf's claim[80] that there already exists an established international custom allowing an attacked state to use force against an attack by an NSA from a third state is premature. While the general right of self-defence in this situation might be recognised, the exact contents of the right need to be further developed along the lines suggested here.

The Syrian case provides a good example for the need to delineate the limits on the right to self-defence against NSAs. Turkey, for instance, bases the legality of its long-term intervention in Syria on claims of self-defence against NSAs.[81] There are, however, indications that its real interest is to block attempts by the Kurdish minority in Syria to achieve any kind of political autonomy, for fear that such claims would spill over to the Kurdish minority in Turkey.[82] This highlights the fact that any claim of intervention in a failed or fragile state based on claims of self-defence should be taken with a grain of salt. Any development of the right of self-defence against NSAs in such states should also include some mechanism to recognise cases in which self-defence is merely a cover for an attempt at political gain from the situation by the use of force.

2.4.3 Assistance by External Forces

Another area in which international law seems to have not adapted to new forms of armed conflict concerns the rights of external governments to intervene at the request of the government of failed states. Even in failed states, only the recognised government can ask other states for assistance, while rebel forces cannot ask other states to intervene.[83] In standard

[78] *Democratic Republic of the Congo* v. *Uganda*, para 147.

[79] In which 2,996 people were killed. The 9/11 attacks were the greatest attack on US land since the Pearl Harbor attack of 1941. They are also considered to have triggered the international community's battle against Islamic terror.

[80] Scharf, 'How the War Against ISIS Changed International Law'.

[81] Lokman B. Cetinkaya, 'Turkey's Military Operations in Syria', *EJIL: Talk!*, 20 February 2018, www.ejiltalk.org/turkeys-military-operations-in-syria/comment-page-1/.

[82] Ibid.

[83] Ronen, 'Israel, Hezbollah and the Second Lebanon War', 135–41.

situations (i.e. those not involving failed states), this rule makes sense. Respect for sovereignty as a means to achieve stability reflects the traditional position of international law.[84] However, this position makes much less sense in the context of intervention in domestic conflict in a failed state. In many such cases, the formal government is government by name only and possesses limited or no actual control on the ground. In these cases, applying the traditional rule of international law actually means that one party to the conflict (supported by the recognised government) is able to invite international forces to participate in the conflict, while the other parties cannot do so, without any interest of stability being served. This situation provides the government with an incentive to invite international forces to participate, simply because the other parties to the conflict would find it difficult to convince other states to intervene. Incentives are thus created that run counter to the interest of the international community. Instead of limiting the conflict to a domestic conflict, at least one party has an interest in internationalising the conflict, a situation which increases the chances of it spilling over to other states in the region.

The Syrian case once more serves to highlight this problem. The Russians wish to intervene in Syria in order to maintain access to the Mediterranean Sea for strategic reasons. The Iranians wish to create a land link with the Hezbollah and perhaps to open another front with Israel on the Golan Heights. Naturally, Israel and Saudi Arabia, threatened by these efforts directed at Iranian expansion, invest monetary, diplomatic, and military capital in order to limit Iranian influence in Syria.[85] The result is that the region is constantly on the verge of crisis.

The application of the traditional rule of *jus ad bellum* in this context requires thinking anew. One possibility is to adopt a position that forbids any international intervention in domestic conflicts in failed or fragile states, absent a clear authorisation on the part of the UN Security Council.[86] That solution would at least not incentivise other states to unnecessarily intervene in domestic conflicts. Eliav Lieblich suggested,

[84] Ben Ari and Cohen, 'Legal Advisors in the Armed Forces'; Smith, *The Utility of Force*, and accompanying article discussion to Note 40.

[85] Isabel Kershner, Anne Barnard, and Eric Schmitt, 'Israel Strikes Iran in Syria and Loses a Jet', *The New York Times*, 10 February 2018, www.nytimes.com/2018/02/10/world/middleeast/israel-iran-syria.html; Anat Kurz and Shlomo Brom, eds., *Strategic Assessment for Israel 2016–2017*, The Institute for National Security Studies (2016), 43, 68.

[86] Naturally, members of the UNSC, and especially the five permanent members, have interests too. Yet the veto power by itself provides some assurance that a decision of the UNSC cannot be adopted if it is in the interest of one specific member and not the others.

alternatively, that intervention in civil wars be subjected to limitations similar to those discussed in Section 2.2.2 regarding humanitarian intervention. Lieblich's view is that a failed or fragile state should be viewed as a place where, at least potentially, civilian society is at significant risk.[87] It seems that this view could be further developed to take account of varying degrees of government control and of actual danger to civilian populations. The stronger the government's position, the more flexibility it should be accorded to receive international assistance, since the chances of international manipulation decrease.

Of course, part of the problem is that there is no agreed-upon definition of a failed or fragile state. Even if such a definition could be developed, the international community should develop international law in a way which takes account of the different nature of these states and the need for solutions tailored to this nature.

2.5 Conclusion

This chapter claims that international law is in the process of adapting to new kinds of domestic conflicts taking place in failed states. It briefly surveys aspects of *jus ad bellum* which need to be adapted to these conflicts. These are: self-defence actions against NSAs acting from another country; humanitarian intervention; and the rule against international involvement without the domestic government's approval. All of these must be adapted to the new forms of conflict, and, in some cases, they are indeed undergoing such a process.

The current conflict in Syria reflects everything that is problematic about the current state of affairs in international relations (and to some extent also in international law?). The UNSC is under a permanent Russian veto and thus cannot act. Many states chose to intervene in the conflict under the cloak of legal claims but are driven by the desire to gain substantial advantages of their own from the deteriorating state of Syria.

In the areas discussed in this chapter, international law needs to be rethought. It should take into account the interests of the states involved and limit the intervention of foreign states in domestic conflicts, so as to prohibit them from exploiting the situation. Of course, altering international law would probably not change a whole lot on the ground, but it is a first step in the correct direction.

[87] Lieblich, *Intervention in Civil Wars*, chapter 8.

3

Legal Classification of the Conflict(s) in Syria

TOM GAL

3.1 Introduction

International law distinguishes between two types of violence: armed conflicts and mere civil disturbances or demonstrations. Armed conflicts are further divided into two types: international armed conflicts (IACs) and non-international armed conflicts (NIACs). This chapter identifies and classifies the different legal types of conflicts or violence that occurred in the territory of Syria since March 2011. Adopting the fragmentation approach, this chapter argues that both of these types of conflicts coexisted in Syria[1] and analyses them according to the legal classifications. Section 3.2 presents and discusses shortly the legal definitions of IAC and NIAC and addresses the importance of the distinction between them. Section 3.3 delineates the geographical and temporal scope of the discussion in this chapter. Sections 3.4 and 3.5 apply the theoretical discussion in the former chapters to an analysis of the conflicts that took place in Syria – international and non-international respectively.

3.2 Legal Definitions: IAC vs NIAC

An armed conflict, which is distinguished from mere disturbances and demonstrations,[2] was defined two decades ago by the International Criminal Tribunal for the former Yugoslavia (ICTY) as 'a resort to armed force between states or protracted armed violence between

[1] Hence, for example, the fact that Turkey operates along the northern border of Syria, or that the Western alliance operates in areas controlled by ISIS, does not affect the classification of the hostilities between Syrian forces and other armed groups.

[2] For a discussion of the beginning of the events in Syria in March 2011 as a civil unrest, see Chapter 5 of this volume.

governmental authorities and organised armed groups or between such groups within a state'.[3] Defining hostilities as an armed conflict entails the applicability of international humanitarian law (IHL) as treaty and/or customary law. IHL is the set of rules governing the conduct of the parties to an armed conflict, limiting the parties' use of force against each other and meant to serve the protection of victims of armed conflicts (i.e. the sick and injured, prisoners of war, and civilians).[4] It applies equally to all parties to a conflict, irrespective of which party was responsible for beginning the conflict.[5]

The ICTY also provided for definitions of the two types of armed conflicts: IAC and NIAC,[6] basing those definitions on the Pictet Commentary to the 1949 Geneva Conventions.[7] The main difference between the two is the identity of the actors. An IAC takes place between two or more states,[8] and IHL applies as of the first shot between two states or more. In a NIAC, at least one of the parties to the armed conflict is an armed group.[9]

Contrarily, and due to political motives of states, the threshold of a NIAC is higher and requires preconditions such as organisation and intensity.[10] In addition, a NIAC differentiates between two types of conflicts: those covered by Common Article 3 to the 1949 Geneva Conventions; and those also covered by the Additional Protocol II (AP II) to those Conventions.[11]

[3] *Prosecutor* v. *Tadić*, IT-94-1-AR72, Decision on the Defence Motion for Interlocutory Appeal on Jurisdiction, 2 October 1995, para 70 [Tadić 1995].

[4] Also referred to as hors de combat.

[5] For elaboration on the meaning of IHL, see Christopher Greenwood, Definition of the Term 'Humanitarian Law', in *The Handbook of Humanitarian Law in Armed Conflicts*, ed. Dieter Fleck (Oxford: Oxford University Press, 1995), 1–15.

[6] Tadić 1995.

[7] J. S. Pictet, ed., *IV Geneva Convention Relative to the Protection of Civilian Persons in Time of War – Commentary* (Geneva: ICRC, 1958), 46–47 [GCIV Pictet Commentary].

[8] Common Article 2 to the Geneva Conventions of 12 August 1949 [Common Article 2]; Commentary of 2016 to the Geneva Conventions edited by the ICRC (available online: https://ihl-databases.icrc.org/applic/ihl/ihl.nsf/Treaty.xsp?documentId=4825657B0C7E6BF0C12563CD002D6B0B&action=openDocument) [2016 ICRC Commentary] §§ 201–2.

[9] Geneva Convention Relative to the Protection of Civilian Persons in Time of War, 12 August 1949, 6 U.S.T. 3516, 75 U.N.T.S. 287 [hereinafter GCIV], Common Article 3 to the Geneva Conventions of 12 August 1949 [Common Article 3]; Pictet Commentary to GCIV, 35–37; 2016 ICRC Commentary §§ 384–92.

[10] In case the level of violence falls below this threshold, IHL will not apply and violence will be curbed by law enforcement measures (policing measures).

[11] Protocol Additional to the Geneva Conventions of 12 August 1949, and Relating to the Protection of Victims of Non-International Armed Conflicts (Protocol II) 8 June 1977, 1125 U.N.T.S. 610 [hereinafter AP(II)]. Two additional protocols were added to the Geneva Conventions (1949) in 1977 to develop IHL, mostly adding significant protections to victims of armed conflicts and especially the civilian population. The first protocol is Protocol

While Syria is not a party to AP II, other states which operate in its territory (such as France) are. The definition and thresholds provided by both provisions will be reviewed shortly.

A NIAC covered by Common Article 3 exists once a conflict arises between a state and an armed group, or among several armed groups. The armed group does not necessarily have to act against a state while based or controlling a territory within the state's boundaries; for example, al-Qaeda was operating against the United States while it was based in Afghanistan.[12] However, the armed group should be organised and the conflict should meet a level of intensity – that is, not sporadic incidents. The term 'organised' encompasses different indicators, inter alia, the existence of a responsible command, some insignia identical to all the group's members, and the ability to conduct concrete military operations. These are neither exclusive nor cumulative.[13] In this respect, two remarks should be made: first, the requirement of a responsible command is indispensable as this is a strong sign of organisation. Yet, it does not necessarily mean the existence of a hierarchical structure – that is, vertical hierarchy.[14] Second, while control over territory is not a sine qua non requirement, it can be a crucial sign of organisation, as well as of the group's ability to comply with international law.

Regarding the requirement of intensity, the jurisprudence first used the notion of 'protraction' aiming at the length of the conflict. However, as protraction of the conflict can only serve as a measure ex post, the ICTY changed this notion to the term 'intense'. A conflict can be determined intensive even if only one attack occurred (e.g. the 9/11 attack). What may indicate that the conflict is intense is the type of operations that are being conducted by the group (in other words, if it is sufficiently armed and organised) and the type of force the state needs to use in order to repress it. If the state's regular police forces are not sufficient for repressing the violence, then the conflict is considered intense. The ICTY later added more criteria for assessing the intensity of the conflict relating, for example, to its effects on the civilian population.[15]

Additional to the Geneva Conventions of 1949, and Relating to the Protection of Victims of International Armed Conflicts (Protocol I) 1977, 1125 *UNTS* p. 3, [hereinafter AP(I)].

12 See e.g. L. Blank and B. R. Farley, 'Determining When the Armed Conflict with Al Qaeda Started', *Just Security*, 11 March 2016 (available online: www.justsecurity.org/29898/determining-armed-conflict-al-qaeda-started/).

13 Tadić 1995; ICTY *Prosecutor* v. *Haradinaj* IT-04-84 Trial Chamber Judgment 3 April 2008, paras 41–52 [Haradinaj]; 2016 ICRC Commentary §§ 422–37.

14 S. Sivakumaran, *The Law of Non-International Armed Conflict* (Oxford: Oxford University Press, 2012), 170–2.

15 See discussion in Section 3.5.1.

According to AP II, the preconditions for a NIAC are even more limited. A NIAC will be subjected to the rules of this Protocol – assuming that the territorial state(s) are parties to the Protocol – only under the following conditions: 1) the conflicts take place between the territorial state and an armed group; and 2) the group controls part of that territory which allows it to implement the Protocol and carry out its military operations.[16] As explained by legal scholar Sandesh Sivakumaran, the level of control required is not high and is not similar to that required to establish occupation.[17]

The division of 'armed conflict' into two types – international and non-international – has been disputed in the last two decades by some commentators and states. They have argued for a third type: an internationalised armed conflict. This type describes a conflict between a state and an armed group, though only in the form of a cross-border conflict. That is, the military hostilities are not confined to (or do not occur at all in) the territory of the belligerent state.[18] This author does not subscribe to this view and supports, in this chapter, the view that a conflict can be either international or non-international; yet the non-international conflict may have some *internationalised* characters.[19] The importance of the dichotomic division is that a clear body of law is applicable – either that of an IAC addressed by the Geneva Conventions (1949) and Additional Protocol I to the Geneva Conventions (AP I)[20] or that of a NIAC addressed by Common Article 3 to the Geneva Conventions and AP II. A NIAC may become international due to the change in the actors' identities (and, to some extent, vice versa).[21]

To conclude this section, an explanation of the relevance and importance of the distinction between the types of armed conflicts is required. In many domains in international law and especially in international humanitarian law, the differences in the applicable law have decreased or disappeared completely. Regarding armed conflicts, however, there are some key differences between the different types of conflicts that should be taken into consideration. The first one is the applicability of legal regimes relevant in one type of armed conflict but not in the other. This concerns, inter alia, the regimes of protected persons,[22] occupation, and criminal responsibility for

16 Article 1, Protocol II.
17 Sivakumaran, 185–8.
18 Such was the case with the US fighting against al-Qaeda and the Taliban.
19 As provided by M. Milanović, 'The Applicability of the Convention to the "Transnational" and "Mixed" Conflicts', in A. Clapham, P. Gaeta, and M. Sassoli, *The 1949 Geneva Conventions: A Commentary* (Oxford: Oxford University Press, 2015).
20 For those states who are parties to the Protocol.
21 Milanović.
22 GC IV Art. 4.

grave breaches of the Geneva Conventions (war crimes in IACs), which are relevant only in IACs. Other differences relate to state or individual responsibility for breaches of international law. In IACs, all parties – that is, states – bear international responsibility for their actions. In NIACs, only one party – that is, the state – will be subjected to such responsibility, while the armed groups will not. From a criminal law perspective, the crime of aggression currently applies only to state officials, not to those of armed groups.

3.3 Temporal and Geographical Scope

Having addressed the reasons for classification of the conflict(s) in Syria, a note about the geographical and temporal scope of this chapter is also required. The geographical scope is limited, first and foremost, to the borders of Syria. This limitation is notwithstanding the fact that armed groups operating in Syria move across its borders to neighbouring countries (or even to Europe). However, the starting point is that all relevant actors (states or armed groups) operate within Syria's borders, even if their military operations spill over outside those borders. The military hostility between the Islamic State of Iraq and Syria (ISIS) and European states, as discussed in Section 3.4, involved, among others, the attack in the Bataclan Theatre.[23] While this attack occurred in Paris, France, both actors – ISIS and France – also operate in Syria.

The temporal scope should be identified as well, so as not to include all hostilities or situations of belligerency in which Syria has been involved in the past century. As the temporal scope of the book includes the events in Syria since March 2011, Syria's belligerency with Israel as of October 1973 and the Armistice between the two is not included in this chapter. However, any military acts between these two states that occurred following March 2011 – and specifically since 29 April 2011, when the UN Human Rights Council held its 17th Special Session[24] – are included and addressed. This timeline is still ongoing, as the conflict(s) in Syria are yet to be resolved. Therefore, the discussion includes the Turkish military operation 'Olive Branch' (20 January 2018),[25] the encounters between the Israeli Air Force and

[23] For more information on the Paris Attacks, see 'Paris 13 Novembre 2015', *Le Parisien*, http://atelier.leparisien.fr/sites/attentats-novembre-2015-paris/.

[24] Held on 29 April 2011; see www.ohchr.org/EN/HRBodies/HRC/SpecialSessions/Session16/Pages/16thSpecialSession.aspx (accessed 9 February 2018).

[25] See announcement in Turkey http://www.byegm.gov.tr/english/agenda/turkish-army-announces-operation-olive-branch-in-afrin/123919 (accessed 9 February 2018).

Syrian/Iranian anti-aircraft defence,[26] and the US, France, and UK attacks on Syrian targets following the alleged use of chemical weapons in Douma.[27] The delineation of the temporal scope also has implications for the distinctions between IAC and NIAC. While an IAC may end once hostilities cease, a NIAC requires the final conclusion of hostilities and the peaceful settlement of the conflict.[28]

3.4 International Armed Conflicts in Syria

The IACs addressed in this chapter are those between the Syrian army (and its proxies, such as the shabiha militia) and the international coalition led by the United States,[29] as well as the conflicts involving Turkey, Israel, and Iran. This section discusses when and to what extent the law of IAC applies to these four IACs, with the exception of Iranian involvement through its proxy Hezbollah,[30] which will only be discussed as a relevant factor related to the Israeli attacks on Syrian territory.[31] In terms of the applicable law, it should be mentioned that Syria is a party to the Geneva Conventions as well as to AP I.[32] This information is relevant in determining the legal obligations of both Syria and other parties to the different conflicts. This chapter will not, therefore, revise the situation between Syria and Israel in the Golan Heights, though

[26] Incidents from 10 February 2018, see, inter alia, reports in the *Guardian*, www.theguardian.com/world/2018/feb/10/israeli-fighter-jet-shot-down-by-syrian-fire-says-military (accessed 10 February 2018).

[27] See, for example, the report of the US Department of State of 7 April 2018, www.state.gov/r/pa/prs/ps/2018/04/280313.htm (accessed 25 October 2018).

[28] Tadić 1995 para 70.

[29] RULAC Project, the Geneva Academy of International Humanitarian Law and Human Rights, www.rulac.org/browse/countries/syria#collapse1accord (accessed 27 March 2018); A. Bellal, ed., *The War Report: Armed Conflicts in 2016*, Geneva Academy of International Humanitarian Law and Human Rights (March 2017), 36. According to these resources, members of the USA-led coalition are: Belgium, Canada, Denmark, France, Germany, Italy, Jordan, Morocco, Netherlands, Saudi Arabia, Turkey, United Arab Emirates, and the United Kingdom. Also see 'Identical Letters dated 17 September 2015 from the Permanent Representative of the Syrian Arab Republic to the United Nations Addressed to the Secretary General and the President of the Security Council', UN doc S/2015/719, 21 September 2015.

[30] For an analysis of this proxy war, see Section 3.4.3.

[31] A. Bellal, ed., *The War Report: Armed Conflicts in 2014* (Oxford: Oxford University Press, 2014), 57.

[32] Information on the status of the Syrian Arab Republic regarding its IHL treaty obligations can be found on the ICRC website, https://ihl-databases.icrc.org/applic/ihl/ihl.nsf/vwTreatiesByCountrySelected.xsp?xp_countrySelected=SY&nv=4 (accessed 3 April 2018).

according to international law this may be considered as a state of occupation and thus covered by the law of IAC.[33]

3.4.1 *Western Countries' Involvement: USA-Led Coalition and US Strikes*

During 2017 the United States conducted several targeting operations against the Syrian Armed Forces as well as against forces allied with the Syrian government. The following incidents created short-period IACs between Syria and the USA (outside the context of the USA-led coalition against ISIS). In April 2017, the USA conducted several missiles strikes against a Syrian military airfield following the Syrian government's reported use of chemical weapons.[34] In May and June of that same year, the USA targeted pro-Syrian forces and a Syrian jet that were threatening US positions in Syria.[35] As of the beginning of 2019, the USA still holds approximately 2,000 soldiers on the ground in Syria.[36]

As the United States is not a party to AP I, the applicable instruments in this respect are the Geneva Conventions, notably Convention IV, which addresses the status of civilians, as well as customary law relating to the

[33] RULAC Project; see also Report of the Secretary General on the United Nations Disengagement Force for the Period from 2 March to 16 May 2017, UN doc S/2017/486, 8 June 2017; Report of the Secretary General on the United Nations Disengagement Force for the Period from 1 March to 20 May 2016, UN doc S/2016/520, 8 June 2016. For a discussion of Israel's involvement in the Syrian conflict, see Chapter 9 of this volume.

[34] US Department of Defense, 'Statement from Pentagon Spokesman Capt. Jeff Davis on U.S. Strike in Syria', Press Release, 6 April 2017, https://dod.defense.gov/News/News-Releases/News-Release-View/Article/1144598/statement-from-pentagon-spokesman-capt-jeff-davis-on-us-strike-in-syria/. For further information about the use of chemical weapons in the Syrian conflict, see Chapters 4 and 5 of this volume.

[35] T. Gibbson-Neff, 'U.S. Conducts New Strikes on Pro-Syrian Government Forces Threatening U.S. Special Operations Base', *The Washington Post*, 6 June 2017, https://www.washingtonpost.com/news/checkpoint/wp/2017/06/06/u-s-conducts-new-strikes-on-pro-syrian-government-forces-threatening-u-s-special-operations-base/; M. Ryan, 'U.S. Launches Rare Intentional Strike on Pro-Government Forces in Syria', *The Washington Post*, 19 May 2017, https://www.washingtonpost.com/world/national-security/us-launches-rare-intentional-strike-on-pro-government-forces-in-syria/2017/05/18/9e4e2830-3bf0-11e7-8854-21f359183e8c_story.html; T. Gibbson-Neff and K. Fahim, 'U.S. Aircraft Shoots Down a Syrian Government Jet Over Northern Syria, Pentagon Says', *The Washington Post*, 18 June 2017, https://www.washingtonpost.com/news/checkpoint/wp/2017/06/18/a-u-s-aircraft-has-shot-down-a-syrian-government-jet-over-northern-syria-pentagon-says/.

[36] L. Loveluck and J. Hudson, 'U.S. Military Announces Start of Syria Troop Withdrawal', *The Washington Post*, 11 January 2019, https://www.washingtonpost.com/world/middle_east/us-military-announces-start-of-syria-troop-withdrawal/2019/01/11/77455bda-1585-11e9-90a8-136fa44b80ba_story.html.

conduct of hostilities. In addition to US attacks, a joint air strike on Syrian facilities occurred on 14 April 2018 in response to the alleged use of chemical weapon in Ghouta by the Syrian government. The United States, France, and the United Kingdom hit multiple targets in Syria, including military bases and chemical weapons research and storage facilities.[37] These strikes are also governed by the law of IAC. However, as the United Kingdom and France are parties to AP I, a question arises as to the applicability of this Protocol. The law governing conduct of hostilities (i.e. the rules of targeting) is mostly, if not entirely, considered part of customary law. In this respect the difference between applying the Protocol as a treaty or as part of customary law will not make much difference. Respectively, one could follow such reasoning and review the decision-making process and the rules of engagement decided upon between the different militaries and ensure that the United Kingdom and France did not violate their international obligations.

In addition to these short-period IACs between the US and Syria, all states belonging to the US-led coalition are also involved in military operations in Syria's territory against ISIS. While the conflict against ISIS is considered a NIAC (and will be discussed in Section 3.5), the states involved are also considered parties to an IAC as long as they encounter Syrian civilians and/or property during their operations.[38] As for the applicable law in these incidents, both the Geneva Conventions and customary law apply. The applicability of AP I will depend on the different parties and the constellation of the military forces; that is, whether the forces are comprised of the militaries of a few states or that of only one. As not all states in the USA-led coalition (and primarily the United States) are parties to AP I, it might, as a treaty, not be applicable to these incidents.[39]

[37] J. Borger and P. Beaumont, 'Syria: US, UK and France Launched Strikes in Response to Chemical Attack', *The Guardian*, 14 April 2018, https://www.theguardian.com/world/2018/apr/14/syria-air-strikes-us-uk-and-france-launch-attack-on-assad-regime.

[38] See for example how the hostilities between the IDF and Hezbollah during the summer of 2006 were classified in Human Rights Council, Report of Commission of Inquiry on Lebanon pursuant to Human Rights Council resolution S-2/1, A/HRC/3/2, 23 November 2006, www.ohchr.org/Documents/Publications/HR_in_armed_conflict.pdf; I Scobbie, 'Lebanon 2006', in E. Wilmshurst, ed., *International Law and the Classification of Conflicts* (Oxford: Oxford University Press, 2012), 402–8.

[39] Unlike the NATO-led security mission in Afghanistan (ISAF), whereby at the time Afghanistan was not a party to API, thus the question was never raised. See F. J. Hampson, 'Afghanistan 2001 Onwards', in E. Wilshurst, ed., *International Law and the Classification of Conflicts* (Oxford: Oxford University Press, 2012). As Afghanistan became party to the Additional Protocols in 2009, it has been argued that at least those forces of states who are parties to APII should apply it in their operations in Afghanistan. It has also been argued that

Nonetheless, AP I should apply to these hostilities, as a minimum in respect to humanitarian standards and protection of civilians. This view is inspired by the fact that parties to AP I should respect and ensure respect of the Protocol.[40] Furthermore, from a practical point, a joint coalition in which different parties do not respect the same legal boundaries may create confusion and, to a certain extent, cause states to violate their international obligations. Finally, while it is true that AP I does not apply as a matter of treaty, nonetheless most AP I standards regulating the conduct of hostilities (i.e. choice of targets, weapons, precautions, etc.) are considered to be part of customary international law[41] and therefore applicable as a matter of law.

3.4.2 *Turkey*

In the summer of 2015, Turkey increased its involvement in the Syrian conflict in the context of both IAC and NIAC. Turkey joined the USA-led coalition against ISIS[42] but also used its involvement in the area to subvert the activities of Syrian Kurdish armed group the People's Protection Units (YPG).[43] Turkey is involved in separate NIACs against ISIS and the YPG while simultaneously being a party to an IAC with Syria, as it is operating in its territory without consent. Moreover, Turkey initiated two separate military operations against the YPG and ISIS: Operation Euphrates Shield in August 2016;[44] and Operation Olive Branch in January 2018.[45] The former, which ended on 29 March 2017 and occurred mainly in the vicinity of the northern Syrian cities of Jarablus and Al-Bab, ensured not only the pushback

even though the USA, for example, is not a party to APII, it should comply with it, as it was conducting its operation in the territory of Afghanistan. However, this argument was based on the ISAF agreement requiring that all forces of the coalition will respect the law in Afghanistan. See A. Bellal, G. Giacca, and S. Casey-Maslen, 'International Law and Armed Non-State Actors in Afghanistan', *IRRC* 881 (March 2011): 47, 59–61.

40 API Art. 1(1); this idea is very much reflected in Bellal, Giacca, and Casey-Maslen.

41 See, inter alia, the ICRC Customary IHL Database (available online: https://ihl-databases.icrc.org/customary-ihl/eng/docs/home).

42 G. Tuysuz and Z. Bilginsay, 'Ministry: Turkey Joins Coalition Airstrikes Against ISIS in Syria', *CNN*, 29 August 2015, https://edition.cnn.com/2015/08/29/europe/turkey-airstrikes/index.html.

43 RULAC Project, the Geneva Academy of International Humanitarian Law and Human Rights, n.14, www.rulac.org/browse/countries/syria#collapse1accord (accessed 27 March 2018).

44 K. Shahbeen, 'Turkey sends tanks into Syria in operation aimed at Isis and Kurds', *The Guardian*, 24 August 2016, www.theguardian.com/world/2016/aug/24/turkey-launches-major-operation-against-isis-in-key-border-town.

45 Turkey's Office of the Prime Minister, 'Turkish Army Announces Operation Olive Branch in Afrin', 20 January 2018, www.byegm.gov.tr/english/agenda/turkish-army-announces-operation-olive-branch-in-afrin/123919.

of ISIS forces from Turkey's borders but also prevented the YPG from gaining more territories in the area.[46] At the time of writing, the latter is still ongoing, mainly in the area of the predominantly Kurdish city of Afrin.[47] These two military operations – each lasted more than few months of constant military presence of Turkey's armed forces within Syria territory (without its consent)[48] – arguably established a state of occupation.[49]

A territory is considered occupied once it is placed 'under the authority of the hostile army'.[50] This precondition was interpreted as requiring the hostile army to exercise effective control over a territory.[51] Effective control requires that the armed forces are present on the ground without consent, that they prevent the effective local government at the time from exercising its power, and that the armed forces exercise their own authority.[52] In respect to the activities of Turkey, its forces remained in Syrian territory even though Turkey admitted that Operation Euphrates Shield had achieved its goals.[53] Turkey also admitted that, while the operation was over, the forces that remained in Syria will operate under a different military operation status.[54] In addition, Turkey has oversight of the humanitarian aid going into the

[46] BBC, 'Turkey "ends" Euphrates Shield campaign in Syria', 30 March 2017, www.bbc.com/news/world-middle-east-39439593.

[47] Office of the Prime Minister, Statement of 5 April 2018, www.mfa.gov.tr/article-by-h_e_-mr_-mevlut-cavusoglu_-the-minister-of-foreign-affairs-of-turkey-the-_meaning_-of-operation-olive-branch.en.mfa.

[48] Sana, 'Syria Strongly Condemns Turkish Aggression on Afrin', 20 January 2018, https://sana.sy/en/?p=124986.

[49] S. Reeves and D. Wallace, 'Has Turkey Occupied Northern Syria?', Lawfare Blog, 22 September 2016, https://www.lawfareblog.com/has-turkey-occupied-northern-syria; R. Goodman, 'Turkey's US-Backed Operation in Syria Has Created an International Armed Conflict', *Just Security Blog*, 17 October 2016, https://www.justsecurity.org/33643/us-backed-turkey-operation-syria-creates-international-armed-conflict/.

[50] Convention (IV) Respecting the Laws and Customs of War on Land, with Annex of Regulations, 18 October 1907, 36 Stat. 2277, T.S. No. 539, Article 42.

[51] ICTY Prosecutor *v.* Naletilić IT-98-34-T Trial Chamber Judgment, 31 March 2003, paras 209–11; M. Sassoli, 'The Concept and the Beginning of Occupation', in Clapham, Gaeta, and Sassoli; T. Ferraro, 'Determining the Beginning and End of an Occupation under International Humanitarian Law', *IRRC* 885 (2012): 139–40.

[52] Naletilić para 217; Sassoli 1397; Ferraro 143–7.

[53] RULAC Project, the Geneva Academy of International Humanitarian Law and Human Rights, n.14, www.rulac.org/browse/countries/syria#collapse1accord (accessed 27 March 2018); S. Asrar, 'Syria: Who Controls What?', *Al Jazeera*, 20 November 2017.

[54] Al Jazeera, 'Turkey Ends "Euphrates Shield" Operation in Syria', 30 March 2017, https://www.aljazeera.com/news/2017/03/turkey-ends-euphrates-shield-operation-syria-170329211428970.html.

area.[55] Moreover, while Turkey's armed forces did not control all of the territory where the operation took place, the Free Syrian Army (FSA) supported by Turkey did.[56] In October 2017, and afterwards in January 2018, Turkey renewed its air and ground campaign in the province of Idlib and Afrin,[57] supported yet again by the FSA.[58]

All of this sheds light on the effective control exercised by Turkey in the area of northern Syria as of August 2015 onward either by its armed forces or together with the FSA. The presence of Turkish armed forces, its control of the humanitarian aid, its ability to launch concrete and continuous attacks while deploying more forces into the area, and the lack of Syrian government control thereof all imply that areas of northern Syria are in fact under the control of Turkey and therefore are subjected to the law of belligerent occupation.[59]

Furthermore, the information available indicates that even if Turkey did not control the entirety of the territory by the presence of its own armed forces (which according to jurisprudence is not required),[60] it did so through its proxies, mainly the FSA. It should be noted that the Turkish government granted refuge to prominent anti-Assad activists, and, along with Qatar, Turkey provided rebel groups with arms and military equipment.[61] An occupation by proxy occurs when a state exercises overall control over an armed group and that group exercises

[55] A. Stein, H. Abouzahr, and R. Komar, 'How Turkey Is Governing in Northern Aleppo', Syria Deeply, 20 July 2017, https://www.newsdeeply.com/syria/community/2017/07/20/how-turkey-is-governing-in-northern-aleppo.

[56] H. Haid, Post-ISIS Governance in Jarablus: A Turkish-led Strategy, Research Paper, Chatham House, 26 September 2017.

[57] RULAC Project, the Geneva Academy of International Humanitarian Law and Human Rights, n.14, www.rulac.org/browse/countries/syria#collapse1accord (accessed 27 March 2018); K. Shaheen, 'Turkey Starts Ground Incursion into Kurdish-Controlled Afrin in Syria', *The Guardian*, 21 January 2018.

[58] 'Turkey Deploys Thousands of FSA Rebels at Syria Border', *Al Jazeera*, 20 January 2018, https://www.aljazeera.com/news/2018/01/turkey-deploys-thousands-fsa-rebels-syria-border-180120070616740.html; S. Al-Khalidi, 'FSA Commander Says 25,000 Syrian Rebels Back Turkish Force in Syria', Reuters, 21 January 2018, https://www.reuters.com/article/us-mideast-crisis-ria-turkey-rebels/fsa-commander-says-25000-syrian-rebels-back-turkish-force-in-syria-idUSKBN1FA0OK; K. Shaheen, 'Syrian Rebels Gamble on Turkish Alliance to Fight Kurds and Assad', *The Guardian*, 27 January 2018, https://www.theguardian.com/world/2018/jan/27/syrian-rebels-gamble-turkish-alliance-fight-kurds-assad.

[59] Naletilić paras 206–21; Sassoli 1399–1400, Ferraro 158–60; T. Gal, 'Unexplored Outcomes of Tadić: Applicability of the Law of Occupation to War by Proxy', *JICJ* 12, no. 1 (2014) 59.

[60] Ibid.

[61] Hasan Hanna, 'Turkey's Changing War in Syria', *Middle East Monitor*, 7 December 2017, www.middleeastmonitor.com/20171207-turkeys-changing-war-in-syria/.

effective control over the territory.[62] It is apparent that Turkey was training and supporting the FSA and that the FSA supported Turkey and its military operations and aims in the region. There is ample information to warrant the conclusion that Turkey had overall control over the FSA, at least in regard to its military operations in northern Syria against ISIS (during the period of Operation Euphrates Shield) and against the YPG and the Syrian government (during the ongoing Operation Olive Branch). To this extent, and until Turkish forces and its proxy cease to control the territory, it should be governed by the law of occupation. As Turkey is not a party to AP I, the applicable legal regimes are Geneva Convention IV as well as customary law applicable to occupied territory.

3.4.3 Israel

This section assesses the military involvement of Israel in the Syrian hostilities with regards to two aspects: the spillover of the hostilities in the area of the Golan Heights; and the recent hostilities between the Israeli Defence Forces (IDF) and Syrian armed groups.

Since 2012, hostilities between Syrian government and anti-government armed groups have occurred in the area of Quneitra Governorate.[63] Quneitra is sensitive for two main reasons. First, it is located in the Syrian Golan Heights, extremely close to the ceasefire line[64] with Israel.[65] Second, it has a Druze community (such as in the village of Hader) that is considered a religious minority.[66] The Druze in this

[62] ICTY, Prosecution *v.* Prlić, IT-04-74-74-T Trial Chamber Judgment (29 May 2013), para 96. The Appeals Chamber did not dispute this approach of the Trial Chamber in its judgment of 29 November 2017; Gal; Ferraro, 160.

[63] G. Fiske, 'Battle rages over Golan Heights Border Crossing', *The Times of Israel*, 6 June 2013, https://www.timesofisrael.com/syrian-rebels-capture-golan-heights-border-crossing/; A. Cowel, 'Syrian Rebels Take Control of Crossing in the Golan', *The New York Times*, 27 August 2014, https://www.nytimes.com/2014/08/28/world/middleeast/golan-heights-al-qaeda-israel-syria.html.

[64] The ceasefire line between Syria and Israel is the result of the Israel–Syria Disengagement Agreement of 1974, following the 1973 conflict. The disengagement line serves until today as the de facto border between the two states; for further information see, for example, 'Golan Heights Profile', *BBC*, updated 19 June 2018, www.bbc.com/news/world-middle-east-14724842 (accessed 20 October 2018).

[65] See reporting of UN peacekeeping forces: inter alia, B. Ratner and M. Mogato, 'Syrian Army, Rebels Fight on Golan where Peacekeepers Held', *Reuters*, 1 September 2014.

[66] 'Violence Hits Druze Village Hader in Syria's Quneitra', Al Jazeera, 3 November 2017, https://www.aljazeera.com/news/2017/11/violence-hits-druze-village-hadera-syria-quneitra-171103142854755.html.

area have family ties with those located in the Israeli-controlled part of the Golan Heights. In other words, clashes between Syrian government forces and armed groups in the area were likely to affect the Druze community,[67] as well as the demilitarised zone and the 1974 ceasefire agreement.[68] These hostilities include rockets that fell in the Israeli-controlled Golan Heights and Israeli targeting of military posts in the Syrian part.[69] Addressing these incidents from a *jus ad bellum* point of view – that is, assessing their legality, justification, or qualification – is beyond the scope of this chapter. Nonetheless, with respect to the application of IHL, these hostilities – spillover of the internal conflict in Syria to Israel's territory – which caused casualties[70] are governed by the law applicable to IAC as long as the parties involved in the incidents are Syrian and Israeli military forces. This legal framework may change once the actors are no longer states.

Besides the incidents already mentioned – that is, the spillover of the Syrian conflict and the military response by Israel thereto – Israel has been involved in several military attacks within Syria.[71] Two different motives can be identified in respect to these attacks: first, preventing the

[67] It is not this chapter's intent to address the different justifications for protecting the Druze community in the Israeli side of the Golan Heights by using force against Hader and the Druze community in Quneitra; however, it should be noted that Israel did announce it will protect the community facing jihadists (Al Jazeera, ibid.).

[68] For reports on the different incidents of spillover and reaction of Israel, see, inter alia: Israel's complaint to the UNSC from 5 November 2012, UN Doc 11302-Add.1. S/11302/Add.1; 'Syria Crisis: Israeli Tanks "Hit Syrian Units" in Golan', *BBC*, 12 November 2012, https://www.bbc.co.uk/news/world-middle-east-20302503; 'Syria Conflict: Rebels Launch Quneitra Offensive', *BBC*, 17 June 2015, https://www.bbc.co.uk/news/world-middle-east-33166040.

[69] Examples include: the downing of a Syrian warplane that had entered the airspace of the Golan Heights in September 2014 – see 'Israel Shoots Down Syrian Warplane', *CBS/Associated Press*, 23 September 2014, https://www.cbsnews.com/news/israel-shoots-down-syrian-warplane/; the bombing of Syrian army positions in March 2014, December 2014, and September 2015 – see L. Smith-Spark and M. Schwartz, 'Israel Retaliates in Syria After Roadside Bomb Attack Against Israeli Troops', *CNN*, 19 March 2014, https://edition.cnn.com/2014/03/19/world/meast/israel-syria-violence/index.html; P. Beaumont, 'Israeli Jets Bomb Syria, Says Damascus', *The Guardian*, 7 December 2014, https://www.theguardian.com/world/2014/dec/07/israeli-jets-bomb-syria-says-damascus; 'Israel Strikes Syria After Stray Rockets Land in Golan', *Al Jazeera*, 28 September 2015, https://www.aljazeera.com/news/2015/09/israel-strikes-syria-golan-heights-150927200119081.html.

[70] For example: Y. Lapin and A. Ben-Solomon, '14-year-old Killed in Golan Heights in Cross-Border Fire from Syria', *The Jerusalem Post*, 22 June 2014, https://www.jpost.com/Defense/One-killed-2-injured-in-explosion-on-Syria-border-360158.

[71] Yet, like the activities discussed in the former paragraph, the legality or justification of Israel's attacks in Syria's territory discussed here is not addressed in this chapter.

transfer of weapons to Hezbollah;[72] and, second, a reaction to Iran's activities in the region.[73] As for the former motive, whether, in these incidents, Hezbollah is a proxy of Iran and/or Syria is relevant for their classification. If the required link between Hezbollah and Iran and/or Syria can be proven,[74] then all of these incidents' aspects will be governed by the law of IAC.[75] In this respect, if it is proven that Iran exercises overall control over Hezbollah or that Syria exercises such control, or in fact incorporated to some extent Hezbollah into its armed forces, then all of the hostilities occurring between Israel and Hezbollah would be considered as part of an IAC, to which Iran and Syria are also parties.

As for the latter motive of responding to Iranian activity in the region, several hostilities occurred. On 10 February 2018, the IDF intercepted an Iranian drone crossing its northern border with Syria and shot it down.[76] Following this incident, Israel launched an air strike targeting the airfield from which it claimed that the drone was launched and operated.[77] During this strike, an Israeli F-16 fighter jet was shot down by Syrian air-defence systems.[78] This incited a second air strike by Israel, targeting Syrian military

[72] RULAC Project, the Geneva Academy of International Humanitarian Law and Human Rights, n.14, www.rulac.org/browse/countries/syria#collapse1accord (accessed 27 March 2018); 'Israel Bombs Hezbollah-bound Missiles in Syria: Official', *Reuters*, 4 May 2013, https://uk.reuters.com/article/uk-syria-crisis-israel-usa/israel-bombs-hezbollah-bound-missiles-in-syria-official-idUKBRE94300U20130504; 'Israeli Airstrikes Hit Damascus Outskirts, Syrian Reports Says', *The Guardian*/Associated Press, 30 November 2016, https://www.theguardian.com/world/2016/nov/30/israeli-airstrikes-hit-damascus-outskirts-syrian-reports-say; P. Beaumont, 'Israel Reported to Have Bombed Syrian Chemical Weapons Facility', *The Guardian*, 7 September 2017, https://www.theguardian.com/world/2017/sep/07/israel-airstrike-syria-chemical-weapons-facility.

[73] See, inter alia, T. Lazarov, 'Netanyahu: U.S. Support Escalated Israeli Response to Iran in Syria', *The Jerusalem Post*, 21 December 2018, https://www.jpost.com/Arab-Israeli-Conflict/Netanyahu-US-supports-our-response-to-Iran-in-Syria-574994; 'Israel Strikes Iranian Targets in Syria', *BBC*, 10 May 2018, https://www.bbc.co.uk/news/av/world-middle-east-44065528/israel-strikes-iranian-targets-in-syria; J. Hincks, 'Israel and Iran are Waging a Secret War in Syria. Here's How it Finally Went Public', *Time*, 25 January 2019, https://time.com/5513411/israel-iran-secret-war-syria/.

[74] The relations between Hezbollah and Iran and Syria are discussed in Section 3.4.3.

[75] For the purpose of classification of the ICTY, see *Prosecutor* v. *Tadić*, IT-94-1 Appeals Chamber Judgment, 15 July 1999.

[76] T. Richell, 'Iranian Drone Shot Down by Israeli Military After Crossing its Border with Syria', *The Independent*, 10 February 2018, https://www.independent.co.uk/news/world/iran-drone-shot-down-israeli-defence-force-syria-border-a8204376.html.

[77] 'Two IAF Pilots Hurt After F-16 Downed during Retaliatory Strike in Syria', *Ynet*, 10 February 2018, https://www.ynetnews.com/articles/0,7340,L-5103264,00.html.

[78] Ibid.; 'Israeli F-16 Shot Down by Syria Fire, Says Military', *Al Jazeera*, 10 February 2018, https://www.aljazeera.com/news/2018/02/israel-shot-iranian-drone-syria-180210053946323.html.

bases which hosted air-defence systems.[79] Adding to the February 2018 strikes, it has been reported (with no comment, confirmation, or denial by Israel) that on 9 April 2018, following the reported use of chemical weapon in Ghouta, Israel attacked a T4 Syrian base near Homs,[80] aiming at disabling Iranian support.[81] All of these incidents, regardless of their justifications or legality, are governed by the law of IAC. This is so, as the parties (Iran, Syria, and Israel) are all states. To the extent that Russian personnel or objects were hit during these strikes (as happened in the 17 September 2018 air strike)[82] the classification will not change. In this respect, the law applicable will be the Geneva Conventions as well as customary law. As only Syria is a party to AP I, it seems that only its customary rules will be applicable.

3.5 Non-international Armed Conflicts in Syria

Three types of NIAC persist in the territory of Syria: the conflict between the Syrian government and anti-government armed groups within the framework of a civil war; the conflict between various armed groups; and lastly the conflict between foreign states against armed groups located and operating in the territory of Syria (namely ISIS and the YPG).

Clearly, the armed groups involved in the different conflicts should meet the requirements for IHL application. Though some of the states involved in Syria are parties to AP II, Syria is not. Applying AP II, however, in many ways will not change the legal framework applicable. First, unlike the suggested framework by the well-known scholars Bellal, Giacca, and Casey-Maslen, here the responsibility to *ensure respect* might not be as applicable as in the US attack of al-Qaeda in Afghanistan (2001).[83] This is so, among others, as Syria itself is not a party to the Protocol. Moreover, while the threshold of AP II

79 O. Holmes, 'Israel launches 'large-scale' attack in Syria after fighter jet crashes', *The Guardian*, 10 February 2018, https://www.theguardian.com/world/2018/feb/10/israeli-fighter-jet-shot-down-by-syrian-fire-says-military.

80 K. Dilanian and K. Cube, 'U.S. officials confirm Israel hit Syria after suspected Ghouta Chemical Attack', *NBC News*, 9 April 2018, https://www.nbcnews.com/news/world/israel-blamed-airstrike-syria-after-suspected-ghouta-chemical-weapon-attack-n863821.

81 B. Hubbard and D. M. Halbfinger, 'Iran–Israel Conflict Escalates in Shadow of Syrian Civil War', *New York Times*, 9 April 2018, https://www.nytimes.com/2018/04/09/world/middleeast/syria-russia-israel-air-base.html.

82 'Syria Fired Missiles for 40 Minutes After Israeli Strike, Hitting Russian Plane', *The Times of Israel*, 21 September 2018, https://www.timesofisrael.com/syria-fired-missiles-for-40-minutes-after-israeli-strike-hitting-russian-plane/; assuming the hit of the Russian plane could be attributed to Israel, which currently is still controversial.

83 Bellal, Giacca, and Casey-Maslen.

seems, at first glance, higher than that of Common Article 3, the indicators for both are similar. That is, in identifying, inter alia, armed groups, we shall look for the same requirements, whether suggestive or sine qua non.[84] Yet, as Syria is not a party to AP II, it is redundant to address its threshold. This section reviews the different actors in the NIAC(s) taking place in Syria and explains how these different armed groups meet the threshold of IHL and whether any outside intervention affects the classification of the conflict.

It is widely agreed that by summer of 2012 one or more NIACs existed in the territory of Syria. The Independent Impartial Commission of Inquiry on the Syrian Arab Republic (CoI Syria), in its third report, released in July 2012 but covering a six-month period starting in February 2012, declared the application of IHL – that is to say, that the violence has become a NIAC.[85] Bashar al-Assad admitted that Syria was in a state of war on 26 June 2012.[86] In a May 2012 statement, the International Committee of the Red Cross (ICRC) had already referred to IHL standards, though not officially classifying the situation as an armed conflict.[87] However, in a subsequent statement made in July 2012, it explicitly stated that the violence in Syria amounted to an NIAC.[88] The CoI Syria started to apply IHL to the situation in Syria only in its report from August 2012.[89] A report prepared by Chatham House distinguishes (somewhat artificially) the requirements of intensity from that of organisation, the latter focusing on the structure of the armed group(s). The report sustains that the intensity of violence in Syria amounted to that required in armed conflicts already in spring/summer 2011.[90] Nonetheless, according to the same report (as will be elaborated in Section 3.5.2.), the level of organisation of the parties (the armed

[84] See M. Milanović, 'The End of Application of International Humanitarian Law', *IRRC* 96, no. 893 (2014), 179.

[85] Report of the Independent International Commission of Inquiry on the Syrian Arab Republic UN Doc. A/HRC/21/50, 16 August 2012.

[86] 'Syria in State of War, Says Bashar Al Assad', *BBC News*, 27 June 2012, https://www.bbc.co.uk/news/world-middle-east-18598533.

[87] 'Syria: Parties to the Fighting Must Distinguish Between Civilians and Fighters', *ICRC News Release*, 27 May 2012, www.icrc.org/eng/resources/documents/news-release/2012/syria-news-2012-05-27.htm.

[88] 'Syria: ICRC and Syrian Arab Red Crescent Maintain Aid Effort amid Increased Fighting', *ICRC Operational Update*, 17 July 2012, www.icrc.org/eng/resources/documents/update/2012/syria-update-2012-07-17.htm.

[89] Report of the Independent International Commission of Inquiry on the Syrian Arab Republic, UN doc A/HRC/21/50, 15 August 2012, para 12.

[90] L. Arimatsu and M. Choudhury, 'The Legal Classification of the Armed Conflicts in Syria, Yemen and Libya', *Chatham House*, 15 March 2014.

groups involved in the conflict) was reached only in March 2012.[91] Accordingly, by March 2012 at a minimum, a NIAC existed, triggering the application of IHL.

3.5.1 *Intensity of the Conflict(s)*

A NIAC under Common Article 3 requires intensity of the hostilities and a level of organisation of the groups themselves.[92] In order to determine whether the hostilities are sufficiently intense, different aspects are assessed, such as the character of the violent incidents (how many, over what period of time); the type and number of forces used in the confrontations; the amount of casualties in the fighting (dead, injured, and those fleeing the area); the level of destruction; and the international community's involvement (such as the UN Security Council or other international bodies).[93]

By April 2011, the Syrian government was already brutally suppressing protests, using heavily armed troops.[94] The violence in Syria spread during 2011, and by November 2011 the CoI Syria assessed that the conflict was rising to – but had not yet reached – the level of an internal armed conflict.[95] Shortly before the Commission published its report, first clashes between the FSA and Syrian government forces were reported.[96] The first wave of refugees was reported in June 2011,[97] near the Turkey–Syria border. On February 2012, the Syrian military launched a wide attack on the city of Homs.[98] By autumn 2012, hostilities escalated dramatically, leading, among others, to the long-standing front in the city of Aleppo.[99] Furthermore, by

91 Ibid.

92 Haradinaj, para 60.

93 RULAC Project, the Geneva Academy of International Humanitarian Law and Human Rights, n.14, www.rulac.org/browse/countries/syria#collapse1accord (accessed 27 March 2018).

94 See the UN Human Rights Council 16th Special Session, held 29 April 2011; Chatham House Report, 15.

95 Report of the Independent International Commission of Inquiry on the Syrian Arab Republic, UN doc A/HRC/S-17/2/Add.1, 23 November 2011, para 97.

96 Ibid., para 27.

97 M. Chulov, 'Syrian Refugees in Turkey: People See the Regime Is Lying. It Is Falling Apart', *The Guardian*, 9 June 2011, https://www.theguardian.com/world/2011/jun/09/syria-turkey-refugees-denounce-regime.

98 R. Gladstone and N. MacFarquhar, 'UN Officials Rebukes Syria over Violence', *The New York Times*, 13 February 2012, https://www.nytimes.com/2012/02/14/world/middleeast/syrian-forces-continue-attack-on-homs.html.

99 G. Abdul-Ahad, 'Syria: The Foreign Fighters Joining the War Against Bashar Al-Assad', *The Guardian*, 23 September 2012, https://www.theguardian.com/world/2012/sep/23/syria-foreign-fighters-joining-war.

spring 2012 the armed groups, and specifically the FSA, were able to receive regular supply of weaponry and light non-lethal military aid.[100]

In April 2011, the UN Human Rights Council convened a special session on the deteriorating situation in Syria. As early as April 2011, the UN Security Council addressed the situation in Syria.[101] In October 2011, Russia and China vetoed a resolution condemning the violence in Syria.[102] Since then, the Security Council has been engaged with the Syrian conflict on repeated occasions.[103] Since March 2011, twelve resolutions on a variety of issues – including referral of the situation in Syria to the International Criminal Court, and extending the mandate of the Organisation for the Prohibition of Chemical Weapons: UN Joint Mission (OPCW-UN), established to determine the parties responsible for the chemical attacks in Syria[104] – have been vetoed by Russia and/or China.[105]

3.5.2 *The Various Armed Groups and Their Level of Organisation*

3.5.2.1 The Free Syrian Army (FSA)

While the violence in Syria was already quite intense in 2011, IHL was not applied to the hostilities until approximately March 2012 (or a bit before) given the level of organisation of the armed groups involved. Consequently, the threshold of a NIAC was not met.[106] Respectively, defining and interpreting the threshold of intensity in the Syrian case may prove counterproductive, as while the hostilities occurring in Syria exceeded the threshold of intensity, the armed groups involved, as discussed, were not sufficiently organised.[107] Therefore, whether the level of intensity was high enough or not does not affect the applicability of the legal framework.[108]

As for the threshold of organisation, the intention of the draftsmen of Common Article 3 was clearly not to set it high.[109] Respectively, the existence

[100] Chatham House Report, 11. The arming of the different groups operating in Syria will be explored further in Section 3.5.2.

[101] See Security Council Report (NGO) website covering all UN Security Council's activities, www.securitycouncilreport.org/syria/index.php?page=19.

[102] UN Security Council draft resolution S/2011/612, https://www.un.org/en/ga/search/view_doc.asp?symbol=S/2011/612.

[103] See Security Council Report (NGO).

[104] 'UN Security Council Fails to Adopt Three Resolutions on Chemical Weapons Used in Syria', *UN News*, 10 April 2018.

[105] UN Security Council draft resolutions: S/2012/77; S/2012/538; S/2014/348; S/2016/346; S/2016/1026; S/2017/315.

[106] The threshold discussed by the ICTY in Tadić 1995 and elaborated in Haradinaj.

[107] Chatham House Report, 15.

[108] Chatham House Report, 17–18.

[109] Sivakumaran, 170.

of a hierarchical structure, with a recognised responsible command, reflects on the group's level of organisation.[110] That is, that effective authority is exercised by one over another.[111] As stated in Section 3.5, the CoI Syria did not apply IHL to the conflict until mid-February 2012, due to lack of hierarchical structure. However, in its later report, and though a single unified command for all armed groups was not identified,[112] the CoI Syria determined that IHL applied, as the armed groups were able to execute organised and concrete military operations and challenge the government's control over Syrian territory.[113] This may as well be a strong indicator of a sufficient level of organisation required for designating this conflict as an armed conflict and for the application of IHL.[114] This determination reflects that many of the indicators for organisation adopted by jurisprudence and custom are more relevant for establishing the intensity of the conflict than for establishing concretely the structure of the group.[115]

The FSA was established during the Syrian government's crackdown on the 2011 protests. The protests were part of a wider movement, dubbed the Arab Spring, calling for democratic reforms in the Syrian government: inter alia, the release of political prisoners and regime reform to allocate powers outside of the Alawite group that was governing Syria.[116] While the protests were held mostly peacefully, the authorities used violent means to disperse them, including live ammunition, imprisonment, and heavy beatings. The violence by the Syrian military continued, and in June 2011 the killing of Syrian soldiers by armed groups were reported. The violence morphed into calls for the fall of the Assad government.[117] Against this backdrop, the FSA formed as a loose alliance between different brigades consisting of deserting soldiers and civilian volunteers. The FSA also encouraged soldiers currently serving in the military to join them.[118] The FSA was the first armed opposition. It adopted a code of conduct,[119] made several unilateral declarations

[110] Chatham House Report, 18; Sivakumaran, 174; Pictet Commentary GCIV, 36.
[111] Sivakumaran, 174–5.
[112] The groups' activities were not coordinated or managed under a proper unified chain of command. Chatham House Report, 15.
[113] CoI Report, 5 February 2013, para 10.
[114] Chatham House Report, 18.
[115] Sivakumaran.
[116] Chatham House Report, 7.
[117] Ibid.
[118] 2016 War Report, 36–7.
[119] 'Code of Conduct of the FSA', The Geneva Call Database: *Their Words. Directory of Armed Non-State Actor Humanitarian Commitments*, available online as of 2012 – http://theirwords.org/media/transfer/doc/sy_fsa_2012_01-670a046d8c995deb933cec25f062ea7e.pdf. The code was not scrupulously followed and violations were discovered. See Human Rights Council, Human Rights Abuses and International Humanitarian Law Violations in the Syrian Arab Republic, 21 July 2016–28 February 2017, A/HRC/34/CRP.3, 10 March 2017.

regarding the applicability of IHL, and signed the deeds of commitments of the Geneva Call.[120] Though consisted mainly of Sunni Arabs, it also encompassed other minorities such as Palestinians, Kurds, and Druze.[121] By March 2011 the FSA had nominated a spokesperson,[122] and in summer 2011, in a military base in Turkey, it was officially established.[123] Notwithstanding these developments, only in March 2012 was it possible to identify some sort of command and coordinated military operations, which also enabled the recruitment of new members.[124] By the end of 2012, the Supreme Military Council was established and many rebel groups operating in Syria had affiliated themselves with it.[125]

The FSA, as of summer of 2012, was supported in one way or the other by Western states[126] and Turkey.[127] Additionally, and as already elaborated, the FSA assisted and continues to assist Turkey in its campaign against the YPG in northern Syria.[128] However, the support granted to the FSA by Western states does not meet the threshold for the FSA to become a proxy of the West.[129] This is so as, contrarily to the support received by Turkey and the furthering of Turkey's military objectives by the FSA, Western states only supplied it with non-lethal means (e.g. body armours) and diplomatically and morally supported it. According to the test developed in jurisprudence, a higher level of support and/or link is required to establish proxy relations. The FSA also participated in several of the peace talks organised and held in Geneva or took part in the coalition of the opposition that participated in them.[130] As already discussed in Section 3.5, as early as March 2012 the FSA meets the threshold of organisation, has been able to conduct concrete

However, this fact does not diminish the significance of the adoption of the code and its implications for the assessment of FSA's level of organisation.

120 Geneva Call, 'Four Brigades of the Free Syrian Army Commit to Prohibit Sexual Violence and the Use of Child Soldiers', 3 July 2017, https://genevacall.org/syria-4-brigades-free-syrian-army-commit-prohibit-sexual-violence-use-child-soldiers/.

121 2016 War Report, 36; RULAC Project.

122 Chatham House Report, 15.

123 'Guide to the Syrian Rebels', *BBC News*, 13 December 2013.

124 Chatham House Report, 15.

125 Guide to the Syrian Rebels.

126 M. Hosenball, 'Obama Authorizes Secret Support for Syrian Rebels', *The Guardian*, 2 August 2012, https://www.theguardian.com/world/middle-east-live/2012/aug/02/syria-crisis-damascus-massacres-live?page=with%3Ablock-501aa5b9b579c24ed0437b28.

127 K. Shaheen, P. Torpey, P. Gutierrez, C. Levett, and the Institute for the Study of War, 'Who Backs Whom in the Syrian Conflict', *The Guardian*, 2 August 2015, https://www.theguardian.com/world/ng-interactive/2015/oct/09/who-backs-whom-in-the-syrian-conflict.

128 See Section 3.4 of this chapter discussing the IAC taking place in Syria.

129 As the provision of supply or diplomatic efforts is not a sufficient link.

130 For example, M. Casey-Baker and J. Haber, 'FSA Will Not Halt Fighting for Syria Peace Conference', *Foreign Policy*, 26 November 2013; E. Camilli, 'Syria: Free Syrian Army Set Conditions to Participate in Geneva II Peace Talks', *ESISC*, 15 November 2013.

military operation, and its commander(s) are identifiable; thus it becomes a party to a NIAC with Syria.

3.5.2.2 The Islamic State of Iraq and Syria (ISIS)

The Islamic State (also known as ISIL or *Daesh*) emerged from al-Qaeda in Iraq.[131] In 2004, Abu-Musab al-Zarqawi established al-Qaeda in Iraq, and by 2006 it tried to spark a sectarian war in Iraq. Following al-Zarqawi's assassination by a US air strike, Abu Ayyub al-Masri took over as leader of al-Qaeda in Iraq and by the end of 2006 announced the creation of the Islamic State in Iraq, with Abu Omar al-Baghdadi as its leader. In 2010, Abu Bakr al-Baghdadi became leader of ISIS, after both al-Masri and Abu Omar were killed in a joint Iraqi–US strike. By 2012, ISIS, which began to gain significant strength in Iraq, got involved with the Syrian conflict along with other Islamist groups.[132] In mid-2013, in an attempt to create a united Islamist front, ISIS leader al-Baghdadi announced that rival Islamists groups the al-Nusra Front and al-Qaeda in Syria will be merging with ISIS under the command of al-Baghdadi (both groups sufficiently organised).[133] However, both groups, who saw themselves affiliated with the local Syrian revolution and less with the broader vision of establishing a Califate, never accepted the merger or the leadership of al-Baghdadi.[134] This resulted in ISIS operating independently in Syria[135] and put it in a hostile relationship with other armed groups, including the al-Nusra Front and al-Qaeda in Syria. Respectively, as of 2012, the al-Nusra Front was recognised by al-Qaeda in Iraq and gained growing support from the Syrian population.[136] It is only in July 2016 that al-Nusra cut all ties with al-Qaeda in Iraq and later on merged with smaller factions forming a new alliance (February 2017).[137]

131 The information in the following paragraph is based on several reports and information available online from both media and research: 'ISIS Fast Facts', *CNN Library*, updated 3 September 2018; RULAC Project, n 15; 'ISIS' in History, www.history.com/topics/21st-century/isis.

132 RULAC Project, the Geneva Academy of International Humanitarian Law and Human Rights, n.14, www.rulac.org/browse/countries/syria#collapse1accord (accessed 27 March 2018).

133 2016 War Report, 37.

134 Ibid.; RULAC Project, 'Al-Qaeda Disowns ISIL Rebels in Syria', *Al Jazeera*, 3 February 2014.

135 *Stanford University Mapping Militant Groups Project*, last update 23 October 2017, http://web.stanford.edu/group/mappingmilitants/cgi-bin/groups/view/1?highlight=Islamic+State.

136 Pomegranate, 'Jabhat al-Nusra – Syria's Jihadists', *The Economist*, 17 December 2012, https://www.economist.com/pomegranate/2012/12/17/syrias-jihadists.

137 'Tahrir al-Sham: Al-Qaeda Latest Incarnation in Syria', *BBC News*, 28 February 2017, https://www.bbc.co.uk/news/world-middle-east-38934206.

During its campaign in Syria, ISIS occupied a significant (though poorly populated) portion of central and north-eastern Syria and established bases in different cities, the biggest of which was in Raqqa, its de facto capital.[138] The group also managed to control most of the border passing between Iraq and Syria until its withdrawal from most parts of Syria (and Iraq).[139] Until its uprooting in 2018, ISIS exercised effective – and in many instances exclusive – control over vast territories. It was able to fund itself through different sources (including the sale of oil and antiquities) and to execute organised and concrete military operations in Syria and Iraq (and abroad to some extent).[140] In 2018, the fight against ISIS in both Iraq and Syria was declared successful,[141] though some 'pockets' of ISIS-controlled territory still exist.[142] This success – that is, driving ISIS troops away from most of the territories it controlled – was the result of cooperation between the USA-led coalition and the Syrian Democratic Forces, a USA-backed multi-ethnic coalition of armed groups, which is still largely led and composed of the YPG.[143] Notwithstanding the successful fight against ISIS, it has been reported that ISIS still operates to some extent in Syria (and Iraq), mainly by kidnapping, issuing violent attacks on civilian population (such as car bombing) and especially by its re-emergence as a guerrilla force – that is, fighting foreign troops and beheading foreign nationals.[144]

[138] Ibid.

[139] Ibid.

[140] Ibid.; 2016 War Report, 37; 'Islamic State: Where Does Jihadist Group Get Its Support', *BBC News*, 1 September 2014, https://www.bbc.co.uk/news/world-middle-east-29004253.

[141] A. Wong, 'The Fall of ISIS in Syria Could Spell More Trouble for the US', *CNBC*, 23 February 2018, https://www.cnbc.com/2018/02/23/the-fall-of-isis-in-syria-could-spell-more-trouble-for-the-us.html; P. Cockburn, 'Preview 2018: After a String of Defeats in Iraq and Syria What 2018 Means for ISIS', *The Independent*, 1 January 2018, https://www.independent.co.uk/news/world/middle-east/isis-defeat-syria-latest-iraq-2018-survive-a8107891.html; see also map provided in 'Islamic State and the Crisis in Iraq and Syria in Maps', *BBC News*, 28 March 2018, https://www.bbc.co.uk/news/world-middle-east-27838034.

[142] L. Dorigo, 'ISIL Continues to Wreak Havoc in Syria's Deir Az Zor', *Al Jazeera*, 14 November 2018, https://www.aljazeera.com/indepth/inpictures/isil-continues-wreak-havoc-syria-deir-ez-zor-181028182030798.html.

[143] Ibid.; 2016 War Report, 37. The Syrian Democratic Forces is consisted of several armed groups, including the YPG and the Syrian Military Council, created to fight ISIS but also other armed groups. See discussion of those groups in Chapter 13 of this volume.

[144] C. Cornish and A. Khattab, 'ISIS Returns to Insurgent Roots after Battlefield Defeats', *Financial Times*, 4 December 2018, https://www.ft.com/content/c46be2aa-f3cd-11e8-ae55-df4bf40f9d0d.

3.5.2.3 The People's Protection Units (YPG)

The YPG is the military branch of the Syrian Kurdish Democratic Unity Party[145] (which is also active in south-east Turkey). Following the withdrawal of the Syrian Army from the north-east area of Syria, the YPG assumed control over these Kurdish territories in mid-2012, handling both military and administrative aspects there.[146] In 2014 the YPG has signed the Geneva Call Deeds of Commitment (on both anti-personnel mines and sexual violence).[147] The YPG's ability to protect, control, and administer vast territories, as well as the participation of the armed group's representatives in the Geneva Call process, underline the structure – that is, the level of organisation – of the YPG and its link with the Kurdish Democratic Unity Party and reflect that the YPG meets the thresholds for the application of IHL as of at least mid-2012. The YPG is estimated to have approximately 30,000 fighters. It is also the major leading member of the Syrian Democratic Forces, backed by the United States, to fight against ISIS.[148] Indeed, with US assistance, the YPG was able to liberate the city of Kobane from ISIS control in January 2015.[149] The YPG was responsible for the August 2014 ground operation that saved the Yazidi population trapped in Mount Sinjar in northern Iraq[150] and is also primarily responsible for the advance on and taking of Raqqa city from ISIS in June 2017.[151]

145 'Who are the Kurds', *BBC News*, 31 October 2017, https://www.bbc.co.uk/news/world-middle-east-29702440.

146 RULAC Project, the Geneva Academy of International Humanitarian Law and Human Rights, n.14, www.rulac.org/browse/countries/syria#collapse1accord (accessed 27 March 2018).

147 Geneva Call, 'Syrian Kurdish Armed Non-State Actor Commits to Ban Anti-Personnel Mines, Sexual Violence and Child Recruitment', 16 June 2014, https://genevacall.org/syrian-kurdish-armed-non-state-actor-commits-ban-anti-personnel-mines-sexual-violence-child-recruitment/.

148 2016 War Report, 38; E. Schmitt, 'U.S.-Backed Militia Opens Drive on ISIS Capital in Syria', *The New York Times*, 6 November 2016, https://www.nytimes.com/2016/11/07/world/middleeast/us-backed-militia-opens-drive-on-isis-capital-in-syria.html.

149 Graham-Harrison, 'Kobani: destroyed and riddled with unexploded bombs, but its residents dare to dream of a new start', *The Guardian*, 31 January 2015, https://www.theguardian.com/world/2015/jan/31/kobani-kurdish-forces-retake-isis-destroyed-power-sanitation-bombs-residents-hopes.

150 I. Tharoor, 'A U.S. Designated Terrorist Group Is Saving Yazidis and Battling the Islamic State', *Washington Post*, 11 August 2014, https://www.washingtonpost.com/news/worldviews/wp/2014/08/11/a-u-s-designated-terrorist-group-is-saving-yazidis-and-battling-the-islamic-state/. The YPG is connected to and cooperates with the PKK and the Peshmerga forces in Iraq.

151 R. Said and E. Francis, 'Revenge for Sinjar: Syrian Kurds Free Islamic State Slaves', *Reuters*, 14 June 2017, https://uk.reuters.com/article/uk-mideast-crisis-syria-yazidi/revenge-for-sinjar-syrian-kurds-free-islamic-state-slaves-idUKKBN1950M0.

Despite the YPG's major role in fighting ISIS and supporting the USA-led coalition, after the peace process with Turkey collapsed[152] it found itself facing another front against Turkey. Respectively, Turkey has been involved militarily (directly or using the FSA) to target the Kurdish territories in northern Syria and specifically targeting YPG fighters for their assumed link with the Kurdistan Workers' Party (PKK) in Turkey. The pressure from Turkey resulted, among other things, from the USA halting its support to the YPG.[153]

3.5.2.4 Miscellaneous and Fluctuating Armed Groups

Beyond these three main groups, there are other armed groups operating in Syria[154] as well. While it is important to mention their existence, they do not affect the classification of the conflict(s) in Syria, as their names, members, size, and affiliations have changed throughout the conflict(s). In 2017, some effort has been made by the armed groups themselves to unite into a single front; however, the success of this effort is questionable.[155] Among these groups are al-Qaeda and affiliated groups, such as: Ahrar al-Sham,[156] the al-Nusra Front, and the Islamic Front, a loose alliance or coalition of seven Islamist opposition armed groups, led by the former leader of the SILF (Syrian Islamic Liberation Front, a coalition of Islamist factions aligned with the FSA).[157] Though these groups are not as relevant to the classification of the conflict(s) in Syria, their existence, organisation, and ability to conduct concrete military operations reflect the intensity of the conflict. This does, however, raise a question as to whether IHL will apply to *all* armed groups operating in Syria, at *all* times, even if these groups do not meet the required threshold.[158]

[152] K. Nazish, 'Turkey and PKK 'Back to Square One'', *Al Jazeera*, 30 July 2015, https://www.aljazeera.com/news/2015/07/turkey-pkk-square-150730074312972.html.

[153] 'US Military: No 'Support' for Kurdish YPG in Afrin', *Al Jazeera*, 17 January 2018, https://www.aljazeera.com/news/2018/01/military-support-kurdish-ypg-afrin-180116202955100.html. For further information on Turkey's operation against the YPG in northern Syria, see Section 3.4 of this chapter discussing the IACs taking place in Syria.

[154] For a short review of the different groups operating in Syria, see 'Guide to Syrian Rebels', *BBC News*, 13 December 2013, https://www.bbc.co.uk/news/world-middle-east-24403003.

[155] On the establishment of the Unified National Army, see S. Abboud, 'Who Are Syria's Opposition Alliances?', *Al Jazeera*, 10 October 2017, https://www.aljazeera.com/news/2017/10/syria-opposition-alliances-171010075809951.html.

[156] 2016 War Report, 38.

[157] Guide to Syrian Rebels; 'Leading Syrian Rebel Groups Form New Islamic Front', *BBC News*, 22 November 2013, https://www.bbc.co.uk/news/world-middle-east-25053525.

[158] Chatham House Report, 18.

3.5.3 *International Interventions*

While for the applicability of Common Article 3, and therefore IHL, it suffices that armed groups are fighting among themselves, classifying the different conflicts taking place in Syria depends on the states parties to these Instruments. As explained in Section 3.4, states that are fighting against armed groups in Syria (like the USA-led coalition against ISIS, or Turkey against the YPG) should comply with the law of IAC with regards to their activities that affect the territorial state (such as when civilians or civilian objects are affected). In this respect, parallel conflicts exist – an IAC and a NIAC.[159] Yet the mere support (by training or supply given by states to armed groups)[160] does not suffice by itself for establishing the required link which will internationalise the conflict.[161] The same analysis is relevant to Turkey in its fight against ISIS and the YPG. Nonetheless, Turkey considers its fight against the YPG as a branch of its NIAC fought in its own territory against the PKK.[162] In its fight against the YPG, Turkey has established effective control in northern Syria and has used the support of the FSA in the process. Assuming that the FSA is for the purpose of this conflict the proxy of Turkey,[163] neither classification changes.

The largest intervention so far in the Syrian conflict is the support given by Russia to the Syrian government.[164] Since the beginning of the conflict, Russia supported Syria diplomatically and by providing military supply. This was seen as early as Russia's first veto of the conflict in the Security Council, 4 October 2011, and by January 2012 it included weapon supplies.[165] In September 2015, Russia intervened actively in the conflict and started

[159] See Sections 3.4 and 3.5 of this chapter as well as RULAC Project, the Geneva Academy of International Humanitarian Law and Human Rights, n.14, www.rulac.org/browse/countries/syria#collapse1accord (accessed 27 March 2018).

[160] I.e., the support allegedly given by the USA to different armed groups, among them the YPG in their fight against ISIS.

[161] Inter alia: *Nicaragua* v *United States of America* [1986] I.C.J. 14, paras 209, 246; Milanović; on US involvement in the conflict, see also Chapter 2 of this volume.

[162] Letter Dated 24 August 2016 from the Permanent Representative of Turkey to the United Nations Addressed to the President of the Security Council, UN doc S/2016/739, 25 August 2016.

[163] Yet not only Turkey's proxy. Other states were also involved in directing the activities of the FSA.

[164] The support granted by Iran through Hezbollah is discussed in Chapter 9 of this volume; nonetheless, and as will be explained, since the support is granted to the *state* participating in the conflict, it does not change the classification.

[165] R. Galpin, 'Russia Arms Shipments Bolster Syria's Embattled Assad', *BBC News*, 30 January 2012, https://www.bbc.co.uk/news/world-middle-east-16797818.

conducting air strikes against ISIS and 'other terrorist groups'.[166] Most of its documented strikes, however, have been on territory held by anti-government armed groups, with very minimal targeting of ISIS positions. Since then, Russia has been supporting the Syrian government not only by supply and training but also by joining and taking active part in military operations.[167] This intervention also led to the 2015 USA–Russia de-confliction agreement to avoid incidents between US drones and airplanes and Russian activities.[168] This agreement was suspended when the USA attacked Syrian army positions in 2017.[169] The tension between Russia and the USA increased in 2018, when Russian contractors were killed during an attack held by the USA over military positions in Syria.[170]

Russian support and intervention has enabled the Syrian government to advance in its war efforts and regain control of many areas in the Syria.[171] Parallel to its involvement in the conflict(s), Russia is also supporting, leading, and hosting different peace talks to end the conflict,[172] the latest round held in Sochi.[173] As this intervention of Russia is in support of the Syrian government, it does not change the classification of the conflict between Syria and the armed groups operating in Syria as a NIAC. Nor does US intervention against ISIS (perceived as a branch of the conflict in Iraq) change this classification. It does, however, raise the question as to whether the attacks on Syrian facilities carried out by different states, such as the USA (and its

[166] 'Russia Joins the War in Syria: Five Key Points', *BBC News*, 1 October 2015, https://www.bbc.co.uk/news/world-middle-east-34416519.

[167] RULAC Project.

[168] N. MacFarquhar, 'U.S. Agrees with Russia on Rules in Syrian Sky', *The New York Times*, 20 October 2015, https://www.nytimes.com/2015/10/21/world/middleeast/us-and-russia-agree-to-regulate-all-flights-over-syria.html.

[169] M. Bulman, 'US Air Strikes in Syria: Russia Suspends Agreement Preventing Direct Conflict with American Forces', *Independent*, 7 April 2017, https://www.independent.co.uk/news/world/middle-east/us-russia-air-strikes-syria-suspend-agreement-memorandum-direct-conflict-military-donald-trump-putin-a7671631.html.

[170] A. Troianovski and A. Roth, 'Russian Mercenaries Said to Be Killed by U.S. Airstrike in Syria', *The Washington Post*, 13 February 2018, https://www.washingtonpost.com/world/russian-mercenaries-reported-killed-by-us-airstrike-in-syria/2018/02/13/c15f5db4-10d7-11e8-a68c-e9374188170e_story.html.

[171] A. Chughtai, 'Syrian Civil War Map: Who's in Control Where?', *Al Jazeera*, 15 April 2018, https://www.aljazeera.com/indepth/interactive/2015/05/syria-country-divided-150529144229467.html.

[172] N. Cumming-Bruce, 'Golden Opportunity Missed: Syria Peace Talks Falter Again', *The New York Times*, 14 December 2017, https://www.nytimes.com/2017/12/14/world/middleeast/syria-peace-talks-un.html.

[173] O. Caroll, 'Russian Syria Peace Talks Achieve Little Beyond Further Division as Fighting Continues in Afrin', *Independent*, 30 January 2018, https://www.independent.co.uk/news/world/europe/syria-civil-war-russia-sochi-talks-assad-lavrov-protests-boycott-a8186371.html.

allies) or Israel, create a second IAC involving those states and Russia. Currently, besides some diplomatic clashes between the different actors, and a suspended memorandum of understanding, this does not seem to be the case from a diplomatic or legal standpoint. For example, the 17 September 2018 incident, in which Syrian anti-aircraft missiles targeting Israeli jets hit a Russian plane instead, did not escalate the relations between Russia and Israel into a full armed conflict, though it did cause some diplomatic tension between the two states.[174] Arguably, military incidents, or hostilities between these actors, are regulated by the law of IAC.

3.6 Conclusion

The active hostilities taking place in Syria have involved different actors – states and armed groups. The identity of these actors varies and changes on a regular basis,[175] hence, the conflict(s) taking place during this period vary, and the alliances change rapidly. The purpose of the classification of the conflicts and identifying their participants is not merely academic but also provides tools and practical understandings for how to regulate these hostilities and protect the victims. Providing this legal framework facilitates the right application of the existing legal instruments. Several armed conflicts are taking place in Syria simultaneously. Hence, actors in the Syrian context may actually be involved in more than one conflict, regulated by different legal frameworks and sets of rules. These actors are forced, consequently, to comply with different sets of rules in different incidents. Notwithstanding the claim of possible confusion under these circumstances, the basic rules of the conduct of hostilities remain the same in both IACs and NIACs. Yet classification has several implications, such as states' and individuals' responsibility for violations of international law. If IHL is not applied correctly, and respective to the shift in actors and the roles they play, as well as the dynamic changes in the territorial control, the immediate and eventual victims will be civilians in these territories.

[174] 'Russian Aircrew Deaths: Putin and Netanyahu Defuse Tension', *BBC*, 18 September 2018, https://www.bbc.co.uk/news/world-europe-45563304.

[175] For example, as of 2016, Canada is no longer actively involved in the USA-led coalition and assists only by air-fuelling and providing supply. See RULAC Project, the Geneva Academy of International Humanitarian Law and Human Rights, n.14, www.rulac.org/browse/countries/syria#collapse1accord (accessed 27 March 2018).

4

The Syrian Government's War against Its People

EYAL ZISSER

As the war in Syria entered its eighth year in March 2018, it seemed – at least from the military aspect – that the war was nearing its end, with Bashar al-Assad and his government victorious. This victory, however, belongs even more to his allies, Russia and Iran. Russia succeeded in its efforts to ensure Bashar al-Assad's continued hold on power, and in the long run Assad will likely be successful in reasserting his rule over the whole of Syrian territory.[1] However, Assad's victory raises the question of accountability and of the Syrian government's responsibility for this devastating war which tore up the Syrian state and society.

Russia's success in ensuring Bashar al-Assad's survival was made possible by Moscow's – and Iran's – military intervention in the Syrian civil war beginning in September 2015. By December 2016, this intervention led to the fall of Aleppo, the second-largest city in the country, to the Syrian government and its allies, as well as the partial collapse of the rebel camp.[2] The conventional belief prior to this Russian and Iranian involvement was that none of the warring parties in Syria had the ability to defeat its adversary, as both the government and its opponents had shown exhaustion. The Russians and Iranians – alongside Lebanese Hezbollah's warriors and members of Shi'a militias recruited by the Iranians in Iraq, Afghanistan, and Pakistan – were thus able to determine the war's likely outcome. With this outside involvement, the conflict ceased to be a war of the Syrians and morphed into a regional and even international conflict, with foreign actors becoming those who would determine its eventual outcome.

It is the Syrian people, however, who pay the heavy price of the ongoing warfare. The civilian population found itself trapped between

[1] Eyal Zisser, 'The War in Syria: What Lies Ahead?' *Strategic Assessment* 20, no. 2 (July 2017): 23–32.

[2] Taylor Luck, 'Fall of Aleppo Could Tip Syria from Civil War to Insurgency', *Christian Science Monitor*, 14 December 2016, www.csmonitor.com/World/Middle-East/2016/1214/Fall-of-Aleppo-could-tip-Syria-from-civil-war-to-insurgency.

the government and its opponents, overwhelmed with a sense of indifference and apathy to the fighting and struggling for survival, trying to attain some basic form of existence for the individual, the family, and the community.

The fighting in Syria has been accompanied by acts of cruelty that amount to war crimes against the civilian population, most of whom were not involved in the fighting and found themselves caught in the crossfire between the government and its opponents. War crimes have been committed by multiple stakeholders: by the government and its allies (Russia, Iran, Hezbollah, and the Shi'a militias recruited by Tehran from Iraq, Pakistan, and Afghanistan) on the one hand and the rebel forces (most prominent of whom were Salafi-Jihadi Islamic groups, the most prominent among them being ISIS) on the other.[3]

The Syrian government should be judged more harshly than it is currently for the cruelties it perpetrates for three reasons. First, the government is still recognised by the international community as the legitimate representative of the Syrian state and the Syrian people. The Syrian government claims to adhere to international law, not only in order to justify the continuation of its rule but also to justify its actions. The government's allies follow suit. Assad has described the widespread killing carried out by his army as a legitimate move made by a legitimate and internationally recognised government fighting terrorism and seeking to protect its citizens. Russia and Iran, meanwhile, justify their military intervention in Syria by claiming that it was undertaken in response to a request submitted by Syria's legitimate government.[4] Second, the government has at its disposal military capabilities and governmental authority far greater than any in the hands of the rebels. The government has used these extensively, indiscriminately, and without restraint. This makes the government's actions far more blameworthy than the actions of the rebels and even ISIS.

Third, the government's cruelties should be judged more harshly because these acts were the result of a systematic, calculated, and purposeful policy dictated from above[5] and anchored in a strategy of systematic

[3] See Chapters 5 and 6 of this volume.

[4] 'Lavrov: Iranian Presence in Syria "Legitimate"', *Ynet*, 14 November 2017, www.ynetnews.com/articles/0,7340,L-5042845,00.html; Shaun Walker, 'Vladimir Putin Makes Triumphant Visit to Syria Airbase', *The Guardian*, 11 March 2017, www.theguardian.com/world/2017/dec/11/vladimir-putin-visit-to-syria-airbase-bashir-al-assad.

[5] See Chapter 5 of this volume, discussing war crimes, and Chapter 6, relating to crimes against humanity committed by the Syrian government.

war.[6] The government's assumption seemed to be that to achieve a decisive victory is not only to fight to end those opponents who bore arms against the government's forces but also fight their supporters within the civilian population. Doing so would cause the civilian supporters to seek refuge outside the country, thus cleansing Syria of all those elements within the society from which the rebels came and which gave the protest movement and the rebellion their support. In other words, if there are no inhabitants, there will be no rebels. The government's acts of cruelty were not limited acts of murder and expulsion carried out by undisciplined soldiers or military units fighting on various battlefields throughout the country. On the contrary, the government did little to conceal that it was waging a total war against its opponents and their supporters, and it likely aimed to publicise this policy to deter its enemies and encourage its supporters.

The Syrian government's acts of cruelty will most likely engender hatred that will last for many years and cast a shadow over what happens both within Syria and in neighbouring countries. If Assad survives the war and manages to remain in power, as it now appears he will, the new demographic reality his government has created will make it easier for him to regain control over the entire territory of Syria.

4.1 The Syrian Civil War, Its Origins, and Bashar's Strategy

The Syrian civil war began in the spring of 2011 as a limited, non-violent protest that erupted among Sunni Arabs inhabiting the rural and peripheral areas of the country. This protest was part of the Arab Spring that had broken out in large parts of the Middle East, from Tunisia to Egypt and Libya and finally to Yemen and Syria.[7] The Syrian protest movement was rooted in the country's unique socio-economic circumstances, of which one of the main features was rapid population growth. Syria's population jumped from 6 million in 1970 to 25 million in 2010. This growth was accompanied by severe social and economic distress, intensified by the policies of the government in Damascus aimed at opening

[6] This notwithstanding, ISIS acts were also systematic. Therefore, the conduct of ISIS and other rebel groups was also investigated by the Independent International Commission of Inquiry on the Syrian Arab Republic (CoI). See Chapter 6 discussing the genocide ISIS committed against the Yazidis.

[7] For more on the origins of the Syrian civil war, see David W. Lesch, *Syria: The Fall of the House of Assad* (New Haven, CT: Yale University Press, 2012); William Harris, *Quicksilver War: Syria, Iraq and the Spiral of Conflict* (London: Hurst, 2018).

Syria to the global economy. The deepening economic and social crisis was intensified by unfavourable weather conditions. For several years, the country suffered severe drought such as it had not known for nearly a century. This affected most severely the agricultural sector, a pillar of the Syrian economy.[8] The inhabitants of the rural and peripheral areas of the country, mainly Sunni, suffered most from the developing economic crisis and became the kindling for the sparks of revolt. Members of other minority communities, such as the Druze and the ʾAlawites, remained loyal to the Assad dynasty, whose origins were in the ʾAlawite community. These groups' loyalty stemmed from the fact that they had little to no choice and from the fear that the protest would assume (as indeed happened) a religious character and turn against them as members of minority communities. Such religious hostility was felt throughout the entire territory of both Syria and Iraq.

Notably, the Sunni rural sector was a loyal pillar of the Syrian Baath government. The rural Sunni community was part of the grand coalition of social forces established by Hafez al-Assad when he came to power in November 1970, and it stood at the base of his government throughout his rule. This coalition was formed following the Baath revolution of 8 March 1963. Its aim was to unify the minority communities in Syria and the Sunni rural sector under the leadership of the ʾAlawites in the struggle against the old Syrian elite. The latter was based in the notable families from the big cities who had ruled the Syrian Lands (*Bilad al-Shaʾm*) for centuries and had become the rulers of the modern Syrian state during the French Mandate period and the years following Syrian independence. It is therefore quite significant that the Sunni rural community, which had been so loyal to the Assad/Baathist establishment, now came out against the government because they felt the government had turned its back on them.[9] Indeed, as in Tunisia and Egypt, human rights activists and civil society groups and organisations were operating in Syria prior to the eruption of the revolution in March 2011, such as the 'Damascus declaration initiative' of 2005 and earlier reformers who sought change during the Damascus Spring of 2001. However, these groups were not the driving forces behind the eruption of the protests in Syria in 2011 and failed to take the lead of these waves of protest.

[8] Fouad Ajami, *The Syrian Rebellion* (Stanford: Hoover Institution Press, 2012); Samer N. Abboud, *Syria* (Cambridge: Polity Press, 2016).

[9] Hanna Batatu, *Syria's Peasantry, the Descendants of Its Lesser Rural Notables and Their Politics* (Princeton, NJ: Princeton University Press, 1999); Eyal Zisser, 'The Renewal of the "Struggle for Syria": The Rise and Fall of the Ba'th Party', *Sharqiyya* (Fall 2011): 21–9.

What began as a relatively peaceful protest deteriorated into a popular uprising, then into a civil war, and finally into a religious war of jihad fought by radical Islamic groups and factions in Syria. At first, the protesters did not employ violence or take up firearms and manifested no Islamic characteristics. Provoked by the violent means adopted by the Syrian government in its efforts to suppress the protest, the situation deteriorated. In time there were even those who blamed the authorities in Damascus for encouraging the protest or at least contributing to its radicalisation and, especially, the perception of its deterioration into a war of jihad. In the view of these critics, the government did so by releasing inmates belonging to radical Islamic groups from Syrian prisons. The government allegedly hoped that these figures would give an Islamic tone to the protest movement and the revolution. In doing so they would deter the moderate elements within the Syrian society – the middle classes and the elites in the big cities – from joining the protest or continuing to support it.[10] However, it is possible that the intervention of foreign countries such as Turkey and especially Saudi Arabia and Qatar in Syria's affairs may have also contributed to the Islamic character of the Syrian war. Additionally, the disintegration of state and social frameworks throughout the Middle East led to a rise in the power of radical Islam.

From the very beginning, the government reacted to the anti-government rioting with unrestrained violence. Initially it deployed the security forces, then the police, and even members of irregular militias (*shabiha*), who acted with unrestrained brutality. Photos and videos streamed on social networks show security forces beating, abusing, and humiliating residents in the areas where demonstrations broke out. When it became apparent that the revolution was too large for the police and security forces to suppress, the government sent regular military units into the fray. The first to suffer was the city of Daraa, where anti-government demonstrations began on 18 March 2011. Troops were sent in on 25 April, and during the following days and weeks military units were deployed to additional towns and cities throughout the country. The army used live ammunition against the demonstrators. In response to the government's large-scale use of the army, the local population turned to armed resistance, largely led by defectors from the Syrian

[10] See Bashar al-Assad's response to such arguments in an interview given to the Radio and Television of Portugal (RTP). For the Arabic version of the interview, see SANA (Syrian Arab News Agency, Damascus), 22 November 2016, http://sana.sy/en/?p=93569.

armed forces. The army reacted by employing tanks, artillery, fighter planes, attack helicopters, and even surface-to-surface missiles. This led to a dramatic increase in the number of casualties. Dozens, even hundreds, of people were killed or wounded every week.[11]

The use of violence, including military force, is an important element in the legacy left by the government's founding father, Hafez al-Assad. From 1976 to 1982 he successfully used violence to suppress the Islamic revolt against his government, culminating in the February 1982 massacre in the city of Hama.[12] However, Bashar al-Assad's employment of military force since 2011 only served to escalate the crisis in Syria into a bloody civil war. During the early stages of the fighting Assad tried to evade any personal responsibility for what was happening throughout Syria. Numerous times he claimed that the means of suppression employed against the demonstrators were not the result of a decision from above, and certainly not the result of instructions he himself gave, but rather a result of the lack of experience and expertise of the security forces and the police. Later, Assad denied that his forces had carried out any killings of his opponents and denied that his government used chemical weapons. One example of this is seen in his 7 December 2011 interview with Barbara Walters of ABC. Walters tried to corner Assad with detailed questions about acts of repression and killings reported by Western media, but Assad was steadfast in his answers. In response to Walters' question 'Do you think that your forces cracked down too hard?', Assad answered: 'They are not my forces, they are military forces [that] belong to the government ... [T]here is a difference between having [a] policy to crack down and between having some mistakes committed by some officials. [T]here is a big difference.' Walters' rejoinder, 'Okay, but you are the government', was rebuffed: 'I don't own them. I am [the] president. I don't own the country, so they are not my forces.' Walters persisted: 'No, but you have to give the order.' Assad responded: 'We don't kill our people, nobody kill[s]. No government in the world kill[s] its people, unless it's led by [a] crazy person.'[13]

[11] Lesch 2012; Eyal Zisser, 'Syria: Between Dar`a and Suwayda: Communities and State in the Shadow of the Syrian Revolution', in Brandon Friedman and Bruce Maddy-Weitzman, eds., *Inglorious Revolutions: State Cohesion in the Middle East after the Arab Spring* (Tel Aviv: The Moshe Dayan Center for Middle East and African Studies, Tel Aviv University, 2014): 107–120.

[12] Raphael Lefevre, *Ashes of Hama, The Muslim Brotherhood in Syria* (London: Hurst, 2013).

[13] Bashar al-Assad, interview by Barbara Walters, ABC, 7 December 2011, audio, 06:28, http://abcnews.go.com/International/transcript-abcs-barbara-walters-interview-syrian-president-bashar/story?id=15099152&singlePage=true.

As the crisis in the country deepened, however, it became less possible to make a distinction between Bashar al-Assad and his associates and subordinates. Just as it had gradually become clear during the first decade of Bashar al-Assad's rule as president that he stood directly and firmly behind various policies and steps undertaken by the Syrian government in the spheres of both domestic and foreign policies, so now it became clear that he was behind the policy of using strong-arm tactics against his opponents and was by no means an uninvolved observer from the side or an innocent sheep caught up among a pack of wolves – that is, the security forces and the army.[14]

4.2 From Suppression and Terror to Total War

Despite the extensive use of force, the government failed to impede the momentum of the protest movement which, provoked by the violence used against it, turned into a popular uprising, then an armed rebellion, and ultimately a civil and proxy war of jihad. The government's failure to end the protests is all the more striking in view of several accompanying circumstances: the opposition began as a purely local and spontaneous phenomenon; it lacked a guiding and organising hand; it had no effective leadership or military command; and the radicalisation that developed in the ranks of the rebels deterred many of those who had supported the uprising in the beginning.

As time progressed, the position of the Syrian government deteriorated. The situation became particularly dire towards the end of 2012 and the beginning of 2013. In July 2012 the top ranks of the government's security forces were killed in an attack in Damascus. This was followed by the spread of the conflagration to Aleppo, the country's second-largest city. In March 2013 the capital city of al-Raqqa province on the northeast bank of the Euphrates River fell to the rebels.[15] Assad and the people around him finally came to understand that the rebels' activities had developed into an existential threat. The result was the adoption of a new strategy, of which a main element was to launch a total war against the government's opponents. Assad's decision to do so was based on his assumption that it would be difficult to put down the rebellion without

[14] Eyal Zisser, 'Alone at the Top: Bashar al-Assad and the Struggle for Syria', *Strategic Assessment* 16, no. 3 (October 2013): 57–65.

[15] Eyal Zisser, 'Can Assad's Syria Survive Revolution?', *Middle East Quarterly* 20, no. 2 (Spring 2013): 36–42; Eyal Zisser, 'The Deadlocked Syrian Crisis: The Fable of the Ants and the Elephant', *Strategic Assessment* 16, no. 2 (July 2013): 35–46.

'dealing' with the civilian population that provided shelter and support to the rebels, as well as a steady supply of newly enlisted fighters. In practice, the implication was to abandon the former tactic of employing fear, intimidation, and terrorisation in favour of the cleansing and purging of whole areas of their inhabitants.

4.3 The Ideology behind the Policy

The violence employed by the Syrian government was inspired by and rooted in attitudes prevailing among the upper echelons of the Syrian government and among many of its supporters. Like Assad himself, they viewed the war against the rebels as a war of survival. This assumption was given greater weight by the religious radicalisation spreading among the rebel ranks and the increasing strength of radical groups.

Members of the religious minorities were particularly concerned in this regard. Not only were they verbally threatened by the Salafi-Jihadi groups, but the threats were also carried out, with minority groups suffering death and destruction at the hands of rebel groups. The pragmatic groups among the Islamic rebels, such as the al-Nusra Front, limited themselves to the demand for Islamisation; they insisted that the people under their rule adopt Sunni Muslim practices. At the beginning of 2015, Sunni Islam was imposed on the isolated Druze communities in the Jabal Samak area of Idlib province in northern Syria.[16] It is no wonder, therefore, that supporters of the government say, 'Assad or We Burn the Country.' On the other hand, Assad's opponents from the pragmatic and even secular camps have been quoted as threatening to drown Syria in blood until they were relieved of the plague of Bashar al-Assad's government.[17] At the same time, the Sunni elites in the big cities were also concerned about the Islamic radicalism preached by some of the rebel groups. These elites did not hide their contempt for those they considered riff-raff coming in from the rural and peripheral areas. This disdain has a long tradition; it stems from the class tension existing within Sunni society between the urban and rural sectors.

[16] Aymenn Al-Tamimi, 'The Massacre of Druze Villagers in Qalb Lawza, Idlib Province', *Syria Comment*, 15 June 2015, www.joshualandis.com/blog/the-massacre-of-druze-villagers-in-qalb-lawza-idlib-province/.

[17] Emile Hkayem, '"Assad or We Burn the Country": Misreading Sectarianism and the Government in Syria', *War on the Rocks*, 24 August 2016, http://warontherocks.com/2016/08/assad-or-we-burn-the-country-misreading-sectarianism-and-the-government-in-syria.

In several statements, Assad gave his personal approval for the extreme brutality employed by his government against its opponents. He thus revealed his perception of the character and essence of the conflict and, consequently, the manner in which he thought the threat should be handled. These statements made it clear the actions on the battlefield were the result of directives that came from above. Assad laid the ideological foundations for an all-out war against his opponents. In a speech before Syrian clergymen in April 2014, he explained:

> We must recognize the fact that we are facing tens of thousands of terrorists who are the sons of Syria. I don't mean the terrorists who came from outside Syria. When we talk about tens of thousands of Syria's sons who became terrorists we must recognize the fact that they had a social environment that supported them: families, relatives, and neighbours, and of course friends and other people. That is, we are speaking about hundreds of thousands or even millions of Syrians. And even if it is only 1 million, this is already a six-digit [sic] number. This may not be so large a number with respect to the overall size of Syria's population, but when we are dealing with a million or even several hundred thousand from a population of 23 million, one cannot avoid the conclusion that what is at stake is a social and moral failure, and ultimately a national failure.[18]

In reporting the confrontations between the Syrian army and the rebels, particularly when reporting military success on part of the government, official Syrian media channels used terms such as 'cleansing' or 'purging' the country of 'terrorists' or the 'liquidation' of the 'terrorists'. Assad used this terminology as well. In an interview with Russian newspaper *Komsomolskaya Pravda* in early October 2016, he promised that the city of Aleppo would be 'cleansed' of terrorists and their supporters. Thus, he claimed, the way would be opened to liberating the whole of northern Syria from the grip of 'terror', and the 'terrorists' would be pushed into Turkey.[19] Assad also referred to his medical background in justifying his actions. While speaking before the Syrian People assembly on 4 June 2012, he justified the use of force against his opponents with the

[18] 'Asad: Millions of Syrians Support Terrorism', *CNN Arabic*, 29 April 2014, http://arabic.cnn.com/middleeast/2014/04/29/syria-assad-speech, translated by Eyal Zisser; 'President Asad Addresses a Group of Religious Clerics', *Damas Press*, 23 April 2014, www.dampress.net/?page=show_det&category_id=5&id=42942&lang=ar, translated by Eyal Zisser.

[19] Laura Smith-Spark and Pete Burn, 'Assad: Syrian Forces Must "Clean" Aleppo', *CNN*, 14 October 2016, http://edition.cnn.com/2016/10/13/middleeast/assad-syria-aleppo-springboard.

following words: 'What sane person likes blood? Of course, there is no such person. But when a surgeon goes into the operating room he is often obliged to open a bleeding wound and even to excise, amputate, or cut off an organ from the body. Would we say, in such a case, that he has blood on his hands, or, on the contrary, salute him for having saved the patient's life?'[20]

Notably, Assad did not consider this to be a war against the entire Sunni community. Assad's wife, Asma' al-Akhras, comes from a Sunni family from the city of Homs. Many Sunnis support him and serve as loyal allies and officials in his government. Wael Nader al-Halqi served as prime minister from 2012 to 2016. He was succeeded by Imad Khamis in July 2016. Fahd Jassem al-Freij became minister of defense in 2012. All three are members of the Sunni community. Many other Sunnis served in Assad's government as well. Furthermore, the majority of the Sunnis belonging to Syria's middle class and living in the big cities support the government or at least prefer to sit on the fence and not join the revolt against the government.

In many cases, those Sunnis who did oppose the government and were subsequently subdued were given the option of becoming 'reconciled' – that is, the opportunity to surrender, turn over their weapons, and accept the government's authority. In other cases, when government forces closed in on an area they gave the rebels and their supporters the opportunity to leave or be evacuated to other areas, such as the rebel-controlled Idlib province.

The members of the Sunni community in Syria were not in and of themselves a target of the government's war against its enemies. The enemy had certain clearly defined characteristics. They were mostly Sunnis inhabiting the rural and peripheral areas of the country or migrants from those areas to the slums surrounding the big cities. Assad's war of extermination, while having a focused religious and even ethnic aspect, also has a definite socio-economic aspect.

4.4 Bashar al-Assad's Total War

With the strategy of total war, the Syrian government has used its military forces against both urban population centres and rural villages held by the rebels. The government forces have employed conventional

[20] 'Syria Crisis: Investigating Jisr al-Shughour', *BBC*, 22 June 2011, www.bbc.com/news/world-middle-east-13857654.

weapons, including artillery fire, aerial bombardment, and advanced surface-to-surface missiles. In areas where it has been unable to purge its enemies, the government has imposed blockades or sieges. This has led to widespread hunger, which the government views as a step in preparing the way for launching an assault, unless the suffering brings about the rebels' surrender first.

Examples of this process can be found in the al-Ghouta al-Sharqiya rural area east of Damascus and in small towns such as Madaya, as well as Darayya and Qudssaya near Damascus. In August 2016, an agreement was reached under the auspices of the United Nations to evacuate rebel fighters and their families from the town of Darayya and, a few days later, also from the town of Muadamiyat al-Sham. In October 2016 the rebels were evacuated from the town of Qudssaya, and in April 2017 from the towns of al-Zabadani and Madaya.[21] The opposition claimed that by sponsoring these agreements the UN and the international organisations involved gave legitimacy to the Syrian government's intended demographic changes (commonly – but not necessarily legally – understood as 'ethnic cleansing') as the agreements included arrangements for the evacuation of the civilian population that supported the rebels.[22]

4.5 Chemical Weapons

The use of chemical weapons is one of the manifestations of the war declared by Bashar al-Assad against his people. One high-profile case of a chemical attack by the Syrian government took place on 21 August 2013, when two opposition-controlled areas in the al-Ghouta al-Sharqiya rural area east of Damascus were attacked. Nearly 1,400 people were killed in the chemical attack, most of them women and children. The attack has been documented extensively; photos and videos of people injured in the attack have been distributed widely, spreading awareness of the atrocity all over the world.[23] Prior to this, on 19 March 2013, the government had used gas at Khan al-Asal near

[21] 'Militants from Syria's Qudsaya Prepare to Leave for Idlib', *Al-Monitor*, 14 October 2016.

[22] Karim el-Bar, 'Ethnic Cleansing on an Unprecedented Scale: Rebels, UN Criticize Assad Tactics', *Middle East Eye*, 3 September 2016, www.middleeasteye.net/news/ethnic-cleansing-unprecedented-scale-rebels-un-criticize-assad-tactics-954614280.

[23] 'Syria Chemical Attack: Key UN Findings', *BBC*, 30 January 2014, www.bbc.com/news/world-middle-east-24130181; '"Clear and Convincing" Evidence of Chemical Weapons Use in Syria, UN Team Reports', *UN News*, 16 September 2013, www.un.org/apps/news/story.asp?NewsID=45856#.Wm4dy6gjRnI.

Aleppo. However, that incident was ignored by the media, and the Syrian government hastened to say that it was not in any way involved or responsible for what happened. Several weeks later, Brigadier General Itai Bron, head of the research department of the Military Intelligence Directorate of the Israel Defence Forces (IDF), confirmed that the Syrian government was responsible for the chemical attack.[24]

On 21 August 2012, US President Barack Obama had warned Bashar al-Assad that if he used chemical weapons he would be crossing a red line. In practice, however, Obama refrained from responding to the Syrians' use of chemical weapons at Khan al-Asal in March 2013, and Bashar may have seen this as a green light for continued use of chemical weapons. However, following the 21 August 2013 chemical attack in al-Ghouta al-Sharqiyya, Obama could not continue ignoring the situation in Syria. The scale of the atrocity was too great, and the photographs and videos of the victims, many of them women and children, were widely distributed. Under pressure from American public opinion, the Obama administration was compelled to threaten that it would respond militarily. However, the preparations for an American military move proceeded very slowly, especially as they received no international backing, even from the European Union. This enabled Russia to come to Assad's aid and propose a compromise that would free him from any threat of US intervention. On 14 September 2013 the foreign ministers of Russia and the United States made a proclamation stating that, along with Syria, they agreed to the elimination of Syria's chemical weapons store by mid-2014. The Russian-American agreement in effect granted Bashar al-Assad breathing space from any future US military action so long as he refrained from continued use of chemical weapons.[25] Following this agreement, the media issued reports that the Syrian government had retained and was concealing chemical weapons.[26] Furthermore, the Syrian government continued to use weapons such as chlorine and 'air-gas' bombs, which

24 United Nations Mission to Investigate Allegations of the Use of Chemical Weapons in the Syrian Arab Republic, https://unoda-web.s3.amazonaws.com/wp-content/uploads/2013/12/report.pdf; Yaacov Lappin, 'IDF Official: Assad Government Is Using Chemical Weapons', 23 April 2013, www.jpost.com/Defense/IDF-intelligence-research-head-Assad-used-sarin-gas-310773.

25 Eyal Zisser, 'The Syrian Deadlock – Bashar al-Assad and Bara[c]k Obama's Moment of Truth', e-International Relations, 15 September 2013, www.e-ir.info/2013/09/15/the-syrian-deadlock-bashar-al-assad-and-barak-obamas-moment-of-truth/.

26 Adam Entous and Naftali Bendavid, 'Mission to Purge Syria of Chemical Weapons Comes Up Short', *Wall Street Journal*, 23 July 2014, www.wsj.com/articles/mission-to-purge-syria-of-chemical-weapons-comes-up-short-1437687744.

proved to be no less deadly than the Sarin gas the Syrians had used up to September 2013. In response, Obama said:

> While chlorine itself is not listed as a chemical weapon, its use in such attacks may be prohibited. And so we're working with the international community to investigate that. If we have the kinds of confirmation that we need, we will once again work with the international community and the organization charged with monitoring compliance by the Syrian government, and we will reach out to patrons of Assad like Russia to put a stop to it.[27]

In March 2015, the UN Security Council approved Resolution 2209 condemning 'any use of chemicals in Syria'.[28] Russia had no problem in supporting the resolution since it refrained from pointing an accusing finger at any of the warring parties. In a typically cynical move, Russia reached an agreement with the United States to establish a mechanism that would examine the matter and determine which of the warring parties in Syria was responsible for the use of illegal weapons.[29]

In August 2016, the findings of a special UN team and the Organisation for the Prohibition of Chemical Weapons were published in New York. The investigators examined a series of reports regarding the use of chemical weapons in the war in Syria. They found that Bashar al-Assad's government had used chlorine bombs at least twice in the previous two years. In April 2014, Syrian airplanes bombed the village of Talmans in Idlib province, and in March 2015 they bombed the small town of Sarmin near the city of Idlib. The investigative team also found that ISIS used chemical weapons, evidently sulphur mustard gas, during fighting in August 2015 near the city of Aleppo.[30]

On 28 February 2017, the UN Security Council discussed the findings of the report. A resolution was brought before the Council to impose

[27] 'Obama: US Helping Investigate Reports of Chlorine in Bombs in Syria', *Reuters*, 15 May 2015, www.reuters.com/article/us-mideast-crisis-syria-obama/obama-u-s-helping-investigate-reports-of-chlorine-in-bombs-in-syria-idUSKBN0NZ2I820150515.

[28] United Nations Security Council, S/RES/2209, 6 March 2015.

[29] Tim Hains, 'Obama on Why Syria "Red Line" Has Not Been Crossed: Chlorine "Has Not Been Listed as a Chemical Weapon"', *Real Clear Politics*, 15 May 2015, https://www.realclearpolitics.com/video/2015/05/15/obama_on_why_syria_red_line_has_not_been_crossed_chlorine_has_not_been_listed_as_a_chemical_weapon.html.

[30] 'Syria, ISIS responsible for chemical weapons attacks, UN inquiry finds', *Fox News*, 24 August 2016, www.foxnews.com/world/2016/08/24/syria-isis-responsible-for-chemical-weapons-attacks-un-inquiry-finds.html; 'Syrian government and Isis carried out chemical attacks, say UN investigators', *The Guardian*, 25 August 2016, www.theguardian.com/world/2016/aug/25/assad-government-isis-chemical-attacks-syria-un-investigators.

sanctions on twenty-one Syrian individuals, companies, and organisations for their role in the chemical weapons attacks against Syrian civilians. The draft resolution also provided for placing a ban on the supply of combat helicopters to Syria, since, according to UN investigators, such aircraft had been used in the chemical attacks. However, Russia and China vetoed the resolution and so prevented its adoption.[31]

4.6 Russian and Iranian Intervention on the Model of Chechnya: Aleppo as a Case Study

The Russians and the Iranians arrived on Syrian soil in September 2015 with the aim of participating in Assad's war. Russia's involvement shielded the government from any possible American action and added another dimension to the war it was waging against its opponents. The Syrian government followed now the 'Chechnya model' used by the Russians in the First Chechen War (1994–1996). The application of this model in Syria was based on a two-pronged military effort. One prong involved the systematic and deliberate destruction of urban and rural spaces by means of aerial bombardments or shelling from the ground. Such attacks inevitably harmed the civilian population suspected of supporting the rebels. The civilians either fled or were compelled to leave, and wide areas of the country were depopulated. The second prong of the military effort involved a joint Iranian-Syrian attack on the ground comprising the Syrian government, Iranian Revolutionary Guards, and Hezbollah fighters. The ground campaign was intended to complement the Russian air campaign and enable the reoccupation of areas the Syrian government had lost to the rebels since the outbreak of fighting.[32]

Like Assad, the Russians had no intention of waging a sectarian war against the Sunni Muslims. Like Assad, they were prepared to reach reconciliation agreements with the rebels, provided the latter put down their weapons and, in some cases, left together with their supporters for areas in northern Syria still under rebel control. In general, though, the Russians' behaviour showed little interest in the fate of the civilian population negatively affected by the shockwaves of the ongoing warfare.

[31] Somini Sengupatafeb, 'Russia and US Clash Over Syria in Security Council Vote', *The New York Times*, 28 January 2017, www.nytimes.com/2017/02/28/world/middleeast/united-nations-security-council-syria-sanctions-russia-trump.html.

[32] Eyal Zisser, 'Russia's War in Syria', *Strategic Assessment* 19, no. 1 (April 2016): 41–9.

Syria's second-largest city, Aleppo, located in the north of the country, has become a perfect archetype of the war. Roughly 2.5 million people lived in the city before the war; only 1.5 million remain. The rebel-held areas are home to only 300,000 people. As Russia's involvement in Syria deepened, the number of civilian casualties rose considerably. Towards the end of 2016, after the Russians began concentrating their efforts on Aleppo and its environs, the number of casualties from Russian attacks reached roughly 4,500 killed and several thousand wounded. This number, however, is only a part of the Russian impact. While Russia's main effort was concentrated around Aleppo, areas held by the rebels all over were being crushed under a combined Russian-Syrian-Iranian campaign.[33]

The purpose of their attacks was to destroy the civilian infrastructure that made it possible for the rebels to continue their fighting in the war zones. Of particular interest were institutions such as medical centres, schools, marketplaces, food supply centres, etc. The attacks entailed large-scale civilian casualties.[34] The UN Security Council attempted to adopt a French-drafted resolution aimed at alleviating the situation in Aleppo, but this effort failed on 8 October 2016 due to a Russian veto. Notably, a Russian draft resolution with a Russian formula for ending the fighting in Syria also failed to be adopted by the Security Council due to a Western veto.[35]

The rebels in Aleppo had little chance against the Russian-Iranian war machine. They continually lost their positions in the eastern parts of the city and finally had no choice but to withdraw. The final end of the battle over Aleppo, and perhaps evidence of the real stakeholders of that battle, came when, on 20 December 2016, the Russians reached understandings with Turkey and Iran (the 'Moscow Declaration') regarding the partition of Syria into 'protected areas', which were spheres of influence in which the regional players had influence and a physical presence. In the framework of this agreement, tens of thousands of the inhabitants of the eastern neighbourhoods of Aleppo were evacuated to Idlib province, which was held by the rebels. Those evacuated included many armed

[33] '4500 Killed Since the Collapse of the Russian-American Truce', *Syrian Observatory for Human Rights*, 22 October 2016, www.syriahr.com/en/?p=52953.

[34] Kareem Shaheen, 'Aleppo Bombing Will Continue until Rebels Leave, Russia Says', *The Guardian*, 9 December 2016, www.theguardian.com/world/2016/dec/09/aleppo-bombardment-syria-questions-over-russia-ceasefire-pledge.

[35] 'Security Council Fails to Adopt Two Draft Resolutions on Syria, Despite Appeals for Action Preventing Impending Humanitarian Catastrophe in Aleppo', *United Nations*, 8 October 2016, www.un.org/press/en/2016/sc12545.doc.htm.

men but also civilians who supported the rebels or who simply wanted to flee the city. On 30 December 2016, Russia brought the Moscow Declaration to the UN Security Council for approval. It was adopted as Resolution 2336, with the support of the United States and the European Union. A month later, on 23 January 2017, peace talks were held in Astana, Kazakhstan, with the participation of representatives of Assad and his opponents, under Russian, Iranian, and Turkish sponsorship, with the aim of diminishing the violence in Syria and stabilising the ceasefire that had been announced a month earlier.[36]

4.7 Assad's Second Strike – The Chemical Attack against Khan Shaykhun

Despite avoiding international repercussions and American actions, and despite situations in Syria apparently moving in his favour, Assad once again used chemical weapons. On the morning of 4 April 2017, Syrian air force planes launched a chemical attack on the northern town of Khan Shaykhun in Idlib province. Reports indicated the Syrian attackers had used sarin gas and killed over a hundred residents of the town, injuring several hundred more; most of the victims were women and children.[37]

On 8 August 2017, a Commission of Inquiry appointed by the UN to investigate allegations of violations of international law in Syria published a report stating that it had detected thirty-three chemical attacks since the beginning of the civil war. Twenty-seven of those had been carried out by forces of the Syrian government, with seven between March and July 2017 alone, including the attack on Khan Shaykhun. The committee said it was unable to discover who was behind the other attacks. Its report added that '[Syrian] government forces continued the pattern of using chemical weapons against civilians in opposition-held areas. In the most serious case, the Syrian air force used sarin gas in Khan Shaykhun, Idlib Governorate, and killed dozens of people, mostly women and children.'[38]

36 Laila Bassam, Angus McDowall, and Stephanie Nebehay, 'Battle of Aleppo Ends after Years of Bloodshed with Rebel Withdrawal', *Reuters*, 13 December 2016, www.reuters.com/article/us-mideast-crisis-syria/battle-of-aleppo-ends-after-years-of-bloodshed-with-rebel-withdrawal-idUSKBN1420H5.

37 Michael R. Gordon, Helene Cooper, and Michael Shearapril, 'Dozens of US Missiles Hit Air Base in Syria', *The New York Times*, 6 April 2017, www.nytimes.com/2017/04/06/world/middleeast/us-said-to-weigh-military-responses-to-syrian-chemical-attack.html.

38 'Syria: UN Probe Documents Use of Chemical Weapons and Other Crimes Against Civilians', *UN News*, 6 September 2017, www.un.org/apps/news/story.asp?NewsID=57468#.WjrKJN8jRnI.

Western media reported that the horrific scenes from Khan Shaykhun played a decisive role in US President Donald Trump's decision to respond with an attack on Syria two days after the chemical attack. On 7 April 2017, before daybreak, two destroyers of the US Sixth Fleet in the Eastern Mediterranean, the USS *Ross* and the USS *Porter*, fired fifty-nine Tomahawk missiles at Syria's Shuʾayrat air base near the city of Homs, from which the Syrian aircraft had taken off to carry out the chemical attack.[39] However, it became clear that the American move was symbolic at best and had no effect in deterring Assad from continuing on his chosen path. Washington refrained from formulating an all-encompassing strategy to deal with the Syrian crisis and instead concentrated on destroying ISIS. This was the case following another American retaliatory attack against Syrian military bases after the government once again used chemical weapons in Douma, east of Damascus on 7 April 2018.[40]

As such, Russia and its allies were able to continue their efforts to implement a settlement. On 5 May 2017 (again in Astana), Russia, Turkey, and Iran signed a 'memorandum of understanding' committing themselves as guarantors for the establishment of four 'de-escalation' or 'protected' zones. One of these zones was Idlib province and parts of the neighbouring provinces in the north of the country, near the border with Turkey. Another was the region between the cities of Hama and Homs. A third zone was the rural area to the east of Damascus, al-Ghouta al-Sharqiyya. The fourth zone included parts of Daraa and Quneitra provinces near the border with Israel and Jordan. Armed military operations were prohibited in these zones, including activity by the Syrian air force. The memorandum also stipulated that humanitarian aid would be extended to the four zones and that the provision of public services, water, and electricity would be restored. Finally, the three guarantor states agreed to deploy their military forces at crossing, inspection, and observation points to supervise the implementation of the agreement. At the same time, a struggle began over who would control the eastern desert (al-Badia), an unpopulated region but a vital one for creating land continuity linking Tehran, Baghdad, Damascus, and Beirut.[41]

[39] 'Evolution of Trump's Statements on Syria', *Fox News*, 6 April 2017, www.foxnews.com/politics/2017/04/06/evolution-trumps-statements-on-syria.html.

[40] BBC, 'Syria War: What We Know About Douma Chemical Attack', 10 July 2018, www.bbc.com/news/world-middle-east-43697084.

[41] 'Syria's "De-escalation Zones" Explained', *al Jazeera TV*, 4 July 2017, www.aljazeera.com/news/2017/05/syria-de-escalation-zones-explained-170506050208636.html.

The ease with which the Russians succeeded in advancing these arrangements and having the rebel groups accept them – at least those moderate rebel groups supported by the Arab states and the West – was evidence of how significantly revolutionary fervour and fighting spirit had declined in Syria. The fatigue and inaction of the international community, in particular the Western states led by the United States, contributed to the decline. Other factors were involved as well, such as the rebels' failure to overcome their tendency to split and quarrel among themselves, their failure to develop effective political and military leadership, and their failure to prevent religious extremism from spreading in their ranks. Indeed, during 2018, the Syrian army supported by the Russians and the Iranians was able to take over most of the 'de-escalation' or 'protected' zones all over country, especially in Southern Syria and east of Damascus.

Washington's willingness to accept Russia's moves and its decision to focus on the struggle to eradicate ISIS in eastern Syria support this analysis. In late June 2017, US President Donald Trump decided to stop the assistance former President Obama had given various rebel groups in Syria. With this, Trump ended American involvement in the civil war itself.[42] A year and a half later, on 20 December 2018, US President Trump tweeted his decision to withdraw US forces from Syria, although 2,000 American soldiers still remain on Syrian soil.[43]

4.8 The Human Price

The feeling that the war in Syria has entered its final stretch makes it possible to turn to the human price it has exacted. On 26 June 2013, the Syrian Observatory for Human Rights (SOHR) (*al-Marsad al-Suri liHquq al-Insan*) reported that the number of people killed in the Syrian civil war had reached 100,000. This estimate was slightly higher than that by the UN, which that same month put the death toll in Syria at 93,000. On 3 December 2014, the SOHR updated the number of fatalities to 200,000. In mid-2016 the Syrian Centre for Policy Research (SCPR) spoke of

[42] 'Syria War: Trump "Ends CIA Arms Programme for Rebels"', *BBC*, 20 July 2017, www.bbc.com/news/world-middle-east-40667229.

[43] Timothy Bella, '"Trump Gets No credit": As Republicans Question Syria Withdrawal, Trump Tweets to Defend Himself', *The Washington Post*, 20 December 2018, www.washingtonpost.com/nation/2018/12/20/trump-gets-no-credit-republicans-question-syria-withdrawal-trump-tweets-after-midnight-defend-himself/?noredirect=on&utm_term=.864bb76e2f48

470,000 fatalities. At the end of 2016 there were those who estimated the number exceeded 600,000.[44] Notably, at the beginning of 2014 the UN Office of the High Commissioner for Human Rights stopped counting the number of people killed in the fighting in Syria when the number, by their estimation, passed the 100,000 mark. This was due to the difficulties encountered when trying to investigate and, in particular, verify the reports issued from the field regarding the number of battlefield victims.[45]

On the first day of the revolution, on 18 March 2011, two demonstrators were killed in the southern city of Daraa, and three more were killed the following day when disorder broke out during the funerals of those killed the day before. The following week, on 25 March 2011, demonstrations broke out at the end of Friday prayer services in the mosques. Between seventy and one hundred people were killed throughout the country in the Friday demonstrations and during the disturbances in the following days. After that, the number of fatalities increased dramatically as a result of several developments. Demonstrations and rioting spread throughout the country and were no longer confined to Fridays. Furthermore, in April 2011 the government began dispatching regular army units against the insurgents.[46] By April 2012 the number of fatalities had risen to several hundred a week, and by the beginning of 2013 over a hundred people were recorded as killed every day in the fighting throughout the country. The greatest number of victims in a day was recorded following the 21 August 2013 chemical attack in al-Ghouta al-Sharqiyya, with nearly 1,400 people killed. In May 2011 the total number of fatalities since the beginning of the revolution passed the 1,000 mark. In March 2012 the number of killed was estimated to be 10,000, and by December 2012 it reached 50,000. In June 2013 the number was already close to 100,000; in December 2014 it was estimated at 200,000, and by mid-2016 it had reached roughly 470,000.[47]

The declining number of fatalities in Syria suggests the war is nearing its end. Statistics show that in 2016, which ended with the battle over the city of Aleppo, 13,617 civilians were killed, a number similar to that of 2015. By contrast, as the year 2017 approached its end, a relatively low

[44] 'Assad Killed 600,000 in Syria, Says Turkish FM', *Orient TV*, 2 December 2016, www.orient-news.net/en/news_show/128024/Assad-killed-600000-in-Syria-says-Turkish-FM.

[45] 'Syrian War Monitor Says 465,000 Killed in Six Years of Fighting', *Reuters*, 13 March 2017, www.reuters.com/article/us-mideast-crisis-syria-casualties/syrian-war-monitor-says-465000-killed-in-six-years-of-fighting-idUSKBN16K1Q1.

[46] Amar Abdulhamid, Syrian Revolution Digest, www.syrianrevolutiondigest.com.

[47] Death toll archives, Syrian Network for Human Rights, http://sn4hr.org/blog/category/report/monthly-reports/victims-death-toll/.

number of civilians (5,600) had been killed. An equally dramatic decrease occurred in the number of soldiers and fighters killed. While roughly 35,000 non-civilians were killed each year in 2015 and 2016, towards the end of 2017 the number stood at roughly 22,000. In all, according to various estimates, Western coalition forces killed roughly 2,100 civilians, while Russian forces killed about 5,300 civilians.[48]

The Syrian government and its allies were pursuing a course intended to bring about mass flight from areas held by the rebels. It is likely that many of those who fled the country will not return. As a result, the remaining population, due to its ethnic composition and socio-economic characteristics, will be more amenable to Assad's control. The refugee phenomenon, which is expected to peak at roughly one-third of the Syrian population, began at the end of April 2011. At the time, it was reported that approximately 250 refugees from Syria had crossed the border into Turkey in the area north of Jisr al-Shughur in northwest Syria. A month later, in mid-May 2011, it was reported that roughly 500 residents of the city of Talkalakh, on the Syria–Lebanon border, had sought shelter in northern Lebanon. The flow of refugees from Syria to neighbouring countries continually increased and by the beginning of 2012 had reached 100,000, most of whom went to Turkey and Lebanon. In the month of August 2012, with the fighting having reached Aleppo, roughly 100,000 people fled, mostly to Turkey – the highest number to flee Syria in the span of one month. August 2012 brought the total number of Syrians seeking refuge in neighbouring countries to roughly 250,000. By 6 May 2013, according to the UN High Commissioner for Refugees (UNHCR), the number of Syrian refugees seeking shelter outside Syria had passed the 1 million mark.[49]

According to estimates issued in mid-2017, over 10 million people, nearly half of Syria's population, had fled from their homes during the fighting. The number of refugees who fled the country stood at 5,842,368, finding refuge in the following locations: Turkey, 2,910,281; Lebanon, 1,011,366; Jordan, 656,170; Iraq, 233,224; Egypt, 117,591; North Africa, 29,275; and Europe, 884,461.[50] These estimates may be low and relate only to those refugees registered in the UN refugee camps. The summer of 2015 saw Syrian refugees increasingly looking towards Europe. Prior

[48] Zvi Bar'el, 'As Syrian Death Toll Dips, So Does World's Attention', *Ha'aretz*, 19 August 2017, https://www.haaretz.com/middle-east-news/syria/.premium-1.807065.

[49] 'UNHCR's Guterres: Syria Refugees Reach One Million', *UNHCR*, 6 March 2013, www.unhcr.org/neu/757-unhcrs-guterres-syria-refugees-reach-one-million.html.

[50] 'Syrian Refugees: A Snapshot of the Crisis – in the Middle East and Europe', http://syrianrefugees.eu/.

to then, the numbers of those seeking refuge in Europe had been negligible, estimated in early 2015 at roughly 30,000. By July 2015 that number had reached 107,500, and by the end of 2015 the number reached roughly 1 million.[51] Notably, as of early September 2015, 2,349 refugees trying to reach Europe by boat drowned in the Mediterranean.[52]

4.9 The Demographic Change in the Character of Syrian Society

The years of warfare in Syria have been destructive to both the state and society. The delicately woven fabric which bound together several ethnic and religious communities in a fragile network was ripped apart and its elements scattered in all directions. Christians, who numbered over 10 per cent of the Syrian population prior to the outbreak of the crisis, emigrated en masse. Proportionally, Syrian Christians are highly represented among the 8 million Syrian refugees. Notably, among the Syrian refugees, the Christians are those most likely to be successfully absorbed in Western Europe and the United States, especially as there are few bonds to keep them attached to their old homeland.

The future of Syria and the character of the country and its society will be dramatically affected by the shrinking Christian community as well as other demographic changes. In March 2017 the UNHCR estimated that roughly 19 million residents remained in Syria from the 24–25 million who had lived there on the eve of the outbreak of hostilities. Roughly 13,234,837 lived in the areas controlled by the Syrian government, 2,457,897 in the Kurdish areas in northern Syria, 1,796,156 in rebel-controlled areas (before they fell into the government's hands), and 1,323,483 in the region controlled by ISIS (before its defeat).[53] Of Syria's approximately 19 million current residents, the members of the Sunni community constitute less than half.[54] They thus yield the position

[51] Ibid.; 'Syria Regional Refugee Response', *UNHCR*, http://data.unhcr.org/syrianrefugees/regional.php.

[52] Stephanie Nebehay, 'UN Urges Greece to Take Charge of Refugee Crisis', *Reuters*, 18 August 2015, www.reuters.com/article/us-europe-migrants-greece-unhcr/u-n-urges-greece-to-take-charge-of-refugee-crisis-idUSKCN0QN14920150818.

[53] 'Syria Regional Refugee Response', *UNHCR*, http://data.unhcr.org/syrianrefugees/regional.php.

[54] Fabrice Balanche, How Sectarianism Can Help Explain the Syrian War, Syria Deeply, 6 March 2018, www.newsdeeply.com/syria/articles/2018/03/06/how-sectarianism-can-help-explain-the-syrian-war; Fabrice Balanche and Mary Kalbach Horan, *Sectarianism in Syria's Civil War* (Washington DC: The Washington Institute for Near East Policy, 2018).

of demographic primacy to the rest of the population, made up of ʾAlawites and other minority groups, such as the Druze, Shiʾa, Kurds, and Christians.

4.10 Economic Damage

Approximately three-quarters of the Syrian economy and its infrastructure has been severely damaged or destroyed as a result of the fighting. In particular, educational, health and welfare institutions, electricity and water installations, transportation, oil and gas fields, and food and grain storage facilities have been lost. Little remains of the Syria over which Bashar al-Assad and his rivals began fighting. For the most part the physical destruction was carried out by the government with the aim of putting pressure, intimidating, or terrorising the civilian population that supported the government's opponents.

In his article 'The Economic Devastation of Syria: Strategic Implications', economist Eran Yashiv wrote that:

> GDP per capita fell to less than a third of its pre-war level .... Total cumulative GDP loss is estimated to be over $160 billion; the capital stock fell to 43 percent of its pre-conflict level .... Currently 85 percent of the population is below the poverty line, and the unemployment rate has reached 53 percent .... the damage to physical capital and human capital will probably require hundreds of billions of dollars to rebuild .... Even with foreign aid, it would take the Syrian economy decades to recover to its previous level: the International Monetary Fund estimates 20 years of reconstruction.[55]

Conclusions

Syria's civil war turned into a systematic war carried out by the Syrian government against its own people with the aid of Russia and Iran. The crimes committed by the Syrian government equal or even exceed in scope the crimes committed by ISIS. True, the rampaging of the latter has been felt not only in Syria and Iraq but also by various other targets around the world as a result of the global war of terror undertaken by ISIS. ISIS's acts provoked the international community to declare a war

[55] Eran Yashiv, 'The Economic Devastation of Syria: Strategic Implications', *INSS Insight* no. 850 (19 August 2016), www.inss.org.il/publication/the-economic-devastation-of-syria-strategic-implications/.

against the organisation, which was portrayed as the 'the face of evil'.[56] At the same time, however, the world appears willing to ignore that the Syrian government was responsible for most of Syria's fatalities and refugees.

As of this writing, it appears that Assad's war against his people is successful and that he is likely to emerge victorious – or at least remain in power. As such, the conflict cost him little personally and, moreover, actually improved his chances of winning. True, what the victor of the war will inherit is a broken and devastated country whose social fabric has been torn to shreds, and Assad's legacy will be one of oppression, massacre, and ethnic cleansing. However, these methods have so far worked well for him. Assad's legacy may very well be one that other rulers in the region, and perhaps even outside it, will be happy to adopt and emulate.

[56] Jim Miklaszewski and Halimah Abdullah, 'Obama on Paris Attack: "ISIS Is the Face of Evil"', *NBC News*, 16 November 2015, www.nbcnews.com/storyline/paris-terror-attacks/obama-discuss-paris-attacks-isis-fight-conclusion-g20-summit-n464061.

5

All the Red Lines

The Syrian Conflict and Its Assault on International Humanitarian Law

SARETA ASHRAPH

The Syrian war's most fundamental characteristic is the systematic disregard for the most basic rules of international law – and notably international humanitarian law – displayed by its belligerents. The result has been unparalleled human suffering, the scale, complexity, and severity of which are yet to be fully understood.

An estimated half a million men, women, and children have been killed in the violence, which first erupted in March 2011 and has not abated since that time.[1] Millions have been maimed and injured. Over 85,000 Syrians have disappeared, leaving behind anguished, and often impoverished, families.[2] Tens of thousands languish in official and makeshift detention centres. Almost 2 million children no longer attend school and are now all too commonly referred to as 'Syria's lost generation'.[3] Some, mainly boys, have been forcibly recruited to fight in the hostilities.[4] Others, mainly girls, have been forced into early marriages amidst the physical and financial insecurities that flow from

1 Syrian Observatory for Human Rights, 'About 500,000 Persons Were Killed in Syria during 81 Months after the Syrian Revolution Started', 10 December 2017, www.syriahr.com/en/?p=80436.

2 Syrian Network for Human Rights, 'Where Are They?', 30 August 2017, 4, http://sn4hr.org/wp-content/pdf/english/Enforced_disappearance_is_a_weapon_of_war_in_Syria_en.pdf.

3 United Nations Children's Fund (UNICEF), 'No Place for Children', 10 March 2016, http://childrenofsyria.info/wp-content/uploads/2016/03/SYRIA5Y-REPORT-12-MARCH.pdf.

4 UN Office for the Coordination of Humanitarian Affairs (UNOCHA), '2017 Humanitarian Needs Overview', 1 December 2016, https://reliefweb.int/sites/reliefweb.int/files/resources/2017_Syria_hno_161205.pdf; Al Jazeera, 'Syria's Lost Generation: Refugee Children at Work', 12 August 2017, www.aljazeera.com/indepth/features/2017/07/syria-lost-generation-refugee-children-work-170704134535613.html.

the war.[5] An estimated 69 per cent of the Syrian population live in extreme poverty.[6]

The Syrian conflict has revealed not only how swiftly the laws of wars could be cast aside but also how ineffectual international institutions have been when it comes to holding warring parties to account for the ensuing violations. As early as 2014, international law was being described as 'Syria's latest victim'.[7]

International humanitarian law was established to protect civilians and those participating in hostilities from unnecessary suffering. In Syria, however, inflicting suffering on civilians and hors de combat fighters has been consistently documented as a deliberate strategy of various warring parties to punish individuals and communities for their refusal to submit. Much of the conflict has served to emphasise the terrifying power the belligerents employ to crush any whisper of dissent. The strategies, and the violations of international law inherent to them, vary. Some attacks targeted particular segments of Syrian society, notably medical personnel, human rights defenders, and journalists. Many other attacks were wholly indiscriminate, including ground and air assaults on densely populated areas that made little to no attempt to distinguish civilians from the potentially legitimate military targets within. While they have killed far fewer people than conventional weapons, the repeated use of chemical weapons, including nerve agents, has underlined the eclipsing of international law in the Syrian war.

This chapter looks briefly at the unrest that preceded the conflict before focusing on those violations of international humanitarian law which quickly became hallmarks of the Syrian war. It will give particular focus to the use of chemical weapons on the battlefield and the investigations to determine the perpetrator(s). Finally, it asks whether the Syrian conflict represents a nadir in the international community's response to a war where international humanitarian law is breached with impunity and, if so, whether the value of the law of wars is being eroded.

5 United Nations Population Fund, 'New Study Finds Child Marriage Rising among Most Vulnerable Syrian Refugees', 31 January 2017, www.unfpa.org/news/new-study-finds-child-marriage-rising-among-most-vulnerable-syrian-refugees.

6 UNOCHA, '2018 Humanitarian Needs Overview', 21 November 2017, https://reliefweb.int/sites/reliefweb.int/files/resources/hno_2018_summary_171120_0.pdf.

7 David Miliband, 'Syria's Latest Victim: International Law', *Time Magazine*, 26 March 2014, http://time.com/35697/syrias-latest-victim-international-law.

5.1 Civil Unrest (March 2011–mid-February 2012)

In February 2011, small demonstrations began, inspired by the Arab Spring but motivated by more immediate grievances. Syrians took to the streets to protest issues such as rural poverty and corruption, and to demand more expansive democratic rights and the release of political prisoners.[8] It was not until mid-March, however, that mass protests began. The first, in the southern city of Daraa, was ignited by the arrest of a group of boys accused of spray-painting anti-government graffiti on their school walls.[9] Security forces fired on protesters outside the Al-Omari mosque, killing four – the first recorded deaths of the violence that would soon engulf the country.[10]

By the end of March 2011, government forces had killed dozens of unarmed protesters. The crackdown, which included government forces firing on a funeral procession in the town of Izra,[11] caused protests to erupt across Syria. The government's response escalated as it began military operations in restive areas, the first taking place in Daraa city on 25 April 2011.[12] A militia, initially referred to as shabiha and reportedly armed by the government, soon joined the government's armed assaults on restive neighbourhoods.[13]

Although years later sieges would become a very public facet of the conflict, the government made the strategic use of sieges part of its earliest attempts to stamp out the growing rebellion. Daraa was one of the first cities to be besieged, with state forces blocking the passage of food, water, medicine, and people. On 29 April 2011, thousands of protesters carrying olive branches attempted to break

[8] International Independent Commission of Inquiry on the Syrian Arab Republic ('CoI Syria' or 'Syria Commission'), A/HRC/S-17-2/Add.1, 23 November 2011, para 27. The CoI Syria published several reports under the same title, hereinafter referred to by their serial number rather than their title. The Syria Commission was established by the United Nations Human Rights Council in August 2011 to investigate all alleged violations of international human rights law since March 2011. See United Nations Human Rights Council, A/HRC/RES/17/S-1, 22 August 2011; 'Syria Unleashes Force on Protesters Demanding Freedom as Unrest Spreads', *The Guardian*, 26 March 2011, www.theguardian.com/world/2011/mar/25/syria-protest-spreads-troops.

[9] CoI Syria, A/HRC/S-17-2/Add.1, para 27.

[10] Katherine Marsh, 'Syria: Four Killed in Deraa as Protests Spread across South', *The Guardian*, 23 March 2011, www.theguardian.com/world/2011/mar/22/syrian-protests-troops-kill-deraa.

[11] '"Nine Killed" at Syria Funeral Processions', *Al Jazeera*, 23 April 2011, www.aljazeera.com/news/middleeast/2011/04/201142311695872 70.html.

[12] CoI Syria, A/HRC/S-17-2/Add.1, para 28.

[13] CoI Syria, A/HRC/19/69, 22 February 2012, para 39.

the siege.[14] They came under fire from security forces near Sayda. More than fifteen people were killed, including women and children.

Between March 2011 and February 2012, Syrian security forces detained thousands of Syrians – mainly (but not solely) men between the ages of eighteen and fifty – during raids and at checkpoints. Mass arrest campaigns took place across Syria. Five hundred Syrian men, women, and children were arrested during a search of Baniyas on 7 May 2011; one week later, over 400 were arrested in Jisr Al-Shughour.[15]

Many subsequently disappeared. Years later, the fate and whereabouts of thousands of people who were arrested or abducted by government forces in 2011 remain unknown. These include medical staff suspected of treating anyone not in support of the government.[16] Those who were released, or who bribed their way to freedom, came bearing stories of torture, ill treatment, and rape in government detention. Detainees also witnessed the death of cellmates in detention. Among the dead were Thamir Al Sharee, aged fourteen, and Hamza Al-Khateeb, aged thirteen, who were arrested in Sayda in April 2011 and whose mutilated bodies were later returned to their families.[17]

In August 2011, as violence mounted, the United Nations Human Rights Council voted to establish a Commission of Inquiry on Syria, which was charged not only with determining where violations had occurred but also with identifying, where possible, those responsible, 'with a view of ensuring that perpetrators of violations, including those that may constitute crimes against humanity, are held accountable'. In October 2012, the Commission's mandate was expanded to include the investigation of 'abuses and violations of international law'.[18] As of March 2018, the Syria Commission has published over twenty reports and is continuing its investigations. The Syrian government has never permitted the Commission access to Syria.[19]

14 Anthony Shadid, 'Syrian Forces Shoot at Protesters in Dara'a Siege', *The New York Times*, 29 April 2011, www.nytimes.com/2011/04/30/world/middleeast/30syria.html.

15 CoI Syria, A/HRC/S-17-2/Add.1, para 54.

16 Ibid., para 81.

17 CoI Syria, A/HRC/S-17-2/Add.1, para 62; CoI Syria, A/HRC/31/CRP.1, 3 February 2016, para 22; Liam Stack, 'Video of Tortured Boy's Corpse Deepens Anger in Syria', *The New York Times*, 30 May 2011, https://www.nytimes.com/2011/05/31/world/middleeast/31syria.html. As described in the *New York Times* article, the video of the boy's body contains a voiceover saying, 'Where are human rights? Where are the international criminal tribunals?'

18 United Nations Human Rights Council, A/HRC/RES/21/26, 17 October 2012.

19 The Commission's investigations rely on the first-person accounts of those who've fled Syria, encrypted communications with people still inside, and a wealth of documentary evidence including photographs, videos, medical records, and satellite imagery.

By the fall of 2011, the number of defectors from the government's military and security forces was rising. Many began to organise themselves into the Free Syrian Army (FSA).[20] By November 2011, armed confrontations with government forces and an increasingly organised FSA intensified in Rif Damascus, Idlib, Hama, and Homs governorates. As armed groups, many operating under the banner of the FSA, seized control of villages and neighbourhoods in larger towns and cities, the government attacked with heavy weaponry, including rockets and mortar bombs, causing mass civilian casualties and the destruction of homes and infrastructure.[21] In December 2011, following the government's retaking of villages in the province of Idlib, the bodies of defectors and activists evidencing signs of summary execution were found by local residents.[22]

Media and human rights defenders also came under government attack. On 19 November 2011, security agents arrested cameraman Ferzat Jarban while he was filming an anti-government protest in Al-Qaseer. He was found dead the next day, his eyes gouged out.[23] On 29 December, Basil Al-Sayed was shot dead by security forces while filming a violent crackdown on a demonstration in Homs.[24] In February 2012, security forces arrested human rights defenders from the Syrian Center for Media and Freedom of Expression.[25]

By mid-February 2012, intense, protracted armed confrontations were taking place between government forces and anti-government armed groups, though levels of violence varied across Syria. Anti-government armed groups, most operating under the rubric of the FSA, showed increased organisational capabilities. Both of these factors – the intensity and duration of the armed confrontation and the increased organisation of the armed groups[26] – led the Syria Commission and the International

[20] Some defectors, in subsequent interviews with the Syria Commission, detailed state forces shooting indiscriminately at unarmed protesters and confirmed that they had received orders to shoot at unarmed protesters without warning. CoI Syria, A/HRC/S-17-2/Add.1, para 41.

[21] CoI Syria, A/HRC/19/69, paras 39–46.

[22] Ibid., para 42.

[23] CoI Syria, A/HRC/S-17-2/Add.1, para 55.

[24] Ibid.

[25] The three were released, finally, in July and August 2015. The last to be released was Mazen Darwish, who received the Bruno Kreisky Human Rights Prize while imprisoned. 'Mazen Darwish, Prominent Syria Human Rights Activist, freed', *BBC News*, 10 August 2015, www.bbc.com/news/world-middle-east-33853443.

[26] International Criminal Tribunal for the Former Yugoslavia (ICTY), *Prosecutor* v. *Dusko Tadić* Decision on the Defence Motion for Interlocutory Appeal on Jurisdiction, IT-94-1-A,

Committee of the Red Cross to independently declare that the unrest in Syria had tipped over into a state of non-international armed conflict.[27]

As Syria descended into a civil war, government forces concentrated their firepower on restive neighbourhoods of Homs city. State forces shelled and fired rockets into Khaldiyah and Bab Amr, with army snipers and shabiha posted at strategic positions targeting civilians trying to flee. According to the Violations Documentation Centre, at least 787 civilians, including fifty-three women, twenty-six girls, and forty-nine boys, were killed in Syria in the first two weeks of February 2012 alone.[28] The largest number of victims died in Homs city.

As the FSA became more active, members were implicated in the torture and killing of suspected shabiha and collaborators. In late November 2011, an FSA group operating in Damascus tortured and killed a member of the security forces.[29] In late January 2012, in Karm Al-Zeitoun, FSA members lynched a man suspected of working with the state security forces and paraded his body through the streets.[30]

In its February 2012 report, the Syria Commission determined that the Government had 'manifestly failed in its responsibility to protect the population; its forces have committed widespread, systematic and gross human rights violations, amounting to crimes against humanity, with the apparent knowledge and consent of the highest levels of the state'.[31] The Commission did not specify which crimes of humanity it was contemplating, but it is likely, given the facts known at the time, that they would have included murder, torture, rape, enforced disappearance, and other inhumane acts.

International humanitarian law only applies when there is a state of armed conflict. While international humanitarian law did not, therefore, apply prior to mid-February 2012, it is essential to understand that much of the conduct that would later constitute violations of the laws of war was manifest in the time of Syria's civil unrest.

2 October 1995, para 70, for a summary of the factors which determine when a non-international armed conflict has come into being.

27 CoI Syria, A/HRC/21/50, 16 August 2012; 'Syria in Civil War, Red Cross Says', *BBC News*, 15 July 2012, www.bbc.com/news/world-middle-east-18849362.

28 CoI Syria, A/HRC/19/69, para 41.

29 Ibid., paras 114–19.

30 Ibid.

31 Ibid., para 126. The Commission also found that '[a]nti-Government armed groups have also committed abuses, although not comparable in scale and organization with those carried out by the State'.

On 4 October 2011, Russia and China vetoed a UN Security Council resolution calling for an immediate halt to the Syrian government's crackdown on protesters and other opponents. In February 2012, the same two Permanent Members vetoed a Security Council resolution that backed an Arab League plan calling for President Assad to step down. This diplomatic development came a day after hundreds of casualties were reported in a major assault by government forces on Homs city's Khaldiyah neighbourhood.

A culture of impunity, bolstered by paralysis in the Security Council, took root from the earliest months of the unrest. It would serve to underpin a conflict so brutal that it would destroy millions of lives and livelihoods and call into question the value of international law.

5.2 Civil War (Mid-February 2012–Present)

As unrest evolved into civil war, armed violence spread across the country, drawing in an increasing number of local and foreign actors on all sides. The intensity of fighting fluctuated among the different governorates, depending on the belligerents involved and the strategic value of the objectives at stake.

Throughout 2012 and into 2013, anti-government armed groups engaged government forces (as well as pro-government forces such as the shabiha and, later, the National Defense Forces or NDF) in asymmetrical warfare.[32] By mid-2013, the coalition of groups fighting under the FSA banner weakened, arguably in part because of the inconsistent and inadequate support of their international backers, which included the United States, the United Kingdom, Turkey, and the Gulf States.[33]

By the summer of 2012, several radical armed groups emerged, the most organised of which was the al-Nusra Front. Linked to al-Qaeda,[34] al-Nusra emphasised the Syrian, rather than global, nature of their jihad.[35] Alongside a growing number of foreign fighters, the discipline

[32] CoI Syria, A/HRC/ 22/59, 5 February 2013, paras 20–8; CoI Syria, A/HRC/23/58, 18 July 2013, paras 18–29.

[33] CoI Syria, A/HRC/24/46, 16 August 2013, paras 29–31; 'No More, for Now', *The Economist*, 12 December 2013, www.economist.com/blogs/pomegranate/2013/12/american-and-british-aid-syrias-rebels.

[34] 'Profile: Syria's al-Nusra Front', *BBC News*, 10 April 2013, www.bbc.com/news/world-middle-east-18048033.

[35] Thomas Pierret, 'External Support and the Syrian Insurgency', *Foreign Policy*, 9 August 2013, http://foreignpolicy.com/2013/08/09/external-support-and-the-syrian-insurgency/.

and operational abilities of al-Nusra's fighters, combined with better access to reliable sponsors, allowed them to outmatch the fractious moderate groups. By 2015, the armed groups, sometimes including al-Nusra and despite ideological differences, would form ad hoc operations rooms, allowing them to coordinate strategies and resources for specific attacks. In 2016, al-Nusra changed its name to Jabhat Fatah al-Sham and severed ties with al-Qaeda.[36]

ISIS emerged in northern and eastern Syria in 2013 after overrunning large portions of Iraq. The group quickly gained international notoriety for its brutal executions, videos of which it released on its social media channels. In contrast to al-Nusra and the anti-government armed groups, ISIS was motivated by securing territory to establish its quasi-state rather than by overthrowing the Assad government. Until late 2016, the Syrian government, and later Russia, directed the vast majority of their aerial attacks on areas held by anti-government armed groups, leaving the territory held by ISIS relatively untouched.[37]

At its peak, ISIS controlled huge swathes of territory in northern and eastern Syria, including oil-rich Dayr az-Zawr. After declaring its caliphate in June 2014, it attracted more experienced and ideologically motivated foreign fighters. ISIS battled anti-government armed groups, including al-Nusra, as well as Kurdish armed groups and, to a lesser extent, government forces. The desire to defeat ISIS was one of the few points in the conflict around which the international community would coalesce. Under the onslaught of attacks from a global coalition, ISIS began its decline in 2016 and, by November 2017, had abandoned its last city stronghold in Syria.[38]

The Kurdish People's Protection Units (YPG) became visible in 2012 as it fought mostly to defend Kurdish-majority areas. In early 2015, the YPG emerged victorious over ISIS in the battle for Kobani, during which it began to receive air and ground support from the USA-led coalition. In late 2015, the YPG founded the Syrian Democratic Forces upon the

[36] Liz Sly and Karen DeYoung, 'Syria's Jabhat al-Nusra Splits from al-Qaeda and Changes Its Name', *The Washington Post*, 28 July 2016, www.washingtonpost.com/world/middle_east/syrias-jabhat-al-nusra-splits-from-al-qaeda-and-changes-its-name/2016/07/28/5b89ad22-54e6-11e6-b652-315ae5d4d4dd_story.html?utm_term=.ec58a5f0d444.

[37] Aryn Baker, 'Why Bashar Assad Won't Fight ISIS', *Time*, 26 February 2015, http://time.com/3719129/assad-isis-asset/.

[38] Sarah El Deeb, 'ISIS militants Evacuate Last Stronghold in Syria Following Government Offensive', *The Star*, 9 November 2017, www.thestar.com/news/world/2017/11/09/daesh-militants-evacuate-last-stronghold-in-syria-following-government-offensive.html.

urging of the United States as an umbrella group to better incorporate Arabs and other ethnic and religious minorities.

The Syrian government's eventual dominance of the battlefield owed less to their own forces than to external intervention and support. This included Hezbollah's integral role in the recapture of al-Qusayr in June 2013, the on-the-ground support of Iraqi Shi'a militias, and the logistical, technical, and financial support provided by Iran and Russia. Most significant, however, was the Russian military intervention which officially began in September 2015 and was indispensable to the December 2016 retaking of eastern Aleppo city, the last major city in which anti-government armed groups held territory.

In the eight years that have elapsed since the violence in Syria first flared, the United Nations and the League of Arab States have appointed three consecutive Joint Special Envoys.[39] All attempts at political negotiations and ceasefires have ended in failure. Future prospects for a political solution to the conflict are poor; the Syrian government's interest in negotiations is perceived to have waned as military victory has become more likely. Between March 2011 and December 2017 there have been twenty-two resolutions adopted by the Security Council concerning the Syrian conflict,[40] many of which noted the continuing violations of international law committed in Syria and none of which referred the matter to justice. A further ten resolutions have been vetoed by Russia (six of which were also vetoed by China), including one referring the situation in Syria to the International Criminal Court.[41]

In December 2016, faced with the lack of action in the Security Council regarding accountability, the General Assembly adopted its own resolution establishing the Syria Mechanism, a sui generis body mandated to 'collect, consolidate, preserve and analyse evidence of violations of international humanitarian law and human rights violations and abuses and to prepare files in order to facilitate and expedite

[39] The Joint Special Envoys have been: Kofi Annan, who served from 23 February 2012 to 2 August 2012; Lakhdar Brahimi, who served from 17 August 2012 to 13 May 2014; and Staffan de Mistura, who has served from 10 July 2014 until the time of writing.

[40] Security Council Report, UN Documents for Syria: Security Council Resolutions, www.securitycouncilreport.org/un-documents/search.php?ctype=Syria&rtype=Security%20Council%20Resolutions&cbtype=syria&search=%22Security%20Council%20Resolutions%22%20AND%20%22Syria%22&__mode=tag&IncludeBlogs=10&limit=15&page=1 (accessed 29 December 2017).

[41] Security Council Report, UN Documents for Syria: Other https://www.securitycouncilreport.org/un-documents/syria/ (accessed 29 December 2017).

fair and independent criminal proceedings' in national, regional, or international courts or tribunals.[42]

5.3 Assault on International Humanitarian Law

The United Nations, international and national NGOs, and the media have chronicled the myriad violations of international humanitarian law that quickly came to characterise the Syrian war. These have included unlawful killings of civilians and hors de combat fighters; torture; rape and other forms of sexual violence; attacks on medical centres, schools, markets, water, and food sources; the use of starvation of civilians as a method of war; intentional attacks on civilians; indiscriminate and disproportionate attacks; and use of chemical weapons. Here, we examine two principal violations which came to symbolise the horror of a conflict unbound by law.

The first, that of indiscriminate attacks, breaches the foundational principle of international humanitarian law: the principle of distinction. This principle, first implicitly recognised in the preamble to the St. Petersburg Declaration of 1868,[43] holds that parties to a conflict must at all times distinguish between civilians and combatants (and, in non-international armed conflict, persons directly participating in hostilities).[44]

The second violation examined by this chapter is the use of chemical weapons, a method of war absolutely prohibited in both international

[42] United Nations General Assembly, A/Res/71/248, 21 December 2016.

[43] 'Declaration Renouncing the Use, in Time of War, of Explosive Projectiles Under 400 Grammes Weight'. Saint Petersburg, 29 November/11 December 1868, 138 C.T.S. 297, https://ihl-databases.icrc.org/ihl/INTRO/130?OpenDocument, the preamble to which reads, in part, 'the only legitimate object which States should endeavour to accomplish during war is to weaken the military forces of the enemy'.

[44] The principle of distinction is now codified in Articles 48, 51(2), and 52(2) of Additional Protocol I, which applies to international armed conflict, and to which no reservations have been made. See Protocol Additional to the Geneva Conventions of 12 August 1949 and Relating to the Protection of Victims of International Armed Conflicts (Protocol I), 8 June 1977, 1125 U.N.T.S. 3 [hereinafter Additional Protocol I]; Article 13(2) of Additional Protocol II, which applies to non-international armed conflict but to which Syria is not a party, prohibits making the civilian population, as well as individual civilians, the object of attack. It is widely recognised that the obligation to make a distinction between civilians and combatants is customary in both international and non-international armed conflicts. See Protocol Additional to the Geneva Conventions of 12 August 1949 and Relating to the Protection of Victims of Non-International Armed Conflicts (Protocol II), 8 June 1977, 1125 U.N.T.S. 609 [hereinafter Additional Protocol II].

and internal armed conflicts.[45] Despite this, and following independent investigations by several UN entities, it is apparent that chemical weapons have been used on multiple occasions on the Syrian battlefield. This fact remains unchanged despite the published results of those investigations and the international outcry which followed.

5.3.1 *Indiscriminate Attacks*

By the summer of 2012, the Syrian government's assaults on restive areas began to adhere to a pattern.[46] Prior to an attack, the government would besiege the city or town, cutting the flow of goods, water, fuel, and medicine. With supplies running low and medical care compromised, encircling government forces would shell and fire rockets and surface-to-surface missiles into the localities. Over time, they would also increasingly rely on aerial assaults, using jets and helicopter gunships that would fire or drop a variety of weapons including missiles, cluster munitions, thermobaric bombs, incendiary weapons, and barrel bombs. Snipers from the Syrian Armed Forces and the shabiha (and later the NDF) would fire at anyone attempting to flee. Finally, government forces would commence ground operations.

One such attack took place in Tremseh in July 2012. Prior to the attack, checkpoints, some reportedly manned by shabiha, encircled the town. Water and electricity supplies were cut. Government forces first shelled the town from nearby artillery positions, before helicopter gunships fired from the air directly into the town. Strategically positioned snipers shot those attempting to flee. Similar assaults were documented by the Syria Commission as occurring across Hama, Homs, Idlib, Aleppo, and Damascus governorates throughout the conflict.[47]

By late 2012, as the Syrian conflict became one of multiple front lines, the government had to prioritise use of its ground forces, adopting a strategy that used minimal manpower in favour of heavy bombardment during its operations. Most of the weaponry used by the government,

[45] Organisation for the Prohibition on the Use of Chemical Weapons, Convention on the Prohibition of the Development, Production, Stockpiling and Use of Chemical Weapons and on their Destruction, 13 January 1993, 1974 U.N.T.S. 45 [hereinafter Chemical Weapons Convention], www.opcw.org/fileadmin/OPCW/CWC/CWC_en.pdf.

[46] Whether attacks were disproportionate in relation to the concrete and direct military advantage anticipated remains a live question. The Syrian government has not cooperated with any international inquiries, outside of those related to chemical weapons use, and so, without knowing the intended target, proportionality has been difficult to assess.

[47] CoI Syria, A/HRC/21/50; CoI Syria, A/HRC/22/59, 5 February 2013, paras 45–54.

whether fired from the ground or dropped from the air, were indiscriminate by virtue of where and how they were used.[48]

This has been most evident in the government's reliance on barrel bombs. Barrel bombs, the use of which was first documented in August 2012 in Homs city and al-Qusayr, had the advantages of being cheaper than conventional munitions and deliverable by transport helicopters, thereby freeing up helicopter gunships for other attacks. They are improvised explosive devices: containers packed with explosives, scrap metal, and, in many cases, incendiary material. Manufactured locally in different sizes, shapes, and composition, some were capable of destroying a building while others had the capacity to level city blocks.

Since July 2013, barrel bombs have been dropped on civilian-inhabited areas in Idlib, Hama, Raqqah, Homs, Aleppo, Daraa, and Damascus governorates. The campaign of aerial bombardment using barrel bombs in Aleppo governorate, and in particular Aleppo city, was executed with shocking intensity.[49] In November 2014, the government dropped three barrel bombs on the opposition-held al-Marjeh neighborhood of Aleppo city. According to the Syria Commission, twenty-eight people were killed and twenty-five others injured. All the victims were civilians. Ten civilian homes were also destroyed. On the same day, barrel bombs exploded in a vegetable market in Tariq al-Bab neighborhood, killing twenty-five civilians, many of them women and children. The blast caused a fire which led to further civilian casualties and injuries.[50]

Like all gravity bombs, barrel bombs are capable of targeting military objectives if they are dropped from sufficiently low altitudes from slow-moving planes or helicopters. However, in an effort to evade the anti-aircraft capabilities of the armed groups, the government's helicopters and planes dropped barrel bombs from high altitudes, often while

[48] CoI Syria, 'Statement by Mr. Paulo Sérgio Pinheiro, Chair, The use of barrel bombs and indiscriminate bombardment in Syria: the need to strengthen compliance with international humanitarian law', 12 March 2015, www.ohchr.org/Documents/HRBodies/HRCouncil/CoISyria/CoISyriaIndiscriminateBombardment12032015.pdf, in which it was noted: 'The information collected by the Commission strongly indicates that the manner in which the attacks were carried out, the timing and duration of the attacks demonstrates that the aim of the Government's campaign of barrel-bombing was to terrorise the civilian population present in the areas attacked, with the clear message that no civilian was safe anywhere at any time of the day or night.'

[49] 'Syria's "Circle of Hell": Barrel Bombs in Aleppo Bring Terror and Bloodshed Forcing Civilians Underground', *Amnesty International*, 5 May 2015, www.amnesty.org/en/latest/news/2015/05/syrias-circle-of-hell-barrel-bombs-in-aleppo/.

[50] CoI Syria, A/HRC/25/65, 12 February 2014, Annex VI.

travelling at speed. The use of barrel bombs in this manner is indiscriminate. In areas where armed group fighters were present, it was determined that government forces treated clearly separate and distinct military objectives located in densely populated areas with high concentrations of civilians as a single military objective. The use of barrel bombs in that context constitutes an area bombardment, prohibited under international humanitarian law as a tactic that spreads terror among the civilian population.[51] Some barrel bombs are constructed as rudimentary incendiary weapons, causing superfluous injury and unnecessary suffering.

The government has also used incendiary weapons, the most widely reported incident being the attack on Urum al-Kubra which killed at least thirty-seven civilians – predominantly schoolchildren below the age of sixteen – and injured forty-four.[52] Human Rights Watch recorded at least eighteen incendiary weapons attacks between June and August 2016.[53] The legality of incendiary weapons is determined by how they are used. Protocol III of the UN Convention on Conventional Weapons prohibits the use of airdropped incendiary weapons in civilian areas.[54]

Russia became a party to the conflict on 30 September 2015 when it intervened militarily in support of the Syrian government. Russian jets participated in aerial attacks across northern Syria, prompting reports that some of these attacks were indiscriminate, in violation of international humanitarian law. Confirming this proved difficult, in part because

[51] For international armed conflict, 'area bombardment' is prohibited under Additional Protocol I to the Geneva Conventions. However, the prohibition of 'area bombardment' was not included in Additional Protocol II, applicable to non-international armed conflicts, though it is arguable that it is included by inference within the prohibition contained in Article 13(2) of Additional Protocol II on making the civilian population the object of attack. The prohibition of 'area bombardment' is contained in the Amended Protocol II to the Convention on Certain Conventional Weapons. See Convention on Prohibitions or Restrictions on the Use of Certain Conventional Weapons Which May Be Deemed to Be Excessively Injurious or to Have Indiscriminate Effects, 10 October 1980, 1342 U.N.T.S. 137 [hereinafter CCW] (Protocol II). Furthermore, state practice establishes this prohibition as a norm of customary international law applicable in both international and non-international armed conflicts.

[52] 'A Special Report on the Use of Incendiary Bombs in Aleppo and Dara'a Governorates: Burning to Death', *Violations Documentation Centre in Syria*, October 2013, www.vdc-sy.info/index.php/en/reports/1382274490#.Wrdkvi5uYdV.

[53] 'Syria/Russia: Incendiary Weapons Burn in Aleppo, Idlib: Increasing Attacks on Civilian Areas Since Joint Operation Began', *Human Rights Watch*, 16 August 2016, www.hrw.org/news/2016/08/16/syria/russia-incendiary-weapons-burn-aleppo-idlib.

[54] CCW (Protocol III), https://ihl-databases.icrc.org/applic/ihl/ihl.nsf/Article.xsp?action=openDocument&documentId=14FEADAF9AF35FA9C12563CD0051EF1E.

the altitude and speed made it difficult for those on the ground to document the markings of the jets conducting the bombing. Moreover, the Syrian government often uses Russian-made delivery systems and weaponry, including Sukhoi jets, rocket launchers, and munitions,[55] in its attacks. Consequently, video footage of jets and examination of exploded munitions near the impact sites often did not shed light on which state was responsible for a particular attack. In March 2018, however, the Syria Commission released its fifteenth mandated report in which it determined that Russia was responsible for air strikes on a market in Atarib on 13 November 2017 which killed eighty-four people and injured 150 others.[56] The Commission found that 'information available indicates that the strikes were conducted by a Russian fixed-wing aircraft using unguided weapons, including blast weapons. The use of such weapons in a densely civilian-populated area was certain to impact civilians.'

Anti-government armed groups have engaged in indiscriminate attacks, through the routine firing of improvised rockets and mortars into neighbourhoods, villages, and towns under government control. Such was the case of Nubl and Zahra villages, which were encircled by armed groups from mid-2012 until early 2016. During this time, various armed groups, including Ahrar al-Sham, Liwa al-Tawheed, and al-Nusra, fired undirected artillery and home-made rockets into the villages.[57] Similarly, areas of government-held Damascus, such as Jaramana and Sayda Zeinab, were subjected to improvised rocket attacks throughout the conflict, as were the residents of western Aleppo city.[58]

Al-Nusra and affiliated groups used suicide bombings and vehicle-borne improvised explosive devices (IEDs). While in 2011 these bombings were directed at military targets, groups soon began to carry out bombings in populated areas without obvious legitimate targets. Between January 2012 and April 2014, seventeen car bombs and other IED attacks took place in Damascus city, rural Damascus, and Homs city.[59] Car bombs exploded in commercial and residential areas, squares in the

[55] Maria Antonova, 'What Weapons Is Russia Sending Syria?', *The Times of Israel*, 26 September 2015, www.timesofisrael.com/what-weapons-is-russia-sending-syria/.

[56] CoI Syria, A/HRC/37/72, 1 February 2018, paras 77–9, and Annex IV.

[57] CoI Syria, A/HRC/31/68, 11 February 2016, www.ohchr.org/Documents/HRBodies/HRCouncil/CoISyria/A-HRC-31-68.pdf.

[58] CoI Syria, A/HRC/27/60, 13 August 2014.

[59] '"He Didn't Have to Die": Indiscriminate Attacks by Opposition Groups in Syria', *Human Rights Watch*, 22 March 2015, www.hrw.org/report/2015/03/22/he-didnt-have-die/indiscriminate-attacks-opposition-groups-syria.

centre of towns, and, in one incident, at a local cemetery during a funeral. In February 2016, ISIS claimed responsibility for a string of suicide bombings near a Shi'a shrine in Damascus city as well as in the pro-government neighbourhood of al-Zahra in Homs city, which killed over 150 people.[60] The circumstances of most of the bombings after 2011 suggested that many of the attacks were intended primarily to spread terror among the civilian population, in violation of international humanitarian law.

In its 1996 Advisory Opinion in the *Nuclear Weapons* case, the International Court of Justice stated that the principle of distinction was one of the 'cardinal principles' of international humanitarian law and one of the 'intransgressible principles of international customary law'.[61] Almost thirty years earlier, in 1969, Israel's Military Court in Ramallah recognised the immunity of civilians from direct attack as one of the basic rules of international humanitarian law.[62] Throughout the conflict, the warring parties in Syria operated in flagrant disregard of their obligation under international humanitarian law to distinguish between civilians and persons directly participating in hostilities. In February 2014, the Security Council adopted Resolution 2139 demanding that 'all parties immediately cease all attacks against civilians, as well as the indiscriminate employment of weapons in populated areas, including shelling and aerial bombardment, such as the use of barrel bombs, and methods of warfare which are of a nature to cause superfluous injury or unnecessary suffering'.[63] Nevertheless, unlawful attacks by the warring parties in Syria increased and were carried out with impunity.

5.3.2 *Use of Chemical Weapons*

In July 2012, the Syrian government publicly acknowledged that it was in possession of chemical weapons, with its Foreign Ministry spokesperson stating that the weapons would never be used against the Syrian people.

[60] Maher al-Mounes with Nicholas Revise, 'IS Blasts Kill More Than 150 as US, Russia Press Syria Truce', Yahoo!, 22 February 2016, www.yahoo.com/news/double-bomb-attack-kills-14-syrias-homs-075829593.html.

[61] International Court of Justice, 'Legality of the Threat or Use of Nuclear Weapon (Advisory Opinion) of 8 July 1996', 8 July 1996, www.icj-cij.org/files/case-related/95/095-19960708-ADV-01-00-EN.pdf.

[62] Israel, Military Court sitting in Ramallah, *Military Prosecutor* v. *Omar Mahmud Kassem and Others*, Judgment, 13 April 1969, as set out in E. Lauterpacht, ed., *International Law Reports*, vol. 42 (Cambridge: Grotius Publications Limited, 1971), 470–83.

[63] UN Security Council, S/Res/ 2139 (2014), 22 February 2014.

He emphasised that 'all of these types of weapons are in storage and under security and the direct supervision of the Syrian armed forces and will never be used unless Syria is exposed to external aggression'.[64] By itself, this was concerning, given the absolute prohibition on the use of chemical weapons under international law.[65] On 20 August 2012, US President Obama, speaking at an impromptu news conference at the White House, said, 'A red line for us is we start seeing a whole bunch of chemical weapons moving around or being utilised.'[66]

In December 2012, the first allegation of chemical weapons use on the Syrian battlefield was made; seven people in the Khaldiyah neighbourhood of Homs city were alleged to have been killed by a 'poisonous gas'.[67] A State Department cable, dated 15 January 2013, from the US Consul General in Istanbul, stated that there was 'compelling evidence' the Syrian government had used a chemical weapon, Agent 15, also known as BZ, in the attack.[68] The Syrian American Medical Society interviewed witnesses and victims of the attack and described the 'probable' use of BZ.[69] A day later, a spokesperson for the US National Security Council said the information concerning the attack in Homs was 'not consistent' with what the US Administration knew about the Syrian government's chemical weapons programme.[70]

[64] 'Syrian Regime Makes Chemical Warfare Threat', *The Guardian*, 23 July 2012, www.theguardian.com/world/2012/jul/23/syria-chemical-warfare-threat-assad.

[65] Public abhorrence of chemical warfare in World War I led to a specific international ban on the use of chemical and biological weapons in 1925. States further strengthened this prohibition with agreement of the Convention on the Prohibition of the Development, Production and Stockpiling of Bacteriological (biological) and Toxin Weapons and on their Destruction, 10 April 1972, 1015 U.N.T.S. 163.

[66] James Ball, 'Obama Issues Syria a "Red Line" Warning on Chemical Weapons', *The Washington Post*, 20 August 2012, www.washingtonpost.com/world/national-security/obama-issues-syria-red-line-warning-on-chemical-weapons/2012/08/20/ba5d26ec-eaf7-11e1-b811-09036bcb182b_story.html?utm_term=.46ed82885092.

[67] Stuart Winer, 'Rebels Say Assad Regime Used Chemical Weapons in Attack', *The Times of Israel*, 24 December 2012, www.timesofisrael.com/rebels-say-assad-regime-used-chemical-weapons-in-attack-on-homs/.

[68] Josh Rogin, 'Exclusive: Secret State Department Cable: Chemical Weapons Used in Syria', *Foreign Policy*, 15 January 2013, http://foreignpolicy.com/2013/01/15/exclusive-secret-state-department-cable-chemical-weapons-used-in-syria/.

[69] Eliot Higgins, 'A History of Sarin Use in the Syrian Conflict', Bell¿ngcat, 6 September 2017, www.bellingcat.com/news/mena/2017/09/06/history-sarin-use-syrian-conflict/.

[70] 'U.S. Plays Down Media Report that Syria Used Chemical Weapons', *Reuters*, 15 January 2013, www.reuters.com/article/us-syria-usa-chemical/u-s-plays-down-media-report-that-syria-used-chemical-weapons-idUSBRE90F00P20130116.

On 19 March 2013, a chemical weapons attack was reported in the opposition-held Khan al-Assal neighbourhood of Aleppo city. The government and the armed opposition blamed each other for the attack. On 20 March, President Obama, in a press conference with Israeli Prime Minister Netanyahu, called the use of chemical weapons 'a game changer'.[71] On the same day, the Syrian government contacted the UN Secretary General to request 'a specialized, impartial and independent mission' to investigate Khan al-Assal, with other member states requesting an investigation of all chemical incidents reported in Syria. By 26 March, the UN Secretary General had appointed Professor Åke Sellström to head the UN Fact-Finding Mission, which would include experts from the World Health Organization (WHO) and the Organisation for the Prohibition of Chemical Weapons (OPCW), to investigate the use of chemical weapons in Syria.[72]

Allegations of the use of chemical weapons by the Syrian government mounted. Chemical weapons attacks were reported in Adra on 24 March 2013; Jobar on 11, 13, and 14 April; the Kurdish Sheikh Maqsoud neighbourhood of Aleppo city on 13 April; and Saraqib on 29 April 2013. On 4 June 2013, the French government stated that it had 'no doubt' the Syrian government had used sarin, a nerve agent, in multiple incidents in Jobar.[73] It was not until April 2017, after the attack on Khan Sheikhoun, that the French government released its 'national evaluation', which included findings that sarin had also been used by the Syrian government in the April 2013 Saraqib attack.[74]

[71] Mark Landler and Rick Gladstone, 'Chemicals Would Be "Game Changer" in Syria, Obama Says', *The New York Times*, 22 March 2013, www.nytimes.com/2013/03/21/world/middleeast/syria-developments.html.

[72] 'Ban Appoints Swedish Scientist to Lead Probe into Alleged Chemical Weapons Use in Syria', *UN News Centre*, 26 March 2013, https://news.un.org/en/story/2013/03/435562-ban-appoints-swedish-scientist-lead-probe-alleged-chemical-weapons-use-syria#.WkhWAyPMyCQ.

[73] Helen Carmichael, 'French Convinced Sarin Used in Syria', *Chemistry World*, 11 June 2013, www.chemistryworld.com/news/french-convinced-sarin-used-in-syria/6257.article. The findings of the French government were based on the testing of clothing, hair, urinem, and blood samples collected by an investigative team from *Le Monde*, who were present in Jobar at the time of the attacks. *Le Monde* published its investigation of reports of chemical weapon attacks in Damascus against the armed opposition in Jean-Philippe Rémy, 'Chemical Warfare in Syria', *Le Monde*, 27 May 2013, http://www.lemonde.fr/proche-orient/article/2013/05/27/chemical-war-in-syria_3417708_3218.html.

[74] 'Chemical Attack in Syria – National Evaluation Presented by Jean-Marc Ayrault Following the Defense Council Meeting (26 April 2017)', *France Diplomatie*, 26 April 2017, www.diplomatie.gouv.fr/en/country-files/syria/events/article/chemical-attack-in-syria-national-evaluation-presented-by-jean-marc-ayrault.

In August 2013, wrangling with the Syrian government over the scope of the UN Fact-Finding Mission, more widely known as the Sellström team, was resolved. It was mandated to establish whether chemical weapons were used but not who used them. The separate mandate of the Syria Commission did allow for the identification of alleged perpetrators, where possible, but – unlike the Sellström team – the Syria Commission was not permitted to enter Syria.

On 21 August 2013, Ghouta, a besieged opposition-held area in Damascus governorate, came under attack. Thousands of people were rushed to hospital with symptoms such as convulsions, suffocation, coughing up blood, and foaming at the mouth. The number of people killed has never been confirmed and ranges from 281 to 1,729, many of them children killed in their beds.[75] The Security Council held an emergency meeting and produced a statement demanding clarity as to what had occurred.[76]

Ultimately, the Sellström team would investigate seven of the sixteen allegations of attacks reported to the Secretary General by Member States: Khan al-Assel on 19 March 2013; Sheikh Maqsoud on 13 April 2013; Saraqib on 29 April 2013; Ghouta on 21 August 2013; Bahhariyeh on 22 August 2013; Jobar on 24 August 2013; and Ashrafiah Sahnaya on 25 August 2013.[77]

On 29 August 2013, the British Joint Intelligence Committee released a report determining that chemical weapons were used and that it was

[75] The lowest estimated number of casualties (281) was reported by the French government based on 'methodical technical analysis of 47 original video tapes' of the 21 August attack in 'Syria/Syrian Chemical Programme – National Executive Summary of Declassified Intelligence', France-Diplomatie – Ministry of Foreign Affairs and International Development, 3 September 2013, www.diplomatie.gouv.fr/IMG/pdf/Syrian_Chemical_Programme.pdf. The highest estimated number of casualties (1,429, including 426 children) came from the US government and was based on 'human, signals, and geospatial intelligence as well as a significant body of open source reporting', reported in 'Government Assessment of the Syrian Government's Use of Chemical Weapons on August 21, 2013', The White House – Office of the Press Secretary, 30 August 2013, https://obamawhitehouse.archives.gov/the-press-office/2013/08/30/government-assessment-syrian-government-s-use-chemical-weapons-august-21.

[76] Dominic Evans and Khaled Yacoub Oweis, 'Syria Gas "Kills Hundreds", Security Council Meets', *Reuters*, 21 August 2013, www.reuters.com/article/us-syria-crisis/syria-gas-kills-hundreds-security-council-meets-idUSBRE97K0EL20130821.

[77] The Sellström team stated that it did not receive sufficient or credible information in respect of nine other alleged incidents, namely: Salquin on 17 October 2012, Homs on 23 December 2012, Darayya on 13 March and 25 April 2013, Otaybah on 19 March 2013, Adra on 24 March and 23 May 2013, Jobar between 12 and 14 April 2013, and Qasr Abu Samrah on 14 May 2013.

'highly likely' that the Syrian government was responsible for the August 2013 attacks.[78] A day later, the White House released a US government assessment, reaching the same conclusions.[79] On 31 August, President Obama made a statement saying he would seek authorisation from Congress for a limited military strike in Syria 'to deter further chemical weapons use and uphold international norms'.[80]

Calls for military actions were quieted by a Russian proposal that Syria place its chemical weapons stockpile under international control and dismantle them. On 14 September 2013, representatives of the United States and Russia reached an agreement on a detailed plan for the accounting, inspection, control, and elimination of Syria's chemical weapons. The Security Council, through its Resolution 2118, approved the plan.[81]

Two days later, on 15 September 2013, the UN Secretary-General delivered a report on the work of the Sellström team, which concluded that 'the environmental, chemical and medical samples we have collected provide clear and convincing evidence that surface-to-surface rockets containing the nerve agent Sarin were used' in the August 2013 attack on Ghouta.[82] It noted that the chemical weapon had been used 'also against civilians, including many children, on a relatively large scale'.[83] In its final report, released in December 2013, the Sellström team confirmed its finding as to the use of sarin in Ghouta and indicated that it had corroborated or collected, to varying degrees, information relevant to

[78] John Day, 'Syria: Reported Chemical Weapons Use', *Joint Intelligence Committee*, 29 August 2013, www.gov.uk/government/uploads/system/uploads/attachment_data/file/235094/Jp_115_JD_PM_Syria_Reported_Chemical_Weapon_Use_with_annex.pdf.

[79] 'Government Assessment of the Syrian Government's Use of Chemical Weapons on August 21, 2013', The White House – Office of the Press Secretary, 30 August 2013, https://obamawhitehouse.archives.gov/the-press-office/2013/08/30/government-assessment-syrian-government-s-use-chemical-weapons-august-21.

[80] 'TRANSCRIPT: President Obama's Aug. 31 statement on Syria', *The Washington Post*, 31 August 2013, www.washingtonpost.com/politics/transcript-president-obamas-aug-31-statement-on-syria/2013/08/31/3019213c-125d-11e3-b4cb-fd7ce041d814_story.html?utm_term=.2501dd0a725e.

[81] United Nations Security Council, S/Res/2118 (2013), 27 September 2013, www.securitycouncilreport.org/atf/cf/%7B65BFCF9B-6D27-4E9C-8CD3-CF6E4FF96FF9%7D/s_res_2118.pdf.

[82] 'United Nations Mission to Investigate Allegations of the Use of Chemical Weapons in the Syrian Arab Republic: Report on the Alleged Use of Chemical Weapons in the Ghouta Area of Damascus on 21 August 2013', A/67/997-S/2013/553, 15 September 2013, https://s3.amazonaws.com/unoda-web/wp-content/uploads/2013/09/SG_Report_of_CW_Investigation.pdf, para 28.

[83] Ibid., para 27.

chemical weapons used in Khan al-Assal, Saraqib, Jobar, and Ashrafiah.[84] It was unable to corroborate the allegations of chemical weapons use in Sheikh Maqsoud or in Bahhariyeh.[85] As per its mandate, it did not broach the issue of responsibility.

The Syria Commission, in its seventh report released in February 2014, found that

> significant quantities of sarin were used in a well-planned indiscriminate attack targeting civilian-inhabited areas [in Ghouta], causing mass casualties. The evidence available concerning the nature, quality, and quantity of the agents used on 21 August indicated that the perpetrators likely had access to the chemical weapons stockpile of the Syrian military, as well as the expertise and equipment necessary to safely manipulate large amounts of chemical agents.

The Commission also found that the chemical agents used in the Khan al-Assal chemical attack in March 2013 'bore the same unique hallmarks as those used in al-Ghouta'. It made no explicit finding regarding a perpetrator.[86]

In October 2013 a UN-OPCW Mission arrived in Syria to commence the destruction of Syria's chemical weapons stockpile. Throughout 2014, the Syrian government transferred its chemical weapons stockpile to a port in Latakia to be shipped out of the country. On 11 April 2014, however, reports emerged of chlorine gas being used to attack Kafr Zeta.[87] An opposition-controlled village, Kafr Zeta was reportedly attacked with chlorine gas seventeen times between 11 April and 28 August 2014. Talmanes village was reportedly attacked with chlorine on 21 and 24 April 2014. A nearby village, al-Tamanah, was said to have been attacked five times, on 12, 18, and 30 April and 22 and 25 May 2014.[88] Chlorine, notably, was not included in the agreement which governed the destruction of Syria's chemical weapons, as the Syrian government hadn't added it to a list submitted to international monitors of the chemical weapons it possessed. Unlike nerve gas,

[84] 'United Nations Mission to Investigate Allegations of the Use of Chemical Weapons in the Syrian Arab Republic, Final Report', 12 December 2013, https://unoda-web.s3.amazonaws.com/wp-content/uploads/2013/12/report.pdf, paras 108–18.

[85] Ibid., paras 119–22.

[86] CoI-Syria, A/HRC/25/65, 12 February 2014, para 128.

[87] Graeme Baker, 'Syrian Regime Accused of Chlorine Gas Attacks', *Al Jazeera*, 16 April 2014, www.aljazeera.com/news/middleeast/2014/04/syrian-regime-accused-chlorine-gas-attacks-201441703230338216.html.

[88] OPCW, Third Report of the OPCW Fact-Finding Mission in Syria – Key Findings, S/1230/2014, 18 December 2014, Annex 2, p 17.

chlorine is legal for countries to possess for water purification and other civilian purposes; however, its use as a weapon is prohibited under the Chemical Weapons Convention.

The OPCW announced it would send a Fact-Finding Mission to investigate, though security concerns prevented them from visiting all sites.[89] On 10 September 2014, the OPCW Fact-Finding Mission released an interim report making 'a compelling confirmation that a toxic chemical was used as a weapon, systematically and repeatedly, in the villages of Talmanes, al Tamanah, and Kafr Zeta' and stating that it concluded 'with a high degree of confidence, that chlorine, either pure or in mixture, is the toxic chemical in question'.[90] While the Mission did not assign blame, its report repeated the testimonies of survivors that the chlorine was contained in barrel bombs dropped from helicopters – which were only in use by the Syrian government. These findings were confirmed in the OPCW Fact-Finding Mission's third report, released in December 2014.[91]

In mid-August 2014, the UN-OPCW Mission announced that the destruction of the chemical weapons stockpile declared by Syria was complete.[92] Despite this, reports of chemical weapons use continued. Between April 2014 and August 2015, dozens of reports of chemical weapons use on the Syrian battlefield surfaced, including attacks on multiple towns in Idlib. There were also accounts of ISIS using chemical weapons in the areas of Syria under its control.

On 7 August 2015, confronted with the continuing allegations, the Security Council responded by adopting Resolution 2235, by which it established a distinct entity, the OPCW-UN Joint Investigative Mechanism (JIM), to determine the parties responsible for the chemical attacks in Syria.[93] Its work would continue alongside that of the OPCW Fact-Finding Mission (the remit of which was limited to determining when and, if so, which chemical weapons had been used) and the Syria

89 Martin Chulov, 'Chemical Weapons Body to Investigate Claims of Chlorine Gas Use in Syria', *The Guardian*, 29 April 2014, www.theguardian.com/world/2014/apr/29/syria-chemical-weapons-chlorine-gas.

90 OPCW, Second Report of the OPCW Fact-Finding Mission in Syria – Key Findings, S/1212/2014, 10 September 2014, para 29; 'Syria Crisis: Chlorine Gas Used in Attacks, Says OPCW', *BBC News*, 10 September 2014, www.bbc.com/news/world-middle-east-29146039.

91 OPCW, Third Report of the OPCW Fact-Finding Mission in Syria – Key Findings, S/1230/2014, 18 December 2014.

92 OPCW, 'U.S. Completes Destruction of Sarin Precursors from Syria on the Cape Ray', 13 August 2014.

93 UN Security Council, S/Res/2235 (2015), 7 August 2015.

Commission (which was charged with investigating both whether international law had been violated and by whom, but to which the Syrian government would not permit access to Syria).

On 29 October 2015, the OPCW Fact-Finding mission presented a report on 'alleged incidents in the Idlib governorate ... between 16 March and 20 May 2015' in which it examined approximately a dozen allegations in six locations in Idlib.[94] Noting the limitations under which it worked,[95] the Mission concluded that 'sufficient facts were collected to conclude that incidents ... likely involved the use of a toxic chemical as a weapon' but indicated there was insufficient evidence to reach 'any firm conclusions as to the identification of the chemical, although there are factors indicating that the chemical probably contained the element chlorine'.[96]

Also on 29 October 2015, the Fact-Finding Mission released a separate report on an alleged incident in ISIS-controlled Marea in August 2015, in which it determined 'with the utmost confidence' that two people had been exposed to sulphur mustard gas and that it was likely that a third person, an infant, had died as a result.[97]

Meanwhile, JIM continued its own investigative mission, and on 24 August 2016 it released a report determining that the Syrian government was responsible for using chlorine gas in a delivery system (likely barrel bombs) dropped from helicopters in Talmenes in April 2014 and in Sarmin in March 2015.[98] It also found that ISIS had fired artillery shells filled with sulphur mustard in its attack on Marea in August 2015.[99] In a report released in October 2016, JIM determined that the government was responsible for dropping a barrel bomb containing a toxic substance, not confirmed to be a chemical weapon, in Qmenas in March 2015.[100]

94 OPCW, Report of the OPCW Fact-Finding Mission in Syria Regarding Alleged Incidents in the Idlib Governorate of the Syrian Arab Republic between 16 March and 20 May 2015, 29 October 2015.

95 Security concerns prevented the Mission from accessing the sites, with the consequence that the team could neither identify their own witnesses nor take their own samples. Furthermore, the supportive value of correlating physical reality, such as visible infrastructure, original records, and impact sites with information supplied by interviewees, was also not possible.

96 OPCW Report supra, note 94, para 5.19.

97 OPCW, Report of the OPCW Fact-Finding Mission in Syria regarding alleged incidents in Marea, Syrian Arab Republic, August 2015, 29 October 2015, para 4.6.

98 JIM, Third report of the Organisation for the Prohibition of Chemical Weapons-United Nations Joint Investigative Mechanism, S/2016/738, 24 August 2016.

99 Ibid.

100 JIM, Fourth report of the Organisation for the Prohibition of Chemical Weapons-United Nations Joint Investigative Mechanism, S/2016/888, 21 October 2016. In five other

On 16 September 2016, Umm-Hawsh was attacked with mortars. Allegations of chemical weapons use and a request for action by the Syrian government led to the OPCW Fact-Finding Mission's investigation. In its May 2017 report, the Mission concluded that two female casualties involved in the Umm-Hawsh incident 'were exposed to sulphur mustard'.[101]

On 4 April 2017, reports appeared claiming there had been a chemical weapons attack on Khan Sheikhoun, resulting in scores killed and hundreds injured. Photographs and videos on social media suggested a nerve agent attack, in what would be seen as the first since the August 2013 sarin attack on Ghouta.[102] The Security Council called an emergency meeting on 5 April to discuss the attack. On 6 April, the United States used missiles to target the base from which it believed the Syrian government launched the attack.[103] Less than a week later, the USA would release a declassified report stating that the Syrian government had conducted a chemical weapons attack using sarin, accusing Syria and Russia of peddling 'false narratives'.[104]

The OPCW Fact-Finding Mission released a Status Update on 12 May 2017 which indicated that its investigation of the Khan Sheikhoun incident was ongoing but included the results of its sample analysis showing that biomedical, biological, and environmental samples had been exposed to sarin or a sarin-like substance.[105] In its June 2017

cases – Kafr Zeta (11 and 18 April 2014), Al-Tamanah (29 and 30 April and 25 and 26 May 2014), and Binnish (24 March 2015) – JIM assessed that the information obtained and analysed did not allow for the identification of actors involved owing to 'inconsistencies that could not be resolved'.

101 OPCW, Report of the OPCW Fact-Finding Mission in Syria regarding the incident of 15 September 2016 as reported in the Note Verbale of the Syrian Arab Republic Number 113 dated 29 November 2016, S/1491/2017, 1 May 2017.

102 Caution should be exercised when making this characterisation as alleged chemical attacks in Uqairabat (Hama) on 12 December 2016 and Latamneh (Hama) on 30 March 2017 were described in the annex of the French National Evaluation as having a 'strong presumption of use of sarin by the Syrian regime'. See 'Chemical Attack in Syria – National Evaluation presented by Jean-Marc Ayrault following the Defence Council Meeting (26 April 2017)', *France Diplomatie*, 26 April 2017, www.diplomatie.gouv.fr/en/country-files/syria/events/article/chemical-attack-in-syria-national-evaluation-presented-by-jean-marc-ayrault. These incidents were unfortunately not investigated by the OPCW Fact-Finding Mission or JIM.

103 Michael R. Gordon, Helene Cooper, and Michael D. Shear, 'Dozens of U.S. Missiles Hit Air Base in Syria', *The New York Times*, 6 April 2017, www.nytimes.com/2017/04/06/world/middleeast/us-said-to-weigh-military-responses-to-syrian-chemical-attack.html?_r=0.

104 'Declassified U.S. Report on Chemical Weapons Attack', *The New York Times*, 11 April 2017, www.nytimes.com/interactive/2017/04/11/world/middleeast/document-Syria-Chemical-Weapons-Report-White-House.html.

105 OPCW, Status Update of the OPCW Fact-Finding Mission in Syria regarding a reported incident in Khan Shaykhun, 4 April 2014, S/1497/2017, 12 May 2017.

report, the Fact-Finding Mission concluded that sarin was used in the attack on Khan Sheikhoun and that fatalities had resulted.[106]

On 8 August 2017, the Syria Commission published its fourteenth report in which, among other reported violations, it examined alleged chemical weapons use in Syria.[107] The Commission concluded that 'there are reasonable grounds to believe Syrian forces dropped an aerial bomb dispersing sarin', while casting doubt on the alternate theory, provided by the Syrian and Russian governments, that sarin had been present in an armed group's weapons depot which was struck during the attack.[108]

On 26 October 2017, JIM – whose mandate had been renewed for one year on 17 November 2016 by virtue of Security Council Resolution 2319[109] – released its report on the incidents in Umm-Hawsh and Khan Sheikhoun. JIM pronounced itself 'confident' both that ISIS was responsible for the use of sulphur mustard in the attack on Umm-Hawsh and that the Syrian government was responsible for the release of sarin in the attack on Khan Sheikhoun.[110] Russia and Syria accused JIM of making political judgements, criticised the team for its use of remote investigations, and singled out its head, Edmond Mulet, as 'an instrument of the West'.[111] The Security Council made multiple attempts to extend JIM's mandate, which Russia vetoed on three separate occasions.[112] On 17 November 2017, JIM's mandate expired.

In the first two months of 2018, the Syrian government was accused of using chlorine gas in its attacks on Saraqeb (Idlib) and on eastern

[106] OPCW, Report of the OPCW Fact-Finding Mission in Syria regarding an alleged incident in Khan Shaykun, Syrian Arab Republic, April 2017, S/1510/2017, 29 June 2017.

[107] CoI-Syria, A/HRC/36/55, 8 August 2017, paras 67–77 and Annex II. Aside from its finding as regards Khan Sheikhoun, the Commission also determined there were reasonable grounds to believe that the Syrian government dropped bombs containing an unidentified chemical weapon in Al-Latamneh (Hama) on 30 March 2017 and held that people in Ghouta showed symptoms of exposure to chlorine following a rocket attack from Government forces on 29 March 2017.

[108] Ibid.

[109] UN Security Council, S/Res/2319 (2016), 17 November 2016.

[110] JIM, Seventh report of the Organisation for the Prohibition of Chemical Weapons-United Nations Joint Investigative Mechanism, S/2017/904, 26 October 2017.

[111] Edmond Mulet, 'How the Security Council Failed the Syria Chemical Weapons Investigators and Victims', *The New York Times*, 29 December 2017, www.nytimes.com/2017/12/29/opinion/syria-chemical-weapons-united-nations-security-council.html?_r=0&referer=https%3A%2F%2Ft.co%2FpW8JQI9IOJ%3Famp&mtrref=undefined&gwh=4E310347111E2AE55467AD4B31D80608&gwt=pay&assetType=opinion.

[112] 'Russia Blocks Bid to Probe Syria Chemical Weapons Use', *Al Jazeera*, 16 November 2017, www.aljazeera.com/news/2017/11/divided-syrian-chemical-weapons-probe-171116165101126.html.

Ghouta.[113] French Foreign Minister Jean-Yves Le Drian stated that 'all indications show us today that the Syrian regime is using chlorine gas at the moment' in attacks on rebel-held areas.[114] In February 2018, the United Nations also charged that North Korea has been shipping supplies that could be used in the production of chemical weapons to the Syrian government.[115]

On 7 April 2018, a chemical attack was reported in Douma, a town in eastern Ghouta. Douma had been out of government control since October 2012[116] and under siege since April 2013.[117] At the time of the April 2018 attack, it was one of the few remaining areas controlled by armed groups. The attack reportedly killed over seventy people, with local medics saying a mix of sarin and chlorine gas was used.[118] Recriminations began almost immediately, with armed groups, residents, NGO, and healthcare staff in Douma casting blame on the government. Internationally, the United States, France, the United Kingdom asserted that the Syrian government was responsible.[119] The Russian Defence Ministry claimed the attack did not occur, saying the videos of the attack's aftermath had been staged by British intelligence.[120]

[113] Krishnadev Calamur, 'Assad Is Still Using Chemical Weapons in Syria', *The Atlantic*, 6 February 2018, www.theatlantic.com/international/archive/2018/02/syria-chemical-weapons/552428/; Anthony Deutsch, 'Exclusive: Chemical Weapons Watchdog Investigates Ghouta Attacks – Sources', *Reuters*, 27 February 2018, www.reuters.com/article/us-mideast-crisis-syria-chemicalweapons/exclusive-chemical-weapons-watchdog-investigates-ghouta-attacks-sources-idUSKCN1GB12O.

[114] 'Global Chemical Weapons Watchdog Investigates Allegations of Attacks in Syria', *The Washington Post*, 7 February 2018, www.washingtonpost.com/world/global-chemical-weapons-watchdog-investigates-allegations-of-attacks-in-syria/2018/02/07/37171ea6-0c10-11e8-998c-96deb18cca19_story.html?utm_term=.80e53369851e.

[115] Michael Schwirtz, 'UN Links North Korea to Syria's Chemical Weapons Program', *The New York Times*, 27 February 2018, www.nytimes.com/2018/02/27/world/asia/north-korea-syria-chemical-weapons-sanctions.html.

[116] Janine Di Giovanni, 'Denial Is Slipping Away as War Arrives in Damascus', *The New York Times*, 20 October 2012, www.nytimes.com/2012/10/18/world/middleeast/syrian-war-reaches-damascus.html.

[117] 'UN Convoy Delivers Aid to Eastern Ghouta Amid "Calm"', *BBC News*, 9 March 2018, www.bbc.co.uk/news/world-middle-east-43343266.

[118] Louisa Loveluck and Erin Cunningham, 'Dozens Killed in Apparent Chemical Weapons Attack on Civilians in Syria, Rescue Workers Say', *The Washington Post*, 8 April 2018, www.washingtonpost.com/world/middle_east/dozens-killed-in-apparent-chemical-weapons-attack-on-civilians-in-eastern-ghouta–rescue-workers/2018/04/08/231bba18-3ac0-11e8-af3c-2123715f78df_story.html?noredirect=on&utm_term=.6442cf106486.

[119] Patrick Sawer, 'Evidence Shows Syria "Attacked Own People with Chemical Weapons", say US, UK and France', *The Telegraph* (UK), 14 April 2018, www.telegraph.co.uk/news/2018/04/14/evidence-shows-syria-attacked-people-chemical-weapons-say-us/.

[120] TASS, 'Russian Top Brass Reports It Has Proof of UK's Involvement in Douma Chemical Incident', 13 April 2018, http://tass.com/defense/999641; TASS, 'Envoy to

The Security Council met five times in the week following the Douma attack to discuss the incident and attempt to mandate investigations. On 10 April, a number of competing resolutions were put to a vote, all of which failed. Russia introduced two resolutions: the first, to create a new investigative body whose findings would be subject to UN Security Council approval before release; and the second, to support an OPCW fact-finding mission to Syria that would be restricted to predetermined sites. Neither resolution received enough votes to pass. The United States introduced a resolution to create an investigative body with a one-year mandate to determine responsibility for chemical weapons use in Syria. The resolution received thirteen votes but was vetoed by Russia.[121]

On 13 April, the United States, the United Kingdom, and France carried out a series of military strikes against three Syrian facilities, one in the Damascus area and two west of Homs, described as being associated with the Syrian government's chemical weapons programme.[122] The US ambassador to the United Nations, Nikki Haley, in justifying the decision to resort to military action, cited the lack of diplomatic progress on accountability.[123]

The Syrian and Russian governments invited the OPCW Fact-Finding Mission – mandated to determine whether chemical weapons were used but not to make any determinations as to the party or parties responsible – to investigate the attacks. Despite the OPCW team arriving in Syria on 11 April, Russia and Syria blocked its access to the impact sites, citing security concerns. The United States, France, and the United Kingdom voiced concerns that the delay was due to ongoing efforts by the Russian and Syrian governments to destroy evidence.[124] An attempt on 17 April to reach an area outside of Douma was curtailed when the OPCW team

OPCW Says Russia Found Participants of Staged "Chemical Attack" Video in Syria', 16 April 2018, http://tass.com/politics/1000124.

121 Ceren Senkul, 'Russia Vetoes Syria Chemical Weapons Inquiry', *Sky News*, 11 April 2018, https://news.sky.com/story/russia-vetoes-syria-chemical-weapons-inquiry-11325688.

122 'Syria Air Strikes: US and Allies Attack "Chemical Weapons Sites"', *BBC News*, 14 April 2018, www.bbc.co.uk/news/world-middle-east-43762251.

123 'Ambassador Haley: After 6 Diplomatic Attempts, "We Acted" in Syria', *Jerusalem Post*, 14 April 2018, www.jpost.com/Breaking-News/Ambassador-Haley-After-6-diplomatic-attempts-we-acted-in-Syria-549802.

124 Richard Pérez-Peña and Rick Gladstone, 'Chemical Arms Experts Blocked From Site of Syria Attack', *The New York Times*, 16 April 2018, www.nytimes.com/2018/04/16/world/middleeast/syria-douma-chemical-attack.html?hp&action=click&pgtype=Homepage&clickSource=story-heading&module=first-column-region&region=top-news&WT.nav=top-news.

came under small arms fire, with the OPCW statement not laying blame on any of the belligerents.[125] It was not until 21 and 25 April that the OPCW Fact-Finding Mission was able to collect samples. At the time of this writing, its report is pending.

5.4 Conclusion

The Syrian conflict is one of the most heavily documented in history. While undoubtedly much is still to be understood, what has resulted is the startling realisation that the vast majority of Syria's warring parties are utterly unrestrained by international humanitarian law. By turning away from the 'hard-headed, high-priced lessons from brutal conflicts of the past two centuries',[126] Syria's war of attrition has eroded Syria both as a country and as a nation.

Whether it has also eroded the value of international humanitarian law is far more debatable. The Syrian conflict along with the horrors belligerents have unleashed largely upon their own people have uniformly and consistently resulted in an outcry over the violations, followed swiftly by demands for justice. Over the course of the last eight years, the warring parties have acted with impunity in their conduct on the Syrian battlefield, in utter disregard of international humanitarian law. While the international community, and notably Security Council members, may argue over which party is responsible and whether violations occurred as described by particular sources, there has never been any attempt to frame recognised violations as anything other than deserving of condemnation and accountability, the latter of which has not been forthcoming.

The full reckoning of the impact of Syrian conflict on the laws of war is likely only be visible in a post-conflict Syria. In that time and space, Syrians and the Security Council alike will have to perform what now seems an impossible task: to reconcile the inviolability of international humanitarian law with the seeming resilience of Assad government and the selective justice that may follow.[127]

[125] OPCW, Update by the Director-General on the Deployment of the OPCW Fact-Finding Mission to Douma, Syrian Arab Republic, to the Executive Council at its Fifty-Ninth Meeting, 18 April 2018, www.opcw.org/fileadmin/OPCW/EC/M-59/en/ecm59dg02_e_.pdf.

[126] David Miliband, 'Syria's Latest Victim: International Law', *Time*, 26 March 2014, http://time.com/35697/syrias-latest-victim-international-law/.

[127] For elaboration on several trajectories for post-conflict justice, see Chapter 12 of this volume.

What the Syrian conflict has done, however, more so than any other in recent history, is to emphasise the Security Council's inability – or perhaps unwillingness – to rise above the geopolitical strategic interests of its Permanent Members in order to fulfil its primary responsibility of maintaining international peace and security. The Syrian conflict has sent a message globally that, with the right backers, it is possible for warring parties to wrestle a military victory at any cost, free from fear of the consequences of violating international law. It is a dangerous message to transmit to a world full of conflict and hardly lacking in unstable leadership.

6

Scorched Earth in Syria

Between Crimes against Humanity and Genocide

HILLY MOODRICK-EVEN KHEN AND YAEL SIMAN

6.1 Introduction

After eight devastating years, the armed conflict in Syria seems to be nearing its end, yet the humanitarian crisis is still ongoing. This is due to the enormous scale of international crimes, including war crimes, crimes against humanity, and genocide, characterising the conflict and committed by different parties to the conflict. This chapter discusses the commission of crimes against humanity and genocide since the beginning of the uprisings[1] and focuses on a legal analysis of some of those crimes.

A striking lack of adherence to international law, shown from the earliest days of the unrest, prompted multiple investigations by NGOs, civil society, and the UN. As the number of deaths and injuries climbed,[2] an urgency emerged to document and analyse allegations of violations of international law by the warring parties. Information and evidence collected resulted in reports, notably by the Independent Impartial Commission of Inquiry on the Syrian Arab Republic (CoI Syria), which stated that many of the belligerents – including the Syrian government, a diverse array of anti-government armed groups, and recognised terrorist groups such as the al-Nusra Front and ISIS – had committed war crimes and crimes against humanity. In the case of the attack by ISIS on the Yazidi ethno-religious group, the Commission of Inquiry on Syria

[1] See Chapter 5 of this volume.

[2] Half a million people are estimated to have been killed and millions are estimated to have been injured. In terms of forced displacement from and within Syria, half of Syria's population has been displaced; 5.5 million registered refugees and over 6 million people are internally displaced.

and the US Holocaust Memorial Museum (USHMM) determined the attack constituted genocide.[3]

The discussion of crimes against humanity in this chapter focuses on specific conduct and the two crimes most documented by the CoI Syria and by Human Rights Watch and Amnesty International: torture and extermination of prisoners in detention facilities of the Syrian government. Regarding genocide, the chapter surveys the evidence for the commission of genocide of the Yazidis by ISIS and focuses on the CoI Syria's factual and legal analysis.[4]

The analysis of conducts and offences is legal and based on the theoretical conceptions of crimes against humanity and genocide laid out in this chapter. Both genocide and crimes against humanity are international crimes that share common features distinguishing them from ordinary crimes; they are committed by either state officials or private individuals in the context of either an armed conflict or in peacetime and with a political or ideological dimension.[5] In contrast to ordinary crimes based on personal goals, these crimes are often committed with a connection to state or organisational policy, which reflects their international element.[6] Moreover, they involve the commission of atrocities that defy the fundamental values of humanity and deeply shock its conscience.

Nevertheless, these crimes are also legally distinguished from each other according to the factual and mental elements that are at their foundation. The legal distinctions of these crimes are elaborated throughout the chapter; these distinctions will be used in order to explain who, among the various parties to the conflict in Syria, is responsible for each crime and the justifications for the allegations against each party.[7]

3 The United States Holocaust Memorial Museum has expressed profound concern about the 'genocidal violence' committed by ISIS against the Yazidi community. See https://www.ushmm.org/confront-genocide/speakers-and-events/all-speakers-and-events/vian-dakhil.

4 While ISIS also committed crimes against humanity against the Yazidis, this chapter focuses on the crime of genocide.

5 Antonio Cassese, *International Criminal Law*, 2nd ed (Oxford: Oxford University Press, 2008), 54.

6 Ibid.

7 Legal responsibility for the crimes analysed in this chapter lies both with Syria as a state (according to the legal concepts of state responsibility) and with individual perpetrators (who bear criminal responsibility according to international criminal law). While only states and not organisations can bear state responsibility, all individuals, regardless of whether they are members of armed forces of the government or members of organisations, bear criminal responsibility and can be prosecuted for the commission of the crimes discussed here. For elaboration on the notions of international criminal law, see, for example, Cassese, Note 5.

The legal definitions of crimes against humanity and of genocide referred to in this chapter are those adopted by the Statute of the International Criminal Court (ICC Statute),[8] whose 'jurisdiction [is] limited to the most serious crimes of concern to the international community as a whole',[9] and by the Elements of Crimes,[10] a complementary instrument to the ICC Statute that elaborates on the elements of the crimes listed in the Statute.[11] The ICC Statute is considered reflective of customary international criminal law.[12] Hence, the customary nature of these definitions sets them as the legal common ground for the analysis of the conduct surveyed in this chapter.

6.2 Crimes against Humanity

6.2.1 Legal Definition

Crimes against humanity are, according to the ICC Statute acts, those that include the harshest threat to human lives – that is, murder, acts which aim at threatening a person's physical integrity, such as torture or rape, and 'other inhumane acts … intentionally causing great suffering, or serious injury to body or to mental or physical health'.[13] Additionally, those acts are committed as part of a widespread or systematic attack directed against a civilian population, either in- or outside of a state of armed conflict. Such acts, specified in Article 7 of the Statute, include murder; torture; extermination; enslavement; deportation or forcible transfer of population; imprisonment or other severe deprivation of physical liberty in violation of fundamental rules of international law; persecution against identifiable groups; rape and other forms of sexual violence; enforced disappearance of persons; and apartheid.

8 Also known as the Rome Statute of the International Criminal Court, opened for signature 17 July 1998, 2187 UNTS 3 (entered into force 1 July 2002).

9 ICC statute art. 5.

10 ICC-ASP/1/3 at 108, UN Doc. PCNICC/2000/1/Add.2 (2000) [hereinafter: Elements of Crimes].

11 The other complementary instrument is the Rules of Procedure and Evidence.

12 Or, in the words of the International Law Commission, 'crimes under general international law [which are] … a norm of international law accepted and recognised by the international community of States as a whole as being of such a fundamental character that its violation gives rise to the criminal responsibility of individuals'. ILC 1993 working group report page 110, cited by Willian A. Schabas, *The International Criminal Court* (Oxford: Oxford University Press, 2010), 103–4.

13 ICC Statute, art.7 (1) (k).

The first recognition of the notion of crimes against humanity was made in a 1919 declaration by France, Great Britain, and Russia denouncing the massacres of Armenians by the Ottoman Empire during World War I;[14] however, it only emerged as a category of international criminal law in 1945 with the Charter of the International Military Tribunal at Nuremberg.[15] Since then, it has been acknowledged by several international instruments as part of international criminal law with much consistency in its definition.[16] Its most updated definition is contained in Article 7 of the ICC Statute.

The category of crimes against humanity was required in international law for several reasons. Most importantly, the prevailing law at the time of World War II used the category of war crimes and so could not incriminate the acts of a government perpetrated against its own citizens and intended to infringe upon their rights.[17] Furthermore, crimes against humanity can be committed both in war and in peacetime.[18] War crimes, on the other hand, and as their name suggests, can only be committed during armed conflicts. Lastly, crimes against humanity are committed as part of a widespread or systematic attack on the civilian population and in that sense are more limited than war crimes.

6.2.1.1 Widespread and Systematic Attack

The notion of 'widespread and systematic' was already developed in 1949 by the UN War Crimes Commission,[19] which defined crimes against humanity

[14] Christopher K. Hall, 'Crimes against Humanity', in Otto Triffterer, *Commentary on the Rome Statute of the International Criminal Court*, 2nd ed (München: Beck, 2008), 167.

[15] Charter of the International Military Tribunal – Annex to the Agreement for the prosecution and punishment of the major war criminals of the European Axis ('London Agreement'), 8 August 1945, STAT. 1544, 82 U.N.T.S. art. 6 [hereinafter: IMT Statute].

[16] Hall, supra Note 14, at 167. The category of crimes against humanity was adopted by the statutes of the following tribunals: International Military Tribunal for the Far East (1946) (Tokyo Tribunal), www.un.org/en/genocideprevention/documents/atrocity-crimes/Doc.3_1946%20Tokyo%20Charter.pdf; International Criminal Tribunal for the Former Yugoslavia (1993), SC res. 827, UN SCOR 48th sess., 3217th mtg. at 1–2 (1993); 32 ILM 1159 (1993) [hereinafter: ICTY Statute] and the International Criminal Tribunal for Rwanda (1994) SC res. 955, UN SCOR 49th sess., 3453rd mtg, UN Doc. S/Res/955 (1994); 33 ILM 1598 (1994) [hereinafter: ICTR Statute].

[17] Cassese, supra Note 5, at 103.

[18] There has been some disagreement over this issue in the preparatory procedures for the establishment of the ICC, see Hall, supra note 14, at 168, n. 11; and yet, the ICC Statute does not require an armed conflict as a precondition for the perpetration of crimes against humanity. See art. 7, ICC Statute.

[19] The commission was established in 1943 – before the establishment of the UN – and was dissolved in 1949.

as '[crimes which] by their magnitude and savagery or by their large number or by the fact that a similar pattern was applied ... endangered the international community or shocked the conscience of mankind'.[20] This notion was adopted by later international instruments[21] and finally by the ICC Statute defining these crimes as those 'committed as part of *a widespread or systematic attack* directed against any civilian population'.[22] The ICC Statute also requires that the attack be committed 'pursuant to or in furtherance of a State or organisational policy'.[23]

The concepts of 'widespread' or 'systematic' stress both the magnitude and the organised or methodical nature of the conduct included in the category of crimes against humanity. The ILC Draft Code of Crimes against Peace and Security of Mankind used the term 'large scale' for the notion of a 'widespread attack' and referred it to a large number of victims.[24] This interpretation was supported by the ICTY (International Criminal Tribunal for the Former Yugoslavia)[25] and the ICTR (International Criminal Tribunal for Rwanda).[26] The ICC added that as 'widespread' refers to the 'large-scale nature of the attack',[27] it should be massive and frequent and could refer either to the large geographical area or the large number of victims.[28]

The term 'systematic' was interpreted by the ICTY and the ICC as excluding random and isolated acts and stressing the organised nature of the acts.[29] The ICC stated that the organised nature of systematic attacks could either refer to the existence of 'an organised plan in furtherance of a common policy' or to 'patterns of crimes' such that the crimes

20 Hall, supra Note 14, at 169, note 16.

21 See Draft Code of Crimes against Peace and Security of Mankind with commentaries, *Yearbook of the International Law Commission*, vol. 2, part 2 (1996): 17–56 [hereinafter: ILC Draft Code]; ICTR Statute.

22 ICC Statute, art. 7; italics added.

23 Ibid.

24 ILC Draft Code, supra Note 21, at 47.

25 See, for example, *Prosecutor* v. *Tadić*, IT-94-1-T, Opinion and Judgement, 7 May 1997, para 656; *Prosecutor* v. *Kordić*, Case No. IT-95/14/2-A, Judgment, Appeals Chamber, 17 December 1994; *Prosecutor* v. *Blaskić*, Case No. IT-95-14-A, Appeals Chamber, 29 July 2004, para 101.

26 See, for example, *Prosecutor* v. *Muvunyi*, Case No. ICTR-00-55A-T, Judgment, Trial Chamber, 12 September 2006, para 512.

27 ICC-02/05-01/09, Decision on the Prosecution's Application for a Warrant of Arrest against Omar Hassan Al Bashir, 4 March 2009, para 84.

28 ICC-01/05-01/08, Decision Pursuant to Article 61(7)(a) and (b) of the ICC Statute on the Charges of the Prosecutor Against Jean-Pierre Bemba Gombo, 15 June 2009, para 83.

29 See, for example, Kordić, supra Note 25, at para 94; Blaskić, id., at para 101. For ICC decisions, see Bashir, supra Note 27, para 81.

constitute a 'non-accidental repletion of similar criminal conduct on a regular basis'.[30] Relating to some ICTY decisions, legal scholar William A. Schabas notes that 'the existence of a political objective and an acknowledged policy or plan pursuant to which the attack is perpetrated, the preparation and use of significant public or private resources, [and] the participation of high-level political or military authorities'[31] should be taken into consideration when appraising the widespread or systematic character of an attack.

An acknowledged plan pursuant to which the attack is perpetrated is also a specific requirement for crimes against humanity as made by Article 7 of the ICC Statute.[32] The Elements of Crimes stress that a policy to commit an attack is recognised when 'the state or organisation *actively promote or encourage* such an attack against the civilian population' [emphasis added].[33] Nevertheless, the policy need not be formalised. The ICC explains that when the attack 'is planned, directed, or organised', and is not spontaneous or consists of isolated acts of violence, the criterion is satisfied.[34]

An attack is 'directed against' any civilian population if the civilian population is the 'primary object of the attack'.[35] A population may be considered as 'civilian' even if certain non-civilians are present – it must simply be 'predominantly civilian in nature'.[36] Factors to determine whether the attack was directed against a civilian population include: the means and methods used in the course of the attack; the number of victims; the status of the victims; the discriminatory nature of the attack; the nature of the crimes committed in the course of the attack; and the extent to which the attacking force complied or attempted to comply with the precautionary requirements of international humanitarian law.[37]

Yet, all of the characteristics discussed (i.e. widespread or systematic and the requirement of a policy or plan) were interpreted as referring to

[30] Katanga et al. ICC-01/04-01/07 Decision on the Confirmation of Charges, 30 September 2008, para 397.
[31] Schabas, supra Note 12, at 149.
[32] ICC Statute, art. 7.
[33] Elements of Crimes, supra Note 10, art. 7, Crimes Against Humanity, Introduction, para 3.
[34] Katanga, supra Note 30, para 398.
[35] *Prosecutor* v. *Naletilić and Martinovic,* Trial Judgment, 31 March 2003, para 235.
[36] *Prosecutor* v. *Kordić and Cerkez,* Trial Judgment, 26 February 2001, para 180; *Prosecutor* v. *Naletilic and Martinovic,* para 235; *Prosecutor* v. *Jelisić,* Case No. IT-95-10-T Trial Judgment, 14 December 1999, para 54; *Prosecutor* v. *Blaskić,* Trial Judgment, 3 March 2000, para 214.
[37] *Blaskić,* AJ, para 106; Kunarac et al., AJ, para 90.

the attack as a whole and not to each individual act. This interpretation is supported by the ICC Statute requiring that the acts form *part* of the widespread or systematic attack; hence, they need not be in and of themselves of such character but must be perpetrated in the context of a widespread and systematic attack. This was stressed by the ICC stating that even 'a single act of murder by a perpetrator may constitute a crime against humanity as long as the legal requirements with regard to the contextual element of crimes against humanity, including the nexus element, are met'.[38]

Lastly, despite the fact that the conducts forming crimes against humanity are part of an organisational or governmental policy, the perpetrators themselves need not necessarily be government officials or members of an organisation. They can practise in their private capacity as long as they find support for their act in a general state or organisational policy.[39]

6.2.1.2 The Subjective Element: Intent or Knowledge

To commit a crime against humanity, the perpetrators must fulfil objective and subjective elements of the crime. Generally in criminal law, and also specifically in the context of crimes against humanity, the objective elements are the specific acts that make up the offence. These elements will be discussed in Sections 6.2.2.1 to 6.2.2.2, in the context of the specific allegations against Syrian government officials. The subjective element in criminal law is the mental state of the perpetrator, most often the requirement that he or she has knowledge (in terms of awareness) of the objective elements or intent to cause the outcomes of his or her acts, specified by the offense.

The subjective element of crimes against humanity is twofold: it includes the subjective element required for the specific act committed by the suspect (i.e. any of the offences included in the list made by Article 7) and 'knowledge of the attack'. Knowledge of the attack was interpreted by the Elements of Crimes as either the perpetrators' acknowledgement of their conduct *as part* of a widespread or systematic attack directed against a civilian population or as their intention that the conduct be part of such an attack.[40] That is, the perpetrator need only be aware of the overall context in which his or her acts occurred.[41] As the ICC Trial

[38] Bemba, supra Note 28, para 151.
[39] Cassese, supra Note 5, at 116.
[40] Elements of Crimes, supra Note 10, art. 7, Crimes Against Humanity, Introduction, para 3.
[41] *Kordić*, supra Note 36, para 185.

Chamber in the Katanga case determined, the perpetrator need not necessarily know all of the characteristics of the attack or the precise details of the plan or policy.[42] The ICTY clarified that the perpetrator should have been aware of a link between the misconduct and the widespread or systematic practice or at least aware of a risk that the act is part of the attack.[43] The ICTY also detailed the sources from which such knowledge could be inferred: the functions of the accused when the crimes were committed and his or her position in the political or military hierarchy; the scope and gravity of the acts perpetrated; and the nature of the crimes committed.[44]

6.2.2 *Extermination and Torture in Syrian Detention Facilities as Crimes against Humanity*

Since the start of the uprising in March 2011, Syrian authorities have detained tens of thousands of civilians broadly perceived as associated with the opposition.[45] These civilians were held in detention centres and prisons in various areas of Syria, including main cities such as Damascus, Aleppo, Hama, Daraa, and Homs,[46] and yet 'out of sight, far from the raging battlefield'.[47] Several Syrian government agencies, such as security and intelligence authorities, the Syrian army, and the Syrian police,[48] carried out arrests, searches, interrogations, and detentions.[49]

[42] Katanga, supra Note 30, para 401.

[43] Cassese, supra Note 5, at 114–15 citing ICTY decisions.

[44] Blaskić, supra Note 25, paras 258–9.

[45] The broad conception of victims as associated with the opposition is evidenced by the State's arrests of residents of opposition-controlled areas, relatives of suspected members of armed groups, activists, defectors, military personnel suspected of sympathising with the uprising, those believed to be providing medical care to the opposition, and civilians suspected of taking active part in armed hostilities. *Out of Sight, Out of Mind: Deaths in Detention in the Syrian Arab Republic*, CoI Syria, 3 February 2016, A/HRC/31/CRP.1 [hereinafter: CoI Syria report, February 2016], 2, 4.

[46] Report of the independent international commission of inquiry on the Syrian Arab Republic, A/HRC/25/65, 12 February 2014, Annex V, pp. 46–49 [hereinafter: CoI Syria report, February 2014].

[47] CoI Syria report, February 2016, supra Note 45. This report establishes that these are deaths for which military necessity cannot be invoked as legal justification.

[48] Department of Military Intelligence, Political Security Directorate, General Intelligence Directorate – known as State Security – and Air Force Intelligence Directorate. *If the Dead Could Speak: Mass Deaths and Torture in Syria's Detention Facilities*, Human Rights Watch, 2015 [hereinafter: HRW], 21.

[49] Ibid.

Those arbitrarily arrested and detained were mainly civilian males above the age of fifteen, though some cases of women and children prisoners as young as seven years old were also documented. These civilians were forcibly disappeared and taken into detention during mass arrests, house searches, at checkpoints, and in hospitals, while almost always denied any means of contacting their families.[50]

Mass arrests of civilians by Syrian forces were conducted as part of a 'country-wide pattern'.[51] Investigations by the CoI Syria, Human Rights Watch, and Amnesty International show that both killings and torture have been 'rampant' and that both torture and extermination were systematic and widespread practices of Syrian authorities against civilian detainees, thus constituting crimes against humanity.[52] Evidence collected from a large number of qualitative interviews, documentary material, and the forensic analysis of 'Caesar's'[53] photographs appeared to provide proof of a state policy to eliminate the government's opponents in a context of civil war.

Human Rights Watch interviewed twenty-seven families of the victims identified in Caesar's photographs. Only eight of these profiles were made public in its report. The first victim profiled was Abdallah Arslan al-Hariri,[54] a 36- or 37-year-old labourer from Namr, Daraa. Abdallah was a leader of anti-government demonstrations in his hometown when protests began in 2011. He later helped Syrian Army defectors who wanted to leave Syria. On 16 June 2012, Abdallah was arrested by the Military Police. Together with his relative Tal'at, Abdallah was arrested, handcuffed, and blindfolded. According to Tal'at's testimony, Abdallah was beaten while held in the Military Police Department's courtyard. 'I could hear that he was in pain. Abdallah was interrogated about his participation in the protests. They hit him. They told him, "You are

[50] Ibid.

[51] Ibid.

[52] Ibid., 2. USHMM also points to crimes against humanity committed by the Syrian government which include systematic extrajudicial killings and murders, torture, sexual violence, and starvation in detention centres. 'Is the Worst Yet to Come? Ongoing Mass Atrocity Risks in Syria', www.ushmm.org/m/pdfs/Syria_Bearing_Witness_Report_031218.pdf.

[53] Caesar is the codename given to a defector from Syria who was in the service of the military police of the Syrian government and who smuggled out tens of thousands of images of corpses photographed by his colleagues and himself; 'They Were Torturing to Kill: Inside Syria's Death Machine', *The Guardian*, International edition, www.theguardian.com/world/2015/oct/01/they-were-torturing-to-kill-inside-syrias-death-machine-caesar.

[54] HRW report refers to this person's first name as 'Abdullah'. However, in Tal'at's testimony, the name is spelled 'Abdallah'. HRW, supra Note 48, at 39–41.

a fighter." Abdallah responded, "No, I am not armed." The last thing I heard was: "I have an injured terrorist, come and take him from here." Then I heard the sound of a car . . . I never saw him again.'[55]

Amnesty International concludes from its findings that since 2011, the Syrian government has 'purposefully inflicted inhumane conditions on detainees in its custody in a calculated effort to kill them'.[56] This coincides with the conclusion reached in 2016 by the CoI Syria.

Investigations by the CoI Syria, Human Rights Watch, and Amnesty International establish a link between the large-scale and organised nature of the crimes and their authorisation by the highest levels of the Syrian government. It has been documented that several government agencies were involved at different stages in the detentions and ill treatment of prisoners. While army units and security agencies conducted arrests, transfers, and interrogations throughout the country, institutions such as military hospitals, the Military Police, and judiciary institutions played a role in various aspects of the process of gross violations. Most deaths in detention occurred in locations controlled by the Syrian intelligence services, while deaths of civilians were recorded at detention facilities on army bases and at military positions in the custody of the 4th and 9th Divisions of the Syrian Armed Forces and the Republican Guard. The Military Police corps of the Syrian army oversaw a centralised registration system of deaths in detention facilities.[57]

Saydnaya Military Prison[58] has been under the jurisdiction of the Ministry of Defence and operated by the Military Police.[59] According to Amnesty International's report, 'death sentences [were] approved by the Grand Mufti of Syria and by either the Minister of Defence or the Chief of

[55] Testimony given to HRW by Tal'at who was released a few days later after his detention. The family of Abdallah identified him when some of the Caesar photographs were posted on Facebook. HRW, supra Note 48, at 40. The photographs and profiles of Khalid Hadla, Osama Hussein Salim, Ayham Ghazzoul, Oqba al-Mashaan, Mohammed Tariq Majid, Ahmad al-Musalmani (child), and Rehab al-Allawi (woman) are on pages 41–58.

[56] Amnesty International concludes that detainees at Saydnaya Prison and other government-run detention centres have been subjected to such 'inhuman treatment' that constitutes 'extermination', as defined by the ICC Statute. Furthermore, it concludes that the 'extermination' carried out at Saydnaya since 2011 has been perpetrated 'as part of an attack against the civilian population that has been widespread, as well as systematic, and carried out in furtherance of state policy'. Thus, these actions amount to 'crimes against humanity'. *Human Slaughterhouse: Mass Hangings and Extermination at Saydnaya Prison, Syria*, Amnesty International, 2016 [hereinafter: AI], Executive Summary, 6.

[57] CoI Syria report, February 2016, supra Note 45, at 7–8.

[58] See Section 6.2.2.1.1 and in Section 6.2.2 on torture, discussion of the events in this prison.

[59] AI, supra Note 56, section 4.1, at 15.

Staff of the Army, who [were] deputized to act on behalf of President Bashar al-Assad. The sentences [were] also signed by the head and the Military Prosecutor of the Military Field Court and a representative of the security forces. The hangings [were] physically overseen by an execution panel, which includes military officers, as well as prison and medical officials.'[60]

Guards and high-level Syrian officials knew about the execution process at Saydnaya. Autonomous national intelligence agencies increasingly coordinated their actions since 2011 and reported to the highest officials in the Syrian state or even directly to the president.[61]

The CoI Syria concluded that the Syrian state pursued a policy 'to target civilians ... perceived as associated with the opposition'.[62] This is demonstrated by the systematic character of the crimes conducted across geographical areas; the fact that killings and deaths occurred with high frequency, over a long period of time and in multiple locations; the employment of 'significant' state resources in the commission of the crimes; and the participation of and coordination by numerous state institutions throughout the country. Furthermore, military and civilian courts 'consistently failed' to order investigations. The crimes occurred with the knowledge of prison personnel and their superiors, as well as that of high-ranking state officials in central military hospitals and the Military Police corps of the Syrian armed forces. Thus, government authorities administering prisons and detention centres were aware of deaths on a massive scale.[63]

6.2.2.1 Extermination

The crime against humanity of extermination is defined in Article 7 of the ICC Statute as 'includ[ing] the intentional infliction of conditions of life, *inter alia* the deprivation of access to food and medicine, calculated to bring about the destruction of part of a population'. The Elements of Crimes add that those killings should be 'mass' to distinguish exterminations from murder.

Most ICTY and ICTR judgments confirm these characteristics of extermination, determining that to qualify as such it should be committed on a large scale, involve the killing of a large number of persons, and be aimed at a group.[64] Nevertheless, extermination as a crime against

[60] AI, supra Note 56, at 6.
[61] HRW, supra Note 48, at 21. See also CoI Syria report, February 2016, supra Note 45, at 6–7.
[62] CoI Syria report, February 2016, supra Note 45, at 16.
[63] Ibid.
[64] Hall, supra Note 14, at 238–9.

humanity should be distinguished from genocide. As explained in Section 6.3.1.2 of this chapter, the crime of genocide can only be committed against specified groups (national, ethnical, racial, or religious), referred to as protected groups; crimes against humanity, on the other hand, can be committed against any part of the population. More importantly, genocide requires that the perpetrator have a specific intent to destroy the group, while crimes against humanity require only the general intent of the perpetrator.[65]

As the CoI Syria reported, extermination was committed in Syrian detention centres[66] through the establishment of inhumane conditions for the detainees as well as through direct killings. Conditions of detention constituted cruel, inhumane, or degrading treatment or punishment, characterised by a lack of food, water, space, sleep, hygiene, and medical care, leading to deaths of detainees.[67] A paradigmatic case of systematic extermination in Syrian detention facilities is Saydnaya Military Prison, located 30 km north of Damascus, to which detainees were transferred since 2011. The prison was under the jurisdiction of the Ministry of Defence and operated by the Military Police. The prison may hold between 10,000 and 20,000 male detainees in its two buildings. Officers and soldiers were held in the 'white building', while the 'red building'[68] held civilian detainees thought to oppose the government: civilian demonstrators, political dissidents, human rights defenders, journalists, doctors, aid workers, and students.[69]

According to Amnesty International's research, which refers also to the findings of the CoI Syria, the UN Office of the High Commissioner for Human Rights, and Human Rights Watch, 'tens of thousands of detainees have died in Saydnaya and other government-run detention centres since 2011 as a result of the extermination policies' of the Syrian government.[70] In Saydnaya, as well as in other detention facilities, extermination was committed through executions as well as through the systematic establishment and prolonged maintenance of inhumane conditions that lead to large numbers of deaths of civilians in detention.[71] A description of these methods follows.

65 For further discussion, see Section 6.3.1.1.
66 CoI Syria report, February 2014, supra Note 46, at 46–9.
67 Ibid., 11.
68 See AI, supra Note 56, at 6, 9.
69 CoI Syria report, February 2016, supra Note 45, at 4.
70 AI, supra Note 56, section 4.3.4., at 40.
71 Ibid., 14.

6.2.2.1.1 Direct Killings and Executions Since the outset of the uprising in 2011, thousands have died in custody in detention facilities in Syria by several means.[72] According to Amnesty International, from September 2011 to December 2015, between 5,000 and 13,000 were executed by 'mass hangings'[73] at Saydnaya prison.[74] Many others were killed after being tortured and subjected to inhumane conditions.[75]

Estimates of deaths in Syrian detention centres and prisons vary greatly,[76] but they indicate an increase since 2011 and on a massive scale. Human Rights Data Analysis Group identifies at least 17,723 people killed in government custody between March 2011 and December 2015, an average of 300 deaths each month.[77] Yet Amnesty International considers this number conservative.[78] Other Syrian organisations, such as the Violations Documentation Center in Syria and the Syrian Network for Human Rights, document between 7,502 and 11,358 deaths.[79] According to Human Rights Watch, while most died in detention facilities of security branches, some died in military hospitals to which they were transferred.[80]

The 28,707 'Caesar' photographs analysed correspond to at least 6,786 dead individuals.[81] However, the number of bodies from detention facilities in these photographs represent only a part of those who died in detention in Damascus during a 27-month period when the military police and forensic medical authorities produced these photographs.

[72] HRW, supra Note 48, at 1.
[73] AI, supra Note 56, at 6.
[74] Ibid., 5, 17, 24.
[75] Mass hangings are called 'the party' by prison authorities. The procedure for executions includes a 'trial' at the military field court, the approval of a death sentence, collection for 'transfer', transport from the red to the white building, and the witnessing of executions by a panel. The bodies are then loaded into trucks, registered at Tishreen hospital, and taken to mass graves. Ibid., 5, 14, 16, 17–28.
[76] According to HRW, several factors make it 'virtually impossible' to determine the precise number of civilian deaths in Syrian detention centres since 2011: 'lack of access for independent observers', the 'near-complete secrecy' in detention facilities, and the government's 'refusal to provide families' with information about their detained relatives. HRW, supra Note 48, at 25.
[77] AI, supra Note 56, Executive Summary, at 5.
[78] Ibid., 40.
[79] HRW, supra Note 48, at 25.
[80] 601 Military Hospital in Mezze, Tishreen Military Hospital and Harasta Military Hospital. As the number of bodies that arrived at the 601 Military Hospital increased, it ran out of rooms in the morgue's refrigerated compartments and began storing the bodies in a garage. HRW, supra Note 48 at 59, 77.
[81] Dead bodies include mostly men, with only one woman, and at least 100 appear to be children. The bodies were mostly from facilities in the greater Damascus area. Ibid., 31.

With respect to mass graves, there is discrepancy between the findings of Amnesty International (which concludes that dead bodies were transferred from Saydnaya, registered, and buried in mass graves on military land near Damascus)[82] and the findings of Human Rights Watch, which states that, although some witnesses refer to the existence of mass graves, it does not have enough evidence to confirm those graves.

6.2.2.1.2 Inhumane Conditions: Filthy and Overcrowded Cells Syrian authorities have kept detainees in filthy, overcrowded cells without access to fresh air, sunlight, or ventilation for months or years, which results in overheating, humidity, and inadequate sanitation. Detainees were continuously denied access to showers, while they were permitted to use the bathroom only a few times a day at designated times and only very briefly, giving them no time to wash. Detainees were also exposed to extremely cold temperatures during the winter.[83] In these inhumane living conditions, disease and infections spread while lack of rest severely weakened detainees. Thus, fatalities in large numbers resulted from 'preventable' or 'treatable' conditions.[84]

6.2.2.1.3 Inhumane Conditions: Deprivation of Adequate Food and Water Evidence for deprivation of adequate food and water was found in the documentation of detention facilities: 'Many of the 6,786 victims depicted in the "Caesar" photographs appear severely emaciated: their ribs are prominently visible, stomachs shrunken, and pelvis bones dramatically pronounced.' According to one medical estimate, 43 per cent of these victims appear emaciated in the photographs.[85] Detainees were provided 'meagre' amounts of spoiled food and were denied water or provided unclean drinking water.[86] This led to 'malnutrition' and

[82] The information presented by Amnesty International is based on interviews with former guards and officials from Saydnaya in 2016. According to the data collected by Amnesty International, 'the bodies of the victims are transported from Tishreen Hospital to mass graves located on military land near Damascus'. Amnesty International's report includes satellite images of mass graves at Najha, Syria. AI, supra Note 56, 28–30.

[83] HRW, supra Note 48 at 8, 35, 61, 62, 67.

[84] CoI Syria report, February 2016, supra Note 45, at 5–6.

[85] HRW, supra Note 48, at 33. Emaciation resulting from inadequate food is also documented in CoI Syria report, February 2016, supra Note 45, at 6.

[86] Ibid., 5. HRW reports that the detention centres provided 'meager quantities of food' so that detainees completely lost their strength. Poor and spoiled food, together with crowding, filthy cells and lack of medical care, 'exacerbated the conditions in which gastrointestinal infections could flourish'. HRW, supra Note 48, at 61–2.

'starvation',[87] thus leaving detainees particularly vulnerable to contracting serious illnesses such as tuberculosis and gastrointestinal infections.[88] Several testimonies of former detainees provide evidence of such inhumane conditions:

> There was one older detainee . . . He loved sweets . . . He got diarrhoea, and shut down. He stopped eating, and started defecating on himself. On the day of his death, in March [2014], the whole cell prayed for his soul.[89]

6.2.2.1.4 Inhumane Conditions: Lack of Medicine and Adequate Medical Care Sick detainees received few or inadequate medicines (i.e. only paracetamol and over-the-counter painkillers, even in severe cases).[90] Medical attention by physicians was available only in some security branches, while detainees were beaten and abused by some of the doctors. A few detainees interviewed by Human Rights Watch said they received medical treatment at 601 or Tishreen military hospitals but described 'abusive conditions' such as handcuffing. Medical assistance was inadequate even for those with chronic conditions or those seriously wounded after beatings or torture.[91] These conditions have led to prolonged suffering and slow deaths.[92]

To conclude this subsection on extermination, such inhumane conditions, imposed intentionally and systematically by Syrian authorities, led to deaths. Such deaths resulted from different factors. Some were common causes identified by forensic analyses: gastrointestinal infections (with severe diarrhoea and dehydration); skin disease (scabies and unidentified rashes or spots) leading to infection, and torture, including severe beatings.[93] Additional causal factors were mental distress; chronic diseases (hypertension, diabetes, asthma, kidney disease); and starvation. Physicians for Human Rights also found evidence of starvation, violent

[87] AI uses the words 'malnutrition' and 'starvation' to describe the conditions that resulted from the intentional denial of adequate food to detainees at Saydnaya prison. AI, supra Note 56, at 33.

[88] AI, supra Note 56, at 5; HRW, supra Note 48, at 866.

[89] Testimony of Karem, a former detainee who spent nine months in Branch 235 of Military Intelligence. It is part of the testimonial evidence provided by HRW, supra Note 46, at 62.

[90] CoI Syria report, February 2016, supra Note 45, at 5–7.

[91] Ibid., 9, 64, 65.

[92] Ibid., 6.

[93] HRW, supra Note 48, at 60.

blunt-force trauma, suffocation, and torture,[94] all of them leading to deaths that constitute extermination.

6.2.2.2 Torture

According to Article 7 of the ICC Statute, 'torture means the intentional infliction of severe pain or suffering, whether physical or mental, upon a person in the custody or under the control of the accused; except that torture shall not include pain or suffering arising only from, inherent in or incidental to, lawful sanctions'. The prohibition on torture is a peremptory norm (*jus cogens*) and an absolute right permitting no reservations and limitations.[95] As such, it requires a broad definition, as is reflected in several aspects of the perpetrator's mental element and purpose, the nature of the pain inflicted upon the victim, and the torturer's identity.

There is no requirement for a specific purpose for the commission of the crime against humanity of torture. Additionally, while the mental element of the perpetrator requires that he or she intends to inflict severe pain,[96] it is not required that the perpetrator knows the pain was indeed severe.[97] In fact, according to the Elements of Crimes, the knowledge of the perpetrator refers only to the 'conduct [as] part of or [the perpetrator's intention that] the conduct . . . be part of a widespread or systematic attack directed against a civilian population'.

With regards to the nature of the inflicted pain, the ICTY confirmed that 'acts inflicting physical pain may amount to torture even if they do not cause pain of the type accompanying serious injury'.[98] Flexibility is also observed with regards to the connection between the act of torture and the victim's subjection to custody. As legal scholar Christopher K. Hall notes, 'custody includes any form of detention or imprisonment, including arrest by security forces and other restrictions on liberty'.[99] Notably, however, the nature of 'lawful sanctions' that may result in pain

[94] Ibid. Sexual violence (that can be a form of torture, such as when prisoners were subjected to threats of sexual violence against female relatives) was also detected in detention facilities. CoI Syria report, February 2016, supra Note 45, at 7. For a discussion of rape and sexual violence against women in Syria, see Chapter 7 of this volume.

[95] That a right be absolute is rare in international law and this emphasises the significance of the prohibition on torture.

[96] ICC Statute, art. 7.

[97] Hall, supra Note 14, at 252. This was confirmed by the ICC. See Bemba, supra Note 28, para 194.

[98] Cassese, supra Note 5, at 112, citing ICTY Appeals Chamber.

[99] Hall, supra Note 14, at 253.

not counted as torture must be determined by international law and not by state law.

Torture has been a systematic and widespread state practice against civilians in Syrian prisons and detention sites[100] with the intention to crush dissent, inflict terror on the population, and provoke death.[101] According to Amnesty International, torture was a systematic practice in Syria's prisons since 1987, but its magnitude and severity have increased since 2011.[102] In 2012, Human Rights Watch documented the systematic use of specific forms of torture by interrogators, guards, and security force officers in twenty-seven separate Syrian detention facilities.[103] Similar conclusions were reached by the CoI Syria.[104] One of its reports mentions that methods of torture included severe beatings of head and body, prolonged hangings by the arms, and sexual torture[105] and attributed to these acts of torture and other forms of cruel, inhumane, or degrading treatment or punishment 'a widespread character [which] points to an organisational policy'. The report, thus, turned these acts into crimes against humanity.[106]

Methods of torture in security branches included: *shabeh* (suspending detainees by their wrists for hours or days); beating detainees' heads or chests with PVC pipes and sticks; whipping with steel cables on their backs, legs, and soles of their feet (the latter called *falaqa*); electrocution (all over their bodies and genital areas); burning; the use of the 'German chair' (a metal pole is strapped to the detainees' back and bent backwards until it feels as though their back will break); *Bsat al-Reeh* or 'flying carpet' (immobilisation on a flat board so that detainees are unable to defend themselves when beaten); suffocation; and *dulab* or 'tire method' (forcing a victim to bend at the waist and stick his head, neck, legs, and sometimes

100 In particular, the Political Security Branch in Aleppo, the Military Intelligence Branch 227 and the Military Intelligence Branch 215, the Mezzeh Airforce Intelligence facility, the Qaboun Military Police Branch and Sednaya Prison in Damascus, the Gharez Central Prison in Daraa, and the Military Intelligence Branch in Homs. CoI Syria report, February 2014, supra Note 46, at 10.

101 HRW, supra Note 48, at 11, CoI Syria report, February 2014, supra Note 46, at 10.

102 AI, supra Note 56, Executive Summary, at 5.

103 Ibid., 9, 23.

104 CoI Syria report, February 2016, supra Note 45, at 17. This report establishes that civilian prisoners died as a result of severe injuries sustained due to torture. It also documents cases of civilians beaten to death during interrogations and in their cells.

105 CoI Syria report, February 2014, supra Note 46, at 10.

106 Ibid., 11.

arms into the inside of a car tire to provoke immobilisation).[107] As in confinement, silence was generally enforced during torture sessions.

Methods of torture documented at all-male Saydnaya Military Prison also included sexual violence. Omar, a young boy arrested and detained at Saydnaya prison, told Amnesty International:

> I don't even know what term to use to describe what I saw. The guard would ask everyone to take off all their clothes and go to the bathroom one by one. As we walked to the bathroom, they would select one of the boys, someone petite or young or fair. They would ask him to stand with his face to the door and close his eyes. They would then ask a bigger prisoner to rape him . . . No one will admit this happened to them, but it happened so often . . . Sometimes psychological pain is worse than physical pain, and the people who were forced to do this were never the same again.[108]

Torture was conducted since the moment of arrest and during 'welcome parties' (severe beatings upon arrival and interrogation). Torture was used during multiple sessions over the course of days, weeks, or months. Killing, generally done by hanging, was preceded by severe beating during two or three hours. Throughout this process, victims remained blindfolded and were never told that they were going to be executed. The execution followed their condemnation to death in one- to three-minute 'trials' at the Military Field Court in Damascus.[109]

The reports of the CoI Syria, Amnesty International, and Human Rights Watch analysed in this chapter prove that Syrian detention practices have resulted in torture, including dehumanisation and degradation, as well as in hundreds or possibly thousands of civilian deaths that amount to extermination.

Evidence of systematic torture is found in 'Caesar's' photographs. Dead bodies exhibited signs of more than one type of torture, while many detainees sustained multiple blunt-force injuries. Starvation and sleep deprivation led to skin sores and infections including cellulitis of lower extremities. Emaciated bodies had bruises, scars, and other physical marks such as deep wounds.[110] This evidence, together with documented processing of bodies of detainees and the inhumane detention conditions described in Sections 6.2.2.1.2 to 6.2.2.1.4, points to a state policy of enabling mass deaths in state custody.[111] Finally, all described

[107] Ibid., 9.
[108] AI, supra Note 56, at 7.
[109] Ibid., 6, 12, 19, 33.
[110] HRW, supra Note 48, at 34, 61, 71.
[111] Ibid., 11.

conducts were committed with the perpetrators' knowledge of being part of a widespread and systematic attack, thus being crimes against humanity.

6.3 Genocide

Like the section on crimes against humanity, this section is divided into theoretical and factual parts. The theoretical part opens with the legal definition of genocide and an analysis of the mental element: the genocidal intent. It continues with an analysis of the distinction between genocide, ethnic cleansing, and cultural genocide. Making this distinction is important for two reasons: the first is understanding why genocide is attributed only to ISIS and not to the Syrian government; the second is that cultural genocide can serve as evidence supporting the proof of the crime of genocide, as in the Yazidi case. The factual part discusses the conducts ISIS committed against the Yazidis and explains why these conducts are forms of genocide.

6.3.1 Legal Definition

The definition of genocide widely accepted throughout the years as representing customary law appears in the 1948 Genocide Convention,[112] which established genocide as an autonomous crime.[113] It was incorporated, without amendment, in Article 6 of the ICC Statute. According to this definition the crime of genocide can be committed through five acts accompanied by a unique mental element: an 'intent to destroy, in whole or in part, a national, ethnical, racial or religious group, as such'.[114] The enumerated prohibited acts are: (a) killing members of the group; (b) causing serious bodily or mental harm to members of the group; (c) deliberately inflicting on the group conditions of life calculated to bring about its physical destruction in whole or in part; (d) imposing measures

[112] *Convention on the Prevention and Punishment of the Crime of Genocide*, 9 December 1948, United Nations, Treaty Series, vol. 78, p. 277 [hereinafter Genocide Convention]; Case Concerning Application of the Convention on the Prevention and Punishment of the Crime of Genocide (*Bosnia-Herzegovina* v. *Yugoslavia*), I.C.J. Reports 1996, p. 595, para 161 [hereinafter: Bosnian genocide case].

[113] The IMT Statute did not include a crime of genocide, and the conducts that comprise this crime were included under the category of crimes against humanity.

[114] ICC Statute, art. 6.

intended to prevent births within the group; (e) forcibly transferring children of the group to another group.[115]

Despite the existence of a firm legal definition, much controversy surrounds the term of genocide since its inception, and this controversy is related to its conceptual boundaries. In public imagination, and also in some academic writings, genocide has been epitomised as 'the crime of crimes',[116] demanding the organised extermination of masses of civilians. As much as this description of genocide can be, and most often is, a component of the legal definition of the crime, it is incomplete and inaccurate.[117] The legal definition of genocide sets five different conducts through which a genocide may be committed, with killing members of the protected group being simply one of them. Therefore, theoretically, genocide can be committed without a single act of killing, though this has not often been so in reality.[118]

The following discussion relates to three theoretical issues that are relevant to the acts of genocide that were committed by ISIS against the Yazidis (and which are further discussed in this chapter): the specific intent of the perpetrator (mental element), destroying a specific group *as such*, and the distinction of genocide from ethnic cleansing and cultural genocide.

6.3.1.1 The Specific Intent

The mental element of genocide distinguishes this crime from other international core crimes – that is, war crimes and crimes against humanity. For a conviction with genocide, it is neither sufficient that the perpetrator had knowledge of the objective elements of the crime nor that he or she intended its consequences. The perpetrator of genocide must have a specific (aggravated)[119] intent to destroy one of the groups mentioned in the legal definition as such.[120]

[115] Genocide Convention, supra Note 112.

[116] This notion has nevertheless been shared by legal jurisprudence as well. See Schabas, supra Note 12, at 119.

[117] See Larry May, *Genocide: A Normative Account* (2010) 4; UN Human Rights Council, '"They Came to Destroy": ISIS Crimes Against the Yazidis', 15 June 2016, A/HRC/32/CRP.2 [hereinafter: 'They Came to Destroy'].

[118] The academic debate focuses on such questions as how restrictive the legal definition should be, especially regarding the targeted victim groups; that is, religious, national, ethnic, racial or national, leaving out other groups such as political ones, and on the scope of genocidal violence, and the particular acts involved. For a discussion of some of these academic debates, see Jens Meierhenrich, *Genocide: A Reader* (New York: Oxford University Press, 2014), 56–104.

[119] Cassese, supra Note 5, at 137.

[120] ICC statute, art. 6.

Yet, proving the existence of such a specific intent is extremely difficult and 'even impossible to determine'.[121] For this reason, the specific intent is in most cases inferred from 'acts or utterances of the accused'[122] or from a contextual element of an existing plan or policy to destroy a specific group.[123] The Elements of Crimes support this conclusion, stating as a requirement for each and every conduct that comprises the crime of genocide that 'the conduct took place in the context of a manifest pattern of similar conduct directed against that group or was conduct that could itself effect such destruction'.[124]

In the case of Omar al-Bashir (the Sudanese president), the ICC determined that intent is usually inferred from factual circumstances (such as the plan held by the Sudanese government);[125] this practice derives from the rareness of evidence explicitly proving a person's intent (such as documents or declarations regarding such intent).[126] As legal scholar Antonio Cassese notes, '[A]cts of genocide are always part of a larger context, and even though they are not necessarily committed by state officials they are usually perpetrated with the complicity, connivance, and at least the toleration or acquiescence of the authorities.'[127]

6.3.1.2 Destroying a Specific Group As Such

The specific intent of the perpetrator expresses his or her willingness to destroy one of the groups mentioned by Article 6 of the ICC Statute 'in whole or in part as such' – that is, as opposed to the case of all the other international core crimes, victims of genocide are not targeted for their personal capacity but rather because they belong to a certain group.[128] This is the core of the genocidal intent: an intent to destroy a group, not only to commit a crime against individuals. The ICC determined that 'the crime of genocide is only completed when the relevant conduct presents a concrete threat to the existence of the targeted group or a part thereof'.[129]

[121] Case No. ICTR-96-4-T, *Prosecutor* v. *Akayesu*, Trial Chamber, 2 September 1998, para 523.
[122] Ibid.
[123] *Prosecutor* v. *Jelisić*, Case no. IT-95-10-A, AC, 5 July 2001. It should be noted that the ad hoc tribunals decisions preceded the ICC Statute and its additional related instruments, including the Elements of Crimes.
[124] Elements of Crimes, supra Note 10, art. 6.
[125] Bashir, supra Note 27, para 124.
[126] Cassese, supra Note 5, at 141.
[127] Ibid., 144.
[128] Ibid., 137.
[129] Bashir, supra Note 27, para 124.

Debates surrounding the definition of genocide focus to a large extent on the question of whether the list of groups mentioned in Article 6 (and so also in the Genocide Convention) is a closed list or whether other groups can be added and, if not, whether they *should* be added. This debate is beyond the discussion of this chapter, as the Yazidis fit within the category of religious groups mentioned in Article 6. Nevertheless, the 'as such' component requires a note regarding the social value that a protection of groups (and not the protection of the members of the groups as individuals) entails.

With its focus on groups rather than individuals, the crime of genocide captures a value that cannot be protected by other international crimes: the significance of groups. Groups, and especially the groups mentioned in Article 6 (national, ethnical, racial, and religious), have a major social role in forming a person's identity, serving as a source of support by fellow members of the group, and nurturing collective memory.[130] When a group is destroyed, its surviving members are stripped of their group membership and experience what Claudia Card calls 'social death'.[131] Their heritage and even their intergenerational connections may be destroyed. Even though they were not physically exterminated, they lose the role that the group has played in their lives, and this loss of both external recognition and self-acknowledgement is irredeemable.[132]

The loss of group identity is significant even if it affects only part of the group, such as members of a specific area,[133] as is suggested by Article 6's reference to the destruction of a group 'in whole or in part'. While the drafters of the Genocide Convention probably intended to prevent the extension of the crime of genocide to isolated acts of racially motivated violence,[134] they have also recognised the significance of destroying a part of the group, as long as this part is substantial.[135] Destroying a substantial part of the group implies the genocidal intent, as this destruction can have major implications for the survival of the group – for example, when the majority of the men are killed and the women survivors are unable to procreate and conserve the group.[136]

[130] May, supra Note 117, at 89.
[131] Card, cited in Ibid., 85.
[132] May, supra Note 117, at 10, 87. For an elaboration on sociological theories on groups' value for the identity and status of group members, see Ibid., 78–94.
[133] Ibid., 89.
[134] Schabas, supra Note 12, at 127.
[135] *Prosecutor* v. *Krstić* IT-98-33-T, Judgment, 2 August 2001, para 12.
[136] Ibid., para 28.

6.3.1.3 Cultural Genocide and Ethnic Cleansing

The destruction of a group is discernible both from ethnic cleansing and from what is called 'cultural genocide'. Cultural genocide and ethnic cleansing are neither crimes per se nor conducts that comprise the crime of genocide. Nevertheless, they are condemned practices (and the drafters of the Genocide Convention considered including them among the conduct that comprises genocide); moreover, they can serve as evidence in proving conducts that do comprise genocide. Therefore, a short note on these practices follows.

Rafael Lemkin, who is known as the first jurist and scholar to coin the term 'genocide' and to initiate the Genocide Convention, included among 'the objectives of such a plan ... [the] disintegration of the political and social institutions, of culture, language, national feelings, religion, and the economic existence of national groups and the destruction of personal security, liberty, health, dignity, and even the lives of the individuals belonging to such groups'.[137] Indeed, the prohibition on acts of cultural genocide was a part of the first draft of the Genocide Convention drawn in May 1947 by the UN Economic and Social Council.[138] Five alternative methods of attempting to destroy the specific characteristics of the group were included, such as the forcible transfer of children to another human group, forced and systematic exile of individuals representing the culture of a group, and conducts aiming at eliminating the language and culture of the group, such as prohibiting the use of the national language and the destruction of books and historical and religious monuments.[139] Eventually, acts of cultural genocide were not included in the Genocide Convention, and the first draft bequeathed the Convention only with the conduct of forced transfer of children to another group.[140]

Ethnic cleansing was similarly distinguished from genocide. The term 'ethnic cleansing' was used in the context of the 1990s civil war in the former Yugoslavia. Possible definitions of ethnic cleansing were established in the context of the war in the former Yugoslavia by the UN Commission of Experts pursuant to Security Council Resolution 780:

[137] Rafael Lemkin, *Axis Rule in Occupied Europe* (1944), 27–8.

[138] Johannes Morsink, 'Cultural Genocide, the Universal Declaration, and Minority Rights', *Human Rights Quarterly* 21 (1999), 1,023.

[139] Ibid.

[140] David B. MacDonald and Graham Hudson, 'The Genocide Question and Indian Residential Schools in Canada', *Canadian Journal of Political Science* 45, no. 2 (June 2012): 427–49.

'rendering an area ethnically homogenous by using force or intimidation to remove persons of given groups from the area'[141] and 'a purposeful policy designed by one ethnic or religious group to remove by violent and terror-inspiring means the civilian population of another ethnic or religious group from certain geographical areas'.[142]

As much as there are similarities between acts of genocide and acts of ethnic cleansing,[143] the international courts and tribunals pointed to the distinction between those concepts. The International Court of Justice determined in the *Bosnia* v. *Serbia* case that ethnic cleansing can only be a form of genocide if it corresponds to or falls within one of the categories of acts prohibited by Article II of the Genocide Convention. Neither the intent, as a matter of policy, to render an area 'ethnically homogeneous' nor the operations that may be carried out to implement such policy can as such be designated as genocide.[144] The ICTY has observed that ethnic cleansing aims at displacement and not necessarily at destruction.[145] Therefore, '[a] clear distinction must be drawn between physical destruction and mere dissolution of a group. The expulsion of a group or part of a group does not in itself suffice for genocide.'[146]

The conclusions regarding the distinction of genocide from discussions of cultural genocide and ethnic cleansing are reflected in Article 6 of the ICC Statute. This Article refers only to a physical destruction of the group and does not include within the ambit of the crime the forced

[141] Interim Report of the Commission of Experts Established Pursuant to Security Council Resolution 780 (1992), UN SCOR, UN Doc. S/25274 (26 January 1993), at 16.

[142] Final Report of the Commission of Experts Established Pursuant to UN Security Council Resolution 780 (1992), UN SCOR, UN Doc. S/1994/674 (27 May 1994), Annex, at 3, 33. For scholars defining ethnic cleansing, see Andrew Bell-Fialkoff, *Ethnic Cleansing* (New York: St. Martin's Griffin, 1999); Terry Martin and Damir Mirković, 'Ethnic Conflict and Genocide: Reflections on Ethnic Cleansing in the Former Yugoslavia', *The Annals of the American Academy of Political and Social Science* vol. 548; The Holocaust: Remembering for the Future (November 1996), 191–9; Norman M. Naimark, *Fires of Hatred: Ethnic Cleansing in Twentieth-Century Europe* (Cambridge: Harvard University Press, 2001). Naimark conceptually distinguishes between ethnic cleansing and genocide as two different activities. He defines ethnic-cleansing policies as those aimed at 'removing a people and often all traces of them from a concrete territory' (3). For an interesting critique of Naimark's analytical framework, see Adam Jones, 'The Politics of Genocide', *International Studies Review* 4, no. 1 (Spring 2002), 129–39.

[143] Krstić, supra Note 135, at para 562.

[144] Bosnian genocide case, supra Note 112. See also European Court of Human Rights, *Jorgić* v. *Germany* App. No. 74613/01, 12 July 2007.

[145] Bashir, supra Note 27, para 143, citing ICTY ruling in Krstić, supra Note 135.

[146] *Prosecutor* v. *Stakić*, IT-97-24-T, Trial Chamber Judgment, 31 July 2003, para 519.

expulsion of members of the group from a geographical area into another area (ethnic cleansing) or the destruction of a group's religious, historical, or cultural heritage.[147]

However, both the ICC and the ICTY acknowledged that ethnic cleansing and cultural genocide can, under certain circumstances, serve as evidence for the specific intent to destroy the group. This can be the case when 'such a practice ... brings about the commission of the objective elements of genocide ... with the *dolus specialis* to destroy in whole or in part the targeted group'.[148] The ICTY discussed the mass killing of between 7,000 and 8,000 Bosnian Muslims in Srebrenica and suggested that it is often the case that when a physical or biological destruction takes place it is accompanied by attacks on religious property and symbols of the religious group; this can serve as evidence of intent to destroy the group. The ICTY, therefore, saw the destruction of mosques and houses of the Bosnian Muslims as evidence for the specific intent to commit genocide.[149]

6.3.2 *ISIS and the Genocide of the Yazidis*

Yazidis are an indigenous community who live in Syria, Iraq (Sinjar region in northwest part of country), Armenia, and Turkey. Their native tongue is Kurdish. With the exception of Armenian Yazidis, they regard themselves as ethnically Kurdish but followers of the Yazidi religion.[150] The Yazidi faith is several millennia old and, while it has common roots with Zoroastrianism, has its own distinct cosmology. Persecuted throughout history, followers of the Yazidi faith have been influenced by and sometimes taken on aspects of later religions in the region, including Judaism, Christianity, and Islam, arguably in an effort to ward off attack. A distinct Yazidi community living in the environs of Mosul appears in historical sources as early as the middle of the twelfth century. Since then, ensuing clashes with surrounding Muslim rulers who had viewed the Yazidis as apostates and rivals for political power resulted in the waning power of the Yazidis and reduction in their numbers. In the late nineteenth and early twentieth centuries, many of them fled to the Caucasus. Despite their relatively numerically small

[147] For a criticism of the logic of the decision not to include ethnic cleansing and cultural genocide within the definition of genocide, see May, supra Note 117, at 102–8.

[148] Bashir, supra Note 27, para 145; italics in original.

[149] Krstić, supra Note 135, para 580.

[150] 'They Came to Destroy', supra Note 117, at 20.

community[151] and its geographical scattering, the Yazidis have a well-organised society and a distinct faith and are often referred to as an ethno-religious group.[152]

The Kurdish component of the Yazidi community complicates the question of whether they are a separate ethnic group.[153] This notwithstanding, ISIS conceives of the Yazidis as being members of a religious group; ISIS has continually referenced the Yazidi religious beliefs as the basis for their attack and abuse. ISIS fighters have called them 'infidels' and 'dirty *kuffar*'.[154] Forced conversions show ISIS's conception of Yazidism as a religion. Thus, on the basis of both 'objective and subjective definitions', Yazidis are 'a protected religious group' according to the Genocide Convention and Article 6 of the ICC Statute.[155]

ISIS's attack on the Yazidis in Sinjar in northern Iraq and the forced transfer of Yazidis into Syria was documented and investigated mainly by the CoI Syria.[156] ISIS attacked the Yazidis in Sinjar in northern Iraq in early August 2014, summarily executing hundreds of mainly Yazidi men and adolescent boys and 'forcibly transferring'[157] the survivors to ISIS-controlled areas in Syria. Women and girls were registered at various sites within ISIS-controlled Syria and Iraq where they were sold into sexual slavery – held either by ISIS fighters or kept on ISIS bases. Women and girls, many of whom were sold multiple times, were subjected to sustained sexual violence, beatings, and forced labour in fighters' homes. Yazidi boys, on reaching the age of seven years, were forcibly recruited into ISIS training camps, where they were indoctrinated and 'trained to fight'[158] with ISIS forces. There is no definitive information on the whereabouts of captured Yazidi men who survived the attack on Sinjar,[159] yet over thirty-five mass graves have been uncovered holding

[151] Between 200,000 to 1,000,000.

[152] Yazidi, in Encyclopaedia Britannica, https://www.britannica.com/topic/Yazidi.

[153] 'They Came to Destroy', supra Note 117, at 21.

[154] Ibid., 9, 15, 20.

[155] Ibid., 21. The targeted group consists of Yazidi men and boys aged approximately twelve and above, Yazidi women and girls aged nine and above, Yazidi young children held with their mothers, and Yazidi boys aged nine and above.

[156] The report named 'They Came to Destroy' (see Ibid.) is based on forty-five interviews with survivors, religious leaders, smugglers, activists, lawyers, medical personnel, and journalists. Documentary material was also used.

[157] On 'forcible transfer', see Ibid., 26.

[158] Ibid., 19.

[159] YAZDA, Global Yazidi Organization, 'An Uncertain Future for Yazidis: A Report Marking Three Years of an Ongoing Genocide', September 2017, https://www.yazda.org/assets/uploads/report/y1152034125784.pdf.

the remains of Yazidi men, boys, as well as of women who were past child-bearing age.[160]

Before the attack, Sinjar was home to a strong Yazidi community numbering approximately 400,000 people. In its aftermath, no free Yazidis remained in Sinjar.[161] The initial attack on 3 August 2014 'was well organised with hundreds of ISIS fighters acting in concert with each other as they seized towns and villages on all sides of Mount Sinjar'.[162] Information collected strongly suggests that 'the command centre for the operation was based in Mosul, with an important operational centre in Tel Afar'.[163] A 'pre-determined pattern with only minor deviations'[164] was documented by the CoI Syria. ISIS fighters captured thousands of Yazidis in their villages or on the roads between 3 and 5 August 2014, emptying almost all villages within seventy-two hours of the attack.[165] Secondary transfers were also conducted in an 'organised manner' to 'designated' holding sites in Mosul, Tel Afar, and Baaj, deeper inside ISIS-controlled territory. A central committee – the Committee for the Buying and Selling of Slaves – organised the Yazidi slave markets, while local committees and commanders adopted similar functions.[166]

This information serves to prove ISIS's intent to destroy the Yazidis in whole or in part, as it presents ample evidence of the existence of a plan to perform such destruction.[167] Additional support to the claim of ISIS's specific intent is found in ISIS's destruction of Yazidi temples and shrines during their attack on Sinjar,[168] which serves as evidence supporting the specific intent to destroy the Yazidis.[169]

The constitutive acts of genocide – that is, the five acts of genocide enumerated in the Genocide Convention and in Article 6 of the ICC Statute – are analysed in the findings of the CoI Syria, which show that ISIS sought to partially or totally[170] destroy this religious group through the acts described in Sections 6.3.2.1 to 6.3.2.4. Given that thousands of

[160] 'They Came to Destroy', supra Note 117, at 4.
[161] Ibid., 33.
[162] Ibid., 6.
[163] Ibid., 6–7.
[164] Ibid., 7.
[165] Ibid.
[166] Ibid., 13.
[167] See Section 6.3.1.1, discussing special intent of genocide and ways of proving intent.
[168] 'They Came to Destroy', supra Note 150, at 19.
[169] See the discussion of cultural genocide.
[170] 'They Came to Destroy', supra Note 117, at 19.

Yazidi women and children are held by ISIS[171] and thousands of Yazidi men and boys are still missing, it is considered a case of 'ongoing genocide'.[172]

6.3.2.1 Killings

ISIS fighters have captured and 'intentionally killed'[173] members of the Yazidi group. Following the attack of Sinjar, they killed hundreds of Yazidi men and adolescent boys. They have also 'summarily executed'[174] men and older boys who refused to convert to Islam. Men from Yazidi villages captured with weapons in their possession were executed. Executions of male Yazidis occurred in towns and villages, at checkpoints, on roadsides, and in 'lower sections'[175] of Mount Sinjar. Killings were conducted through 'gunshots to the head' or 'throat cutting'. While most killings were of small groups – two to twenty men and boys – mass killings in Kocho and Qani villages were documented.[176] There was also one documented mass killing of Yazidi women from Kocho at Solagh Technical Institute. Killings occurred mostly in Iraq but also in Syria. A Yazidi girl captured by ISIS, detained for seven months and sold once, described how she was forced to witness the beheading of their Yazidi men:

> After we were captured, ISIS forced us to watch them beheading some of our Yazidi men. They made the men kneel in a line in the street, with their hands tied behind their backs. The ISIS fighters took knives and cut their throats.[177]

6.3.2.2 Inflicting Serious Bodily and Mental Harm

ISIS and its fighters conducted acts of enslavement, sexual slavery, rape, torture, inhumane and degrading treatment, and forcible transfer into Syria, causing serious bodily and mental harm to members of the Yazidi group. Yazidi women and girls have been 'enslaved'[178] and 'sexually

[171] This information is updated until June 2016. Currently, the numbers of captives are lower.

[172] 'They Came to Destroy', supra Note 117, Summary, at 2.

[173] Ibid., 21. The CoI Syria concludes that 'ISIS has committed the prohibited act of killing members of a protected religious group, the Yazidis'.

[174] Ibid., 8.

[175] Ibid., 7.

[176] Ibid., 8, 21. Hundreds were killed in Kocho and 80 in Qani.

[177] Ibid., 8.

[178] Ibid., 24. 'Enslavement' is a 'crime distinct from sexual slavery'.

enslaved',[179] while hundreds of Yazidi children have been transferred to ISIS-controlled areas of Iraq and Syria while their mothers were sold and resold multiple times. They were held captive in various locations, including ISIS fighters' homes and apartments, 'makeshift shelters',[180] or gas fields. The only exception were young boys who sometimes accompanied fighters to pray in the local mosque. A Yazidi woman, held captive for twelve months, described how she was sold multiple times by ISIS fighters:

> We were driven into Raqqah city at night and held in a building there. I was there for three weeks before I was sold. Throughout that time, ISIS fighters were coming to buy women and girls. All of us were Yazidi. I think I was sold about 15 times in all. It is hard to remember all those who bought me.[181]

Yazidi women were forced to be domestic servants and were not allowed to wear *abayas*[182] as a measure to prevent their escape.[183] Yazidi men and boys over the age of puberty experienced degrading and inhumane treatment by being forced to work on ISIS projects – construction, cleaning, digging trenches,[184] and looking after cattle – both in Tel Afar and Mosul; execution followed any escape attempts.

Sexual offences were also a way of inflicting mental and bodily harm. Enslaved Yazidi women and girls as young as nine were victims of sexual offences. They were subjected to 'entrenched sexual violence' during their sexual enslavement.[185] Yazidi women and girls were sold into sexual slavery and were victims of rape by ISIS fighters, which took place over extended periods of time.[186] Some women who attempted to escape were subjected to 'gang rapes'. There is ample evidence of rapes, including physical and psychological wounds. ISIS fighters have become 'owners' of enslaved women and girls (*sabaya*). To determine their monetary value, they were registered and sold at slave markets and online auctions.[187]

[179] Ibid., 22–3.
[180] Ibid., 14.
[181] Ibid., 10.
[182] Loose-fitting garment covering body and head, worn in public by females over the age of ten.
[183] Most of the interviewees reported violent daily rapes and brutal violence by their fighter-owners. Girls as young as nine were raped, as were pregnant women. Where Yazidi women and children are injured by rapes or beatings, ISIS fighters do not permit them access to medical care. 'They Came to Destroy', supra Note 117, at 27.
[184] Ibid., 9.
[185] Ibid., 12, 14, 22.
[186] Ibid., 22.
[187] Ibid., 25; Akayesu, supra Note 121, para 732.

Yazidis were tormented, faced threats, and experienced trauma through several actions imposed by ISIS, thereby suffering serious mental harm. These included family separations, forced transfer, witnessing of killings,[188] enslavement, degrading treatment and derogatory language (women were treated like 'chattel' and called 'unclean' and were mocked for 'worship[ing] stones'[189]), beatings, sexual enslavement, and rape. Many Yazidi women described hearing their children screaming and crying outside the door while ISIS fighters raped them in a locked room. Sexual and physical violence together with mental trauma 'rises to the level of torture, causing ... serious physical and psychological harm', leading to the destruction of the spirit and the will to live.[190] Yazidi boys over seven years of age experienced 'serious physical and psychological harm' through their 'violent separation from their families, forced conversions ... indoctrination, recruitment, military treatment – which included beatings, training in suicide bombing, and watching violent propaganda – and ISIS's use of the boys to actively participate in hostilities'. Systematic acts underpinning enslavement, separation, and forcible transfer have been incremental and cumulative steps in the destruction of the individual and the group.[191]

6.3.2.3 The Infliction of Conditions of Life Calculated to Bring about the Group's Physical Destruction

Following the attack on Mount Sinjar on 3 August 2014, a 'humanitarian crisis' unfolded 'as ISIS trapped tens of thousands of Yazidi men, women, and children in temperatures rising above fifty degrees Celsius and deliberately prevented them from accessing water, food, or medical care'.[192] ISIS fighters also attacked planes and helicopters bringing aid and rescue.[193] Many, particularly infants and young children, became very sick, and no medical care was provided. Some Yazidi women were punished by starvation for trying to escape or resisting rapes. In captivity, most interviewees reported regularly having little food and sleeping in

188 'They Came to Destroy', supra Note 117, at 25. Upon their capture, 'Yazidi women and children ... were being forced either to bear witness to the murders of their relatives or to watch them being taken away to an unknown fate.'

189 Ibid., 5.

190 Ibid.

191 This conclusion is based on *Prosecutor* v. *Kayishema*, ICTR-95-1, Trial Judgment, 21 May 1999, para 116, and *Republic of Croatia* v. *Republic of Serbia*, ICJ Judgment, 3 February 2015, paras 362–4, pp. 15, 26, 27.

192 'They Came to Destroy', supra Note 117, at 7.

193 Ibid., 26.

unheated rooms in the winter. The CoI Syria concluded that 'ISIS and its fighters deliberately imposed conditions of life in a calculated awareness that ... particularly when inflicted continuously over a long period of time, would cause the deaths (physical destruction) of Yazidi women and children'.[194]

6.3.2.4 Imposing Measures Intended to Prevent Births

ISIS has prevented Yazidi children from being born through several measures, including separating Yazidi men and women; killing hundreds of Yazidi men on capture;[195] and conducting forced conversions of men and women to Islam.[196] There is evidence that, because of their rape and the ensuing trauma, Yazidi women do not trust those around them, 'particularly men', and feel 'real anxiety' and an unwillingness to marry, which in some cases has also resulted in 'sexual dysfunction' or 'reluctance to procreate'.[197] This is compounded by a sense of lost honour.[198] Thus, rape may be considered a measure to prevent births.[199]

6.3.2.5 Forcibly Transferring Children of the Group to Another Group

Forcible transfers by ISIS of Yazidi children were conducted in two ways. Girls of nine years of age or older were separated from their mothers and sold into sexual slavery. Boys of seven years of age or older were also separated from their mothers and siblings and were sent to ISIS training bases where they were indoctrinated and forced to fight. This forcible transfer of Yazidi children cut them off from beliefs and practices of their own religious community. In this way, 'ISIS intentionally [sought] to destroy' the children's 'concept of themselves' as Yazidi by 'erasing their attachment to the Yazidi religion'.[200]

194 Ibid., 27. On the denial of adequate food to captured Yazidi women and children see Ibid., 15, 26.

195 Under Yazidi religious tradition, both parents must be Yazidi for the child to be of the Yazidi faith.

196 'They Came to Destroy', supra Note 117, at 27, 28. Within days of the attacks in the Sinjar region, men were forced to convert. All Yazidi men and boys were required to go to mosque for prayers; however, forced conversions did not provide them with any protection or equal status.

197 Ibid., 27.

198 The conclusion is based on Akayesu Trial Judgment, supra Note 121, para 508.

199 'They Came to Destroy', supra Note 117, at 27.

200 Ibid., 28.

6.4 Conclusion

The commission of two types of international crimes in Syria were explored in this chapter: crimes against humanity committed by the Syrian government; and genocide committed by ISIS.[201] Part of the discussion was devoted to the legal concepts and characteristics of each crime, thus explaining the similarities and differences between them. The rest of the discussion, based on the legal analysis, was devoted to an inspection and analysis of evidence for the commission of acts of torture and extermination in detention camps by the Syrian government as crimes against humanity and the commission of genocide of the Yazidis by ISIS.

In the section on crimes against humanity, we analysed evidence for the commission of direct killings and executions and for the imposition of inhumane conditions that led to large numbers of deaths of civilians in detention – all of those acts comprising acts of extermination according to the ICC Statute. We also analysed evidence for acts of torture conducted in Syrian detention facilities and prisons.

In the section on genocide, we analysed acts falling under the types of conducts that comprise the crime of genocide according to the ICC Statute: killings; acts of enslavement, sexual slavery, rape, and torture that inflict both severe bodily and mental harm; inflicting of conditions of life calculated to bring about the group's physical destruction, such as the deliberate prevention of water, food, or medical care; imposition of measures intended to prevent birth such as separating Yazidi men and women and killing hundreds of Yazidi men on capture; and forcibly separating Yazidi children from their mothers, thus cutting them off their Yazidi identity.

The empirically based analysis of the acts constituting crimes against humanity and genocide conducted in this chapter is significant for various reasons. Adding to our knowledge and conceptualisation of these crimes committed both by the government and by non-state actors, it serves as further input for decision-makers and civil society at large to actively respond to a still-ongoing humanitarian crisis, thus promoting ex-post justice.[202] Achieving ex-post justice becomes even more important vis-à-vis the international community's failure in preventing these atrocities. In addition, this analysis is important for the purposes of

[201] See Chapter 5 of this volume.
[202] See Chapter 12 of this volume.

restoring civil society and the Syrian community when the conflict ends. The documentation of the atrocities validates the narratives of the victims, their families, and their communities. It also serves as a basis not only for demanding justice but also for conducting other transitional justice procedures aimed at reconstituting a cohesive society. The analysis of the atrocities is therefore not only backward-looking, for retribution, but also forward-looking, for purposes of restoration of a society torn and ravaged by those very atrocities.

7

Weaponising Gender

Sexual Violence in the Syrian Conflict

LINA BISCAIA

7.1 Introduction

Within months of the beginning of the Syrian uprising in March 2011, reports emerged of Syrian government forces and pro-government militias committing sexual violence against civilians. Owing to the large number of actors documenting war crimes in Syria, the information available eight years on shows that during the unrest and first stages of the armed conflict government forces used a variety of means, especially arrests and killings, to repress opposition. Sexual and gender-based violence against women and men was used from the onset as an integral part of the campaign of arrests and detention, and it subsequently formed part of ground operations against opposition communities.

This chapter outlines a typology of sexual violence committed by government forces. It analyses the reasons why it was used, its consequences (which are closely linked to its reasons), and the extent to which the government forces achieved their goals by using violence of a sexual nature. This analysis shows that the patterns of sexual violence followed the chronology and dynamics of the conflict, becoming more extreme as attempts to repress opposition failed. It is argued that while the types of sexual violence by government forces evolved, its use exploited gender roles and cultural and social norms throughout the conflict. In doing so, sexual violence was effective in fulfilling the government's goal of terrorising, humiliating, and disempowering families and, through them, communities. In detention, sexual violence was also used as a tool of torture to extract information and force confessions. Though addressing sexual violence against men to some extent, this chapter focuses primarily on sexual violence against women, analysing its impact on both genders.

Throughout this chapter, the term 'sexual violence' refers primarily to sexual crimes as defined in international criminal law, which encompasses acts of a sexual nature committed by the perpetrator against a person, as well as acts that caused another to engage in such acts. These acts are not limited to physical violence and may not involve any physical contact. Sexual crimes, therefore, cover both physical and non-physical acts with a sexual element.[1] Beyond the legal definition, sexual violence is not about sex per se but about body parts and socially constructed norms of what is 'sexual', including norms that link the virginity of unmarried girls and women with families' honour[2] and norms that define males as protectors and representatives of the virility, strength, and power of the family.[3]

7.2 Context

While pre-conflict Syria has sometimes been described as relatively progressive because of its rich cultural past and relatively open mentality in urban areas, it has nevertheless remained a strongly conservative society where the patrilineal descent group is the decisive factor of all main aspects of one's life.[4] This includes economic security, religious affiliation, citizenship, social life, and identity. Men are heads of families; women and younger family members occupy a subordinate role. As in other Arab societies, the father has the authority and is the breadwinner, while the mother is typically a housewife who takes care of the children.[5] These gender roles are almost universally reflected in nuclear and extended families and, through them, in communities and in society as a whole.

Concrete factual data shows gender inequality has been pervasive, particularly in rural areas. The role of women in the independence

[1] International Criminal Court Elements of Crimes [hereinafter 'ICC Elements of Crimes'], Articles 7(1)(g), 8(2)(b)(xxii), and 8(2)(e)(vi) as summarised in the 'Policy Paper on Sexual and Gender-Based Crimes' of the ICC's Office of the Prosecutor, June 2014, www.icc-cpi.int /iccdocs/otp/otp-policy-paper-on-sexual-and-gender-based-crimes–june-2014.pdf.

[2] Valerie Oosterveld, 'Sexual Violence Directed Against Men and Boys in Armed Conflict or Mass Atrocity: Addressing a Gendered Harm in International Criminal Tribunals', *Journal of International Law and International Relations* 10 (2014): 122.

[3] Sandesh Sivakumaran, 'Sexual Violence Against Men in Armed Conflict', *The European Journal of International Law* 18, no. 2 (2007): 268.

[4] Esther van Eijk, *Family Law in Syria: Patriarchy, Pluralism and Personal Status Codes*, (London: I. B. Tauris, 2016): 100–1.

[5] Ibid., 100–1.

movement led them to gain the right to vote in 1949, and in the 1960s the Baath party adopted social policies that fostered progress in the health and education sectors, which positively impacted women and girls. By the 1970s, however, women had been shunned from political life and were effectively limited to mobilising women supporters through the party's General Union of Syrian Women, which did not address inequality issues but instead focused on economic objectives of the state.[6] Outside of the framework of the General Union, women's organisations faced repression and were forced to operate illegally.[7] By 1990, only 9 per cent of parliament seats were held by women.[8] In 2010, it was estimated that female participation in the labour market had decreased to the point that 85 per cent of women and girls over the age of 15 were housewives,[9] and by 2011 the Global Gender Gap Report ranked Syria at 124 out of 135 countries.[10] In 2012, the majority of women were estimated to marry at the age of 18,[11] though in the previous decade 13 per cent of all marriages involved a child.[12] Most likely, the minor would have been the girl, since it is not uncommon for men to be 10 to 15 years older than their wives.[13] Despite the increase in divorce rates in the years before the uprising, the institution of marriage had not lost its societal significance.[14]

[6] Khuloud Alsaba and Anuj Kapilashrami, 'Understanding Women's Experience of Violence and the Political Economy of Gender in Conflict: The Case of Syria', *Reproductive Health Matters* 24, no. 47 (2016): 6–7.

[7] Robin Yassin-Kassab and Leila al-Shami, *Burning Country: Syrians in Revolution and War* (London: Pluto Press, 2016), 18–19; Sanja Kelly and Julia Breslin, *Progress and Resistance: Women's Rights in the Middle East and North Africa* (New York: Rowman & Littlefield (2010), 4.

[8] Inter-Parliamentary Union, 'Proportion of Seats Held by Women in National Parliaments', The World Bank, last updated 2018, https://data.worldbank.org/indicator/SG.GEN.PARL.ZS.

[9] Alsaba and Anuj, 'Women's Experience of Violence', 6.

[10] World Economic Forum, 'The Global Gender Gap Report', 2011, www3.weforum.org/docs/WEF_GenderGap_Report_2011.pdf.

[11] United Nations, Department of Economic and Social Affairs, Population Division. World Fertility Report, 2012, www.un.org/en/development/desa/population/publications/dataset/fertility/wfr2012/MainFrame.html.

[12] Syrian Arab Republic Statistics, UNICEF, www.unicef.org/infobycountry/syria_statistics.html.

[13] Cultural Atlas, Syrian Culture, https://culturalatlas.sbs.com.au/syrian-culture/syrian-culture-family.

[14] Maaike Voorhoeve, *Family Law in Islam: Divorce, Marriage, and Women in the Muslim World* (London: I. B. Tauris, 2012): 155.

The legal system reflects the patriarchal family model, with the laws privileging men. Syrian women are disadvantaged in areas such as marriage age, choice of husband, the right to divorce, inheritance, and child custody.[15] Prison sentences for women found guilty of adultery are harsher than those applied to unmarried men.[16] The law obliges the husband to provide for his wife and children, and in return the wife is obliged to obey the husband and take care of the household and children.[17] Marital rape is not criminalised, and male relatives who commit honour killings receive reduced sentences.[18]

Societies in general tend to consider the chastity of females similarly to the virility of males: both are considered the sexual virtue of each sex.[19] In Syria, the concept of honour, not only of the individual but also of her family, is constructed around notions of female virginity before marriage and sexual fidelity afterwards.[20] Honour is based on a collective understanding, as opposed to an individual one, that, in cases of behaviour deviating from social norms, the propensity towards shame, rather than guilt, is intensified because of the heightened exposure of the behaviour to others.[21] An attack on the family's honour demonstrates the man's inability to protect female family members and themselves and represents a stigmatisation of women as the source of the family's shame.[22]

In Arab societies, including Syria, virginity of females is as much the responsibility of women as of men.[23] While all communities and sects of the Syrian society mosaic value virginity, this is especially so in rural areas, where honour killings were more frequent before the conflict.[24] Women are required to remain virgins until they are married, with virginity giving

[15] Van Eijk, *Family Law in Syria*, 100–1.
[16] Syrian Penal Code, Article 473.
[17] Van Eijk, *Family Law in Syria*, 102.
[18] Syrian Penal Code, Article 548; Yassin-Kassab and al-Shami, *Burning Country*, 18.
[19] Sandesh Sivakumaran, 'Male/Male Rape and the Taint of Homosexuality', *Human Rights Quarterly* 27, no. 4, (2005): 1289.
[20] Report of the United Nations Independent International Commission of Inquiry on the Syrian Arab Republic [hereinafter 'CoI Syria'], 5 February 2013, A/HRC/22/59. Annex IX, para 2.
[21] Stefan Brunner, 'Sexual Violence in the Syrian Civil War Is likely a State Strategy' (2014), https://cpb-us-w2.wpmucdn.com/campuspress.yale.edu/dist/a/379/files/2014/02/Brunner-Sexual-Violence-in-Syria-is-Likely-a-State-Strategy-feb-8-20141.pdf, 12.
[22] Brunner, 'Sexual Violence in the Syrian Civil War', 13.
[23] Lama Abu-Odeh, 'Honor Killings and the Construction of Gender in Arab Societies', *The American Journal of Comparative Law* 58 (2010): 917–18.
[24] Katherine Zoepf, 'A Dishonourable Affair', *The New York Times*, 27 September 2007, www.nytimes.com/2007/09/23/magazine/23wwln-syria-t.html.

the woman a stamp of respectability and virtue. Men act as censors of the woman's behaviour. They ensure the virginity of unmarried women in their family by guarding, supervising, and defending incursions perceived as threats to the women's virginity. The required behaviour from both genders upholds a heterosexuality that is honour/shame-based, and failure to do so results in penalties for both sexes. For women, these sanctions include threat of physical punishment, spatial entrapment through segregation of gender spaces, and the mobilisation of social gossip and reputation. A man who does not intervene by killing his wife or his daughter once she has shamed him suffers the loss of his gender. In other words, he is no longer a man; he is 'castrated' and perceived as a woman.[25]

Patriarchal beliefs that men have the right to control women's sexuality meant that violence against women, including sexual harassment and domestic violence, was treated as a private matter. As a result, these issues went largely unaddressed and women were prevented from reporting it, as doing so represented a betrayal of the family and a violation of the social cohesion.[26] The lack of information on sexual violence against men and boys before 2011 is most likely due to a combination of cultural taboos and the fact that homosexuality is criminalised.[27] This meant victims could face criminal charges if they came forward with allegations. In practice this meant that male-on-male sexual violence, like male-on-female sexual violence, went largely unreported.[28]

In this context, the demonstrations that erupted in March 2011 were unsurprisingly led by men, the traditional protectors of the community. It was largely in that masculine role that they later took up arms. Indeed, this was a natural reaction given that, during armed conflicts, men tend to self-identify with masculine stereotypes more strongly.[29] But the uprising also gave women an unprecedented opportunity for involvement in political activities, particularly in 2011 and 2012. Women had key roles in mobilising non-political movements, including two of the largest grassroots coalitions,[30] resulting in a certain degree of recognition and respect from their male counterparts.[31] Women, including those

[25] Abu-Odeh, 'Honor Killings', 917–19.
[26] Alsaba and Anuj, 'Women's Experience of Violence', 8.
[27] Syrian Penal Code, Article 520.
[28] On the distinction between male/female, male/male, female/male, and female rape, see Sivakumaran, 'Male/Male Rape', 1275.
[29] Sivakumaran, 'Sexual Violence against Men', 255.
[30] Yassin-Kassab and al-Shami, *Burning Country*, 67.
[31] Alsaba and Anuj, 'Women's Experience of Violence', 6.

from conservative areas, organised and participated in demonstrations and on occasion organised women-only demonstrations.[32] In Aleppo, women founded a radio station promoting activism and gender equality.[33] Young women joined coordination committees that emerged in towns across the country and formed the nucleus of civil resistance.[34]

With many men having been arrested or having fled the country to avoid conscription by the government, by 2012 women formed the backbone of the activism.[35] As the main targets for arrest and forced conscription, men were forced to rely on women not only to protest but also to carry supplies through checkpoints[36] and provide medical care to the wounded.[37] The protraction of the conflict allowed room for radicalisation of armed groups and the emergence of terrorist groups, such as ISIS, and by 2014 the gains of women in the political arena had vanished.

7.3 Typology of Abuses

Syrian armed forces and pro-government militias began targeting women and girls and men and boys for sexual violence almost in parallel with the beginning of the uprising in March 2011. A report by the United Nations Independent International Commission of Inquiry on Syria (CoI Syria) details the types of sexual violence committed against female and male victims, the extent and widespread nature of those acts, and the context in which they occurred.[38] While the report does not explicitly mention it, all individual incidents by Syrian armed forces and pro-government militias described in it, whether against males or females, were perpetrated by men. The patterns of sexual violence identified in the report show that those acts were closely linked to the chronology and dynamics of the uprising, and later the armed conflict, and to the gender roles of men and women in Syrian society.

In many ways, the fact that government forces used sexual violence and the context in which they used it fits patterns observed in other conflicts. State forces are generally more likely to perpetrate sexual

32 Yassin-Kassab and al-Shami, *Burning Country*, 67.
33 Ibid., 67.
34 Ibid., 65, 87.
35 Yassin-Kassab and al-Shami, *Burning Country*, 64.
36 Ibid., 67.
37 CoI Syria, 'I Lost My Dignity: Sexual and Gender-Based Violence in the Syrian Arab Republic', 8 March 2018, A/HRC/37/72/CRP.1, para 27.
38 Ibid.

violence than armed groups, refuting the misconception that rape is perpetrated primarily by undisciplined rebel forces.[39] Furthermore, evidence suggests that states frequently use sexual violence as a tool of torture, including during interrogations, against detainees as well as during operations against civilians.[40] Finally, sexual abuse of prisoners in detention often commences with enforced nudity, accompanied by verbal threats, which adds to the humiliation. Other more serious forms of sexual violence such as beatings to the genitals and rape then follow.[41] All of these apply to the Syrian context.

According to the CoI Syria report, sexual violence against women and girls occurred during house searches, ground operations, at checkpoints, and in detention. By contrast, the vast majority of sexual violence targeting men and boys took place in detention. The common thread between the different contexts in which government forces perpetrated sexual violence is that the overarching goal was to repress unrest and opposition. In practice, government forces did this primarily by killing, arresting, and detaining opponents and members of their families. This explains why most of the incidents of sexual violence, especially outside of detention, took place in 2011 and 2012. After the formation of armed groups and the escalation of the unrest into armed conflict,[42] both sides started resorting to different tactics: the opposition focused its efforts in arming groups, and the government resorted to shelling and sniping and then to air power.[43] The military escalation through the use of air power meant that there was both less need and fewer opportunities for government forces to resort to sexual violence, and indeed the number of sexual violence incidents reported outside the context of detention after 2012 decreased.[44]

[39] With the exception of ISIS, the CoI Syria's report did not find patterns of physical sexual violence to be present in the conduct of armed groups in Syria. See CoI Syria, A/HRC/37/72/CRP.1, paras 51–6. For a description of ISIS sexual violence against the Yazidis, see Chapter 6 of this volume.

[40] Dara Kay Cohen, Amelia Hoover, and Elisabeth Jean Wood, 'Wartime Sexual Violence: Misconceptions, Implications, and Ways Forward' (2013), United States Institute of Peace Special Report, 4.

[41] Sivakumaran, 'Sexual Violence against Men', 266.

[42] The CoI Syria determined that by February 2012 the unrest had escalated into a non-international armed conflict (CoI Syria, A/HRC/21/50, Annex II, para 12).

[43] CoI Syria, A/HRC/37/72/CRP.1, para 12.

[44] This is concluded from an analysis of the dates of the individual incidents of sexual violence documented by the CoI Syria in its report A/HRC/37/72/CRP.1.

Within months, government forces moved from killing protesters and conducting arrests at demonstrations to carrying out house searches. While the majority of the wanted persons were male, many women were targeted for their own involvement in protests or support to the opposition.[45] House searches involved arrests, killings, looting, destruction of property, and sexual violence. When the search was conducted to arrest a wanted male and he was not found, government forces arrested women to force men to surrender in return for the release of the detainee. By arresting women in lieu of their male relatives, government forces implicitly threatened the women's and their families' honour. In doing so, the arrests leveraged gender roles by forcing males who were part of – or perceived to be part of – the opposition to turn themselves in to the government in order to protect the women's honour. In households, there were two predominant types of sexual violence: rape of women and girls, who were sometimes killed after the rape; and forcing relatives, particularly males, to watch the rapes.[46]

With the emergence of the Free Syrian Army (FSA) around mid-2011, house searches evolved to became part of government forces' ground operations aimed at retaining or regaining control of a town or city. Such operations began with the cordoning off of a targeted area with checkpoints, then shelling and use of snipers as a prelude to incursions by ground forces, including pro-government militias, to dislodge insurgents and their supporters.[47] Defectors, activists, or fighting-aged men were systematically sought out during these operations.[48] Sexual violence against women and girls also occurred during the assault by ground forces. As before, women and girls were raped in their homes, but ground operations also led to new forms of sexual violence including public rapes and forced nudity in the streets,[49] the escalation of the conflict resulting in expanded types of sexual violence. Men who attempted to stop the rape of their female relatives were sometimes killed.[50] Sexual violence against women and girls was documented in twenty-eight ground operations,[51] the high number suggesting sexual violence was a government strategy.[52]

45 Ibid., para 27.
46 Ibid., paras 2–18.
47 CoI Syria, A/HRC/21/50, paras 22 and 52.
48 Ibid., Annex V, para 3.
49 CoI Syria, A/HRC/37/72/CRP.1, para 17.
50 Ibid., para 17.
51 Ibid., para 15.
52 On the difference between sexual violence as a practice and a strategy, see Elisabeth Jean Wood, 'Conflict-Related Sexual Violence and the Police: Implications of Recent

As part of the campaign to arrest, within the first week of protests government forces began setting up checkpoints where soldiers and security agents used lists of wanted persons to conduct arrests. Since the lists consisted mostly of males, women and girls initially enjoyed greater freedom of movement and were able to cross the checkpoints. In 2012, government forces tightened their grip on all those crossing the checkpoints. From then on, women were not only searched but also subjected to sexual violence in locations near checkpoints, such as abandoned houses and military vehicles. At checkpoints, women were raped, sexually harassed, subjected to intimate body searches by male soldiers, and threatened with virginity tests. Many of the women arrested at checkpoints, all of whom were from opposition-held areas, were subsequently transferred to detention facilities.[53]

Despite the lack of statistical data, the considerable amount of information available on sexual violence against women in detention and the fact that many detainees were held for years, suggests that the majority of sexual violence incidents against women and girls took place in prisons and unofficial detention facilities. Unlike house searches and checkpoints, detention provides perpetrators the opportunity of subjecting individuals – women as well as men – to violence, including sexual violence, on multiple occasions over a long period of time.

Women and girls were subjected to sexual violence before even arriving at the detention facility. Upon arrest, soldiers and militiamen groped their breasts and thighs, and insulted them, creating a climate of fear and threat of sexual violence. On arrival to the facility, women were forced to strip naked in front of male guards, who often inserted their fingers into the women's vaginas on the pretext of conducting searches.[54] During the first interrogation, women were asked about their sex lives, including whether they were virgins, and were subsequently threatened with rape. Also during interrogations, women were beaten and electrocuted in the breasts and genitalia and were tortured while naked. Women were raped, sometimes gang-raped, in at least twenty government detention facilities across Syria. Many survivors said that the rapes were so violent they lost consciousness during the events. The rapes resulted in physical injuries that went untreated throughout their detention. On occasion, women

Research', *International Review of the Red Cross* (2014): 461. It has been previously argued that in the Syrian conflict, sexual violence was likely a strategy (Brunner, 'Sexual Violence in the Syrian Civil War').

[53] CoI Syria, A/HRC/37/72/CRP.1, paras 22–6.

[54] Ibid., paras 29–32.

were raped in front of other female and/or male detainees.[55] Unlike in other conflicts such as Bosnia, the CoI Syria did not document incidents of male detainees being forced to rape female detainees.

With the exception of being forced to watch rapes of female relatives during house searches[56] and a small number of rapes during ground operations,[57] sexual violence against men and boys took place inside detention facilities. This illustrates that men and boys are most likely to experience sexual violence during conflict while in detention.[58] Contrary to the abuse suffered by women, there are no indications that men and boys were subjected to sexual violence of types such as groping and sexual humiliation immediately after arrest. Like women, however, upon admission to the detention facility men were subjected to forced nudity during body searches and interrogations. Male detainees also had their genitals beaten and electrocuted during torture carried out as part of interrogation.

The most documented form of sexual assault against men in detention was rape with objects such as batons, wooden sticks, and pipes, a technique documented in fifteen detention facilities and which was not usually used against women. Army officers, soldiers, and militia members also forced detainees to perform fellatio on the officers, and on occasion detainees were gang-raped during torture and interrogation. Men were also raped by guards in front of other detainees, sometimes females but most commonly males, including inside the cell the detainee shared with other inmates. In some instances, male detainees were forced to rape other male detainees, including a number of cases involving blood relatives.[59] Finally, men were targeted for genital mutilation.[60]

7.4 Reasons

Wartime sexual violence against women *and* men is about asserting masculine power – both forms of violence involve similar constructions of masculinity and heterosexualised masculine dominance.[61] Broadly speaking, both sexual violence against females and sexual violence

55 Ibid., paras 33–42.
56 Ibid., para 14.
57 Ibid., para 16.
58 Oosterveld, 'Sexual Violence Directed against Men', 117.
59 CoI Syria, A/HRC/37/72/CRP.1, paras 43–9.
60 Ibid., para 50; CoI Syria, 'Out of Sight, Out of Mind: Deaths in Detention in the Syrian Arab Republic', 3 February 2016, A/HRC/31/CRP.1, para 24.
61 Valorie K. Vojdik, 'Sexual Violence Against Men and Women in War: A Masculinities Approach', *Nevada Law Journal* 14 (2014): 926.

against males aim at multiple, similar ends: asserting domination, terrorising, coercing, humiliating, and disempowering.[62] In this regard, male- and female-directed sexual violence are clearly intertwined, as the two are intimately linked to socially constructed gender norms that victimise individuals as well as communities.[63] Rape is a sexual manifestation of aggression that leads to greater acknowledgement of the modes to subjugate an enemy group in armed conflict.[64] This subjugation is particularly visible in the increase of violent rapes during conflict,[65] including in Syria where there is a considerable number of gang rapes and rapes with objects resulting in loss of consciousness and serious physical injuries.

In the Syrian context, sexual violence served all the ends outlined in this chapter, particularly terrorising, humiliating, and disempowering. Government forces did this by using sexual violence as one of a set of means to quell demonstrations and later armed opposition. It was not the only tool, and it should be understood as part of a broader strategy of the Syrian government to repress opposition. As noted by Elisabeth Wood, an organisation's sexual violence repertoire is part of its overall repertoire.[66] In Syria, that repertoire changed over time, with sexual violence falling into two categories: outside of detention (during house searches, ground operations, and at checkpoints) and in detention.

Prior to 15 March 2011, which marks the start of the uprising, the government used threats of violent repression and sexual violence to pre-empt protests. These threats are strong indicia of intent to later use sexual violence. These threats were successful, which explains why Syria was one of the last countries to join the Arab Spring. When a first 'Day of Rage' was called for 4–5 February 2011, the riot police were deployed, and the scheduled demonstration did not take place.[67] On 6 March, in what became the symbol of the uprising, government forces arrested a group of teenage boys in Daraa for spraying graffiti calling for revolution. When their families pled for their release, the local head of political security replied, 'Go sleep with your wives and make new [children] or send them to me and I will do it.'[68] In April, the body of one of the boys was returned

[62] Oosterveld, 'Sexual Violence Directed against Men', 117.
[63] Ibid., 109.
[64] Ibid., 119.
[65] Wood, 'Conflict-Related Sexual Violence', 464.
[66] Ibid., 461.
[67] Yassin-Kassab and al-Shami, *Burning Country*, 36.
[68] Ibid., 38.

to his family with signs of severe torture, including sexual mutilation.[69] Also in March, government-allied armed gangs drove in the streets of Latakia, a government stronghold, screaming threats of rape and murder.[70]

If threats of violence – including sexual violence – instilled fear in the population, effectively preventing demonstrations and delaying the uprising, once protests took off the immediate response of the government was violent crackdowns and the killing and arrest of demonstrators. This pattern is observed as early as the first two weeks of the Syrian uprising. On 15 March 2011, known as the second Day of Rage, thousands of people gathered in cities across Syria to demonstrate. Though the demonstrations were peaceful, dozens were arrested. As demonstrations continued in the following days, government forces attacked protestors and continued to carry out arrests.[71] Throughout the month of March alone, government forces arrested and killed protesters in the governorates of Daraa, Damascus, Homs, Rif Damascus, and Tartous.[72] By 23 March, government soldiers and police were abducting people and setting up checkpoints.[73]

The campaign of arrests and killings exploited gender roles and as such impacted men and women differently. Men were targeted for their personal role in the revolution, whether as activists or protesters. Owing to their active role in the revolution, women, like men, were targeted for their activism, but unlike men they were also arrested for being related to male protesters as a way to pressure these men to surrender.

While initially the stage of killings and arrests were public areas, such as squares and streets where the demonstrations took place, this quickly changed when government forces resorted to house searches, giving all-male government forces access to family households, the women's traditional domain. At this point, humiliation of families through sexual means was restricted to the household. There was no need, yet, to resort to sexual violence in other contexts. This changed when, despite violent repression, the unrest continued. Government forces accordingly resorted to other tactics, namely shelling and sniping, followed by

[69] CoI Syria, A/HRC/31/CRP.1, para 22.
[70] Yassin-Kassab and al-Shami, *Burning Country*, 48.
[71] Ibid., 37.
[72] Report of the High Commissioner for Human Rights on the Human Rights Situation in the Syrian Arab Republic, 15 September 2011, A/HRC/18/53, paras 34–63.
[73] Yassin-Kassab and al-Shami, *Burning Country*, 39.

ground operations. During ground operations, men were arrested or killed and women were raped in their homes, often more than one at a time and sometimes in the presence of their male relatives, which humiliated the victim and her family and symbolically degraded her community.[74] Survivors of sexual violence and defectors of the Syrian army have specifically linked the arrests of men to the rape of women, with the rapes considered punishment for rebellion and a way to deter opposition.[75]

By entering and committing sexual violence in households, government forces attacked the family space where women would be particularly vulnerable and the place where children were more likely to be victimised, including by witnessing direct violence against their parents and siblings. Through sexual violence in households, government forces sent two messages. The first was that there was no safe place from sexual violence, not even at home. At any time, government forces could enter a household and rape the women, and there was nothing that their male relatives could do to prevent it. Female rape functioned as a form of communication between men, reinforcing the 'conquered status' of masculine impotence.[76] The second was ensuring that the family and the community of the victims knew what had happened, thus terrorising them. This meant that staying in the community equalised living with the shame and the dishonour that the rapes brought on the family, as well as risking future sexual violence. The fact that the rapes occurred together with killings, arrests, destruction of property, and looting terrorised the civilian population with the aim of repressing opposition.[77]

Unlike house searches in the early days of the uprising, ground operations targeted communities as a whole rather than specific individuals. It is therefore more accurate to speak of collective targeting based on identity as members of a town or village, which overlaps with the political alliances of its residents.[78] During ground operations, the rape of women and girls, including at home, was used to weaken enemy

[74] Vojdik, 'Sexual Violence against Men and Women', 925.
[75] CoI Syria, A/HRC/37/72/CRP.1, para 10.
[76] Sivakumaran, 'Sexual Violence against men', 268.
[77] CoI Syria, A/HRC/37/72/CRP.1, paras 2–18.
[78] Wood, 'Conflict-Related Sexual Violence', 461. The CoI Syria found that some of those targeted during ground operations appear to have been randomly selected (CoI Syria, A/HRC/21/50, Annex V, para 3). It has also been argued that attacks during ground operations by government forces collectively targeted the population that inhabited an area in which the forces are advancing (Brunner, 'Sexual Violence in the Syrian Civil War', 9).

communities by humiliating the women and emasculating their male relatives. New forms of sexual violence such as public rapes and forced nudity in the streets[79] were the means to drastically increase humiliation within the community.

As mentioned, government forces also perpetrated sexual violence against women and girls at checkpoints. The main purpose of checkpoints was to conduct arrests based on lists of wanted persons.[80] As those wanted for arrest were mostly males and men also feared conscription, women initially enjoyed greater freedom of movement. This resulted in an increase of women crossing checkpoints, as they were now obliged to take care of matters that were previously the purview of the husband as head of household. Importantly, some women replaced men in tasks such as carrying supplies and passing information, which added to the role they may have had as activists. The increased number of women at checkpoints, combined with their active role in supporting opposition, inevitably led government forces to change their approach and over time scrutinise women more closely. Unaccompanied by male relatives, women were left particularly vulnerable to sexual violence. At checkpoints, as in detention, sexual violence was used to extract information, and many women who were subjected to sexual abuse at checkpoints were subsequently detained. Sexual violence at checkpoints was also used to discourage women from providing assistance to the opposition and, more broadly, to instil fear in the population.

Most incidents of sexual violence at checkpoints and during ground operations occurred before August 2012.[81] By then the unrest had escalated into an armed conflict, armed groups had emerged, and government forces resorted to air strikes and besieging populations.[82] This resulted in a decrease of incidents of sexual violence committed within the communities – be it during house searches, as part of ground operations, or at checkpoints. In detention, however, sexual violence continued.

In detention, sexual violence took place away from the gaze of the family and the community, taking many forms and serving a wider range

[79] CoI Syria, A/HRC/37/72/CRP.1, paras 17.
[80] Ibid., para 22.
[81] Ibid., para 12.
[82] The first sieges reported by the CoI Syria were laid in February 2012 (CoI Syria, A/HRC/21/50, 12 August 2012, para 43). By mid-2013, the number of sieges laid by government forces, which included indiscriminate shelling, on opposition areas had significantly increased (CoI Syria, A/HRC/24/46, 16 August 2013, paras 172–9).

of purposes. For women, sexual harassment started from the moment of arrest, which served to degrade them and as a threat of future sexual violence in detention. Forced nudity, including invasive searches upon arrival, took these threats and the sexual humiliation to the next level. By gradually adopting more serious forms of sexual violence, government forces sought to instil fear and make female detainees more willing to cooperate during interrogation. Whether women were arrested for their own activism or to force male relatives to surrender, in detention they were sources of information, and the immediate goal of sexual violence was to extract information. During interrogation, detainees – male and female – were severely beaten and electrocuted. Sexual violence, including rape, was used as part of torture to obtain information as to the whereabouts of their male relatives and to force confessions of the women's alleged support to the opposition.[83]

For women arrested for their own involvement in the uprising, sexual violence was also used to end their activism. This was an effective technique for many women, especially those who were brutally raped, who did not continue to be actively involved in the revolution, at least inside Syria.[84] Related to this, sexual violence against women and girls in detention served the broader goal of preventing others from being politically active. Rape of women and girls occurred in at least twenty detention facilities, a number that in reality is likely to be higher because of common challenges in addressing under-reporting in sexual violence investigations. Furthermore, the number of facilities identified refers specifically to where rape occurred and does not include facilities where other types of sexual violence – forced nudity, beating, electrocution of genitals, etc. – took place. This means that sexual violence targeting women in detention was so widespread that its occurrence was generally known and, as such, served as a deterrent for other women to be politically active.

The broad reasons to use sexual violence against men are the same that led to sexual violence against women: to terrorise, to humiliate, and to disempower. But sexual violence directed against men can also be committed for different reasons than female sexual violence: specifically, 'to cast aspersions of homosexuality' and to emasculate.[85] In the Syrian context, forced nudity upon arrival to the detention facility followed by

[83] CoI Syria, A/HRC/37/72/CRP.1, para 34.

[84] Interviews with female survivors of sexual violence conducted by the author between February and April 2018.

[85] Oosterveld, 'Sexual Violence Directed against Men', 109.

threats of rape during interrogation sexually humiliated male detainees and threatened their masculinity. Individuals who are forced to strip naked feel exposed and vulnerable, feelings that are exacerbated when forced nudity is accompanied by threats of a sexual nature.[86] Rape, including prison rape, is a public display of masculinity used to control and dominate others.[87]

While all sexual violence is under-reported due to a combination of feelings of shame, confusion, stigma, and fear, this is even more so for men due to society's specific construct of masculinity. Societies associate manhood with the ability to exert power over others, particularly through the use of force, making victimisation and masculinity incompatible.[88] Yet, in the Syrian context, sexual violence against men in detention is relatively well documented.[89] This is probably because the most documented type of sexual violence is rape with objects during interrogation to extract information. By and large, survivors – and perhaps also perpetrators – did not perceive such acts as rape, technically a legal qualification.[90] Similarly, it is likely that victims perceive beatings and electrocution of genitals as torture and not (also) as sexual violence, so survivors may have been more willing to provide information on these violations. The implication is that the information available on rapes perpetrated by guards against male detainees and of guards forcing male detainees to rape other male detainees is not representative of the actual scale of that type of violence. Male victims of such acts feel reluctant to report sexual violence for feeling they failed to accord with cultural norms of manhood.[91]

There are, nevertheless, reported incidents of male-on-male sexual violence and more specifically of guards raping detainees and forcing detainees to have intercourse with each other.[92] The rape of detainees by guards occurred in two separate contexts. Some took place during interrogations and would have been aimed primarily at extracting information or forcing confessions. In other instances, men were raped by guards

86 Sivakumaran, 'Sexual violence against Men', 269.
87 Sivakumaran, 'Male/Male Rape', 1300; Sivakumaran, 'Sexual Violence Against Men', 267.
88 Sivakumaran, 'Male/Male Rape', 1288–9.
89 CoI Syria, A/HRC/37/72/CRP.1, paras 43–50; 'We Keep It in Our Heart – Sexual Violence against Men and Boys in the Syria Crisis', UNHCR, 2017, https://data2.unhcr.org/es/documents/download/60864#_ga=2.86560600.1161866260.1535337619-800307029.1521160147 (accessed 22 October 2018).
90 ICC Elements of Crimes, at Arts. (7)(1)(g)-(1) and 8(2)(b).
91 Oosterveld, 'Sexual Violence Directed against Men', 109.
92 CoI Syria, A/HRC/37/72/CRP.1, paras 43–50.

in prison cells in front of other inmates or in corridors. In these contexts, the purpose of rapes was not to extract information; their primary goal was to threaten and terrorise those who watched (in cells) or heard the rapes (taking place in corridors), as they were made to believe that the same would happen to them if they did not cooperate.[93] Indirectly, of course, that would have made the secondary victims more willing to provide information or confess during interrogations.

The reported incidents of detainees forced to have intercourse with one another include the case of an uncle and nephew.[94] It is not surprising that the number of reported incidents of this nature are few and far between; under-reporting of such cases is to be expected in any context. The extreme trauma, humiliation, shame, and stigma inflicted by this violence prevents survivors from coming forward. Within the prison context, it would not only be extremely likely to be successful in forcing detainees to provide information or confess but would also inflict considerable trauma and fear on all other detainees.

In instances both of rape by guards and of detainees forced by guards to have intercourse, the perpetrators sought to assault the masculinity of their victims. The victims were heads of households or unmarried men for whom society had clearly defined roles. Those roles, which were perceived as superior to women, were directly attacked. From strong roles in families and communities that were enhanced by these men's active participation in the revolution, they were brought down to a situation – symbolised by the act of rape and even more evidently by genital mutilation – in which they were stripped of their masculinity and, through it, the power they traditionally had or were to have in society.

7.5 Consequences

Eight years of war show that despite the spectrum of tactics adopted by the government at different times of the conflict, those tactics, including sexual violence, failed to achieve the main goal of ending opposition. On the contrary, it has been argued that the use of sexual violence in detention and the rape of women and girls in front of their male relatives is one – if not necessarily the foremost – reason that led the opposition to militarise.[95] While this suggests a collective sense of outrage, it also shows

93 Ibid., para 46.
94 Ibid., para 47.
95 Yassin-Kassab and al-Shami, *Burning Country*, 79.

that, though opposition was not repressed, sexual violence succeeded at spreading terror by shaming women and emasculating men made to feel powerless to protect their wives and daughters. Insofar as it contributed to militarisation, sexual violence led men from opposition communities to reclaim their sense of masculinity and their family honour.

Sexual violence, particularly against women and girls inside their homes and at checkpoints, humiliated and shamed communities. It also instilled fear of future sexual violence, working as a driving factor for families to flee Syria and become refugees abroad.[96] On a case-by-case basis, sexual violence was highly effective against both female and male survivors. Many protesters, mostly women but also some men, subjected to sexual violence in prison gave up their activism after their release. Furthermore, the fact that so many former detainees signed confessions following torture of which sexual violence was a part[97] is indicative that it was effective at obtaining confessions and extracting information. More broadly, the use of sexual violence prevented some women from joining protests out of fear of being arrested and raped in detention, the latter being well known in opposition communities.

The widespread rape of female detainees worked on other levels too. It tainted all female detainees with the stigma of suspicions associated with widespread use of sexual violence.[98] Former female detainees have spontaneously and vehemently denied that they were raped in detention, with some acknowledging that after release their families disowned them regardless because they considered detention to equal rape. Whether married or not, the family's reaction prevents them from fulfilling the traditional role of wife and mother. By breaking up families, sexual violence contributed to the fracturing of communities and the existing social fabric.

In general, brutal rapes – including gang rapes that result in severe physical injuries and trauma – and the rape of women in front of male relatives suggest institutionalised forms of sexual violence adopted for government purposes.[99] This is also the case in the Syrian conflict, where

[96] G. Hassan, P. Ventevogel, H. Jefee-Bahloul, A. Barkil-Oteo, and L. J. Kirmayer, 'Mental Health and Psychosocial Wellbeing of Syrians Affected by the Conflict', *Epidemiology and Psychiatric Sciences* 25, no 2 (2016): 132.

[97] CoI Syria, A/HRC/S-17/2/Add.1., para 61; A/HRC/27/60, para 54; A/HRC/28/69, para 105 and 145–6.

[98] Interviews with former female detainees conducted by the author between February and April 2018.

[99] Wood, 'Conflict-Related Sexual Violence', 471.

the most physically violent rapes documented were against detainees to obtain information and those in households, which were used to terrorise and punish.[100] There is no indication that explicit orders to perpetrate sexual violence were given. Yet the widespread nature of sexual violence evident from the high number of ground operations and detention facilities where rape occurred, the involvement of senior leaders in rapes,[101] and the absence of information that perpetrators were punished suggests that there were, at the very least, implicit orders for rape to be used as a tactic.

Information on pregnancies resulting from rape is extremely scarce. In some instances, women and girls travelled abroad seeking abortions, though they did not tell their families about the procedure unless strictly needed.[102] Reports have emerged of prison authorities giving women medication that prevents them from menstruating or suspected to be birth control.[103] According to medical professionals who treated former female detainees, some would have stopped menstruating due to malnutrition and/or trauma.[104] On the other hand, near absence of information of pregnancies is more likely to result from extreme stigma that the survivors endure. While some victims have been able to receive medical as well as psychological assistance, including from non-governmental organisations operating abroad,[105] many others have not.

Male-on-male rape, both in instances of rape by guards and of detainees forced to have intercourse with each other, struck at the core of the notion that only women can be victims of rape. Sexual violence stripped male detainees of their masculine attributes in a social construct where men are defined by a heterosexual masculinity. Rape of men by men in prison effectively emasculated male detainees. Through rape, perpetrators asserted their power and dominance over the victims, lowering them to the status of women, 'feminising' them[106] in a society where women were considered to be socially inferior. In instances of rape by guards, some survivors also reported to have felt that they lost their masculinity and occasionally reported that after the rapes they questioned their sexual orientation.[107] Survivors of beatings and electrocution of genitals who

[100] Ibid., 463.
[101] CoI Syria, A/HRC/37/72/CRP.1, paras 37–40.
[102] Ibid., paras 97–9.
[103] Ibid., para 36.
[104] Interviews conducted by the author with medical staff between February and April 2018.
[105] CoI Syria, A/HRC/37/72/CRP.1, para 93.
[106] Sivakumaran, 'Sexual Violence against Men', 270–1.
[107] CoI Syria, A/HRC/37/72/CRP.1, para 96.

suffer loss of sexual function and infertility are not likely to seek treatment because of the stigma and fear of social ostracism.[108]

7.6 Conclusion

In one form or another, sexual violence was a part of the Syrian conflict from its very first days, with the use of sexual violence being part of a larger set of means used by government forces aimed at repressing opposition. Types of sexual violence changed over time, escalating with the dynamics on the ground. The use of sexual violence deliberately exploited gender roles and cultural norms throughout the conflict. Immediately before the uprising, government forces used threats of sexual violence to pre-empt protests which could lead to revolutionary movements similar to those taking place in other Arab countries. Together with threats of violent repression of planned demonstrations, threats of sexual violence delayed the uprising.

As they had threatened, government forces violently repressed countrywide demonstrations calling for reform. After decades of being relegated from political life, women joined protests, became politically active, and as such became direct targets for killings and arrests during demonstrations. When this failed to repress opposition, government forces killed and arrested civilians in their homes, where women were raped in front of their families, including their husbands. By using sexual violence in the household, government forces exploited the patriarchal family system, striking at the heart of the family, shaming the women – even if they had not been personally involved in the revolution – and the men who failed to protect them.

As opposition militarised, government forces resorted to ground operations, shelling and sniping before troops went from house to house targeting entire communities rather than specific individuals. In this context, rapes of women served to humiliate the women and emasculate their male relatives, thus weakening the entire community. The escalation of violence was accompanied by an expansion of the sexual violence repertoire of government forces, which by then included public rapes and forced nudity in the streets. Once again, sexual violence against women was closely interrelated with that against men, the women sexually humiliated in a situation where their male relatives could not fulfil the role of protectors.

[108] Vojdik, 'Sexual Violence against Men and Women', 924.

Increased participation of women in the political arena and in assisting newly formed armed groups left them vulnerable at checkpoints that they crossed unaccompanied by male relatives who feared conscription. At checkpoints, women were subjected to sexual abuse that discouraged them from providing assistance to the opposition. Sexual violence at checkpoints also served to instil fear in the population. Together with sexual violence during ground operations, sexual violence at checkpoints were factors for families to seek refuge abroad.

As part of a campaign of arrests that started in parallel with the uprising and continued until 2014, thousands of people were arrested. In detention, both women and men were subjected to progressively serious types of sexual violence meant to instil fear and make them cooperate during interrogation. Chronologically, the acts of sexual violence would begin with forced nudity during searches followed by threats of rape during interrogation, then beating and electrocution of genitals, and finally rape. Rape of women was used as method of torture to obtain information as to the whereabouts of their male relatives and to force confessions of the women's alleged support of the opposition – and, more broadly, to end the woman's activism and prevent others from being politically active out of fear they would also be raped.

Sexual violence directed against men had the overall aims and consequences to shame and emasculate. This happened first when women were raped in the household during the campaign of arrest and later during ground operations, and men's inability to protect them was made manifest by their being forced to watch the rapes. In a cultural context so closely defined by heterosexualised masculinity and where homosexuality is criminalised, when men were themselves directly targeted for sexual violence in detention, their level of shame and emasculation dramatically increased. Rape of male detainees by guards feminised men by shattering the notion that only women can be raped while also replacing their heterosexuality, and therefore their power, with the taint of homosexuality.

The close relationship between sexual violence against women and that against men meant that, combined, they were used to empower the government while weakening the collective of people who opposed it. On the one hand, sexual violence against women humiliated the women and shamed their families, particularly their male relatives. On the other hand, sexual violence against men was a tool to masculinise and empower the perpetrator and to feminise the victim and, through him, his community.

The impact of sexual violence is likely to endure for generations to come. While physical and psychological trauma affects survivors of both genders, women rejected by their families must also find the means to support themselves and often their children who are stigmatised by association. More broadly, the shame brought by sexual violence to opposition communities affects their self-perception of worth, which reinforces the sense of empowerment by communities that support the government. In this context, any attempts at post-conflict community reconciliation must necessarily consider how to address and overcome these perceptions.

A crucial step towards Syrian society acknowledging, understanding, and coming to terms with the extent and impact of sexual violence lies in documenting it. Such allegations must therefore be an integral part of any investigations geared towards future prosecutions. Though significant progress has been made in recent decades, information gaps and inconsistent legal qualification of acts of sexual violence have resulted in partial successes.[109] As it is one of the most well-documented conflicts in modern history, practitioners working on accountability in the Syrian context are in a position to do better.

[109] Oosterveld, 'Sexual Violence Directed against Men', 109–10.

PART II

The Syrian Neighbourhood

8

Proxy Wars in Syria

Exploitation of the Palestinian Issue in the Syrian Crisis

MORAN LEVANONI

8.1 Proxy Powers in the Syrian War

The fast pace of events in the first year of the Syrian conflict, along with the collapse of effective governance in large parts of Syria, created a political vacuum that quickly drew external powers into the Syrian arena. Since the beginning of clashes between the Syrian government and Syrian rebels in early 2011, vast numbers of militia groups, armed forces, and military experts poured into Syria. These groups represented different agendas, effectively turning Syria into the battlefield of a multifaceted proxy conflict. In this chapter, the roles of two of those groups will be explored: Hezbollah, a Lebanese militia; and Hamas, based in Gaza. These groups represent different sets of interests and different stakeholders and, consequently, had different attitudes towards the crisis.

The Iranian Revolutionary Guards (IRG) and Hezbollah militiamen were the first outsiders to become involved in Syria. By invitation of the Syrian government, the IRG and Hezbollah came to assist Syrian Armed Forces against the rebels at the beginning of the uprising in March–April 2011. They were quickly followed by a wave of disparate outside forces, including Russian air force and naval personnel; American troops, CIA agents, and military advisors; European coalition forces; Jordanian air force pilots; volunteers who joined the Kurdish militia, the People's Protection Units (the YPG); Shi'a militias from Iraq, Afghanistan, Pakistan, and Malaysia; Sunni jihadist fighters from Iraq, as well as foreign volunteers from the Arab world and across five continents; Turkey's armed forces; and Turkman militias.

In the complexity of this proxy war, the influence of two organisations, Hezbollah and Hamas, can be difficult to discern. However, the Israeli-Palestinian conflict and the 'axis of resistance' (*Muqawama*) played a key role in the involvement of both organisations in the Syrian crisis. At its heart, the axis of resistance is made up of three understandings: first, resistance must be against imperialists and colonialists – the foreign powers who do not belong to the Middle East and seek to exploit it to the benefit of their own interests. Second, the threat of these great colonial powers' involvement is emphasised by the 'Zionist occupation of Palestine',[1] a result of the hundred-year-old Balfour declaration, British support for the Zionists, and later American intervention in favour of the Zionists. Third, the axis of resistance must struggle against dictators and oppressive regimes, such as the oppression of the Palestinians by the Zionists. In the past, Arab leaders such as Gamal Abdel Nasser, Saddam Hussein, Muammar Gaddafi, and Hafez al-Assad used harsh rhetoric against Israel and emphasised support for the Palestinian cause in order to stimulate the Arab world and provide for themselves a better domestic standing by showing Arab pride. By doing so they also affiliated themselves with the axis of resistance.

This chapter will examine the factors influencing the decision-making for both organisations during their entanglement in Syria through the lens of the *Muqawama* and usage of the Palestinian issue as a tool. The roles of Hezbollah and Hamas in Syria will be examined through the organisations' published announcements and publicised actions as reported in the media, along with their actions on the ground. This will include the speeches of Hassan Nasrallah, the secretary general of Hezbollah; his deputy, Shaeikh Na'im Kasem; and Ibrahim al-Amin, the editor of *Al-Akhbar* newspaper. On the Palestinian side, the speeches of Isma'il Haniya, Hamas's prime minister, will be examined, as will the harsh criticism of Hezbollah's actions in Syria by Dr. Azmi Bishara, former Israeli Member of Parliament and Palestinian supporter of Hezbollah. Additionally, this chapter will look at an article by Nabil Bitari, a Palestinian Syrian Red Crescent worker, activist, and resident of al-Yarmouk refugee camp, concerning the events that took place in the camp in April 2015.

[1] Zionism as the emphasis of the nationalistic ambitions of the Jewish people for a nation state in Israel became a symbol and focal point for the Arab national struggle.

8.2 Hezbollah's First Reactions to the Arab Uprising, March 2011

From the beginning of the popular uprisings, and particularly with the Bahrain uprising in late 2010, where the Shi'a majority rebelled against the Sunni elite, it was clear that Hezbollah would be sympathetic to rebel groups. The organisation was founded upon and shaped by the ideology of Imam Muasa al-Sadr and his *Harkat al-mahrumin,* or 'the movement of the deprived', which was based on supporting the common people against oppressive tyrants. This ideology had its roots in the Shi'a fundamental perception of the struggle of Imam Husayn, the founder of Shi'ism, against the Umayyad Caliphate.

Hezbollah had several other factors influencing its policy. Its patron, Iran, assumed that new Islamic regimes resulting from the revolutions might provide convenient support for the Islamic Republic of Iran. Hezbollah also had unresolved issues with Arab leaders – from Gaddafi of Libya concerning the disappearance of Shi'a leader Imam Musa al-Sadr to President Mubarak of Egypt for arresting Hezbollah activists – and with the rest of the Arab world for refusing to assist the organisation during its 2006 war with Israel.

On 19 March 2011, a mere one week after protests erupted in Syria, some hundreds of Hezbollah supporters assembled in Beirut's *Sayyid al-Shuhada* centre in what was described by the organisers as an assembly in support of the revolutions in Tunis, Egypt, Bahrain, Libya, and Yemen. The highlight of the meeting was a televised speech by Hassan Nasrallah, Hezbollah's secretary-general, in which he claimed:

> We gathered here firstly to express our support for the rebelling people in Tunis, Egypt, Bahrain, Libya, and Yemen. These revolutions that storm the Arab world are genuine ones, and their aim is to topple oppressive leaders. They are not backed by big powers from outside the Arab world. Although the United States is ostensibly supportive of the rebels, their true goal is to keep the tyrants on their thrones while we, Hezbollah, wish to reach out to the revolutionaries, and remind the Arab leaders that they turned a blind eye against us, the *Muqawama,* during the 2006 war.[2]

Later in his speech, the secretary general warned the governments not to retaliate against the revolutionaries 'with an iron fist' and instead negotiate with the rebels.

In an 8 April 2011 speech, Deputy Secretary General Naim Qassem warned the rebels throughout the Middle East not to be tempted by

[2] Speech by Hassan Nasrallah, Moqawama.org, 19 March 2011, www.moqawama.org/essaydetails.php?eid=20205&cid=142 (Arabic). Translated by Moran Levanoni.

American promises for support and not allow the United States to 'hijack the revolution'.[3] As reflected in their speeches, Hezbollah leaders expressed support for the rebels following the tenets of the *Muqawama*, which they saw as hand-in-hand with the 'new Arab spring', and rejected the intervention of outside forces in the uprisings.

8.2.1 The Story of al-Yarmouk Refugee Camp, 2011–2013

The Palestinian issue is usually portrayed as the heart of the *Muqawama*, as it embodies a genuine struggle against an oppressor, the Zionists, backed by great powers, first the British and later the Americans. As such, the proximity of the al-Yarmouk refugee camp to the Syrian capital of Damascus could have been used as a perfect example for the Syrian government to show its devotion to the Palestinian cause and the *Muqawama*. Home to some 150,000 Palestinians before the Syrian uprising, al-Yarmouk was the largest concentration of Palestinians in Syria and housed most of the Palestinian movements and organisations.

According to Nidal Bitari, a Palestinian Syrian Red Crescent worker, activist, and resident of the camp, the Syrian authorities used the Palestinian residents of al-Yarmouk camp and their ambitions as a playing card in the government's hand. In an article published in the *Journal of Palestine Studies*, Bitari described the events the camp experienced during the Syrian uprising.[4] The article portrayed the atmosphere among the Palestinians in al-Yarmouk as nationalistic, with great awareness for national commemoration days and Palestinian culture. Bitari described the extensive cultural and youth activities organised in the camp and argued that during the Syrian uprising much of the Palestinian population of the camp was eager to remain neutral, knowing that the ramifications of Palestinian participation in the protests would result in a strong backlash against them by the Syrian government.

Bitari describes how, on Naqba Day, 15 May 2011, little more than two months after the beginning of the uprisings in Syria, Palestinian demonstrations took place on the Golan Heights border with Israel – demonstrations which were promoted and in part orchestrated by the Syrian government. In an unprecedented move, the Syrian government

[3] Speech by Naim Qassem, naimkassem.net, 18 April 2011, www.naimkassem.net/article.php?id=849&cid=74 (Arabic). Translated by Moran Levanoni.

[4] Nidal Bitari, 'Yarmuk Refugee Camp and the Syrian Uprising: A View from Within', *Institute for Palestine Studies* 43 (2013/2014): 61–79, www.palestine-studies.org/jps/fulltext/162936.

allowed Palestinian demonstrators to gather at the Golan Heights border fences and organised buses to transport demonstrators, mostly from the al-Yarmouk camp, to the border. During this demonstration, three Palestinians were killed by Israeli soldiers as they climbed the border fence into the Israeli-held Golan. Within the camp, this resulted in a growing anger towards the Syrian government for agitating the Naqba Day demonstration, allowing demonstrations to take place on the border, and then leaving the demonstrators defenceless.

Bitari goes on to describe how on 5 June 2011 – Naqsa Day, commemorating the defeat of the Arab armies in the 1967 war against Israel – Syrian security forces sent three minivans to al-Yarmouk camp to transport Palestinians to demonstrations along the border fence with Israel despite camp representatives deciding to refrain from participation in these demonstrations. Nevertheless, some fifty camp residents travelled to the border in the Syrian buses, encouraged by the Syrian government to protest against Israeli occupation. By the end of the demonstration, twenty-three of the camp's youth were killed trying to scale the border, and hundreds more were wounded in the clashes. Funerals for the dead, held the following day at the camp, turned into a massive demonstration against the Syrian government for, as the residents felt, using the Palestinians to further its own cause. The demonstrators, thirty thousand strong, started throwing stones at the headquarters of Ahmad Jibril's Palestinian organisation, the Popular Front for the Liberation of Palestine – General Command (PFLP-GC), as this organisation is known for its entrenched support of the Syrian government. One of the guards opened fire and killed a fourteen-year-old boy. The demonstrators stormed the building and set it on fire, resulting in Ahmad Jibril and his staff having to be rescued by the Syrian army. In total, three people were killed, including the fourteen-year-old boy and a member of the PFLP-GC, and hundreds injured.

The second major turning point Bitari describes happened in late 2012. Ahmed Jibril's PFLP-GC, backed by the Syrian government, was the main armed force in the camp. However, since the summer of 2012, the Free Syrian Army (FSA) and the more radical al-Nusra Front looked for an opportunity to occupy the camp as a 'gateway' to Damascus. This opportunity arrived when, on 16 December 2012, a Syrian MIG fighter mistakenly bombed the camp, causing dozens of civilian casualties. Following this attack, anti-government rebels stormed the camp and drove out Ahmed Jibril's PFLP-GC and other government-backed militias. The PFLP-GC pulled out, holding only a number of checkpoints around the camp. These checkpoints were later fortified, effecting a siege around al-Yarmouk.[5]

Over the next few months, the camp fell into chaos as the rebel groups fought each other to gain ground in the camp at the expense of the Palestinian civilians. Hamas, with its leaders expelled to Qatar, formed a brigade called the Pact of Umar and, in March 2013, began receiving weapons from abroad, which were distributed to its supporters in an attempt to protect them in the camp.[6] Fighting soon broke out between the FSA and the al-Nusra Front, and the integrity of ragtag Palestinian brigades eroded as infighting caused groups to splinter. By summer 2013, Hamas remained the only Palestinian group with any semblance of cohesion.

Bitari's third turning point occurred in July 2013, when the Syrian military and the PFLP-GC issued a blockade around al-Yarmouk. This resulted in the camp having no clean water and pushed the camp's inhabitants towards starvation, with high rates of malnutrition. The situation became so desperate that in October 2013 the imam of the central mosque issued a fatwa giving people permission to eat cats, dogs, and donkeys.

The camp of al-Yarmouk became a focal point in the struggle between the Syrian government and its associated militias on one hand, and the FSA rebels, including the al-Nusra Front, and Palestinian forces such as Hamas on the other. The Syrian government did not hesitate to use the Palestinians and the Palestinian issue as a way of gaining points vis-à-vis the Syrian people and the Arab world, using the Palestinians as a confirmation for being part of the axis of resistance as a way of surviving and maintaining power. The Syrian government, in the name of the axis of resistance, deployed the Palestinians to the frontline of its own struggles and, by drawing some Palestinian militias against the rebels and rebel-supporting Palestinians into the conflict, driving al-Yarmouk's inhabitants into siege and starvation.

8.3 Hamas' Departure from Syria, 2011–2012

Hamas was no stranger to the Syrian arena, with the movement having maintained an active office in Damascus since 1993. As a rejection of the

[5] Bitari.
[6] Ibid., 74.

Oslo Accords and due to the expulsion of Hamas officials from Jordan in 1999, Hamas made Damascus its headquarters.

Hosting the Hamas headquarters placed the Syrian government as a pivotal actor in the axis of resistance and gave its leaders the benefit of acting as the spearhead of the anti-Israel offensive, providing the government legitimacy internally and throughout the Arab and Muslim worlds. Hamas gained a haven in Syria, political backing, and open doors to the other anti-colonial actors such as Libya and Iran, as well as logistical and financial aid. Hamas operated relief activities, as well as educational and cultural organisations in the Palestinian camps, which helped Hamas win the hearts and minds of its political base. As a result, both Hamas and the Syrians were in delicate positions with much to lose in the case of relationship damage.

An op-ed published on 19 February 2012 by Al Jazeera attempted to describe the relations between Hamas and the Syrian government. Al Jazeera is a state-funded channel owned by Qatar, which at the time participated in the Syrian crisis in favour of anti-Assad armed groups, including some which could be described as Islamist groups. Qatar eventually hosted Hamas headquarters after the organisation left Syria in 2012. The op-ed described a meeting between Khaled Mashal, at that time chief of Hamas' politburo,[7] and President Assad in mid-March 2011. During this meeting, Mashal warned the Syrian president of the 'revolution storm winds' blowing across the Middle East, to which Assad replied he hopes the revolution will pass over Syria.[8] No doubt Hamas was wary of the decision it would face when riots erupted in Syria. Hamas saw the revolutions in the Arab world as a great opportunity for the Muslim Brotherhood, Hamas' parent movement, to take over governments across the Middle East, as they did in Egypt in June 2012. Hamas understood it would be necessary to take sides early on in a conflict, either in favour of their Syrian patrons or on the side of the Islamist rebels. A decision to support those fighting the Syrian government could harshly affect the Palestinian population in Syria, which was dependent on the government's good will for its freedoms. The deportation of 30,000 Palestinians from Kuwait after Yasser Arafat declared his support for Saddam Hussein in 1991 remained clear in Palestinian memory.

7 Mashal was replaced by Ismail Haniyeh in May 2017.

8 'Mashal Avoided Meeting Assad before Leaving Damascus', *Al Jazeera*, 12 February 2012, www.aljazeera.net/news/pages/ab318b39-612f-4700-bb4d-6aefc374fc14 (Arabic).

The protests in Syria started in the southern town of Daraa in early March 2011 and consisted of public unarmed demonstrations calling for reform and civil rights. The Syrian government retaliated with live ammunition, causing casualties and an escalation in the violence.[9] As the protests in Syria developed, the government demanded of Hamas firm support in an attempt to isolate the rebels and as a means of showing unity within the axis of resistance. Hamas did not comply, instead publishing a vague statement describing the uprisings in Syria as an 'internal affair'.

Nearly a year later, Hamas changed its stance. In a 15 February 2012 speech at Al-Azhar University, Hamas Prime Minister Ismail Haniyeh congratulated 'the brave Syrian people in their revolution on the way toward democracy and freedom'. The speech was given as part of a rally under the slogan 'Saving Al-Aqsa and victory to the Syrian people', with crowds shouting, 'Not Iran nor Hezbollah, Syria Syria Islamia'. Two factors facilitated Hamas in taking this stance. First, Hamas received a measure of assurance for support from Qatar. Indeed, within three days, Haniyeh announced that Hamas's headquarters had left Damascus[10] (it eventually moved to Qatar). Second, Egypt was, at the time, ruled by Mohamed Morsi of the Muslim Brotherhood, Hamas's parent movement.[11]

Since Iran considered Hamas an ally in the region, by breaking off its connections with the Syrian government and Iran and shifting its patronage to Qatar, Hamas moved from the revolutionary, progressive, anti-Western axis to the more conservative bloc. Notably, Qatar played a pivotal part in the American deployment in the Middle East and was headquarters for the air strikes in Syria and Iraq. By moving to a Qatari patronage, Hamas could be accused of cooperating with the Americans.

8.4 Hezbollah Deepens Its Involvement in Syria, 2012–2015

Hezbollah did not enjoy the same privileges as Hamas. The relations between Iran and Hezbollah are both ideological and material, since the

[9] Azmi Bishara, *Syria, A Path to Freedom from Suffering an Attempt in Contemporary History* (Beirut: Arab Center For Research & Policy Studies, 2013), 95–122 (Arabic).

[10] Pola Astih, 'Hamas Confirms that Its Headquarter Left Damascus', *Al-Sharq Al-Awsat*, 28 February 2012, www.aawsat.com/details.asp?section=4&issueno=12145&article=665742&search=%DE%ED%C7%CF%C9%20%CD%E3%C7%D3&state=true#.UTSZIFf0Bj1 (Arabic). Translated by Moran Levanoni.

[11] 'Haniyeh Salutes "the Hero" Syrian People from the al-Azhar Podium', *Al-Sharq Al-Awsat*, 25 February 2012, www.aawsat.com/details.asp?section=4&issueno=12142&article=665249&search=%CD%E3%C7%D3&state=true#.UTSWR1f0Bj1 (Arabic). Translated by Moran Levanoni.

organisation looks up to Iran as a role model for successful Shi'a revolution and as its financial, political, and operational source.[12] Hezbollah in Lebanon was heavily indebted to Iran and obliged to follow Iranian requests.[13] Naim Qassem wrote in his book *Society and Resistance* (*mujtama' wamoqawama*, 2008):

> Just like the important role of the Islamic Republic of Iran in standing by the resistance against the neo-colonialism project, so the Syrian Arab Republic too stands alongside with the resistance when there has been threats to it [referring to the 2006 war between Israel and Hezbollah].[14]

On 25 May 2011, in his annual speech on the 'freedom commemoration day' in the town of Nabi-Shayth, Hassan Nasrallah denied any Hezbollah involvement in the fighting in Syria. However, rumours of the killing of a high-ranking Hezbollah militiaman named Abu Abbas in Syria raised the question of whether Hezbollah was in fact fighting in Syria,[15] calling into question Nasarallah's statement.[16] In a televised speech on 12 October 2012, Nasrallah claimed that, though the organisation had been accused of involvement in Syria, the fighters who were killed in Syria, including Abu Abbas, were residents of twenty-three villages and seventeen farms in the Syrian Beqaa region who happened to be of Lebanese origin and who were merely defending themselves against terrorist attacks.[17]

The public admittance of Hezbollah's involvement in suppressing the uprisings in Syria came only after two months of clashes between Hezbollah and the FSA over the town of al-Qusayr in the Syrian Beqaa valley in June 2013. During the two months of battle, Hezbollah lost dozens of its fighters in this strategic area but ultimately succeeded in taking control of the town and the surrounding roads. From that moment on, Hezbollah's fighters officially supported the Syrian government and spread to Aleppo, Homs, and Deir ez-Zur, as well as to the fighting in the Syrian Golan Heights and the nearby areas of Daraa and Beit Jinn in the so-called

12 Roschanac Shaerly-Eisenlohr, *Shi'ite Lebanon, Transnational Religion and the Making of National Identity* (New York: Columbia University Press, 2008), 158–99.

13 Eyal Zisser, *Commanding Syria: Bashar Al-Asad and the First Years in Power* (London, New York: I. B. Tauris, 2007), 161–2, 182.

14 Na'im Kasim, *Society and Resistance* (Beirut: Institute Al-Ma'arif Al-hikma, 2008), 1.

15 'Is Hezbollah Fighting in Syria?', *Al-Jazeera*, 5 October 2012, www.aljazeera.net/news/pages/1f1059a3-60e8-4812-b5e9-e26e5ea944dc (Arabic). Translated by Moran Levanoni.

16 'Hezbollah Organized a Big Festivity in the Town of Nabi-Shayth Commemorating the Freedom Day 25.5.2011', Moqawama.org, 26 May 2011, www.moqawama.org/essaydetails.php?eid=20819&cid=142 (Arabic). Translated by Moran Levanoni.

17 'Nassarallah: We Do Not Fight in Syria', *Al-Hayat*, 12 October 2012, http://alhayat.com/Details/443724 (Arabic). Translated by Moran Levanoni.

death triangle between Daraa, Quneitra, and Damascus. Hezbollah maintained a particular presence in the Druze village of al-Hader. To emphasise the importance of Hezbollah to the operations in al-Hader, Hezbollah appointed Samir Quntar as commander of this region. Quntar was a Lebanese Druze and ex-Fatah Palestinian group member who had served time in Israeli prison, joined Hezbollah upon his release, and been assassinated in 2015. Hezbollah and its Iranian patrons made a special effort to set a 'foot on the ground' in the Golan Heights that can be explained by a master plan to create an optional second front with Israel.

This effort was accompanied by indoctrination campaigns and media publications. On 15 October 2016, the Hezbollah-affiliated television channel Al Mayadeen broadcasted an investigative programme titled 'Southern Syria: A Region in Flames' concerning Hezbollah's struggle on the Golan front from 2013 to 2016, supposedly in relation to Israeli policy and the various groups active in southern Syria.[18] The programme provided an insight into Hezbollah's narrative as part of its propaganda campaign in the Syrian Golan Heights, hand in hand with the fighting on the ground.[19] In an effort to prove Israeli intervention in Syria, the report included biased descriptions of battles and military campaigns, emphasising the tactical successes of Islamist groups, such as Jish al-Sham and the Al-Rahman Division, along with various statements by Israeli military officials.[20] In addition, the report claimed that a series of attacks against fifty officers and fighters of the Free Syrian Army had been carried out by jihadists with the involvement of Western intelligence officials and Israel. Al-Mayadeen's report concluded that the Israeli-Western-Saudi front is working actively to plant a compliant Islamist regime in southern Syria at the expense of the moderate FSA. As a result, Hezbollah is portrayed in the report as the region's legitimate representative of the free world.

Hezbollah slowly grew more involved in the fighting in Syria as the conflict progressed, from low-profile support to active troops supporting Assad wherever he lost ground. According to some estimates, the number of Hezbollah troops fighting in Syria rose from several hundred in

[18] 'Al-Mayadeen Documents: The Syrian South, A Region in Flame', uploaded to YouTube on 15 October 2016, video, www.youtube.com/watch?v=e5eNYGE1pTM.

[19] Moran Levanoni, 'The Consciousness Front: Hezbollah's Struggle on the Southern Front in the Syrian Golan Heights', *Beehive* 4, no. 10 (November 2016): 7–9, www.aftau.org/document.doc?id=541.

[20] Ely Zuzovsky, 'UN Soldiers Who Fled from Syria Report a New Situation', *Mako*, 17 September 2014, www.mako.co.il/pzm-magazine/Article-8a8708d57448841006.html.

2013 to several thousand by the end of 2015.[21] Major importance was given by the organisation and its Iranian patrons to set a 'foot on the ground' on the front with Israel. To earn legitimacy, Hezbollah used its participation in the axis of resistance to confront Israel and foreign Western powers when they allegedly collaborated with radical Islamists.

8.5 Azmi Bishara and the Axis of Resistance, 2012

A fascinating debate exists within the axis of resistance between those supporting the Palestinian cause and those supporting the Syrian people against the Assad government. A sample of this debate can be seen in an op-ed published by Dr Azmi Bishara on 6 October 2012 and published in *Al-Akhbar*.[22]

Al-Akhbar, a prominent newspaper in Lebanon, edited by an ex-Hezbollah member, describes itself as follows:

> On 14 August 2006, Beirut-based Al-Akhbar was launched as a 'calculated adventure' by prominent Lebanese journalist Joseph Samaha and a team of like-minded colleagues. The late Samaha (1949–2007) envisioned a publication that would uphold the highest standards of journalistic integrity while *remaining true to the principles of anti-imperialist struggle* [emphasis added], progressive politics, and freedom of expression. Hot on the heels of Israel's war on Lebanon, the launch of the Arabic edition coincided with the onset of a turbulent period *in the history of Lebanon and the Arab-Israeli conflict* [emphasis added].[23]

This attitude made the newspaper a useful media mouthpiece of the axis of resistance and Hezbollah.

Azmi Bishara is the general director of the Arab Centre for Research and Policy Studies. Nazareth-born, Bishara was a member of the Israeli parliament until 2006, when he left Israel for Qatar in response to

[21] Gili Cohen, 'Thousands of Hezbollah Troops Fighting, Hundreds Killed in Syria, Study Confirms', *Haaretz*, 5 June 2013, www.haaretz.com/study-hezbollah-action-in-syria-is-heavy-1.5274284; Avi Issacharoff, 'A Third of Hezbollah's Fighters Said Killed or Injured in Syria', *The Times of Israel*, 15 December 2015, www.timesofisrael.com/a-third-of-hezbollahs-fighters-said-killed-or-injured-in-syria/.

[22] Azmi Bishara, 'Bishara Argues with Hezbollah', *Al-Akhbar*, 6 October 2012, www.al-akhbar.com/Opinion/78366/%D8%B3-%D9%88%D8%B5-%D8%B9%D8%B2%D9%85%D9%8A-%D8%A8%D8%B4%D8%A7%D8%B1%D8%A9-%D9%8A%D9%86%D8%A7%D9%82%D8%B4-%D8%AD%D8%B2%D8%A8-%D8%A7%D9%84%D9%84 (Arabic). Translated by Moran Levanoni.

[23] Alakhbar English, 'About', Facebook, www.facebook.com/pg/AlakhbarEnglish/about/?ref=page_internal.

accusations of cooperation with the enemy after he met with Bashar al-Assad and Hassan Nasrallah during the 2006 Israel–Hezbollah war.[24]

In his article, Bishara argued that Hezbollah is wrong in fighting alongside the brutal Assad government against the Syrian rebels. Bishara described this Syrian government as a '16th-century occupying regime in all aspects', adding that 'nobody comes to the aid of the poor Syrian people'. The Syrian people, Bishara added, are struggling for freedom and self-respect, facing crimes against humanity committed by Syrian forces. Bishara's main argument was that, while the Palestinian problem is valid, it cannot be progressed on account of the Syrian people: the Syrian people must be concerned firstly with Syrian problems as much as the Egyptian people are concerned with Egyptian problems, and the Palestinian problem comes second. Bishara admitted that on his 2006 visit to Syria he felt the oppression imposed on the Syrians, but by his being part of the Palestinian cause he felt committed to the resistance alongside Hezbollah and Assad. From the beginning of the Arab revolutions, he wrote, his heart was with the protesters in Tunis, Egypt, Yemen, and Syria: he was surprised when Hezbollah joined the conflict on the side of the Syrian government in oppressing its people.

These views from a devoted and loyal member of the axis of resistance and a ''48 Palestinian'[25] such as Azmi Bishara could not pass without a stern response. That response came one day later in an op-ed by Ibrahim Al-Amin, editor of *Al-Akhbar* and one of the original founders of Hezbollah.[26] Al-Amin argued that the Palestinian cause and the Syrian regime are one, as they are inseparable parts of the axis of resistance. Every act against the Palestinian cause, he claimed, harms the Syrian regime, and vice versa. There can be no separation of the two issues: the Syrian government and the Palestinians are one and the same, and therefore support for the Syrian government against the rebels is also supporting the Palestinians in their struggle. Al-Amin concluded that Bishara must support the Syrian government alongside Hezbollah in the axis of resistance.

[24] 'Azmi Bishara', Biography, Azmi Bishara, last modified 29 January 2018, www.azmibishara.com/ar/%D9%86%D8%A8%D8%B0%D8%A9/%D8%B9%D8%B2%D9%85%D9%8A-%D8%A8%D8%B4%D8%A7%D8%B1%D8%A9 (Arabic). Translated by Moran Levanoni.

[25] This term refers to Arab residents and citizens of Israel living within Israel's pre-1967 borders.

[26] Ibrahim Al-Amin, 'The Resistance and Syria', *Al-Akhbar*, 7 October 2012, vol. 1853, www.al-akhbar.com/Politics/78444 (Arabic). Translated by Moran Levanoni.

The three tenets of the axis of resistance – anti-colonialism, anti-Zionism, and the struggle against dictatorship – become questionable when looking at the Syrian crisis. The argument between Azmi Bishara and Ibrahim Al-Amin sheds a light on the major paradox of exploiting the Palestinian issue and anti-Zionism in the Syrian war. While Bishara, as a genuine Palestinian representative, condemned using his people's misery as an excuse to oppress the Syrians, Al-Amin contradicted him, demanding him to close ranks with the resistance against Israel and colonialism side by side with the Syrian government and against the Syrian opposition forces. This discussion also brings to light the dilemma facing the different Palestinian groups when considering their moves in the brutal Syrian politics and fighting.

8.6 Palestinian al-Quds Brigade in Aleppo, 2013–2015

Due to the intensity of fighting, the Palestinian policy of neutrality in the Syrian crisis, as described by Nabil Bitari in al-Yarmouk camp, could not last long. Hamas soon declared its allegiance to the al-Nusra Front in al-Yarmouk refugee camp, closing ranks with its new patron Qatar. Ahmad Jibril's PFLP-GC took part in the fighting in Aleppo and its agricultural hinterland in the defence of al-Nayrab refugee camp, the second-largest Palestinian camp in Syria.

In mid-2013, as the war over Aleppo became more brutal, a new military structure was assembled by the Syrian government as a way to mobilise the Palestinian groups. The new structure was called the al-Quds Brigade, or *Liwaa Al-Quds*, and consisted of Palestinian fighters affiliated with the PFLP-GC and the government-backed as-Sa'iqa Palestinian group. Most of the men were mobilised from the al-Nayrab and Handarat refugee camps.[27] The brigade was commanded by General Muhammad al-Saeed, who was known for his coordination with the Syrian Air Force intelligence and alleged assassination of seventeen Palestinian soldiers who defected from the government-backed Free Palestinian Army base in Aleppo early in 2012.[28]

Although the al-Quds Brigade was strictly deployed in the Aleppo area, away from the Israeli front lines, and involved in fighting the FSA and al-Nusra Front, it was interesting to see a report on Kana al-ʿAlam,

[27] Amar al-Bakur, 'Who Are "Al-Quds Brigade" and What Are Their Relations with the Palestinians?', *Orient News*, 6 June 2015, www.orient-news.net/ar/news_show/87996 (Arabic). Translated by Moran Levanoni.

[28] Ibid.

a government-backed internet channel, describing the al-Quds Brigade fighters in Aleppo as fighting the rebels, who were painted as the strong arm of Israel within Syria.[29] This approach – framing the fight against the rebels as fighting the Zionists – was used again by Hassan Nasrallah on a televised speech on 15 July 2015,[30] in which he claimed that the way to free Jerusalem was by freeing Syrian Qalamoun, Zabadani, Homs, Aleppo, Daraa, Hasakeh, and Suweida.

8.7 Conclusions

One of the reasons why the Syrian conflict became so complex and difficult was the involvement of different proxy forces with conflicting agendas and affiliations. This chapter discussed the constant struggle between the formal ideology of *Muqawama* and its implementation on the ground through two organisations, Hezbollah and Hamas. Both these organisations are Islamist-affiliated: Hamas is a Sunni organisation linked to the Muslim brotherhood, while Hezbollah is affiliated with radical Shiʾa Islam, linked to and financed by Iran. Despite their different Islamist affiliations, the two are devoted to the Palestinian cause as part of the axis of resistance. Throughout the fighting in Syria, it became clear that the Palestinian issue was an important slogan exploited by all sides to mobilise public opinion and gain solidarity. It became clear that the Palestinian factions themselves faced a dilemma whether to join the Syrian government and the axis of resistance or support the rebels and the Sunni groups against the Syria–Iran–Hezbollah–Shiʾa alliance.

Before the beginning of the conflict in Syria it was clear to which side each group or power was supportive. The Palestinians supported the revolutionary and radical regimes and powers against Israel. Israel was supported by the United States, which also supported the conservative regimes in the Middle East. However, after 2011, when the uprising erupted in the Arab world, alliances became more complicated. Under President Obama, the United States was supportive of the rebels in Egypt and elsewhere. The Iranians were supportive of the rebels in Egypt, Tunisia, and Bahrain at the start but turned against the rebels in Syria

[29] 'Palestinian Brigade Fights Alongside the Syrian Army Against the "Takfiri" groups', *Al-Alam News*, 5 May 2015, www.alalam.ir/news/1700171/بالفيديو ،-لواء-فلسطيني-يقاتل-التكفيريين-الى-جنب-الجيش-السوري؟ (Arabic). Translated by Moran Levanoni.

[30] Karim Traboulsi, 'Hassan Nasrallah: Road to Jerusalem Passes through Syria', *The New Arab*, 13 July 2015, www.alaraby.co.uk/english/politics/2015/7/13/hassan-nasrallah-road-to-jerusalem-passes-through-syria.

when its own interests were at risk. The Russians – great supporters of the Palestinian cause in the past and in fighting against Israel – started intervening in Syria in 2015, bombing rebel forces (FSA, ISIS, the al-Nusra Front, and other groups) as well as civilians. Western coalition forces also bombed ISIS and supported the Kurds. This had the partial effect of assisting the Syrian government, who, in turn, used heavy arms and chemical weapons against areas held by and perceived to be supportive of the rebels.

As mentioned in Bishara's critique, it became difficult for the Syrian government to affirm its legitimacy within the axis of resistance and, at the same time, be assisted by foreign powers against its own people. Moreover, it is complicated for Hamas to explain its cooperation with Qatar considering the American airbases on Qatari soil used against Hamas's old brothers-in-arms in Syria. Hezbollah and Hamas, who used to be partners in the axis of resistance, have now found themselves in opposing camps. The exploitation of the resistance ideology by Hezbollah and Hamas in the Syrian war was used to legitimise the organisations' behaviour and for the benefit of their patrons. As the war in Syria continues, the Palestinians will continue facing the same dilemma of allegiance. It is not unlikely that another change of alignment will occur in the future, with Hamas rejoining the axis of resistance in allegiance with Iran and Hezbollah. Throughout the conflict, the cry for *Muqawama* was a constant, used as a currency by all sides of the struggling powers to gain public support. These politics, however, have made the phrase itself empty of true meaning and left the Palestinians as oppressed and neglected as ever.

9

A Northern Dilemma

Understanding Israel's Actions Facing the Syrian War

NIR T. BOMS

On 21 July 2018, in the dark of night, movement was observed along the Israel–Syria border. The Israel Defence Forces (IDF) had facilitated the evacuation of hundreds of rescue workers known as 'the White Helmets' and their families from an embattled pocket of southern Syria, helping them travel through Israeli-held territory to reach Jordan and, later, refuge in countries such as the United Kingdom, Canada, and Germany.[1] It was the eleventh hour. Syrian government forces were fast approaching, eliminating the rebel resistance within the southern 'de-escalation' zone along the Israeli and Jordanian borders. The military campaign, involving substantial Syrian forces advised and assisted by Russian military and air force personnel in Syria, would soon regain the provinces of Daraa and Quneitra. Israel would soon cease its humanitarian activities on the other side of the border and close its 'Good Neighbours' operation that had commenced two years prior.[2]

This campaign of the Syrian government forces would later be dubbed 'the last campaign of the South'. The Syrian government and its allies used the full scope of their superior military power, ultimately propelling most of the rebel leaders to surrender or flee. Rebel cities such as Busra al-Sham, the surrounding villages to its south, al-Jieza, and locations to the west along the border with Jordan were among the first to comply with 'reconciliation agreements', requiring the surrender of arms and removal of key rebel leaders. Those who contested the deal were evacuated to the opposition stronghold of Idlib in northeastern Syria. In the meantime, according

[1] Ben Hubbard, 'Israel Aids Evacuation from Syria of Hundreds of "White Helmets" and Families', *The New York Times*, 22 July 2018, www.nytimes.com/2018/07/22/world/middleeast/israel-white-helmets-syria.html.

[2] Ari Judah Gross, 'Operation Good Neighbor: Israel Reveals Its Massive Humanitarian Aid to Syria', *The Times of Israel*, 19 July 2017, www.timesofisrael.com/operation-good-neighbor-israels-massive-humanitarian-aid-to-syria-revealed/.

to UN estimates, the battles had pushed more than 320,000 people out of their homes, mainly towards the Israeli and Jordanian borders. For weeks, impromptu camps mushroomed just across from the Israeli border fences, where Syrians sought last possible refuge.[3] By the end of July 2018, most of those would be gone, their residents having evacuated to Idlib or returned to their villages, now under Syrian government control; by 26 July, the Syrian two-star flag was again stationed at the Quneitra crossing.[4]

However, while the Israeli humanitarian chapter appeared to have neared its end, other chapters in Syria's long war were being written. On 10 February 2018, the peaceful Galilee skies in Israel's northern district were lit up by missiles fired from Syria. One hit an Israeli F-16 jet, causing its two pilots to eject.

'Israel clashed with Syrian and Iranian military forces on Saturday in a series of audacious cross-border strikes that could mark a dangerous new phase in Syria's long civil war', wrote the *New York Times*.[5] The escalation had begun on 10 February, when Israel intercepted an Iranian drone entering its airspace from Syria and responded by taking it down. Israel then launched attacks on multiple Iranian targets. These raids reportedly hit at least twelve targets, including three aerial defence batteries and four targets that were part of Iran's military establishment in Syria.[6] They marked Israel's most substantial involvement in Syria to date, signifying an increasing Israeli involvement in parallel to a sequence of events that appeared to signal the end of the Syrian uprising.

A few weeks later, on 9 April 2018, two days after what was reported to be a devastating chemical attack in the Damascus suburb of Douma,[7] Iranian targets in Syria – including an airbase in Palmyra – were again

[3] Bethan McKernan, 'Syria Civil War: More than 320,000 People Flee Fighting in Deraa in "Largest Displacement Yet"', *The Independent*, 6 July 2018, www.independent.co.uk/news/world/middle-east/syria-civil-war-deraa-refugees-evacuation-assad-regime-rebel-fighting-israel-jordan-a8434706.html.

[4] TOI Staff, 'Regime Fighters Raise Syrian Flag at Crossing with Israel', *The Times of Israel*, 26 July 2018, www.timesofisrael.com/regime-fighters-raise-syrian-flag-at-crossing-with-israel/.

[5] 'Israel Strikes Iran in Syria and Loses a Jet', *The New York Times*, 10 February 2018, www.nytimes.com/2018/02/10/world/middleeast/israel-iran-syria.html.

[6] 'Israel Military Targets Iranian Drone and Strikes Syria, F-16 Crashes', *Fox News*, 10 February 2018, www.foxnews.com/world/2018/02/10/israels-military-strikes-syria-downs-iranian-drone.html.

[7] Ben Hubbard, 'Dozens Suffocate in Syria as Government Is Accused of Chemical Attack', *The New York Times*, 8 April 2018, www.nytimes.com/2018/04/08/world/middleeast/syria-chemical-attack-ghouta.html.

attacked.[8] This time, Israel took no responsibility, though the Russian government quickly indicated that their radars had identified Israeli aircraft as being responsible for the attacks. As the extent of damage caused to Iranian assets and personnel in Syria became clearer, the war of words escalated. Iranian Foreign Ministry spokesperson Bahram Ghassemi announced in a press conference that 'Tel Aviv will be punished for its aggressive action'[9] and that 'the occupying Zionist regime will, sooner or later, receive an appropriate response to its actions'.[10] Reports of attacks on Iranian targets in Syria became much more common in the weeks and months that followed, and in September an Israeli military official stated that Israel had struck over 200 Iranian targets in Syria over the past eighteen months.[11]

This chapter examines the Israeli policy formation and evolution during the Syrian war, leading to the current direct Israel–Iran confrontation on Syrian soil. Israeli policy, which initially saw Israel as a 'passive onlooker' and then as a 'good neighbour' and, more recently, as a declared rival against the Iranian presence in Syria, requires explanation. Its organising principle combined humanitarian and military activity: building bridges on the one hand and maximising Israeli interests on the other. In addition, 'humanitarian diplomacy' – the civilian and government assistance provided in the Syrian Golan Heights area – will be explored, as will its role in the efforts to build a set of common interests between Israel and Syrian opposition groups. Finally, this chapter will address the new challenges and opportunities facing Israel in light of the shifting situation across its north-eastern border.

9.1 Israel and the War in Syria

The civil war raging in Syria for the last eight years has altered the regional arena along with Syria itself, which, until 2011, had experienced

[8] Ben Hubbard and David Halbfinger, 'Iran–Israel Conflict Escalates in Shadow of Syrian Civil War', *The New York Times*, 9 April 2018, www.nytimes.com/2018/04/09/world/middleeast/syria-russia-israel-air-base.html.

[9] Natasha Turek, 'Israel "Will Be Punished" for Its Strike on Iranian Drone Base, Tehran Says', *CNBC*, 17 April 2018, www.cnbc.com/2018/04/17/tehran-israel-will-be-punished-for-its-strike-on-iranian-drone-base.html.

[10] Ibid.

[11] Josef Federman, 'The Latest: Israeli Official Confirms 200 Strikes in Syria', *Associated Press*, 4 September 2018, www.washingtonpost.com/world/europe/the-latest-syrian-state-media-report-israeli-airstrikes/2018/09/04/65b68406-b064-11e8-8b53-50116768e499_story.html?utm_term=.60d2fa3113f3.

some four decades of relative stability.[12] Today, despite the renewed strength of the Syrian government, Syria looks less like a state and more like a domestic and regional battleground between a state, non-state actors, and other interested parties that have managed to exploit the uprising against the central government.

The weakening of the central Syrian government and the rise of other actors in its place have posed fresh dilemmas and challenges for Israel. First, the near-collapse of the Syrian state, at various points in the conflict, led to the creation of areas without an effective central government, some of which have been infiltrated by radical Islamic Sunni elements. In areas still under Syrian government control, Iranian-led militias often became effective authorities on the ground.[13] Both elements, while hostile to each other, were united in their hostility to Israel and are subject to the influence of states whose relations with Israel are extremely strained, such as Turkey and Qatar, or antagonistic and volatile, as in the case of Iran. As the Syrian government and its allies advanced, they have pushed radical jihadist actors closer to the Israel–Syria border in the Golan Heights. Clashes between the rival rebel militias and the Syrian military have, intentionally or unintentionally, spilled over periodically into Israeli territory, forcing the IDF to respond, albeit without much enthusiasm. The early months of 2018, which have been marked by significant bolstering of the pro-Syrian government forces under Russian-Iranian auspices, have seen the beginnings of a status quo that presents new challenges for Israel.

9.2 Evolution of Israeli Policy

With the outbreak of the civil war, Israel preferred to view the events in Syria as a domestic issue. Israel chose to look on from the sidelines and avoid taking a position on the events taking place across the border. This policy of being a passive observer was based on the perception that events in northern and central Syria should not have a major influence on Israel's interests. Continued fighting and the fact that hostilities

[12] See, for example, Eyal Zisser, *The Face of Syria: Society, Regime, and State* (Tel Aviv: HaKibutz Hameuhad, 2003) (Hebrew).

[13] Will Fulton, Joseph Holliday, and Sam Wyer, 'Iranian Strategy in Syria', *Institute for the Study of War* (May 2013), www.understandingwar.org/sites/default/files/IranianStrategyinSyria-1MAY.pdf.

'strayed' closer to the Israeli border,[14] as well as neighbouring areas such as Lebanon, compelled Israel to rethink its course. In 2013, then-Defence Minister Moshe Ya'alon stated: '[L]ooking at the civil war in Syria, we spoke and acted from the outset as a party that is not involved and does not get involved unless our interests are harmed. We therefore established "red lines" – the transfer of chemical weapons to Hezbollah, or an encroachment upon our sovereignty.'[15]

As this statement indicated, Israel had set three clear lines that, if crossed, would necessitate a response: first, exploitation of the war to transfer arms, particularly advanced weaponry, to Hezbollah in Lebanon; second, a spillover of the conflict in the direction of Israel; and third, consolidation of radical elements in the border region (which would later focus on the pro-Iranian axis). Officially, Israel has avoided choosing between the two principal alternatives for an end to the conflict. The first favoured a weakened Syrian government over chaos and a potential takeover of rebel groups that are more extreme in their relation to Israel. The second alternative was to support the rebels – or at least some groups with whom Israel can find common ground – as a proxy of sorts against the emerging pro-Iranian 'axis'. In the absence of a clear-cut decision between the two, Israel focused primarily on maintaining security and repelling threats posed by the war in Syria.

This formal non-intervention policy was coupled with low-profile Israeli military activity. Israel took steps to foil the smuggling of strategic weapons by Hezbollah[16] and block the establishment of staging bases by Iran and Hezbollah in the Golan Heights. From 2011 to 2013, as Israel officially continued to weigh the level of intervention required, a number of Israeli aid organisations in the civilian sphere launched a humanitarian effort. They built channels of cooperation with civil society organisations both within Syria and

[14] In August 2012, Syrian rebels succeeded in driving out Syrian army forces from Jubata al-Khashab in the Golan Heights and declared the region's independence. In February 2013, the first military council was established in the Golan area, and in March of that year the IDF found itself responding to the Syrian army after IDF soldiers were fired on at the Golan border.

[15] Moshe David Ahikam, 'Ya'alon: Inaction in Syria also Has Ramifications for Us', *NRG*, 8 September 2013, www.makorrishon.co.il/nrg/online/1/ART2/505/424.html.

[16] 'Israel Claims to Have "Blocked WMD Smuggling to Hezbollah" After Alleged Strike on Damascus Airbase', *Russia Today*, 8 December 2016, www.rt.com/news/369593-israel-syria-hezbollah-weapons/.

beyond its borders. In 2014, having observed the process, the Israeli government began to follow suit.

9.2.1 *The Civilian–Humanitarian Dimension*

Between 2011 and 2013, concurrent with the Israeli government's hesitation and its policy of acting as a passive observer, Israeli civil society spearheaded an effort to stake out a clearer position by taking humanitarian action that gradually received more formal, official recognition. A number of Israeli groups have taken part in this work, which has resulted in the transfer of over 50,000 tons of supplies between 2013 and 2018.[17] On the whole, Israeli society seems to have enlisted in the 'Syrian effort', with no fewer than ten different organisations taking part;[18] tens of thousands of Israelis have also participated in several public campaigns on behalf of this undertaking. These efforts included, but are not limited to, Israeli assistance to a professional team in refugee camps in Jordan; food distribution inside Syria (itself in an unprecedented collaboration between Israeli and Syrian NGOs); Israeli involvement in the rescue of Syrian refugees on the Greek coast; the establishment of an Israeli field hospital for treating Syrian refugees in Europe; mass mobilisation to collect food and winter clothing, with the participation of the Council of Youth Movements in Israel; distribution of food and emergency equipment in refugee camps in Jordan;[19] the establishment and management of a school for Syrian refugees at the Greek island of Lesbos;[20] and the treatment of wounded Syrians through an Israeli civilian channel. Beyond this, Israeli assistance has focused on the Syrian Golan, quickly joining forces with the 'official' Israeli government effort to tend to the needs of the population on the other side of the border.

[17] This is an estimate by the author based on numbers provided by the IDF and interviews with the organisations cited in this chapter.

[18] The Israeli organisations include Israel Flying Aid; Save a Child's Heart; IsraAID – the Israel Forum for International Humanitarian Aid; the Task Division of the Kibbutz Movement; Multi-Faith Alliance for Syrian Refugees/Jewish Coalition for Syrian Refugees; Hand in Hand with the Syrian Refugees; Jewish–Arab Committee for Humanitarian Aid to the Syrian People; NATAN – International Humanitarian Aid; the Amaliah organisation; Syrians on the Fence; and the Council of Youth Movements in Israel.

[19] Nir T. Boms, 'Israel's Policy on the Syrian Civil War: Risks and Opportunities', *Israel Journal of Foreign Affairs* 11, no. 3 (2018): 327.

[20] Maecus Sheff, 'The Beginnings of Hope in Lesbos', *The Times of Israel*, 27 August 2018, https://blogs.timesofisrael.com/the-beginnings-of-hope-in-lesbos/.

This activity took place in a number of places, including Jordan, Turkey, Europe (along the refugee routes in Greece, Macedonia, and Slovakia), and of course, Syria itself, with a special emphasis on the Golan Heights. Gradually, in parallel with the start of the IDF's humanitarian effort in February 2013, the civilian relief efforts became better synchronised with the official ones. That was needed, for example, when it was necessary to open the border in the Golan Heights or when coordination was required due to the sensitivity of the cooperation with Syrian bodies. Israel, which was still at the deliberation stage, seems to have been more comfortable leaving some of the involvement in this area to civilian groups while keeping an eye open for the hidden opportunities offered by these channels.

Extending Israeli assistance to refugees or the embattled population of Syria is not a simple process that can be carried out without coordination with Syrian counterparts. The difficulties in implementing such initiatives are intensified by the absence of any diplomatic relationship between Israel and Syria. Yet, the scope of the relief work can itself indicate the depth of the relationships developed using these channels.[21] This policy of 'humanitarian diplomacy' has helped overcome the element of fear and forge a path towards Israel's neighbours across the border.

9.2.2 *Shaping Israeli Policy in Syria and Establishment of the Good Neighbours Programme*

Alongside the civilian channels, Israel operates an official humanitarian assistance programme. This arrangement began on 16 February 2013[22] as a local initiative of an IDF commander who gathered a group of seven injured Syrians from the border zone and transferred them to the hospital in Safed. This initiative, which was initially not coordinated beyond the IDF circles, later became policy. The IDF would soon establish a field hospital in the Golan Heights to treat wounded Syrians, transporting the more seriously injured to hospitals inside Israel. Over time, this initiative was institutionalised, with over 5,000 Syrian men, women, and children receiving medical treatment in Israeli hospitals and with more than 200 humanitarian missions carried out. The IDF formed a unit dedicated to operating in the Syrian border zone, through which collaboration with Israeli civilian organisations began. Here, too, it seems that two sets of interests came together:

[21] The author has studied many of these engagements and has actively participated in them.

[22] See testimony of Dr Alejandro Rosenthal, treating physician, Médecins Sans Frontières, *Yisrael Hayom*, 28 September 2017, www.israelhayom.co.il/article/506757 (Hebrew).

the humanitarian and the operational. Ongoing events in the southern Syrian border area have helped highlight these common interests.

9.3 The Nearing of the War to the Israeli Border

In 2013, fighting in Syria continued to move closer to Israel's border. After Israeli soldiers were fired upon while patrolling the border in March of that year,[23] the IDF responded for the first time by launching a missile in the direction of a Syrian military position in the Syrian Golan. Later that year, the Syrian army began to withdraw, leaving a vacuum that was quickly filled with various rebel forces. At the end of the year, IDF Division 210 was formed – a new regional unit charged with blocking incursions from the Syrian side of the 1974 disengagement line.[24] In 2014, the situation escalated, with an attack by the al-Nusra Front on United Nations Disengagement Observer Force (UNDOF) soldiers stationed in the Syrian Golan Heights, during which forty-seven soldiers were taken hostage.[25] In July of that year, the Quneitra border crossing was occupied by al-Nusra forces. In September 2014, Israel shot down a Syrian plane that had crossed into its airspace. In January 2015, Israel struck a convoy in Syria, killing General Mohammad Ali Allahdadi, a high-ranking commander in Iran's Revolutionary Guard, along with six other officers and fighters. In June, Israel contended with the threat of a lynching when an IDF ambulance carrying wounded Syrians was attacked by Druze residents of the Israeli town of Majdal Shams.[26] In late 2015, an Israeli attack assassinated Samir Quntar, the Fatah activist and senior Hezbollah commander in the Syrian Golan.[27] As 2016

[23] Reuters, 'Israel Fires into Syria and Destroys Machine-Gun Position in Golan Heights that Had Been Targeting Border Patrolmen', *New York Daily News*, 24 March 2013, www.nydailynews.com/news/world/israel-fires-syria-destroys-machine-gun-position-golan-heights-article-1.1297766.

[24] 'Gantz Decided to Establish a New Regional Division in the Golan to Block Terrorist Incursions from Syria', *Haaretz*, 10 July 2013, www.haaretz.co.il/news/politics/.premium-1.2068105 (Hebrew).

[25] Colin Freeman, '47 UN Peacekeepers Abducted by al-Qaeda Linked Syrian Rebels', *The Telegraph*, 28 August 2014, www.telegraph.co.uk/news/worldnews/middleeast/syria/11061515/47-UN-peacekeepers-abducted-by-al-Qaeda-linked-Syrian-rebels.html.

[26] Hassan Shaalan, 'Wounded Syrian Killed when Druze Lynch Mob Attacks IDF Ambulance', *Ynet News*, 23 June 2015, www.ynetnews.com/articles/0,7340,L-4671371,00.html.

[27] Anne Barnard and Diaa Hadid, 'Commander of Hezbollah Freed by Israel Is Killed in Syria', *The New York Times*, 20 December 2015, www.nytimes.com/2015/12/21/world/middleeast/samir-kuntar-hezbollah-syria-israel.html.

dawned, the IDF continued to respond to spillover attacks of mortar shells landing in the Golan Heights, along with fighting between rival Syrian factions that continued to draw closer to Israel's border – this time, also under Russia's aegis. However, Israel was now caught less off guard, in part as a result of the relationship established with some of the rebel actors on the other side of the border.

The contact with the rebels on the Syrian side began in order to create channels of communication and improved as greater familiarity was built with local actors operating in the Golan Heights, on the basis of a shared interest in weakening radical Islamic elements, Hezbollah fighters, and the Iranian al-Quds force in the area. These contacts and the experience accumulated in the Golan area led to greater understanding of the importance of the relationship that had begun to develop with the Syrian civilian population and the rebel forces fighting in southern Syria.

The significance of these ties was also reflected in the creation of the Good Neighbours Administration, a military command that specialises in relations with the civilian population and in coordinating the various relief efforts, including civilian.[28] The establishment of the unit in May 2016 can be seen as a further step in recognising the need to integrate the efforts on the northern border, to coordinate civilian and military actions, and to publicise at least some of the work in order to mobilise international support. This last channel began to develop in earnest over the course of 2017: collaborative partnerships were established with several international organisations, including Syrian NGOs, which began cooperating with Israel in transferring aid across the border. This aspect, which included cooperation with Christian, Muslim, and Syrian organisations, is particularly significant in terms of its diplomatic ramifications.

9.4 Across the Border: The Syrian Actors along the Israeli Border

The actors operating in southern Syria include proxy militias, local (armed and non-armed) groups, and Druze. These groups have different ideologies, ethnic affiliations, and sources of financing and influence. At times, villages or militias also switch organisational affiliations and loyalties based on pragmatic and local considerations and shifting balances of

[28] 'At Syrian Border, IDF Seeks Closer Contact with Civilians on Other Side', *The Times of Israel*, 29 May 2016, www.timesofisrael.com/on-syrian-border-idf-sets-up-unit-that-will-work-with-syrian-civilians.

power on the ground. These balances have continued to shift as the fighting approached the southern front and radical groups such as the al-Nusra Front – considered an offshoot of al-Qaeda (but also a group with which Israel maintained a certain degree of communication) – became further entrenched.[29] Potential partners of Israel on the Syrian side shared certain objectives and interests, at times even similar liberal values, and, above all, common enemies. On the southern border, the groups that fit this description were primarily those affiliated with the circle of the Free Syrian Army (FSA), along with a number of independent local armed groups, which take a more moderate/pragmatic line.

The interaction between the FSA and Israel has been influenced by diverse geopolitical factors. In early 2014, the FSA announced the establishment of the Southern Front, which stretched from the Jordanian border through Damascus to the Golan Heights, with some 20,000 fighters[30] deployed in fifty-four rebel groups. In their operations, the groups were only partially coordinated, making it difficult to work with them due to the many different channels. In August of that year, the FSA's Southern Front, alongside al-Nusra, seized most of the Israel–Syria border in the Golan, though it lost some of this territory in 2016 as a result of increased Russian intervention.[31] The Southern Front was considered a moderate player and a partner of the United States and its allies in the fight against the Salafi-Jihadi forces such as the Khalid ibn-Walid Army,[32] a radical Muslim militia that declared its allegiance to ISIS

[29] There have been numerous reports of Israeli contact with, and even aid to, the al-Nusra Front. Israel's alleged cooperation with this group has been raised in several reports and, inter alia, in the public accusations by Israeli MK Akram Hasson. See Jack Khoury, Amos Harel, and Gili Cohen, 'Israel Is Helping Jabhat al-Nusra To Attack Druze in Syria', *Haaretz*, 11 September 2016, www.haaretz.co.il/news/politics/.premium-1.3065151 (Hebrew). Al-Nusra severed its ties with al-Qaeda in July 2016.

[30] Estimates differ as to the number of fighters affiliated with the Southern Front. See 'Free Syrian Army Factions of the Southern Front Unite their Forces Against the Regime and Extremists', *RFS Media Office*, 11 May 2016, http://rfsmediaoffice.com/en/2014/12/13/free-syrian-army-factions-of-the-southern-front-unite-their-forces-against-the-regime-and-extremists/#.V_YRdYVOKM8, which estimates 'nearly 35 thousand fighters'. Alternatively, see Mona Alami, 'What's Keeping Syria's Rebel Forces from Consolidating Power?', *Al-Monitor*, 26 September 2016, www.al-monitor.com/pulse/originals/2016/09/syria-north-south-opposition-groups.html, which estimates 20,000.

[31] 'The Rebels Control the Entire Border Crossing to Occupied Golan', *Syrian National Coalition*, 27 August 2014 (Arabic).

[32] International Crisis Group, 'New Approach in Southern Syria', *Middle East and North Africa*, Report No. 163 (2 September 2015), www.crisisgroup.org/~/media/Files/Middle%20East%20North%20Africa/Iraq%20Syria%20Lebanon/Syria/163-new-approach-in-southern-syria.pdf; Haid, 'The Southern Front: Allies Without a Strategy', *Heinrich Böll*

in 2015 and conquered territory at the meeting point of the borders of Syria, Jordan, and Israel on the banks of the Yarmouk River. To counter the fear that international aid to the Southern Front will bolster radical elements, and to elicit greater support from the international community and enlist its help in promoting political moves to solve the crisis in Syria, several of the groups that make up the Southern Front have announced the severing of all ties with al-Nusra in April 2015.[33]

The Druze community makes up roughly 4 per cent of the Syrian population or 700,000 members. Israel and the Syrian Druze have a long history of contact, beginning in the 1930s with intelligence cooperation following the Great Arab Revolt, continuing through the 1950s, and reaching its peak in a programme conceived by Israeli Minister Yigal Alon following the Six-Day War to extend Israeli control from the Druze villages in the Golan Heights to Jabal al-Druze.[34] Nevertheless, loyal to a minority strategy and to the land they live on, the Syrian Druze have maintained their loyalty to the Syrian establishment and have generally been hostile towards Israel. Throughout the Syrian civil war, the Druze have continued to depend on and cooperate with the Syrian government, though increasing numbers (particularly in the al-Suwayda governorate) have chosen to avoid serving in the Syrian army or, alternatively, have refused to participate in the fighting units outside their areas of residence.

A smaller Druze community, numbering about 26,000, lives on the Israeli side of the Golan Heights and under Israeli control. Unlike the Druze community in the Israeli Galilee, most of the former Syrian Druze in the Israeli Golan had also maintained loyalty to the Syrian government, though that loyalty has weakened as the war progressed.[35] The perception that Assad's government was unlikely to survive, and may well lose influence in Syria (mainly in the beginning of the war, up to 2014), led some Druze in Syria (and the Israeli Golan Heights) to call for a reckoning and a change in approach. This has extended to the establishment of

Stiftung, 21 August 2015, www.lb.boell.org/en/2015/08/21/southern-front-allies-without-strategy.

33 Maysara al-Zoubi, 'The Free Army in Daraa: Ousting al-Nusra Is a Patriotic Decision that Will Serve the Revolution', *Kuluna Shurakaa*, 15 April 2015, www.all4syria.info/Archive/207246 (Arabic).

34 Yossi Alpher, *Periphery: Israel's Search for Middle East Allies* (Lanham, MD: Rowman & Littlefield, 2015), 45.

35 Etta Prince-Gibson, 'Druze in the Golan Heights Have Long Been "on the Fence" between Syria and Israel. Syria's Civil War Has Changed Things', *PRI*, 16 November 2017, www.pri.org/stories/2017-11-16/druze-golan-heights-have-long-been-fence-between-syria-and-israel-syrias-civil.

a militia opposed to the Syrian government, known as Rijal al-Karama (or 'Men of Honour'). Israel has also allowed its own Druze community to participate in the humanitarian effort and support their relatives across the border. Taken together, these factors began to create a new dynamic in relations between the Syrian Druze and Israel. However, once it became clear that Assad will not lose power, these new relationships weakened, and the Druze became more focused on restoring the old arrangements that allowed for a certain degree of contacts and visits between the Syrian Druze and their relatives in the Israeli Golan.[36]

An additional aspect of the relationship between Israel and southern Syria touches on one of the potential scenarios regarding the division of Syria.[37] Representatives of several local armed groups united in the latter half of 2014 in an attempt to promote a plan (with the help of members of the exiled Syrian opposition) to establish an autonomous 'safe zone' in southern Syria, with regional and international backing, that would prevent a takeover of the area by hostile groups, whether Shia or Salafi.

The international community, led by the UN, was asked by some of the stakeholders to guarantee security arrangements that would include enforcing a no-fly zone over southern Syria and the demarcation of a 25-kilometre-wide security zone that would extend along Syria's borders with Israel, Lebanon, and Jordan. The plan received a partial boost from the Astana Initiative,[38] which included southern Syria as a 'de-escalation zone'. The Astana Initiative called for the turning of Syria's southern region into the first link in a secure and thriving new Syrian entity that would serve as a model to be gradually expanded to other areas. Implementation of the proposal would require three stages:

- short term: mobilising international financial and humanitarian assistance organisations, making it possible to provide food, clothing, medicine, tents, and gas;
- medium term: setting up field hospitals, courts, schools, and a police force; and

36 Sana, 'Syrians in Cccupied Golan Call for Exerting Pressure on Israel to Open Quneitra Crossing', *Syrian News Agency*, 24 September 2018, https://sana.sy/en/?p=147504.

37 The notion of the partition/federalisation of Syria is echoed in the Syrian Kurds' identification with the independence referendum in Iraq's Kurdish region and in the establishment of Kurdistan also in northern Syria.

38 The documents are on file with the authors of the original article: 'Project for a Safe Zone in Syria', SAP (Safe Area Project).

- long term: promoting regional cooperative ventures, including Syrian-Israeli collaboration in the fields of technology and water.

Among the initiatives proposed was the formation of a body called the 'Sons of the Golan', led by Syrian exiles in Europe, to appeal for international and Israeli assistance in establishing an IDP/refugee camp in the demilitarised zone on the Israel–Syria border.[39]

9.5 A New Status Quo: Challenges for Israel

Overall, 2017 was marked by a tipping of the scales towards the pro-Syrian government axis, which succeeded in exploiting the exhaustion of Assad's opponents, internal rivalries, and the international community's focus on the battles against ISIS, which consequently began to retreat in both Syria and Iraq. The Syrian army, with Russian and Iranian support, developed a *Sulha* strategy of forced 'reconciliation agreements' that helped further demilitarise rebel strongholds and pushed some of the fighters – at times, under duress – to join pro-government militias.

The ceasefire declared in southern Syria, which took effect in July 2017, is the result of political coordination achieved through direct talks between the United States and Russia and finalised between Russian President Vladimir Putin and US President Donald Trump at their meeting earlier that month. This process took place concurrently with negotiations initiated by Russia in Astana, the capital of Kazakhstan, with the active involvement of Iran and Turkey, with which Russia also reached agreements on their respective spheres of influence in Syria. 'De-escalation zones' were proposed throughout Syria, including the southern region and the provinces of Daraa and Quneitra. According to the Russian plan, they will become safe zones for refugees from combat areas and will serve as the basis for a political settlement in Syria that will bring the civil war to an end.[40]

The Astana process; the Russian–American–Jordanian negotiations; and, concurrently, the Russian–Iranian–Turkish talks have led to a series

[39] See 'Syrian Opposition Members Prepare a Peace Initiative with Israel', *Al Arab Al Yawm*, 27 July 2017 (Arabic), and the response at the conference of the Members of Free Golan (apparently financed by Azmi Bishara), who are opposed to the Golan Peace initiative: *Rabi' al-Thawra*, 6 August 2017 (Arabic), www.arabstoday.net/37/112430-معارضون-سوريون-من-الجولان-يمهدون-لمبادرة-سلام-مع-إسرائيل.

[40] Ron Ben-Yishai, 'Concern in Light of Ceasefire: Iran Will Continue to Move Forward on a Land Corridor to Lebanon', *Ynet*, 9 July 2017, www.ynet.co.il/articles/0,7340,L-4986376,00.html (Hebrew).

of agreements and understandings, the bulk of which have not been revealed, which are intended to create a new status quo in Syria in general and on its southern border in particular. Israel – as well as Jordan – has a clear interest in keeping hostile forces away from its border, including pro-Iranian militias, Hezbollah forces, and Salafi-Jihadi fighters. Various reports have claimed that the Russians and Americans will support a zone of up to 40 kilometres from Israel's border in which Iranian activity will be prohibited.[41] However it is unclear what form these areas will take, especially since reports, such as those published by London's *Asharq al-Awsat*,[42] claim that the American agreements are limited to 8 kilometres from the border, after which the United States will accept the presence of pro-Iranian forces and militias.[43]

Meanwhile, on the ground, it appears that the Iranians, like the Syrian government forces, are choosing to ignore the series of agreements. The closing months of 2017 saw an increase in attacks on the Quneitra and Hermon region under the watchful eyes of the Russians, who deployed their troops and have also been seen in southern Syria and the Quneitra region.[44] Israel's concerns were also reflected in the widely covered meeting between Prime Minister Benjamin Netanyahu and President Putin in late August 2017, in Netanyahu's statement that Iran 'is spreading across the Middle East, in every place from which Daesh [ISIS] retreats', and his statement that Iranian weapons-manufacturing facilities, including a factory for medium-range missiles, are being established in Syria and Lebanon.[45]

Simultaneously but separately, the ties and cooperative efforts have intensified in the Syrian portion of the Golan Heights. Syrian and international organisations have begun taking advantage of the new opportunities opening up unfolding in the Golan to transfer medical and humanitarian

41 'Tripartite Agreement to Support Ceasefire in Southern Syria', *Al Jazeera*, 7 July 2017, www.aljazeera.net/news/arabic/2017/7/7/اتفاق-ثلاثي-لمساندة-وقف-إطلاق-النار-جنوبي-سوريا (Arabic).

42 'Ceasefire in the South on Eve of Astana Meeting', *Asharq al-Awsat*, 4 July 2017, https://aawsat.com/home/article/966196/هدنة-في-الجنوب-عشية-«أستانة» (Arabic).

43 Andrew Illingworth, 'US Will Allow Iranian Forces in Syria to Operate within 8 km of Israel', *AMN*, 1 September 2017, www.almasdarnews.com/article/us-will-allow-iranian-forces-syria-operate-within-8-km-israel/.

44 'Russian Delegation to Border Town between Syria and Israel', *Sputnik News*, 5 March 2017, www.rabic.sputniknews.com/russia/201703051022638756وفد-روسيا-سوريا-اسرائيل-القنيطرة/ (Arabic).

45 Itamar Eichner and Yael Freidson, 'Netanyahu to UN Secretary-General: "We Will Not Allow a Noose; Iran Is Building Precision-Guided Missile Sites Also in Syria"', *Ynet*, 28 August 2017, www.ynet.co.il/articles/0,7340,L-5008625,00.html (Hebrew).

assistance across the border and to a number of clinics, small hospitals, and refugee camps located in the area. Furthermore, the consolidation of the Syrian government and the weakening of the rebel camp have led some rebel factions in the Golan to unite, something that enabled a more orderly engagement with Israel in 2017 and 2018 as the Syrian war neared its end.

9.6 Who Cares about a Bird? Opportunities in Southern Syria

On 5 September 2017, an Israeli NGO activist involved in the dialogue with the Syrian opposition received a text message. A rare vulture with a marking in Hebrew was found injured in Syria and was picked up by a local militia commander. Luckily for the bird, the commander was both a wildlife enthusiast and aware of the transborder relationship. He reported the presence of the wounded bird and was quickly put through to the director of the Gamla Nature Reserve of the Israel Nature and Parks Authority to receive instructions on its care. The militants in Syria were told by the commander to 'get two turkeys a day for the vulture, and bring them alive. [The fighters] ... had been eating bread and water for weeks, but the vulture got meat.'[46] The vulture returned home safely after coordinating the transfer route with three other militias, and those involved recount that it was actually this large bird that managed to bring about a rare instance of cooperation between the warring sides.

Moving stories such as this have emerged in recent years. It is estimated that more than 300,000 Syrians were cared for by the Israeli humanitarian and medical assistance that, at its peaks, supported fifteen clinics and hospitals in Syria.[47] The partnership with allies across the border has enabled, for example, the departure of Jews left in Syria as well as the return of Jewish artefacts and ritual objects to the Syrian Jewish community outside the country.[48] Perhaps of greater interest are the various pieces of information – not only about birds – that were passed to the other side in timely fashion.

[46] Testimony of Gal Lusky, who coordinated the transfer of the vulture following a conversation with the author. See also 'How an Injured Israeli Vulture Returned from Syria', *Channel 2 News*, 7 September 2017, www.mako.co.il/news-military/israel-q3_2017/Article-2a0c4e75c9d5e51004.htm (Hebrew).

[47] Based on field work and interview made by author.

[48] 'After 68 Years, a Syrian Great-Grandmother Comes Home ... to Her Jewish Family in Israel', *The Times of Israel*, 11 December 2015, www.timesofisrael.com/after-68-years-a-syrian-great-grandmother-comes-home-to-her-jewish-family-in-israel/.

Israel – while still asserting that it is not taking sides in the conflict and that it is focused solely on protecting its own citizens and on offering humanitarian aid – has intensified its activities to block the transfer of arms or facilities that could serve the Hezbollah–Iran axis. Israel's interest in keeping these elements, seen as a serious threat, at a distance is clear – but less clear was its declared policy of ambiguity and non-intervention. Moreover, reports – such as a series of articles claiming that Israel is supplying weapons to radical groups on the Golan Heights, backed by photos of crates of ammunition stamped with Hebrew writing[49] – do not assist in clarifying Israel's position; nor does Israel's perceived lack of response as the Syrian army and Hezbollah draw closer to the Israeli border following the fall of the Bet Jann pocket. The fall of this small enclave, which has been aided by Israel for years, posed the first major test for Israel, which has preferred not to cross the line of intervention and not to offer more significant operational assistance so as to halt the Syrian army and Iranian militias. Unfortunately, this episode began to shift the balance of power in the Golan Heights.

All of this indicates something about the Israeli policy in the Syrian south: on the one hand, it is a tactical/humanitarian opportunity that focused on local needs; on the other, it was operational cooperation that begun to signal a different discourse – one of acceptance and partnership, as well as a possible long-term alliance with groups unwilling to accept the Syrian government and its supporters or the radical Islamic axis. The relations on the ground had helped create a broader network of relations between Israelis and Syrians and had found expression in articles, interviews, and public calls of Syrians for recognition of, and cooperation with, Israel. This sentiment has also been reflected in (overt and covert) visits by Syrians to Israel, aimed at creating additional channels of dialogue and cooperation. The notion that Syrian organisations would, surprisingly, be significant partners to the Israeli humanitarian effort was not a given one, and it suggested a new depth of the relations between the two sides. However, the concluding chapter of this new broader dynamic – the Syrian government takeover of the Golan Heights under what was perceived as Israeli approval under the auspices of a Russian

[49] 'Syria Shows Evidence that Western Weapons End Up in Terrorist Hands', *Al-Masdar News*, 10 October 2017, www.almasdarnews.com/article/syria-shows-evidence-western-weapons-end-terrorist-hands.

deal – was seen by some Syrians as an Israeli betrayal which again changed some of these dynamics, as the Syrian government regained complete control of the Syrian south in July 2018.

9.7 Conclusion: A Changing Border Reality

As we begin to examine in retrospect the eight years of war – which extracted a devastating toll of lives, displaced an almost endless stream of refugees, and brought radical groups directly to the Israeli border – Israel's policy score appears to be relatively high. Israel's northern border in the Golan Heights has remained relatively calm throughout the entire period. Despite the presence of Hezbollah, the al-Nusra Front, Iran, ISIS, and other hostile actors, there has been little spillover of the conflict into Israel, and it appears that the IDF has managed to contain the conflict away from the Israeli border while implementing its red lines without significant difficulties or concentration of troops. Russia, the main power broker in Syria, maintained close consultation with Israel throughout the entire period, and Israel became one of the players able to maintain good relations with both the Americans and the Russians, who together helped Israel keep the Iranian elements farther from its border. These results, achieved partially due to the relationships formed inside Syria and the establishment of the 'Good Neighbours' unit, are all indications of the relative success of the Israeli measures. However, that relative success is still limited as Israel looks at the new reality emerging across its border. The emerging threat lies in the creation of a new status quo that cements a much broader and deeper Iranian presence in Syria, coupled with a border that constitutes a front, with Hezbollah forces and pro-Iranian militias, second-circle Iranian bases, and radical Sunni groups still deployed on the other side. The Russian foreign minister's declaration that 'Iran and Hezbollah are allowed to operate in Syria'[50] stands in contrast to reported agreements between Israel, Jordan, and Russia, which set a range of 85 kilometres[51] from Israel's border as being the zone in which Iranian forces will not be allowed to operate. As recent reports indicate, pro-Iranian forces

[50] Leith Fadel, 'Hezbollah, Iran Are Allowed to Operate in Syria: Russian FM', *Al-Masdar News*, 12 September 2017, www.almasdarnews.com/article/hezbollah-iran-allowed-operate-syria-russian-fm/.

[51] Alexey Khlebnikov, 'Can Russia Limit Iran's Influence in Syria?', *Middle East Eye*, 24 July 2018, www.middleeasteye.net/columns/can-russia-limit-iran-s-influence-syria-453630430.

continue to operate despite the declared agreements, often under the cover of the Syrian army or related forces. As the Syrian uprising seemingly comes to a close, another chapter – potentially much more dangerous to Israel – appears to begin involving a direct confrontation with Iran on Syrian soil.

10

The Spillover Effects of the Syrian Civil War

Regional Ramifications for Refugees

JOEL D. PARKER

10.1 Introduction

A few days after Barack Obama was re-elected in 2012, Thomas Friedman wrote a provocative opinion piece in the *New York Times* directed at the president, predicting that the Syrian civil war could explode outwards, effectively destabilising almost every country in the Middle East.[1] Friedman argued that, due to the artificial borders and the transnational identities of the main ethno-religious communities in Syria, the entire political order of the region would collapse without ongoing US military presence. While the United States eventually became ensconced in northern Syria following the multinational effort to defeat ISIS, the collapse of regional central governments has yet to occur. Nevertheless, the results of the Syrian uprising and its suppression have been devastating. The primary cost has been human loss of life (at least half a million dead) and the displacement of half of Syria's 22 million people by the end of 2017, with some 6 million Syrians having fled the country altogether, mostly to surrounding countries.[2] Thanks to several stop-gap efforts pulled together by aid agencies and the UN, as well as donor nations and mostly sympathetic host governments, Syrian refugees have been able to survive and usually find food, shelter, and basic medical care.[3]

[1] Thomas L. Friedman, 'Obama's Nightmare', *The New York Times*, 14 November 2012, https://www.nytimes.com/2012/11/14/opinion/friedman-obamas-nightmare.html.

[2] Throughout this article, most of the large figures on the Syrian displaced people crisis are provided by and updated regularly by UNHCR: The UN Refugee Agency, www.unhcr.org/syria-emergency.html.

[3] Of course, this does not mean to downplay situations where displaced Syrians did not find refuge, as with recent reports of Syrians freezing to death trying to get into Lebanon or the many reports of those who died or were raped while fleeing from the conflict. This is also

However, the aid agencies have had chronic funding shortages from the beginning, which only worsen as war fatigue sets in among the international communities. Furthermore, host governments are under pressure after repeated promises that the Syrian conflict would end and the refugees would soon pack up and leave.

Statistical analysis of civil wars that produce refugees has, moreover, suggested that the spillover effect, aside from the terrible cost to those who flee and the direct impact on host communities, makes violent conflict in the host countries much more likely.[4] This chapter surveys some of what is known about the situation of Syrians outside of Syria who have stayed in the region and argues that, considering the dangers posed by concentrations of impoverished refugees, the international community should take a proactive and pragmatic approach that encourages host countries to absorb Syrians into their sociopolitical systems as much as possible to avoid leaving them in limbo for the undetermined future. In fact, the present chaotic situation, with ongoing instability and violence in Syria, raises larger questions about community cohesion and the longevity of Syrian national identity. Will the present wave of Syrians who were dispersed and displaced since 2011 maintain close social ties to those who remained in the territory of Syria over the long term, or will they perhaps evolve into self-contained communities of Syrian refugees who have no plans to return to Syria?

10.2 The Syrian War and Its Regional Surroundings

The transition from *duyuf* (guests), as they were called by regional governments in the early phase of the civil war, to *laji'in* (refugees) took place over a few years, and a challenge remains for political leaders in Turkey, Jordan, Lebanon, Iraq, and Egypt to determine who can and will return to Syria while admitting that at least some cannot or will not ever return. The challenge of working out the legal details of who stays, who goes, and who should be cared for by international aid organisations requires an enormous amount of macro data which, so far, is concentrated in the hands of the United Nations High Commission for Refugees (UNHCR) and its

not to downplay the trauma of losing a certain quality of life – going from a real house to living in a tent is certainly a shock to some people that can have a long-lasting effect. Nevertheless, in the big picture, the pathways out of the Syrian conflict have often been less treacherous than those faced by Armenians in World War I or by other groups fleeing their homes elsewhere.

4 Idean Salehyan and Kristian Skrede Gleditsch, 'Refugees and the Spread of Civil War', *International Organization* 60, no. 2 (Spring 2006): 335–66.

affiliates. This presents methodological problems, as even they admit, and, in the experience of the United Nations Relief and Works Agency for Palestine Refugees (UNRWA), the numbers of those officially registered can have wide discrepancies when other local and international governmental organisations begin to examine them. In short, counting the Syrian refugees is a challenge that will most likely remain beyond the ability of any individual scholar, lawyer, activist, or academic to meet alone.

On the micro level, there are as many stories of individual refugees and their families as there are refugees, only a few of which have been recorded. Individual testimonies, such as those collected by Wendy Pearlman,[5] have described in detail the urban violence that has characterised the failed civil rebellion and the resulting brutal crackdown by a regime bent on staying in power. As the uprising spread, wide-scale arrests, torture, and assassinations pushed rebels to choose: fight or flight. The Assad regime has used tactics from barrel bombings to chemical attacks, as well as the use of phosphorous and cluster ammunitions, all of which, in addition to killing and maiming, have forced civilians to flee.[6] It is possible that these crude weapons of war were used to cause the civilians to flee urban areas so the regime could attack militants unimpeded. In addition, the various countries involved in uprooting ISIS from 2014 to 2017 also caused a high number of civilian casualties, which no doubt added to the number of civilians fleeing Syria.

For many Syrians the nightmare continues, as mass displacement, siege, and ongoing air strikes belie the propaganda of the regime portraying it as a liberator, freeing the people from 'terrorists'. Lebanon, Turkey, and Jordan have borne the brunt of the refugee crisis, though a significant number of Syrians who were dispersed fled to Iraq and Egypt as well. The full extent of the destruction, death, and mass exodus of people, suffering from physical and psychological traumas resulting from the Syrian conflict, and their impact on the future of the Middle East is impossible to measure in its totality. Young Syrians, for instance, in addition to having lost limbs and loved ones and suffering the long-lasting effects of being uprooted from their place of birth, have often missed whole years of education; conversely, they have learned more than one should ever know about the depths of violence that humanity can experience.

In addition to the millions of internally displaced persons (IDPs) and the regional Syrian refugee crisis, at least 1 million Syrian asylum seekers have

[5] Wendy Pearlman, *We Crossed a Bridge and It Trembled* (New York: Custom House, 2017).

[6] See Chapters 5 and 6 of this volume.

found their way to Europe, with Germany and Sweden leading substantially in the effort to host them.[7] This has led to an intense political debate within Europe,[8] not to mention the deaths of hundreds of Syrians and other migrants in transit through the Mediterranean Sea attempting to reach asylum.[9] Of the Middle Eastern states with significant numbers of Syrian refugees, only Jordan has completely avoided deep political upheaval. Turkey's President Erdoğan was threatened by a military coup in 2015 and has since significantly tightened the reins on his control of the political system and the press. Iraq, likewise, survived the Syrian civil war – but not without significant losses to ISIS, which was only defeated with Iranian involvement in creating Shi'a militias and the heavy militarisation of the Kurdish Regional Government (KRG). Though plans for a Kurdish breakaway state are on hold, the situation could easily change in the coming years. In Lebanon, while the state appears to have stabilised with a unity government that includes Saʿad al-Hariri, it went from April 2014 to October 2016 without choosing a president. Hezbollah, which has a political wing in government and a military wing deeply involved in the Syrian conflict, has increased its influence in Lebanon and wants Syrian refugees to leave. However, the outlook has changed since 2012–2013, when it appeared that Lebanon was going to become a secondary arena for violence and that the Jordanian monarchy was not going to be able to withstand the pressure of so many refugees. Since 2013, the overall state stability in Lebanon and Jordan and Egypt has improved; however, the actual situation of refugees in Egypt and in Lebanon in particular has become more precarious due to the nature of the regimes in power.

Among the difficulties facing a short overview such as this is that it is difficult to separate the problems of the political make-up of each country, its popular discourse, and the socio-economic and bureaucratic issues from the Syrian refugee crisis to which they are intricately tied. For instance, when Erdoğan announced in 2016 that he wanted to grant Syrians a path to citizenship, many Turks argued that this was unreasonable, mainly citing economic concerns – even if deeply held ethnolinguistic

7 For more information, see http://syrianrefugees.eu/; www.unhcr.org/europe-emergency.html. See also Chapter 11 of this volume.

8 Some have even argued that the Syrian refugee crisis was a contributing factor to the British decision to break off from the EU rather than likely be forced to share the burden of hosting refugees. See, for instance, NBC, 'Meet the Press', 26 June 2016, www.nbcnews.com/meet-the-press/video/did-the-syrian-refugee-crisis-help-lead-to-brexit-713110595998.

9 For more specific numbers of migrant deaths since 2013, see The Missing Migrants Project, https://missingmigrants.iom.int/region/mediterranean.

tensions may also exist.[10] Fast forward to early 2018 and Erdoğan decided to carry out 'Operation Olive Branch', ostensibly designed to secure areas of the Turkey–Syria border under Kurdish YPG (PYD) militia influence near Afrin. He then said that it would continue until the Syrian refugees were able to return.[11] The fluid manner in which politicians in the region have been mixing the humanitarian, political, military, and economic dimensions related to the refugee crisis caused by the Syrian civil war shows how difficult it may be to actually resolve the refugee crisis without a final political agreement that ends the Syrian civil war – and the longer it takes for this, the more likely it is that Syrian refugees will put down roots in their host countries.

10.2.1 Turkey

Turkey, more than any other country, enabled the Syrian opposition to transform from a disparate group of civil protesters against a police state into an organised armed movement fighting under the banner of the Free Syrian Army with an exiled political wing based in Istanbul. Yet despite the official policy claiming to oppose Bashar al-Assad for the sake of a more liberal majoritarian-based Syrian political arena, Turkey sought to use the movement to forward its own interests. This can be seen in its very late opposition to ISIS, its cynical demands for an enormous amount of EU and UN funding for the Syrian refugees, and its constant attempts at undermining armed Kurds in Syria who were on the front lines against ISIS until late 2017. As of early 2018, 3,424,237 Syrian refugees have been registered with the UNHCR in Turkey.[12] This means that Turkey has more than three times the number of Syrian refugees than all the rest of Europe combined and contains the most total refugees of any country in the world (though not the most per capita).

While Turkey initially welcomed the Syrians, who were fleeing a government crackdown against civil protests in 2011, it soon became clear that the 822-kilometre border between Syria and Turkey made it

[10] Selin Girit, 'Turkey Hits Back at Erdogan Plan to Give Syrians Citizenship', *BBC*, 5 July 2016, www.bbc.com/news/world-europe-36704791.

[11] *Hürriyet Daily News*, 'Turkey's Military Operations to Continue until 3.5 Million Syrians Return: Government', 23 January 2018, http://www.hurriyetdailynews.com/turkeys-military-operations-to-continue-until-3-5-million-syrians-return-government-126195.

[12] See, for instance, http://data.unhcr.org/syrianrefugees/country.php?id=224. These numbers may not reflect the actual number of Syrian refugees living in Turkey, since some may have returned home or moved elsewhere without 'unregistering' from their asylum status.

impossible to significantly limit what would become a massive influx of refugees in the following years. Moreover, while Turkey cooperated with international aid organisations to create at least twenty-five camps near the border for about 230,000 refugees, the Syrians preferred not to live in the camps and rather spread out throughout Turkey, mostly in the cities near the border with Syria.[13] Though Turkey has been praised for its efforts, which to an extent have been coordinated with the UN and the EU, most Syrian refugees face economic hardship, language barriers, and simply operate off the radar of the formal legal system. All of this is complicated by Turkey's complex approach to the situation in Syria and the rise of President Erdoğan's authoritarian grip on domestic politics. This has included, among other things, crackdowns on independent and critical media, purges throughout the public sector following a failed coup attempt in 2015, and an intense struggle against imported and home-grown Islamist terrorism, as well as an ongoing fight against the Kurdish nationalist PKK and its Syrian affiliate, the Democratic Union Party (PYD). All of this has led many observers to the obvious conclusion that Erdoğan's slide to dictatorship has also been a significant factor in the complete loss of faith in a democratic trend in the Middle East following the Arab Spring uprisings of 2011.[14]

Turkish society at large has shown remarkable generosity, initially defining the fleeing Syrians as guests. However, as it became clear over time that the Syrians were really refugees and, moreover, were not going to be able to return to Syria any time soon, the legal ambiguity began to create problems for the Syrians themselves, as well as for the Turkish people interacting with them. This ambiguity has been highlighted by researchers doing interviews up through 2015, who note that Syrians were only able to get official rights for an identity card (*kimlik*) from the government by registering with the Disaster and Emergency Management Agency (AFAD) in the cities where they resided, and that process had to be repeated if they moved to another city.[15] Turkey did improve its labour laws to include more Syrians in 2016, yet, even with a slight improvement in the legality of Syrian

[13] *The Daily Sabah*, 'Turkish Border Cities Host Almost Half of Syrian Refugees', 8 January 2018, www.dailysabah.com/turkey/2018/01/09/turkish-border-cities-host-almost-half-of-syrian-refugees.

[14] Steven A. Cook, *False Dawn* (Oxford: Oxford University Press, 2017).

[15] Feyzi Baban, Suzan Ilcan, and Kim Rygiel, 'Syrian Refugees in Turkey: Pathways to Precarity, Differential Inclusion, and Negotiated Citizenship Rights', *Journal of Ethnic and Migration Studies* 43, no. 1 (2017): 41–57, DOI: 10.1080/1369183X.2016.1192996.

employment, the types of jobs are often concentrated in physical agricultural labour, where Syrians make less than half of what a Turkish worker would make and may not get paid on time or at all.[16] These sectors, where the Turkish government has actually encouraged employers to take in Syrians, often lead to Syrians taking jobs held by poorer Kurdish workers, which in turn increased tension between local Turkish Kurds and the Syrian refugees. This is compounded by the problem that Turkey's still-active citizenship law from 1934 technically designates only ethnic Turkish people as eligible for citizenship or official refugee status. As a result of this and the 1951 UN Convention Relating to the Status of Refugees, which Turkey signed and arguably only applies to European refugees into Turkey, Turkey works with the UNHCR to designate Syrians as only temporarily in Turkey, with the expectation that they will eventually go home or be transferred to a third state.[17]

Overall the Syrian refugee population in Turkey is highly urban, with only 10 per cent living in the relative predictability of refugee camps, and many are stuck in legal limbo. Syrian youth are working instead of getting an education, and girls are subject to early marriages to older men. That said, the situation in Turkey is somewhat better than in Jordan or Lebanon, due to the Turkish government's attempts at improving the situation and EU money allotted to help Syrian refugees. Despite numerous obstacles including a language barrier, significant portions of Turkish society are sympathetic to the plight of Syrian refugees, as was recently demonstrated by a viral picture of a pudgy Syrian shoeshiner youth standing outside a workout gym. The social media attention led to the gym giving the boy a lifetime free membership, and a second photo went viral of the same boy working out inside the gym he had only previously dreamed of entering.[18]

10.2.2 Jordan

Throughout the Syrian refugee crisis, the Jordanian monarchy has been shored up with international non-governmental organisations, as well as

[16] Anna Lekas Miller, 'Inside the Turkish Camps Where Syrian Refugees Work for $8 a Day', *NewsDeeply*, 5 September 2016, www.newsdeeply.com/refugees/articles/2016/09/05/inside-the-turkish-camps-where-syrian-refugees-work-for-8-a-day.

[17] Fulya Memisoglu and Asli Ilgit, 'Syrian Refugees in Turkey: Multifaceted Challenges, Diverse Players and Ambiguous Policies', *Mediterranean Politics* 22, no. 3 (2017): 317–38, DOI: 10.1080/13629395.2016.1189479.

[18] Borzou Daragahi, Twitter, 9 January 2018, https://twitter.com/borzou/status/950681788715847681.

American and Saudi influence. At the same time, it faces a complex local political climate where the Muslim Brotherhood and the Palestinian majority raise questions about the long-term viability of the last Hashemite kingdom.[19] Currently there are approximately 655,624 Syrians registered with the UNHCR living in Jordan, with just over 20 per cent living in designated camps and the rest in urban areas. According to Jordanian statistics, only half the total number of Syrians in Jordan have registered with the UNHCR.[20] The scale of the problem has levelled off since the intense crisis year of 2013 where numbers went from 120,000 to 576,000 between 1 January and 31 December of that year.[21] In 2014, Jordan took active steps to limit the flow of refugees into Jordan and in June 2016 effectively closed Jordan to further refugees, leaving tens of thousands stranded inside Syria. Though these measures enabled NGOs and the UNHCR to work with the government to manage the problem of people needing to live in camps, they reflect the brutal reality that Syrians currently face, which is the sense that they have nowhere to go. Yet, as time went on, the majority of the immediate problems facing the refugees were related to things that concern all Jordanians, such as housing, education, and jobs. Jordan has noted on several occasions that it is at a breaking point with the number of refugees, with its government estimating more than $12 billion of costs to the economy from 2013 to 2016 and hosting the second-highest rate of refugees per capita in the world at 89:1000, second only after Lebanon.[22]

The security situation in Jordan is quite tense, and this complicates Jordan's relationship with Syrian refugees and the Assad regime in Syria. Due to a series of terrorist attacks, mainly at or near checkpoints close to the al-Ruqban refugee camp in 2016–2017, Jordan essentially closed its border to new refugees.[23] In addition, it has been reportedly

[19] Assessments, 'Jordan Caught between the Muslim Brotherhood and the East Bankers', *Stratfor Worldview*, 26 April 2012.

[20] Mohammad Ghazal, 'Population Stands at 9.5 Million, Including 2.9 Million Guests', *Jordan Times*, 30 January 2016, http://www.jordantimes.com/news/local/population-stands-around-95-million-including-29-million-guests. According to these statistics, foreigners represent 30 per cent of the people living in Jordan. But that also includes over 634,000 Palestinians who do not have ID numbers, who presumably have been in Jordan for a long time.

[21] http://data.unhcr.org/syrianrefugees/country.php?id=107.

[22] Mohammad Ghazal, 'Jordan Second Largest Refugee Host Worldwide – UNHCR', *Jordan Times*, 8 March 2017.

[23] *The New Arab*, 'Car Bomb Hits Syrian Refugee Camp on Jordan Border', 8 April 2017, www.alaraby.co.uk/english/news/2017/4/8/car-bomb-hits-syrian-refugee-camp-on-jordan-border.

deporting some families that have contacts inside Syria, ostensibly for having contacts with ISIS.[24] This is combined with the unusual fact that it allowed Amman to be the Military Operations Centre (MOC) of the armed rebels of the Southern Front, while at the same time it kept dual channels open with Moscow and the United States to, in a sense, hedge its bets on whatever path appeared to be the most stable for the long term.[25] By walking this tightrope between Jordan's desire to return to stability and simultaneously hoping for an outcome in Syria that would be favourable to Jordan and its Gulf State allies (i.e. Sunnis in the region), Jordan has been helping Syrian refugees while warily looking for ways for them to be repatriated to Syria, whether liberated from Assad or not.

As in Turkey above and Lebanon below, the Syrian refugees in Jordan face an informal market where they are subject to exploitation without recourse to legal protection due to the illegality of their labour. Several reports have also noted that female youth are particularly vulnerable to early marriages to help the family offload costs to usually a much older Jordanian, who may already have one or more wives.[26] However, Jordanian thinkers have not been passive and have encouraged an innovative approach to the crisis that involves an economic development approach, for the moment, together with the post–World War II typical aid system that tends to view refugees as sponges for indefinite aid. This idea was put forward by economists, such as Alexander Betts and Paul Collier, who believe that refugee host countries should create Special Economic Zones (SEZs), as they have done in Jordan, designed to encourage manufacturers to hire refugees and gain access to low-interest loans and tax breaks.[27] Yet these ideas have been met with scepticism since even though some Syrians might welcome the shift in perspective by the host towards refugees, from economic threat to economic stimulator, these SEZs can themselves become sophisticated locations for further exploitation and enslavement, just like other

[24] Alice Su, 'Why Is Jordan Deporting Syrian Refugees?', *The Atlantic*, 20 October 2017, www.theatlantic.com/international/archive/2017/10/jordan-syrian-refugees-deportation/543057/.

[25] Youssef Sadaki, 'The MOC's Role in the Collapse of the Southern Opposition', *The Atlantic Council*, 23 September 2016, http://www.atlanticcouncil.org/blogs/syriasource/the-moc-s-role-in-the-collapse-of-the-southern-opposition.

[26] Karin Laub, 'Spike in Number of Syrian Teens Marrying as Child Brides in Jordan', *The Independent*, 7 August 2017, www.independent.co.uk/news/world/middle-east/child-brides-jordan-syrian-teenage-refugees-a7880831.html

[27] Alexander Betts and Paul Collier, *Refuge: Transforming a Broken Refugee System* (London: Allen Lane, 2017).

sectors.[28] Betts and Collier, moreover, view the UNHCR, with its emphasis on triage and setting up isolated camps, as part of the problem more than a contributor to the solution. But for the most vulnerable orphans, widows, elderly, and children, expecting them to become the engine of a lagging economy is naive at best and cruel at worst.

Jordan, in fact, has become an experimental arena for similar projects, starting with the USA-sponsored Qualified Industrial Zones (QIZs) set up in the 1990s to stimulate Jordanian–Israeli–Palestinian cooperation by allowing certain sectors duty-free access to sell in the US markets if they used local products. However, the experience of these QIZs has shown that cultural differences also factor into the function of these areas. In Jordanian society, much like southern Syrian society, it is uncommon for women to work in factories, often because they simply do not want to or because a family member prevents them from doing so. As a result, many of the workers in these economically successful sectors, focused on textile manufacturing, are from South and East Asia.[29] Similarly, Jordanian entrepreneurs and its government, together with the EU, the United Kingdom, and the World Bank, signed the 'Jordan Compact' in 2016 in London, with an aim of creating 200,000 jobs in Jordan with the help of $1.7 billion in grants over three years and offering companies who set up in the new SEZs ten years of tariff-free access to European markets. Yet despite the attempts at recruiting Syrian refugees, primarily women, to work in factories in Jordan, not very many have signed up to do so.[30]

The informal sector provides risk but also more direct benefit for both the employers and the employees. Syrians are officially prohibited from working in many sectors; there are also additional bureaucratic difficulties: Syrians may be required to pay for a permit, and employers may have to file official papers for Syrians to work in those sectors paying minimum wages, from which Jordanians typically decline (such as hard construction or agriculture). Therefore, even in those jobs, many of the estimated 200,000 Syrian refugees already working informally in Jordan prefer to continue to do so under the table. However, this can lead to exploitation and resentment among the Jordanians who are, in some

[28] Heaven Crawley, 'Refugee Economics', *Nature* 544 (April 2017), https://pdfs.semanticscholar.org/3260/ce159b3660d8a7ac385aaa6deff76bb1b4ce.pdf.

[29] Aliza Reznik, 'As Jordan's Garment Sector Grows Activists Push for Better Migrant Workers' Rights', *Middle East Eye*, 13 January 2018, https://www.middleeasteye.net/news/jordans-garment-sector-grows-activists-push-better-migrant-workers-rights.

[30] Daniel Howden, Hannah Patchett, and Charlotte Alfred, 'The Compact Experiment', NewsDeeply, Refugees Deeply Quarterly, December 2017.

cases, undercut by cheaper Syrian labourers. The Jordanian government promotes the Jordan Compact as a 'paradigm shift ... to turn the refugees' challenge into an economic development opportunity ..., which has allowed Jordan and its international partners to make significant strides in supporting Syrian refugees, host communities, and overall the development agenda of Jordan'.[31] Yet it risks stirring up more political opposition, which already boils under the surface, from either the Muslim Brotherhood or the various Jordanian and East Bank communities who feel the government owes them a handout.

10.2.3 Lebanon

The Turkish and Jordanian situations, as bad as they are, pale in comparison to that of Lebanon, which has the highest per capita refugee population in the world. Unlike the authoritarian rulers of Jordan and Turkey, Lebanon's fragile government is stuck in a situation where the Christian President Michel Aoun is in a coalition with Hezbollah and its allies. The Lebanese government has a long tradition of restricting the rights of Palestinian refugees, where, for over sixty years, they were explicitly denied the ability to work in jobs that required education and were forbidden from owning property.[32] In addition, the military wing of the coalition party, Hezbollah, is actively engaged in the fighting in Syria and, by most estimates, is the strongest military organisation in the country. By contrast, the Sunni prime minister, Saʿad al-Hariri, is in the awkward position of ruling alongside Aoun, but, due to his ties to the Saudi government, and indeed his Saudi citizenship (like his father Rafiq, who was assassinated in 2005), he cannot publicly pronounce support for Hezbollah and would prefer Hezbollah to withdraw from Syria altogether. In this sense, Lebanon is, at least politically, and to a large extent also militarily, deeply involved in the Syrian war. This complex and potentially explosive compound adds to the already precarious nature of the Syrian refugee population in Lebanon.

31 Petra [Official Jordanian News Bulletin], 'British PM Commends King Abdullah II's Counterterrorism Efforts', 30 November 2011, www.petra.gov.jo/Public_News/Nws_NewsDetails.aspx?Site_Id=1&lang=2&NewsID=329763&CatID=13&Type=Home&GType=1.

32 May Farah, 'Palestinian Refugees in Lebanon: Worthy Lives in Unworthy Conditions', 274–300, in Anthony Gorman and Sossie Kasbarian, *Diasporas of the Middle East: Contextualizing Community* (Edinburgh: University of Edinburgh Press, 2015).

Roughly 70 per cent of Syrian refugees in Lebanon are living below the poverty line, and yet, despite this, they are often required to pay high rental costs. The good news, perhaps, is that the actual number of Syrian refugees in Lebanon has fallen slightly, from roughly 1,017,000 to 1,001,000 – according to UNHCR statistics – and this may not reflect the actual decline, since refugees often fail to unregister before leaving. However, the bad news is that, as of late 2017, the UNHCR estimated that 74 per cent of all the registered refugees over the age of fifteen were not allowed to reside in Lebanon legally.[33] This is due to the fact that registering for legal permits to be in Lebanon and gain access to basic healthcare and education rights costs $200 per refugee, per year, and, in addition, the refugees are required to submit sensitive information (or hide such information) about employment to prove that they are not working illegally.

In reality, however, many Syrian refugees are working illegally; otherwise they would not be able to cover their expenses. About 19 per cent of all households are headed by women, which creates further vulnerabilities due to the limited job availabilities for women in the somewhat less exploitative sectors where Syrian men can work. This has led to many accounts of sexual abuse and rape of women and minors in return for small favours, rent, or cash from those with access to material things needed for survival.[34] In addition, many Syrian women who have become pregnant, whether by choice or not, and have given birth have to deal with the fact that their baby may be stateless – because the refugees are not registered as legal residents of Lebanon, or they may not be officially registered with the UN, and/or they may be registered legally in Lebanon but fear going to the Syrian embassy for political reasons.[35]

In parallel with the pre-existing communitarian political alliances in Lebanon, Syrian refugees are often broken up into groups supported by the various communities to which they feel closest. This has meant, by definition, that concentrations of refugees have a known identity that can be exploited either by enemies or, potentially, by those who claim to be friends but who do not actually have their interests at heart. For instance,

[33] Vulnerability Assessment of Syrian Refugees in Lebanon (VASYR) for 2017, UNHCR, http://data.unhcr.org/syrianrefugees/country.php?id=122

[34] For just one of many examples, see Amnesty International: Press Release, 'Lebanon: Refugee Women from Syria Face Heightened Risk of Exploitation and Sexual Harassment', 2 February 2016, www.amnesty.org/en/press-releases/2016/02/lebanon-refugee-women-from-syria-face-heightened-risk-of-exploitation-and-sexual-harassment/.

[35] Diana al-Rifai, 'UN: 36,000 Syrian Newborns Stateless in Lebanon', *Al Jazeera*, 11 May 2015, https://www.aljazeera.com/news/2015/05/150506060248502.html.

due to the predominance of Hezbollah's intelligence network and militia in Lebanon and its overt involvement in the Syrian civil war since 2013, many Syrian Sunnis are afraid of being targeted.[36]

The feeling of vulnerability led many Syrian refugees in desperate situations to consider joining ISIS or Jabhat al-Nusra, who were active in Lebanon until 2017. However, until the joint Hezbollah–Syrian regime operation along the Lebanon–Syria border in the summer of 2017, there were significant numbers of armed jihadis camping out in the area around Arsal, where many of their families lived. In the wake of the military operation in Arsal, which effectively dismantled the militants' camps, some 9,000 people were transferred to Syria via an arrangement made with the Assad regime. This move was somewhat opposed by the Lebanese Sunni Prime Minister Saʿad al-Hariri, who has publicly refused to make deals with Assad and has argued for a more comprehensive plan to be enacted in coordination with the UNHCR. Later in 2017, the Lebanese government forced 12,000 Syrian refugees living in informal tent colonies around Riyak to move after labelling that area a military zone due to its proximity to an air force base.[37] The extreme vulnerability of Syrian refugees in Lebanon, who put over $400 million into the Lebanese housing market in 2017 due to the government's prevention of the establishment of formal camps, may speed their return to Syria. Alternatively, it could eventually undermine the credibility of the Lebanese president's continual promises that the Syrian refugees are not meant to stay in Lebanon for the long term. This fear, as well as the ruling preventing the establishment of semi-permanent camps, is based on the negative Lebanese experience with Palestinian refugees. Moreover, the UN's Regional Refugee and Resilience Plan (3RP) only met 38 per cent of its targeted fundraising goals in 2017,[38] which means

[36] One Sunni Arab refugee I spoke to in a lengthy recorded interview from his home in Germany to my office in Tel Aviv recalled how he fled from Damascus University where he was a law student in 2012 due to his family name being associated with key members of the opposition. He fled to Beirut, but after a year he was afraid that he would be captured by Hezbollah operatives or other regime loyalists he referred to as the *shabiha*, who had free rein in the capital. It was then that he was lucky enough to flee to Greece and then on to Germany before that process became extremely expensive. Recorded interview in November 2017 with Amer in Germany, who has not given permission to use his real name.

[37] Abby Sewell and Charlotte Alfred, 'Evicted Refugees in Lebanon Have Nowhere Left to Run', *NewsDeeply: Refugees Deeply*, 28 September 2017, www.newsdeeply.com/refugees/articles/2017/09/28/nowhere-left-to-run-refugee-evictions-in-lebanon-in-shadow-of-return.

[38] http://reporting.unhcr.org/sites/default/files/10%20Sept%202017-3RP%20Interagency%20Funding%20Snapshot-2017%20Syria%203RP.pdf.

that Syrian as well as the Palestinians dependent on the UNRWA,[39] two of the most marginalised, abused, and legally discriminated against populations in Lebanon (both of whom happen to be majority Sunni Muslim), are likely to face increasing challenges in the near to medium term.

10.2.4 Iraq

Iraq is still in a state of flux and appears to have narrowly avoided losing Iraqi Kurdistan to an independence drive, with large areas of the Sunni majority Nineveh province and the historic Sunni city of Mosul in ruins after a nearly successful attempt by ISIS to impose a brutal mediaeval-style Islamic caliphate. In fact, tens of thousands of IDPs have fled these areas, largely to live in the Kurdistan Region of Iraq (KRI). Likewise, Syrian refugees who have fled to Iraq have concentrated their camps in that area. Overall, their situation appears to be somewhat less problematic than the situations in Jordan, Lebanon, and Turkey. This seems to be a result of not concentrating in urban or semi-urban areas where jobs are more prevalent, leading to an estimated 37 per cent living below the poverty line (as opposed to 93 per cent and 70 per cent in Jordan and Lebanon respectively).[40] Additionally, the UN has been able to register the vast majority of the total number of Syrians, as opposed to in Jordan and Lebanon, where significant numbers of Syrians prefer not to register. The number of Syrian children getting education in Iraq is estimated at over 60 per cent, which is higher than in Jordan and Lebanon but lower than in Turkey or Egypt, where nearly all the Syrian children have been enrolled in school (thanks to a decree by Mohamed Morsi in 2012).

Around 230,000 to 240,000 Syrian refugees are presently in Iraq, according to UNHCR numbers, which is a low figure considering its long border with Syria. The reasons likely include the instability in Iraq since the US withdrawal in 2011, as well as the Shi'a majority

[39] The US government, which had long been the main financier of the UNRWA, significantly cut its funding projections in 2017 leading to a $411 million shortage, according to the appeal for aid on their site on 9 January 2017, www.unrwa.org/resources/emergency-appeals/opt-emergency-appeal-2017; this also affects the 120,000 Palestinians registered with the UNRWA who have fled Syria to Jordan and Lebanon, as well as some 400,000 in Syria who may be eligible to receive UNRWA aid, www.unrwa.org/resources/emergency-appeals/syria-emergency-appeal-2017.

[40] 3RP Regional Strategic Overview 2017–2018, UNHCR-UNHDP, www.3rpsyriacrisis.org/the-3rp/strategic-overview/.

government, which has been perceived as biased against Sunni Muslims. The ethnically Arab-Sunni majority provinces, meanwhile, have not been ideal refuge sites due to ISIS. Kurdish-Sunni areas, by contrast, have hosted a large number of refugees. In fact, official Kurdish Regional Government (KRG) figures estimate that as many as 97 per cent of all Syrian refugees in Iraq are in Kurdistan.[41] While this is likely an exaggeration, there may be more than 200,000 Syrian refugees in the KRG in addition to hundreds of thousands of internally displaced Iraqis, creating a situation of uncertainty, in particular since Kurdish national aspirations may clash with the demographics of hosting so many non-Kurds.[42] As long as the situation is viewed as temporary, this issue can continue to be ignored, but if the situation in Syria remains chaotic for the medium term, or if Syrians in Iraq do not have the resources to return to their homes in Syria, tensions between the Arab and Kurdish communities could rise. The government of Baghdad, like all the other governments surveyed here, wants the Syrians to return. Realistically, however, many could stay for the long term, just as many of the more than 1.2 million Iraqis who fled to Syria in the 2000s ended up staying there. The relative ease of reaching urban areas, as opposed to concentration in camps, means that chronic health problems, unemployment, and lack of access to justice and education may go undetected among refugee populations.[43] This generally means that the situation of Syrians in Iraq is uncertain, though presently better than that of most in Lebanon and Jordan. Their situation could change if the status of the KRG changes, but that also is simply uncertain from the vantage point of 2019.

10.2.5 Egypt

Mohamed Morsi's short-lived presidency in Egypt left behind at least one long-lasting decree: granting Syrian refugee children access to Egyptian schools. Morsi's decree in September 2012 – which ordered, for example, that Syrian refugees would pay the same as Egyptians for school – has greatly

41 See http://cabinet.gov.krd/p/page.aspx?l=12&s=000000&r=401&p=479&h=1&t=407.

42 The KRG estimates that up to 1.9 million Iraqi IDPs are in its area, which is likely an overestimate but still indicates that the scale of the problem is very large. Diyar Amin, 'Kurdistan Region – Heaven for Refugees', *Vocal Europe*, 29 May 2017, www.vocaleurope.eu/iraqi-kurdistan-heaven-refugees/.

43 See Shannon Doocy, Adam Sirois, Margarita Tileva, J. Douglas Storey, and Gilbert Burnham, 'Chronic Disease and Disability among Iraqi Populations Displaced in Jordan and Syria', *International Journal of Health Planning and Management*, no. 28 (2013): e1–e12.

benefited the Syrian refugee communities.[44] It has allowed for them to find a sense of stability, sustainability, and rootedness, perhaps more so than in any other country in the region. Though Morsi was deposed by a military coup and replaced by Abdel Fattah el-Sisi in 2013, the policies towards Syrian refugees have remained in place. That said, there were early fears in the months of consolidation when Sisi was reportedly targeting Syrian refugees who were suspected by his regime of being loyal to Morsi as well as sympathetic to the Muslim Brotherhood.[45] The lack of transparency and limits on press freedom in Egypt since the fall of Morsi mean that data on Syrian refugees and their overall well-being is particularly difficult to attain and verify, especially if it might reflect negatively on the current government. The UNHCR reported in early 2017 that there were at least 500,000 Syrians in Egypt, though less than 150,000 have registered as refugees, most by the middle of 2013.[46] While the status of Syrian refugees in Egypt appears on the surface to be among the most encouraging – in particular with respect to education – there may be reason to doubt appearances and even reason to suggest that the educational progress is not as rosy as it could be.[47]

10.3 Conclusions: The Lasting Effects of the Syrian Refugee Crisis

Unlike most of North and South America, as well as a few other countries, most states in Europe, North Africa, and Asia do not have *jus soli* – the 'right of the soil' – which legalises automatic citizenship based on birth in the country.[48] In this sense, Syrian families who have

[44] *Al-Arabiya*, 'Morsi Makes Syrians Equal to Egyptians in School', 18 September 2012, www.alarabiya.net/articles/2012/09/05/236213.html (Arabic). For follow-up articles, see Ahmed Aleem, 'How Egypt Is Promoting Education for Syrian Refugees', *al-Monitor*, 4 September 2017, https://www.al-monitor.com/pulse/originals/2017/09/egypt-syrian-students-classes-education-government-efforts.html.

[45] Vice, 'Life Is Hell for Syrian Refugees in Egypt', www.vice.com/en_us/article/dpw87y/life-is-hell-for-syrian-refugees-in-egypt; incidentally, the activist cited in this article for Vice, Mahienour al-Massry, was herself imprisoned and fined for her political involvement in supporting the rights of Syrian refugees and opposing the presidency of Sisi, https://egyptianstreets.com/2017/11/18/activist-mahienour-al-massry-detained-during-court-hearing/.

[46] UNHCR: 'Vulnerability Assessment for Egypt in 2016', no date but refers to early 2017, http://data.unhcr.org/syrianrefugees/download.php?id=14902.

[47] Nahla ElNemr, 'Syrian Students Struggle in Egypt's Schools', *al-Monitor*, 3 March 2016, https://www.al-monitor.com/pulse/ru/originals/2016/05/egypt-syria-students-refugees-education-schools-challenges.html.

[48] For explanation and criticism of this notion, see Ayelet Shachar, *The Birthright Lottery: Citizenship and Global Inequality* (Cambridge: Harvard University Press, 2009), 120.

children while refugees in the Middle East or out of wedlock by a legally unrecognised father face long-term challenges of not having citizenship. In the view of this author, all the host countries should come up with terms or set conditions whereby Syrians and their offspring[49] may find a path to gain full civic and economic rights, even if not as equal citizens, in order not to repeat the mistakes of the Palestinian refugee tragedy. However, the idea of long-term hosting of refugees is often unpopular, and, despite the insulated nature of most Middle East governments, there is still some fear that their countries will be overwhelmed if they accept refugees on an equal footing, as Jordan once did for Palestinians born in Jordan between 1949 and 1954. Nevertheless, even without an obvious path to citizenship, education and escape from the Syrian authoritarian state system can provide some meaningful hope for refugees in the medium term. Over the long term, Syrians living outside Syria may come to see themselves less as 'refugees' and more as a 'diaspora' similar to the Palestinian, Kurdish, or Lebanese diaspora groups of the world.[50] The evolution of a robust Syrian diaspora depends largely on whether Syrian refugees build transnational ties with each other and come to define themselves as a community that is distinct from Syrians in the homeland.[51] The transformation of identity of refugees into a diaspora has been observed in other cases, such as that of the Somalian community of the United States.[52]

While it may sound trite or even distasteful to note that the plight of Syrian refugees could also open doors to research, this may be one long-term effect of the situation. For instance, because Syrians have been afraid to speak openly to foreigners about the sociopolitical situation in Syria for years, now that Syrians far removed from the direct threat of the

[49] Whether or not those born to one or two Syrian-origin parents are still Syrian by legal definitions depends on who is asking (i.e. the UNHCR, host governments, some other organisation), even if conceptually it seems obvious that the child of Syrian parents would have 'Syrian' identity on some level. In Lebanon for instance, the problem of stateless children born of those who were not citizens is an ongoing issue for the descendants of Palestinians, Syrians, and others. See Samira Trad and Berna Habib, 'Stateless in Lebanon: Between Shame and Shadows', *The Legal Agenda*, 7 January 2016, http://legal-agenda.com/en/article.php?id=3115; and UNHCR Lebanon, Statelessness Update, 2014, https://reliefweb.int/sites/reliefweb.int/files/resources/4.StatelessnessUNHCRMonthlyUpdate-August2014.pdf

[50] For a more in-depth discussion and collection of articles on diasporas in the Middle East, see Anthony Gorman and Sossie Kasbarian, *Diasporas of the Middle East: Contextualizing Community* (Edinburgh: University of Edinburgh Press, 2015).

[51] Osten Wahlbeck, 'The Concept of Diaspora as an Analytical Tool in the Study of Refugee Communities', *Journal of Ethnic and Migration Studies* 28, no. 2 (2002): 221–38.

[52] Abdi Roble and Doug Rutledge, *The Somali Diaspora: A Journey Away* (Minneapolis: University of Minnesota Press, 2008).

mukhabarrat (Syrian military intelligence service) can be interviewed and heard, and something approaching a more authentic voice can be expressed. While certainly some of the voices will prefer to focus on the trauma of being displaced, which is certainly an important element that deserves close attention, others may want to discuss stories of the nature of the Syrian state and its mechanisms for silencing opposition. In Wendy Pearlman's collective autobiography *We Crossed the Bridge and It Trembled*,[53] as well as in Yassin al-Haj Saleh's partially autobiographical work *Impossible Revolution*,[54] Syrians living outside of Syria today are finally able to articulate a critical version of Syrian history which has been missing for decades.

Indirectly, studying the story of Syrian refugees can also reveal the inner workings of societies and governments throughout the region. For instance, the political tension between the various communities in Lebanon, combined with the actual involvement of Hezbollah and some of the family members of Syrian refugees in Lebanon in the ongoing fighting in Syria, can be analysed from the perspective of developments with Syrian refugees in Lebanon. Often the political opposition in Lebanon, afraid to directly confront Hezbollah or Michel Aoun, will criticise other aspects of governmental mismanagement. This type of protest was seen with the recent campaign by Sami Gemayel, Phalange Party Member of Parliament and long-time critic of Hezbollah, to expose the scale of the trash disposal problem.[55] Syrian refugees highlight shortcomings in the confessional-quota system that has been in place since early in the French mandate period, which makes the Christian and Shi'a communities afraid to accept Sunnis into the overall Lebanese national fabric. This has also been the case with Palestinian refugees, but many of the most explosive results of the Palestinian refugee crisis in Lebanon took years to come to the surface; with Syrians these issues are ever-present in the public discourse.

In Turkey, Jordan, Egypt, and Iraq, the actual presence of Syrian refugees is less seen as an 'existential' threat to the extent that some in Lebanon see it, but nevertheless a host of economic, administrative, and long-term problems exist that make life extremely precarious for Syrian refugees as well as for the vulnerable communities in the host states. These challenges are exacerbated by political uncertainty, as in Iraq and Jordan, or overbearing regimes, as in Turkey and Egypt, where

53 HarperCollins, 2017.
54 Hurst, 2017.
55 *Al-Hayat*, 'Sami Gemayel Calls for International Justice and Blames the Whole Government for the Waste [Problem]', 22 January 2018 (Arabic).

information may be obscured by a lack of free press access. This may also limit the role of researchers, but nevertheless, the involvement of international aid agencies may ease one's way into areas that otherwise would have been off limits. In the long run, while some Syrians are stuck in limbo, others will manage to get a freer and better education than they would have if they had never left home. Education is truly the silver lining in the cloud: the more education Syrians receive, the more likely it is that a new elite will emerge and ultimately reshape the very concept of what it means to be Syrian.

11

Syrian Refugees in Europe

Assessing Challenges, Practices, and Integration Policies

FRANCESCO FARINELLI

11.1 Introduction

The year 2015 was a defining one for Europe. An unprecedented number of asylum seekers arrived in Europe, the vast majority fleeing Syria's civil war. According to some scholars, the mass influx of Syrian refugees in countries neighbouring Syria and across Europe represents one of the largest humanitarian crises since World War II. The refugee crisis found European countries unprepared to handle such a dramatic flood of people.

The Syrian civil war and the refugee crisis are undoubtedly among the historical events that mark an era, the scope of which is usually described in numerical terms: how many asylum seekers, how many refugees, how many migrants, how many survivors, how many human deaths, etc. History, however, is not constituted of statistics alone. So many small, individual stories contribute to the creation of a historical event. This chapter offers a snapshot of the main issues related to the integration process of Syrian refugees in Europe, as well as of the good practices and policies so far implemented, providing the reader with both statistic data and concrete examples.

The examples are testimonies collected by the European Foundation for Democracy (EFD), a policy institute based in Brussels which, in 2017, undertook a qualitative research project looking into how different European countries with high numbers of refugees are managing the integration process. The countries researched were Austria, Belgium, Denmark, France, Germany, the Netherlands, and Sweden. Looking at existing policies, legislation and practices, the research took a holistic approach, specifically listening to refugees themselves, as well as government officials, selected civil society organisations (CSOs), integration experts, academics and practitioners, and front-line professionals engaging with refugees. A total of 245 interviews, 131 of which were with refugees, took place to provide analysis into the 2015 refugee crisis and its evolution. This represents a considerable added value compared to the majority of the previous studies on this topic, which were mostly based on secondary sources.

There is no doubt that policy decisions currently being rolled out across Europe will have long-term effects on migration in European societies. For this reason, it is crucial to highlight and share both good practices and vulnerabilities, as well as the main challenges facing the integration policies and practices of European countries.

Personal accounts – ranging from torture, harassment, racism, and solitude to mere misunderstandings, bureaucratic problems, and difficulties in cultural adaptation – are presented in some of the following paragraphs, helping increase an understanding of a topic usually seen from a very factual and statistical angle. Nevertheless, we begin with numbers and statistical data in order to measure the phenomenon quantitatively and to understand the extent of the phenomenon of Syrian refugees fled to Europe.

11.2 Syrian Refugees in Europe: The Numbers

The outbreak of the Syrian civil war in March 2011 has generated a crisis described by António Guterres, the UN High Commissioner for Refugees, in 2014 as 'the biggest humanitarian emergency of our era'.[1] His successor, Filippo Grandi, repeated these same words in 2016.[2] Over eight years of war have caused a mass migration of Syrian nationals seeking asylum into other countries, especially in the Middle East and North Africa (MENA) region. This refugee crisis had an impact also in Europe. To understand the phenomenon, it is important to highlight the numbers and statistics.

Over 5.6 million people have fled Syria since 2011,[3] while 6.1 million remain internally displaced within Syria.[4] The vast majority of those who

1 Adrian Edwards, 'Needs Soar as Number of Syrian Refugees Tops 3 Million', *UNHCR*, 29 August 2014, www.unhcr.org/news/latest/2014/8/53ff76c99/needs-soar-number-syrian-refugees-tops-3-million.html.

2 'Syria Conflict at 5 Years: The Biggest Refugee and Displacement Crisis of Our Time Demands a Huge Surge in Solidarity', *UNHCR*, 15 March 2016, www.unhcr.org/afr/news/press/2016/3/56e6e3249/syria-conflict-5-years-biggest-refugee-displacement-crisis-time-demands.html.

3 'Syria Emergency', UNHCR, www.unhcr.org/syria-emergency.html (accessed 26 October 2017).

4 'Syria: Facts & Figures', European Commission, http://ec.europa.eu/echo/files/aid/countries/factsheets/syria_en.pdf (accessed 25 February 2018).

escaped the Syrian conflict asked for asylum in neighbouring countries.[5] At present, there are more than 3.5 million Syrian refugees registered in Turkey; 2 million in Egypt, Iraq, Jordan, and Lebanon; and more than 33,000 in North Africa.[6] Europe, between April 2011 and July 2017, received 970,316 Syrian asylum applications.[7] Many more Syrians are unregistered with the UN High Commissioner for Refugees (UNHCR). The number of internally displaced people and refugees, therefore, is expected to be significantly higher than current official estimates.

The Syrian civil war began on 15 March 2011, when Bashar al-Assad's government met pro-democracy protests with violence.[8] In April 2011, Syrian security forces opened fire in several towns and villages.[9] The flow of refugees towards Turkey started that month[10] in response to the rise of oppression and violence in the country. According to Amnesty International,[11] in May 2011 thousands of Syrians fled the town of Talkalakh in western Syria, crossing into Lebanon after the Syrian crack-down on anti-government protests.[12] In the same month, the first camps for refugees were opened in Turkey.[13]

Syria became the main country of origin for new asylum applicants in the EU in 2012, with 20,780 asylum applications.[14] In 2013 Syrian asylum

5 For more information on the refugee crisis in Syria's neighbouring countries, see Chapter 10 of this volume.

6 'Syria Regional Refugee Response', UNHCR, https://data2.unhcr.org/en/situations/syria (accessed 24 September 2018).

7 'Europe: Syrian Asylum Applications', UNHCR, http://data.unhcr.org/syrianrefugees/asylum.php (accessed 7 November 2017).

8 'Syria Civil War Timeline: A Summary of Critical Events', Deutsche Welle, www.dw.com/en/syria-civil-war-timeline-a-summary-of-critical-events/a-40001379 (accessed 24 September 2018).

9 'Syria's Crackdown on Protesters Becomes Dramatically More Brutal', *The Guardian*, 25 April 2011, www.theguardian.com/world/2011/apr/25/syria-crackdown-protesters-brutal.

10 'Factbox: Syrian Refugee Numbers Pass 34,000', *Reuters*, 16 March 2012, www.reuters.com/article/us-syria-refugees-idUSBRE82F0L820120316.

11 'Crackdown in Syria: Terror in Tell Kalakh', *Amnesty International*, July 2011, www.amnesty.nl/content/uploads/2016/12/1107_rap_syrie2.pdf?x44743.

12 See the testimony of Mahmoud Orabi, a Syrian national who fled from Talkalakh: 'We decided to come to Lebanon because of the bad scene back home; killing, oppression, destruction, and what can I say. While on the way, they shot at us, a young man and lady died.' In C. Davies and R. Adhami, 'Lebanese open homes to "Arab brothers" fleeing Syria', *CNN*, 10 June 2011, http://edition.cnn.com/2011/WORLD/meast/06/08/syrians.fleeing.into.lebanon/index.html.

13 'Fact Sheet: Timeline and Figures', UNHCR, www.unhcr.org/5245a72e6.pdf (accessed 24 September 2018).

14 ECRE/ELENA, *Information Note on Syrian Asylum Seekers and Refugees in Europe* (2013), 6.

seekers made up 12 per cent of the total number of applicants in the EU, reaffirming Syria as the leading country of origin of the influx.[15] In the first half of September 2013, Germany agreed to resettle 5,000 Syrian refugees under a two-year humanitarian admissions programme, and, at the end of the month, Sweden announced that Syrian asylum seekers would also be granted permanent residency. The year ended with a total of 1,164 UNHCR-assisted resettlement departures from Syria to EU countries.[16]

The number of Syrian asylum applicants in the EU jumped from 50,000 in 2013 to almost 123,000 in 2014. Most of them (70,000) applied for asylum in Germany and Sweden.[17] According to statistics, in the same year Syria also represented the main country of origin for asylum seekers in Austria, Belgium, Bulgaria, Cyprus, Denmark, Romania, Slovenia, Spain, and the Netherlands.[18]

The year 2015 marked a peak in first-time asylum requests for many European countries. According to the UNHCR, roughly half of those crossing the Mediterranean were Syrians fleeing the civil war.[19] In that year, the Syrian Observatory for Human Rights (SOHR) claimed that ISIS had taken control of half of Syria's landmass after taking hold of the historic city of Palmyra.[20] In this regard, a distinction should be made between controlling land and controlling population. Indeed, some lands under ISIS control were desert and not populated. Regardless, the number of Syrian asylum seekers in Europe in 2015 more than doubled from 2014, reaching 362,800.[21] Germany received the largest number of Syrian asylum claims (158,655)[22] and, in the same year, ceased applying the 1990

[15] 'Asylum in the EU28', *Eurostat*, 24 March 2014, http://ec.europa.eu/eurostat/documents/2995521/5181422/3-24032014-AP-EN.PDF/36a73587-7914-4a51-94a4-8e558a086fba.

[16] 'EU Resettlement Fact Sheet', *UNHCR*, www.europarl.europa.eu/meetdocs/2014_2019/documents/libe/dv/8_1_eu_resettlement_factsheet_unhcr_/8_1_eu_resettlement_fact sheet_unhcr_en.pdf (accessed 8 November 2017).

[17] 'Asylum in the EU', *Eurostat*, 20 March 2015, http://ec.europa.eu/eurostat/documents/2995521/6751779/3-20032015-BP-EN.pdf/35e04263-2db5-4e75-b3d3-6b086b23ef2b.

[18] Ibid.

[19] 'Over One Million Sea Arrivals Reach Europe in 2015', *UNHCR*, 30 December 2015, www.unhcr.org/news/latest/2015/12/5683d0b56/million-sea-arrivals-reach-europe-2015.html.

[20] 'Syrian Observatory: ISIS Now Controls 50% of Syria', 28 May 2015, www.syriahr.com/en/?p=18699; 'Isis "Controls 50% of Syria" after Seizing Historic City of Palmyra', *The Guardian*, 21 May 2015, www.theguardian.com/world/2015/may/21/isis-palmyra-syria-islamic-state.

[21] 'Asylum in the European Union Member States', *Eurostat*, 4 March 2016, http://ec.europa.eu/eurostat/documents/2995521/7203832/3-04032016-AP-EN.pdf/.

[22] Ibid.

Dublin Convention to Syrian refugees.[23] The Dublin protocol established that asylum claim must be processed in the first European country to which the asylum seeker arrives. As proof of how it has been difficult to find a balance between security and humanitarian responsibilities, in September 2015 the German interior minister informed the secretary general of the Council of the European Union that Germany was re-establishing temporary border controls under Article 25 of the Schengen Borders Code.[24] Two months later, Sweden also decided to impose temporary border controls due to 'a serious threat to public policy and internal security resulting from the unprecedented migratory pressure'.[25] Since September 2015, other Schengen countries reintroduced temporary border controls due to 'unexpected migratory flow'.[26] According to the International Organisation for Migration (IOM), 'with 3,771 deaths, 2015 was the deadliest year on record for migrants and refugees crossing the Mediterranean trying to reach Europe'.[27] The death of Alan, a three-year-old Syrian-Kurdish boy photographed along Turkey's coastline,[28] became symbolic of the refugee crisis.

In 2016, the number of Syrian first-time asylum seekers decreased slightly to 335,000.[29] In March 2016, the EU announced a deal with Turkey to dramatically reduce the influx of refugees inside EU borders.

In sum, Syria was the main country of citizenship of asylum seekers in Europe from 2012 to 2017. However, it was not just Syrian asylum seekers who were arriving in Europe. Many people were fleeing other parts of the Middle East, southern Asia, and continental Africa, most escaping conflicts in their countries. Furthermore, they were joined by

23 Convention Determining the State Responsible for Examining Applications for Asylum Lodged in One of the Member States of the European Communities (Dublin Convention), 15 June 1990, Official Journal C 254, 19/08/1997 pp. 1–12.

24 See Elspeth Guild, Evelien Brouwer, Kees Groenendijk, and Sergio Carrera, 'What Is Happening to the Schengen Borders?', *CEPS Papers in Liberty and Security in Europe* no. 86 (December 2015): 5.

25 Ibid., 7.

26 AAVV, *Internal Border Controls in the Schengen Area: Is Schengen Crisis-Proof?* (Brussels: Policy Department for Citizens' Rights and Constitutional Affairs, 2016), 15, www.europarl.europa.eu/RegData/etudes/STUD/2016/571356/IPOL_STU(2016)571356_EN.pdf.

27 'IOM Counts 3,771 Migrant Fatalities in Mediterranean in 2015', *IOM*, 1 May 2016, www.iom.int/news/iom-counts-3771-migrant-fatalities-mediterranean-2015.

28 'Looking Back at Alan Kurdi and Other Faces of Syrian Crisis', *The New York Times*, 2 September 2016, www.nytimes.com/2016/09/03/world/middleeast/alan-kurdi-aylan-anniversary-turkey-syria-refugees-death.html.

29 'Asylum Statistics', Eurostat, http://ec.europa.eu/eurostat/statistics-explained/index.php/Asylum_statistics (accessed 9 November 2017).

economic migrants in search of better livelihood prospects. Economic migrants who request asylum represent a major challenge for European countries. Indeed, while the authorities can fast-track manifestly unfounded applications, the process requires considerable resources to provide social and economic support for the high numbers of individuals who in most cases have no chance of being awarded refugee status.[30]

When it comes to discussing how many Syrian asylum seekers have received protection and how many of them are expected to stay in Europe, it is difficult to provide exact figures, as the migratory phenomenon and the civil war are ongoing. However, it is possible to examine data and statistics related to Syrian beneficiaries of the EU international protection that encompass both refugee status and subsidiary protection status.[31]

In 2012, Syrian nationals were granted roughly 10,000 first instance decisions of subsidiary protection statuses and more than 5,000 refugee statuses.[32] Of those, the majority were granted by Germany and Sweden. By 2013, Syrians began to represent 'the largest group granted protection status in half of the Member States and one of the three largest groups in 23 of the 28 Member States',[33] with 35,800 granted protection statuses. Over 60 per cent of those were granted by Sweden and Germany. This percentage remained the same in 2014 when 68,300 Syrians were granted protection status in the EU, representing 'the largest group [. . .] in nearly half of the Member States'.[34] In 2015, the number of positive decisions granting protection status to Syrian asylum seekers more than doubled from 2014, reaching a total of 166,100; Germany, who granted protection to 104,000 Syrian nationals, represented more than 60 per cent of the total decisions.[35]

[30] As emerged during the research undertaken by the EFD the high numbers of Albanian asylum seekers in France is a striking example of this challenge since Albania is included in France's list of safe countries.

[31] See both the definitions provided by the European Migration Network (EMN), 'Asylum and Migration Glossary 3.0' (European Commission, October 2014), 230, 278, https://ec.europa.eu/migrant-integration/librarydoc/asylum-and-migration-glossary-30.

[32] 'Asylum Applicants and First Instance Decisions on Asylum Applications: 2012', *Eurostat*, May 2013, 12, https://emnbelgium.be/sites/default/files/publications/eurostat_2012.pdf.

[33] 'Asylum Decisions in the EU28', *Eurostat*, 19 June 2014, http://ec.europa.eu/eurostat/documents/2995521/5173390/3-19062014-BP-EN.PDF.

[34] 'Asylum Decisions in the EU', *Eurostat*, 12 May 2015, http://ec.europa.eu/eurostat/documents/2995521/6827382/3-12052015-AP-EN.pdf/6733f080-c072-4bf5-91fc-f591abf28176.

[35] 'Asylum Decisions in the EU', *Eurostat*, 20 April 2016, http://ec.europa.eu/eurostat/documents/2995521/7233417/3-20042016-AP-EN.pdf/34c4f5af-eb93-4ecd-984c-577a5271c8c5.

The year 2016 again saw the number double, with 405,600 Syrian nationals granted status in the EU, 294,700 of which were recorded in Germany.[36]

Syrians represented the largest group granted protection in Europe from 2013 to 2017 since they meet international standards for recognition as refugees according to the 1951 Convention Relating to the Status of Refugees (Refugee Convention). However, it is difficult to determine how many Syrians will remain in Europe once the Syrian war is over, taking into consideration both the will of refugees and that of the host countries. A bewildering variety of motivations can influence a person to voluntarily renounce or maintain refugee status, as well as many other reasons which could arise for the status to be revoked. What is certain is that the refugee crisis of 2015 has represented a turning point for Europe, revealing that many countries were unprepared to handle this wave of migrants – even those with a long tradition of welcoming migrants.

The European Union and its member states are the leading donors of international aid to the Syrian crisis.[37] However, the lack of a common policy generated a certain level of chaos at numerous borders, and the influx of refugees did not benefit from careful political planning and long-term strategies. A French government official commented that the fact that Europe found itself surprised by this wave of refugees was reflected in an ad hoc policy process and that France's experience is an example of this phenomenon, saying: 'At least four relevant policy devices were simultaneously put in place during the big 2015 influx: relocation, resettlement, the coordination of Iraqi nationals belonging to persecuted religious minorities, and the need to find a solution to the Calais "jungle" refugee camps.'[38] It is increasingly evident that it is crucial to highlight and share good practices and bad practices, as well as the main challenges facing the integration policies of European countries.

11.3 The Legal Framework

The Universal Declaration of Human Rights (UDHR), proclaimed in 1948, can be considered a milestone document in the history of human rights,

[36] 'Asylum decisions in the EU', *Eurostat*, 26 April 2017, www.europeanmigrationlaw.eu/documents/Eurostat-AsylumDecisions-2016.pdf.

[37] 'Syria', European Commission, http://ec.europa.eu/echo/where/middle-east/syria_en (accessed 9 November 2017).

[38] Interview conducted by the EFD at the Interior Ministry in Paris on 23 March 2017.

stating: 'Everyone has the right to seek and to enjoy in other countries asylum from persecution.'[39] In 1951, the Refugee Convention,[40] a UN multilateral treaty, provided a universal framework for the treatment of refugees on the basis of Article 14 of the UDHR. The Refugee Convention defined 'refugees'[41] and set out their rights and obligations. In 1967, the Protocol Relating to the Status of Refugees[42] expanded the temporal and geographical scope of the Refugee Convention, which originally covered only persons fleeing events occurring within Europe before 1951.

The principle of non-refoulement contained in Article 33 of the Convention can be defined as the cornerstone of refugee protection. According to this article, refugees coming from countries where their life is at risk or where they are in danger of being treated in an inhumane or degrading manner should not be returned. However, refugees who are considered a substantial threat to the host community may not invoke this principle. This latter point has become a major topic of debate in terms of legal and security aspects within the EU.[43]

Enacted on 3 September 1953, the Convention for the Protection of Human Rights and Fundamental Freedoms[44] (ECHR) established the European Court of Human Rights (ECtHR). In 1961, the Court recognised that Article 3 of the EHCR can enclose the principle of non-refoulement.[45] This principle was adopted by a Parliamentary Assembly of the Council of Europe (PACE) recommendation on the granting of the right of asylum to European refugees on 1 October 1965, 'to guarantee refugees the right not to be returned to a country where they

39 GA Res. 217 A (III), UN Doc. A/811, 10 December 1948, Article 14.

40 Convention Relating to the Status of Refugees, 28 July 1951, 189 U.N.T.S. 137.

41 European Migration Network (EMN), 'Asylum and Migration Glossary 3.0' (European Commission, October 2014), 230, https://ec.europa.eu/migrant-integration/librarydoc/asylum-and-migration-glossary-30: 'In the EU context, either a third-country national who, owing to a well-founded fear of persecution for reasons of race, religion, nationality, political opinion or membership of a particular social group, is outside the country of nationality and is unable or, owing to such fear, is unwilling to avail themselves of the protection of that country, or a stateless person, who, being outside of the country of former habitual residence for the same reasons as mentioned above, is unable or, owing to such fear, unwilling to return to it, and to whom Art. 12 (Exclusion) of Directive 2011/95/EU does not apply.'

42 Protocol Relating to the Status of Refugees, 31 January 1967, 606 U.N.T.S. 267.

43 G. Gilbert, 'Undesirable but Unreturnable: Extradition and Other Forms of Rendition', *Journal of International Criminal Justice* 15, no. 1, (1 March 2017): 55–74.

44 4 November 1950, ETS 5.

45 G. S. Goodwin-Gill and J. McAdam, *The Refugee in International Law* (Oxford: Oxford University Press, 2007), 290.

would be in danger of persecution (recognition of the principle of prohibition of return (non-refoulement))'.[46]

The principle of non-refoulement is anchored in Article 78(1) of the Treaty on the Functioning of the EU[47] (TFEU) and Articles 18 and 19 of the Charter of Fundamental Rights of the European Union,[48] a charter that became legally binding for all member states in 2009 in the wake of the Treaty of Lisbon Amending the Treaty on European Union and the Treaty Establishing the European Community.[49] Non-refoulement, together with other factors, such as the lack of travel documents, forms the basis of the impossibility to return a migrant even if he or she is considered as undesirable in the host country. In these cases, the rejected asylum seeker or refugee whose status has been revoked enters a limbo of uncertainty and diminished rights, posing a risk to national security.

As terrorist attacks began to occur with greater frequency across Europe, the non-refoulement principle became a matter of public debate. Furthermore, xenophobic political parties have exploited the humanitarian disaster, which occurred at the same time as increasing numbers of terrorist attacks and terror threats all over Europe. Such parties have used these dual events to foster the false and dangerous fear of a systematic use of migration routes by terrorists. In addition, jihadist groups such as ISIS have sought to play on the fears of 'refugees as terrorists', which aligns with the group's own belief that there are unresolvable divisions between East and West. During the Bataclan attack in Paris in November 2015, for example, one of the Belgian-born attackers kept on him a false or stolen passport of a Syrian asylum seeker, to be found later on his corpse by the authorities.[50] Reality is different from this narrative: most of the attacks – including Paris in January and November 2015; Brussels in March 2016; Berlin in December 2016; Stockholm in April 2017; Manchester in May 2017; and London in June 2017 – were committed by home-grown terrorists radicalised in the European country where they were born and grew up. This reveals that poor integration, especially within second- or

[46] 'Recommendation 434 (1965). Granting of the right of asylum to European refugees', 1 October 1965, http://assembly.coe.int/nw/xml/XRef/Xref-XML2HTML-en.asp?fileid=14471&lang=en.

[47] 13 December 2007, 2008/C 115/01.

[48] 26 October 2012, 2012/C 326/02.

[49] 13 December 2007, 2007/C 306/01.

[50] 'Why Syrian Refugee Passport Found at Paris Attack Scene Must Be Treated with Caution', *The Guardian*, 15 November 2015, www.theguardian.com/world/2015/nov/15/why-syrian-refugee-passport-found-at-paris-attack-scene-must-be-treated-with-caution.

third-generation citizens,[51] and a lack of proper integration policies is the real issue. On the other hand, it is worth noting that these fears should not be totally underestimated. Indeed, according to Europol, '[I]t is indisputable that some terrorists have entered the EU posing as a refugee.'[52] A report written by the Danish Institute for International Studies states that from January 2016 to April 2017 'four asylum-seekers were involved in terrorist incidents, but no actual refugees'.[53] Only one attack has been documented as having been committed by a Syrian refugee. Mohammad Daleel, who had been denied asylum, detonated a suicide bomb outside a wine bar in Ansbach, Germany, in July 2016. He killed only himself but wounded fifteen others. Daleel had been radicalised in Syria and had fought for al-Nusra before pledging allegiance to ISIS.

With the aim of guaranteeing protection and effective procedures for refugees, the EU created a Common European Asylum System (CEAS) in 1999. Five pillars constitute CEAS, supported by an agency, the European Asylum Support Office (EASO):

- Dublin Regulation: determines which member state is competent to process a given asylum application. The main rule is that responsibility lies with the member state where the asylum seeker first entered.
- Eurodac Regulation: establishes a central fingerprint database for asylum seekers in the EU. This prevents refugees from lodging applications in more than one member state.
- Asylum Procedure Directive: establishes harmonisation of asylum procedures and criteria in the EU, such as how to judge an application as 'unfounded' or 'inadmissible'.

[51] On that note, see Gilles Kepel and Antoine Jardin, *Terror in France: The Rise of Jihad in the West* (Princeton, NJ: Princeton University Press, 2017); Sean S. Costigan and David Gold, *Terrornomics* (Abingdon: Routledge, 2016), 60; Vicki Coppock and Mark McGovern, '"Dangerous Minds"? Deconstructing Counter-Terrorism Discourse, Radicalisation and the "Psychological Vulnerability" of Muslim Children and Young People in Britain', *Children and Society* 28, no. 3 (2014): 242–56; Peter Bergen, 'Bergen: A Pattern in Terror Second Generation, Homegrown', 24 May 2017, http://edition.cnn.com/2017/05/24/opinions/homegrown-terrorism-opinion-bergen/index.html; and Valerio de Divitiis, 'Considerations over Factors Empowering Radicalization in the European Union', in *Perspectives on Immigration and Terrorism* eds. G. M. Ruggiero, S. Sassaroli, Y. Latzer, and S. Suchday (Amsterdam: Ios Press, 2011), 53.

[52] Europol, *TESAT: European Union Terrorism Situation and Trend Report* (Europol, 2018), 62; Europol, *Changes in Modus Operandi of Islamic State (IS) Revisited* (Europol, 2016), 9.

[53] 'Europe's Refugee Crisis and the Threat of Terrorism: An Extraordinary Threat?', DIIS, 2017, 4, http://pure.diis.dk/ws/files/910914/Report_05_Europes_Refugee_Crisis_Web.pdf.

- Qualification Directive: establishes common grounds for the rights of refugees, e.g. protection from refoulement, residence permits, travel documents, access to employment, etc.
- Receptions Conditions Directive: determines minimum standards for living conditions, e.g. housing, food, healthcare, etc.

In sum, while every EU member state maintains its own asylum laws, it must align them to EU rules. One of the main issues facing the mass influx of asylum seekers is to determine which country is responsible for processing the asylum claim. According to the Dublin Regulation, this responsibility lies with the country of first arrival. This results in pressure on southern member states such as Italy and Greece simply because of their geographic location, with the Mediterranean countries being the first point of contact for many arriving refugees. Consequently, in September 2015, the member states decided to enact an Emergency Relocation System within the EU, with the aim of transferring asylum seekers and refugees from states under huge pressure to states with fewer arriving refugees. However, as of August 2017, some member states, including Denmark, Austria, and Hungary, were failing to participate in the programme, while others were doing so insubstantially.[54] In addition, the EU created 'hotspots' in Italy and Greece to further ease migratory pressures. These 'hotspots' were established to help front-line member states to 'swiftly identify, register, and fingerprint incoming migrants',[55] though some reports reveal they became overcrowded detention centres.[56]

The resettlement framework is an important tool for helping people in need of protection reach Europe legally and safely. The framework is more a collection of multilateral programmes than a common set of rules and, as far as it concerns Syrian refugees, twenty member states are

[54] European Migration and Home Affairs, 'Member States' Support to Emergency Relocation Mechanism', *European Commission*, 19 October 2017, https://ec.europa.eu/home-affairs/sites/homeaffairs/files/what-we-do/policies/european-agenda-migration/press-material/docs/state_of_play_-_relocation_en.pdf.

[55] European Commission, 'A European Agenda on Migration', *European Commission*, 13 May 2015, 6, https://ec.europa.eu/anti-trafficking/sites/antitrafficking/files/communication_on_the_european_agenda_on_migration_en.pdf.

[56] On that note, see Aspasia Papadopoulou, 'The Implementation of the Hotspots in Italy and Greece', ECRE, 5 December 2016, 11, www.ecre.org/wp-content/uploads/2016/12/HOTSPOTS-Report-5.12.2016.pdf; 'Understanding Migration and Asylum in the European Union', *Open Society Foundations*, www.opensocietyfoundations.org/explainers/understanding-migration-and-asylum-european-union (accessed 24 October 2017).

currently involved in these procedures.[57] In March 2016, for instance, the EU announced a deal with Turkey to curb the flow of irregular migration of Syrian refugees inside its borders. Unfortunately, as of 2017, many member states have not yet started resettling refugees within the EU-level schemes, and thousands of people have continued to travel to Europe with the help of smugglers or have been stuck in camps ever since the Balkan migration route was closed.

According to some analysts, the EU regulatory framework should be comprehensively reassessed, both in developing European border management in line with the European Convention on Human Rights and in handling asylum applications and redistributions.[58] The establishment of an independent and fully qualified EU Agency on Asylum (currently being discussed at the EU legal level) is widely considered an important step in the right direction.[59]

11.4 The EFD's Study

11.4.1 Main Challenges and Vulnerabilities

Integration is a multidimensional phenomenon whose success or failure varies according to individuals, their arrival situation, their cultural background, the duration of their stay, the community that welcomes them, the generation to which they belong, and a further set of variables that are difficult to catalogue. During the research, the EFD found some vulnerabilities and areas of concern that can negatively impact the integration process of refugees.

Most recent asylum seekers have experienced psychological trauma as a result of fleeing civil war and conflict in their home countries. This is particularly the case for Syrians, though not limited to them alone. Although an element of embarrassment and a wish to forget often prevailed when it came to recounting the tragedies, shocks, and physical

[57] 'Resettlement of Refugees: EU framework', *European Parliament*, 13 December 2017, www.europarl.europa.eu/RegData/etudes/BRIE/2016/589859/EPRS_BRI(2016)589859_EN.pdf.

[58] Clémentine d'Oultremont and Anna Martin, 'The Migration Crisis: A Stress Test for European Values', *European Policy Brief*, no. 38 (September 2015), http://aei.pitt.edu/74541/1/38.pdf; Christian Dustmann et al., 'On the Economics and Politics of Refugee Migration', *CESifo*, no. 6111 (September 2016), www.cesifo-group.de/DocDL/cesifo1_wp6111.pdf; Elspeth Guild et al., 'The 2015 Refugee Crisis in the European Union', *Centre for the European Policy Studies*, no. 332 (September 2015), www.ceps.eu/system/files/CEPS%20PB332%20Refugee%20Crisis%20in%20EU_0.pdf.

[59] d'Oultremont and Martin, 'The Migration Crisis: A Stress Test for European Values'.

damages suffered due to the Syrian civil war, the EFD collected some accounts on these themes.[60] Fahad spoke about living conditions in Syria: 'I had no choice but to leave, ISIS was terrible with the population in Deir ez-Zur, you can be jailed for a cigarette or indeed for looking at someone that may be perceived as provocative.' Rajab's tale came out in a whisper: 'I have seen too many horrors, children dying, dismembered bodies, people with mental health wandering and dying on the street.' Majd fled to Europe with his brother after being tortured by Assad's regime: 'We had written some songs to support the spirit of the revolution.' Sayid was abducted in the streets by Bashar al-Assad's secret police for attending a peaceful demonstration, tortured for fifteen days, and then released after his father paid a bribe. Despite this terrible situation, most European governments do not offer psychological trauma-therapy as a standard, though it can be made available on request. In some of the countries surveyed by the EFD, government funding is being reduced for this service.

Housing shortage is reported as a regular hardship asylum seekers and refugees must endure. Overcrowded living quarters in reception centres have been specifically mentioned as places where incidents and violence take place. Rania's tale was emotionally draining: 'I remember it was raining that afternoon and I was sitting by the window at the accommodation centre. I was thinking of everything we'd been through in Syria and during the terrible journey to reach Europe with my husband and my five-year-old son. My son was playing and running inside the centre but for ten minutes he seemed to be hiding. I went to look for him, I heard him weeping in the men's toilet. I came in and a man was sexually assaulting my son. I took him away and I ran to my husband. We called the police but my husband wanted to kill him. The police have not proved the sexual violence and so that man has only been moved to another centre.'

The forced cohabitation of people from different backgrounds, even of those coming from the same country of origin, has also led to sectarian tensions. 'The first months were really hard', said Tariq. 'I did not speak the language, I had no money. I sought help in the other Syrians of the

[60] See 'Refugees in Europe: Review of Integration Practices & Policies', EFD, 2018, http://europeandemocracy.eu/wp-content/uploads/2018/05/2018-Refugees-In-Europe-Full-Version.pdf. All respondents were assured of anonymity and confidentiality in their responses to the survey questions to protect their identity and encourage frankness and increased openness in the interviews. All names used in the EFD's report and in this article have been changed and are not the real names of respondents.

centre but shortly thereafter I decided to stay alone because I saw Assad regime supporters write down my name as a dissident and I was scared.' Marwan's tale strengthens this account: 'There are mainly three kinds of Syrian refugees in Europe: pro-regime, non-militant opposition, and militant opposition. Syrians are generally scared of interacting with each other. A pro-regime person will not engage with somebody against the regime and vice-versa.' Amina explains: 'It is necessary to imagine Syria as a small community. We do not travel so much inside our country and we live mainly in the region of birth. So, we know only a small part of Syria. But when someone, for example, arrives in Europe and is hosted in a reception centre, they find themselves in the midst of so many people of different cultures and religions. It can create many problems.' Some refugees also reported high levels of conservatism in the centres against LGBT people. A number of female refugees reported episodes of harassment from their own menfolk in European host countries because they did not wear the hijab and behaved too much like Western women.

The situation is further complicated by the high concentration of immigrants in some neighbourhoods due to a lack of redistribution policies. This is particularly true for Belgium, France, and Sweden, where distribution of immigrants is unequal, discouraging integration with the host community and fuelling tensions and criminality.[61] In the Netherlands, despite a quota system in each municipality, concentration of migrants and refugees in cities such as Amsterdam or Utrecht have been reported as an issue that makes it more difficult for newcomers to pass language and integration exams.[62]

In Austria, France, and Germany, some refugees reported instances of high levels of intolerance and conservatism in some mosques. According to Aisha, '[T]here are Syrians who have stopped going to mosques because they are scared. I live close to a mosque and I am scared. People there are hard-core Salafists. Syrians have trouble with Salafists everywhere, even in a sandwich shop for instance.' Amjad provides an example of this: 'Syrians often have trouble with Salafists and the most

[61] In Belgium asylum seekers and refugees tend to congregate in Brussels and Flanders; in France there is a high concentration in the Paris/Île-de-France region. In Sweden, concentration and ghettoisation are particularly present in Malmö and Stockholm. Concerning violence, see 'Utsatta områden -sociala risker, kollektiv förmåga och oönskade händelser', *Polisen*, December 2015, https://polisen.se/siteassets/dokument/ovriga_rapporter/utsatta-omraden-sociala-risker-kollektiv-formaga-och-oonskade-handelser.pdf (accessed 18 May 2018).

[62] Interviews conducted from April to June 2017. Refugees in Amsterdam are those who have complained most on this issue.

common example relates to the consumption of alcohol. If a Syrian man goes to a take-away restaurant where there are Salafists and he buys whiskey, Salafists who see him often show aggression.' In France, some Syrian respondents also reported concerns about obscure money-raising schemes in halal butcher shops that were allegedly for relief purposes outside any state control.

Another concern raised was how non-violent radical groups have sought to exploit refugees by encouraging individuals to not integrate or learn the local language and instead remain separate from the host nation. Many refugees cited examples where they believed governments had abrogated responsibility in providing support services to refugees by delegating this to organisations that did not appear to have the same respect for liberal democratic values. In many of the countries surveyed – Sweden, Germany, and the Netherlands in particular – the EFD heard of examples of political-religious organisations that had effectively been permitted to take over tasks such as providing refugee housing, language and integration orientation courses, and other services. A number of refugees in Austria, Germany, and Sweden said they had also encountered Islamist organisations seeking to act as intermediaries between them and the government agencies or assuming self-appointed roles as 'representatives' of certain refugee communities. They rejected these groups because of their overly conservative narratives and non-inclusive approach to integration. For instance, in the Netherlands, some refugees complained that women had been verbally harassed for not wearing the veil in some Arabic and Quranic schools. Some refugees in Sweden saw that Islamist groups were also providing pre-school education support services to young refugee children, a number of which were state-funded for these activities. Most governments surveyed had no formal procedures for qualitatively vetting and assessing the service providers or the services themselves for refugees. This represents a real risk of failing to offer a proper integration process for newcomers and a serious risk of empowering radical elements.

EU authorities admitted that numbers of migrants in 2015 were so vast that the security services of many countries were overwhelmed and unable to properly vet those arriving. At the same time, government respondents in many countries downplayed the risk of 'fake refugees' because of what is considered to be good cooperation between the security services and asylum agencies, which have systems to detect possible inconsistencies in asylum seekers' applications. However, it is possible for individuals to present a plausible case and be considered genuine asylum seekers. This issue, together with other factors – such as the absence of a sense of belonging, the loss of social status, the lack of employment, and the role of some radical ideologies, among others – can create a breeding ground for the possible radicalisation of newcomers. The recent arrest of six Syrian migrants in Germany, all of whom had applied for asylum, suspected of plotting a terrorist attack linked to ISIS,[63] emphasises these risks. A number of testimonies discussed Islamist actors in Germany and Belgium who have been proselytising among newcomers, focusing on young people and unaccompanied minors who represent those categories most at risk for radicalisation and recruitment by terrorists.

Furthermore, interviews with experts in international crime and terrorism reveal that some civil society organisations involved in supporting refugees' integration process do not report to the authorities signs of radicalisation they identify in some of their clients. This is mainly because they fear their reports may have serious negative repercussions for their clients, and also because they do not receive any feedback from the authorities regarding their reports. Therefore, they do not know whether their reports are relevant.

When it comes to talking to newcomers about their first steps in the host countries, many of them reported having been victims of racist insults during asylum procedures. 'I've been called "animal" from a government official', said Leila. 'I had a very bad experience with the personnel in the office where I submitted my asylum application.' Banan reported: 'I had to come back five times to the office before I could start my application and employees did not have much patience.' Some testimonies gave reports about translators who were not sufficiently proficient and about a lack of coordination in managing asylum procedures. Saabir, for instance, explained he was in a very difficult economic situation when he started the asylum procedure, as he did not have a job. However, he had accommodations, and therefore the official who helped him fill out the forms told him to write he did not need state housing. When Saabir asked how he could receive the economic aid that the state made available for newcomers, he was told he could no longer ask for that kind of help as he had refused state housing. It took another two months to solve the problem. Others recount the waiting period for their status

[63] 'Anti-Terror-Razzien in mehreren Bundesländern', *Florian Flade*, 21 November 2017, www.welt.de/politik/deutschland/article170797822/Anti-Terror-Razzien-in-mehreren-Bundeslaendern.htm.

recognition. 'I was eating a sandwich with other migrants when some guys arrived with their shaved heads yelling and insulting us. I did not understand the language so I could not reply. They overturned the table against us and some other people were clapping. I was very scared', says Rami.

The EFD have heard not only about problems and concerns but also about a number of good experiences. Most of those are related to the help and advice Syrian refugees received from civil society organisations or from state initiatives, which facilitate refugees' access to the labour market. This is described well by Mohamed, who said: 'There are some associations that treat refugees with piety and convey a sense of inferiority and malaise to the newcomer. Others have an agenda, such as proselytism. But, luckily, there are many others who understand what the real needs are of an asylum seeker or a refugee and offer help in every field: food, clothing, cultural activities, language courses, and job placement.'

11.4.2 Good Practices and Policies

There is currently no clear agreement regarding how to measure and evaluate practices that facilitate integration. The EFD made a structured assessment based on three pillars of integration policy: socioeconomic, sociocultural, and social inclusion. In order to test initial assumptions, we conducted interviews with asylum seekers and refugees asking them which practices and initiatives had helped them integrate into the host society. Asylum seekers and refugees' satisfaction with some practices should be seen as a process-oriented assessment rather than the end result, as most of the good practices identified are still ongoing while others are at a preliminary stage. On the whole, the assessment was based on a framework of need and response. If the practices offered solutions to central problems that afflict the integration process, they were introduced for their potential contribution.

Most governments examined by the study require asylum seekers to sign a declaration of intent, requiring newcomers to comply with the principles of the host country; these include fundamental liberal democratic values, such as gender equality, respect for different sexual orientations, freedom of religious and non-religious beliefs, and an overall respect for the individual. These declarations are an obligatory part of the integration process. However, comparable documents also exist at the local level, which can be signed on a voluntary basis. For example, the city of Vienna has adopted a charter, drafted together with refugees and asylum seekers, which outlines the fundamental principles that underlie good social coexistence in the Austrian capital. Aamir, a young Syrian refugee in Austria, said: '[P]articipating in writing this Chart was exciting. I felt that my thoughts were important. People listened to my point of view and I listened to the others. I understood better some principles of the society where I am living.' Empowering a refugee to integrate themselves is a good practice, and it is essential that all citizens, including newcomers, abide by the values and principles of a liberal-democratic society in order to maintain a peaceful coexistence.

In this regard, some integration courses, like those offered by the Flemish integration system or by different CSOs throughout Belgium, include components dedicated to intercultural exchanges and civic education on the laws and values of the host country. These efforts to overcome cultural barriers are bolstered by the creation of projects specifically made by refugees for newcomers. An example of these is a pilot project supported by the Belgium Federal Agency for the Reception of Asylum Seekers and run by Afghan volunteers from the Human Welfare Association NGO, which works at educating Afghans in refugee centres on gender equality.

Initiatives relating to the social inclusion of refugees and their host community also emerged from the EFD's study. One such example is the Austrian Integration Fund, which provides language and other services to promote integration and, since 2012, has managed an initiative called TOGETHER: AUSTRIA. This programme organises 'Integration Ambassadors' – successfully integrated migrants – to visit Austrian schools, clubs, and organisations with the hope of motivating young people with a migrant/refugee background to recognise the importance of education and the ways to benefit from the career options offered in Austria.

Peer Youth, an EU-funded sub-project run by the City of Vienna, is another example of social support initiatives. Peer Youth works at connecting groups of refugee or immigrant youths with peers from their neighbourhood and community, particularly regarding issues surrounding integration. Similarly, Zebra helps connect refugees with the local community in the city of Graz, through close cooperation with the municipalities and other stakeholders. In Denmark, certain municipalities train older or former refugees to be mentors to newcomers and act as intercultural bridges between new refugees and the state.

Finding available and affordable housing is described by many refugees as the greatest challenge they face, due to housing shortages, high rent, and a lack of willingness by landlords to rent properties to refugees. In Belgium, where the state economically supports refugees but does not offer them accommodation, Caritas International Belgium and Convivial, two Brussels-based non-governmental organisations, have built a network of *proprietaires solidaires* ('sympathetic landlords') willing to rent to refugees. The organisations act as intermediaries between the two groups. In France, research has detected QuickBed – a management tool to help asylum seekers find accommodation, which is also useful for dispersing newcomers across the country and relieving pressure on any one region.

As mentioned, certain countries do not enact policies of redistribution. This results in the concentration of newcomers in poor neighborhoods, which strains local social services. In order to avoid 'closed' communities, the Danish government requires refugees to stay in the municipality to which they have been allocated for three years before they can receive state integration benefits. This system appears effective in encouraging refugees to integrate into Danish society: according to the information collected during interviews at the Ministry of Justice, most refugees, after some preliminary misgivings, settle in relatively quickly and enjoy living in the area they have been allocated, ultimately managing to integrate successfully. In March 2016, Sweden approved a law obliging all municipalities to each settle a certain number of refugees in order to free up space in the reception system and, by extension, avoid problems associated with high concentrations at the reception centres. Likewise, in the Netherlands, where the state provides refugees with social housing, each municipality is required to house a certain number of refugees.

Regarding the need for the host country to have a greater awareness of asylum seekers and refugees, some initiatives deserve to be mentioned. In Belgium, non-governmental organisations such as DUO for a JOB, Refugees Got Talent, and Our House Project promote the integration of refugees with their host society. The Humanity House initiative in the Netherlands organises events where the historical and humanitarian dimensions of migration and refugeeism are presented from different perspectives. Moreover, in Germany a number of municipalities have created structures with the aim of favouring roundtable discussions and information campaigns about refugee-related issues.

At the level of civil society, several initiatives and programmes address intercultural interaction between refugees and local communities in

Sweden. One example is Hej Främling! (Hello Stranger!) which organises outdoor excursions and physical activities for refugees and their families: 'It has been nice to participate in activities that the Swedes are most passionate about. I had new experiences and I met new friends. I really felt part of a great new community', said Kamal. In France and Germany, the SINGA organisation does important work in bringing together refugees and local communities to dissolve false myths and ignorance surrounding the refugee phenomenon; in 2017 it organised more than 150 outreach events across France.

It is critical that each newcomer receives information on the asylum process, ways to find basic goods, social assistance options, and how to find jobs, among other things. Both the Start Vienna programme and Paris' weanswer.ue are examples of good practices that provide essential information on how to start life in those cities.

Even though they can present some critical issues, offering volunteer opportunities to asylum seekers and refugees is another good practice widely implemented across the countries in the study. Such initiatives include the Ankommen App, which helps refugees navigate the maze of rules and regulations of the German asylum procedure, as well as offering an understanding of the German way of life. Similarly, in Belgium, asylum seekers have the right to social assistance from a social worker. This acts as a way to inform newcomers of the asylum process and their social rights (including the rules of the reception centres) and to offer assistance in case of urgent or dangerous individual circumstances. Angehort is a Berlin-based CSO founded by social workers, lawyers, and students, which works to explain the application process as well as help prepare applicants for their interview at the Federal Office for Migration and Refugees. A volunteer-based organisation called Venligboerne (Kind Neighbours) has more than ninety Facebook groups based in different districts, towns, and cities in Denmark and abroad. Its members (about 150,000) and many refugees widely praise it as being one of the country's most accessible support networks for newcomers. For many, it offers the first tangible opportunity to participate in the labour market and receive practical information on different domains. A similar initiative is Action Emploi Réfugiés, a French NGO that launched a project aiming to connect refugees looking for work with employers prepared to recruit refugees. It is important, however, that if governments encourage civil society organisations to intervene along the asylum chain, they must carry out constant checks and evaluations of the quality of the services provided.

Developing language skills and finding skill-relevant and appropriate work are among the most critical challenges refugees face. Most governments do not permit asylum seekers to benefit from state-funded language and other pre-integration services. They do, however, encourage volunteers and volunteer organisations to provide these services. Moreover, many governments support interesting initiatives to facilitate refugees' access to the labour market. Some governments have developed early skills and education mapping of asylum seekers and locate successful applicants to live in relevant areas where their skills are needed. Some private sector initiatives in several countries surveyed have specific skill shortages, including, for example, on-the-job training and remunerated conversion courses for Syrian engineers (e.g. in Denmark). Initiatives such as this seem to be highly appreciated by refugees.

One of the most vulnerable categories in need of specific services is that of unaccompanied minors. Stichting Nidos is a Dutch organisation, a national shelter providing guidance and support for unaccompanied minors seeking asylum in the Netherlands. The shelter provides professional guardians to protect minors. Its main purpose is to take care of children in family circles regardless of whether or not they have refugee status. This is a good practice to be replicated in all the European countries.

11.5 Final Remarks

According to the UNHCR, by February 2018 over 77,000 Syrian refugees had returned to their home country.[64] The cities of Aleppo, Hama, Homs, and Damascus received the most returnees during the first half of 2017, primarily from Turkey.[65] Since the war is still ongoing, it is highly unlikely that the return of refugees will occur in safe and dignified conditions. In Europe, it seems too early to talk about return for Syrian refugees. In 2016, German Chancellor Angela Merkel said during a regional meeting of her Christian Democratic Union that refugees should return home once the war is over and ISIS has been defeated.[66]

64 'Syria: February 2018', *UNHCR*, February 2018, www.unhcr.org/sy/wp-content/uploads/sites/3/2018/02/Syria-Fact-Sheet-2017-2018.pdf.

65 'UNHCR Seeing Significant Returns of Internally Displaced amid Syria's Continuing Conflict', *UNHCR*, 30 June 2017, www.unhcr.org/news/briefing/2017/6/595612454/unhcr-seeing-significant-returns-internally-displaced-amid-syrias-continuing.html.

66 'Germany's Merkel Says Refugees Must Return Home Once War Is Over', *Reuters*, 30 January 2016, https://in.reuters.com/article/europe-migrants-germany-refugees/germanys-merkel-says-refugees-must-return-home-once-war-is-over-idINKCN0V80IR.

In the meantime, Syrian refugees in Europe are trying to build new lives in their host country, opening businesses, getting married, and having children who will grow up in Europe for as long as the war continues. Furthermore, the reconstruction of Syria, both in terms of buildings and economic reorganisation, will take many years. Additionally, many of the refugees will not willingly return to a country led by the same regime from which they fled, in the event of Bashar al-Assad remaining in power at the war's conclusion. These are among the primary reasons Europe cannot delay investing in the integration of refugees.

With over 1 million Syrian refugees likely to stay in Europe, the challenges of integration and absorption are both critical and urgent. Based on the EFD's study of seven EU member states, the EFD concluded that Europe still has much to do. Indeed, over the course of this study it became clear that considerable problems relating to the 2015 migration crisis persist on both a local and international level. Governments in most EU countries have similar asylum and immigration policies, although application processes can take significantly longer in certain jurisdictions: in March 2017, applications took as long as thirteen months to process.[67] The changing political climate towards refugees in Europe has seen governments considerably tighten the rules on granting asylum.

The main problems facing the refugee issue in Europe include the lack of integration courses and job opportunities, tensions among asylum seekers or refugee communities, a lack of monitoring and evaluation of organisations that claim to 'represent' groups or particular religious faiths while they approach asylum seekers, and the unequal distribution, or 'ghettoisation', of refugees. All this could lead to violence and other serious societal issues. However, Europe has also experienced a number of good practices that can be extended and serve as a model for other countries to adopt. These are actions relate to the social inclusion of refugees with their host community, guidance to asylum seekers during administrative procedures, initiatives to facilitate refugees' access to the labour market, and other activities which appear effective in terms of sociocultural integration in the liberal-democratic framework.

It is paramount that refugees understand and accept that the foundations of liberal democratic systems in Europe are based on a set of inviolable principles established as part of the Enlightenment – respect for the rule of law, freedom of expression, individual liberty and conscience, gender equality, the right to choose or change one's religion, etc.

[67] This was particularly the case in France and Austria.

Syrian urban society is not a stranger to these principles. The 2011 pro-democratic protests in Daraa are the tangible proof.

Failure to integrate refugees into liberal-democratic European societies creates voids that may be filled by extremist forces of different types that increase fragmentation and polarisation. The international community has failed to protect the Syrian people from their own government and other forces over the past six years. Hundreds of thousands of refugees are now in need of the protection of many EU member states. Europe has a duty of care and a responsibility to protect them from exploitation, predation, and attack while preserving the values upon which its liberal-democratic societies are built.

There is but a short time frame in which Europe can create and enforce robust integration policies and practices. To do so will require political strength, forward planning, and intellectual honesty from all political players and civil society participants. Such changes are essential not only for the current crisis but also for the future unity, safety, and security of Europe. Therefore, it is necessary to find an equilibrium between security, humanitarian responsibilities, and the protection and promotion of liberal democratic values and principles.

PART III

A New Syria in a New World Order?

Assessing Legal and Political Implications

12

Transitional Justice Without Transition

The International Community's Efforts in Syria

BETH VAN SCHAACK

12.1 Introduction

The concept of transitional justice refers to the range of measures – judicial and non-judicial, formal and informal, retributive and reconciliatory – that may be employed by societies in response to a legacy of authoritarianism or mass violence following a period of political transition.[1] Most of the work around building a transitional justice response has historically occurred during the final phases of a conflict or in the post-conflict period,[2] when the guns have fallen silent (though perhaps not been fully holstered). The situation in Syria, by contrast, presents an interesting experiment at attempts by the international community to lay the groundwork for a credible transitional justice process pre-transition, while the conflict continued to rage. Many of these efforts carried with them the potential to facilitate or hasten the desired transition. These objectives were central to the policy of the United States vis-à-vis the conflict in Syria. Working primarily through the State Department and the US Agency for International Development

This chapter benefited from the support of the Center for Advanced Study in the Behavioral Sciences at Stanford University. I am grateful to the following individuals for their wise feedback on this paper: Sareta Ashraph, Stephanie Barbour, Priscilla Hayner, Louise Malinder, Hilly Moodrick-Even Khen, Blake Peterson, Ambassador Stephen Rapp, and Ron Slye.

1 See generally Paul Van Zyl, 'Promoting Transitional Justice in Post-Conflict Societies', in *Security Governance in Post-Conflict Peacebuilding: Second Edition*, eds. Alan Bryden and Heiner Hänggi (Geneva: Lit Verlag, 2005): 209.

2 Ever hopeful, the drafters of the Geneva communiqué of 30 June 2012 (A/66/865, annex), which is one of the major terms of reference of the political settlement in Syria, state that transitional justice should be an integral part of the comprehensive framework for amnesty and national reconciliation.

(USAID),[3] the United States deployed strategic messaging and multilateral engagement coupled with dedicated assistance programmes to support a range of accountability and transitional justice projects focused on Syria. Other donor states followed suit.

These wartime projects reflected a number of overarching foreign policy priorities: to send a clear message that perpetrators of international crimes, regardless of affiliation, would be held to account; to provoke defections and deter further abuses; and to begin to socialise the value of pursuing a holistic and inclusive transitional justice programme, particularly when it comes to marginalised segments of society, victim groups that may have been singled out for special abuse, and other key Syrian stakeholders. These lines of effort were pursued with the goal of enabling a peaceful democratic transition, establishing future stability, and encouraging social cohesion among the myriad Syrian communities torn asunder by the conflict. Many of these initiatives did not depend upon Syrian consent or a multilateral consensus and so could be pursued notwithstanding Assad's unapologetic intransigence or Russia's propensity to veto any coercive measures proposed within the Security Council.

This effort at pre-transition transitional justice has been fraught with challenges and uncertainty. For one, many transitional justice practitioners argue that any transitional justice programme must develop organically from within the affected society itself, with international involvement largely limited to the provision of technical assistance and funding rather than the imposition of a fully formed agenda. It has been difficult, however, to ensure that any course of action is Syrian-led when it is unclear which Syrians will be in a position to eventually lead such a process. In addition, secure access to the country has been largely foreclosed, so most work had to be done on the periphery – in refugee camps and neighbouring countries, within the diaspora and exile communities, and with Syrians courageous enough to brave a border crossing. Many of these projects were conceptualised and implemented in an era when President Bashar al-Assad appeared to be operating from a position of growing weakness and the conflict seemed to be coming to a close. These endeavours became infinitely more complicated with the subsequent metastasis of the battlefield following the emergence of ISIS on the scene and the involvement of Western superpowers who are at

[3] Beth Van Schaack, 'US Policy on Transitional Justice', *Just Security*, 29 June 2016, www.justsecurity.org/31722/us-policy-transitional-justice/, identifying State/USAID policy papers on the US approach to transitional justice.

once allies (against ISIS) and adversaries (vis-à-vis the regime). Prospects for a holistic transitional justice process are even dimmer now as it becomes increasingly apparent that President Assad will remain in power in some capacity, at least in the immediate future.

This chapter focuses on the role of the international community in fostering pre-transition transitional justice. This is a project that can take multiple forms. For many years, the United Nations and individual states laid emphasis on the documentation of abuses 'on all sides', including by leveraging tools available through the UN Human Rights Council in the absence of a consensus around any other accountability options within the Security Council. The General Assembly ratcheted up the prospects for criminal accountability in 2016 with the establishment of the International, Impartial, and Independent Mechanism to Investigate Serious Crimes in Syria (IIIM) to help coordinate these efforts.[4] States and NGOs also surveyed and trained Syrian actors to prepare them for undertaking a programme of transitional justice. Other proto-accountability exercises included naming and shaming the regime and individual perpetrators, though this was not pursued to the full extent possible in Syria. Individual states and norm entrepreneurs explored more robust options. With access to the International Criminal Court effectively barred by Russia's veto, these alternatives included promoting a potential regional tribunal or specialised chambers that could be inserted within the Syrian judicial system,[5] as well as national trials under principles of extraterritorial jurisdiction.[6] However, no concrete steps towards justice were taken on the multilateral front, notwithstanding the emergence of a number of penal initiatives. This was due in part to persistent ambivalence about the potential for vigorous criminal accountability to complicate peace negotiations and future processes of reconciliation.

[4] G.A. Res. 71/248 (21 December 2016); UN Doc. A/71/L.48 (19 December 2016), www.securitycouncilreport.org/atf/cf/%7B65BFCF9B-6D27-4E9C-8CD3-CF6E4FF96FF9%7D/a_res_71_248.pdf.

[5] See S. 905, Syrian War Crimes Accountability Act of 2017, www.congress.gov/bill/115th-congress/senate-bill/905, calling for the president to support efforts to ensure accountability for war crimes and for the completion of a feasibility study of potential transitional justice mechanisms for Syria (including a hybrid tribunal) to address crimes committed.

[6] For example, both Sweden and Germany have brought suits involving Syrian perpetrators. '"These are the Crimes we are Fleeing": Justice for Syria in Swedish and German Courts', *Human Rights Watch*, 3 October 2017, www.hrw.org/report/2017/10/03/these-are-crimes-we-are-fleeing/justice-syria-swedish-and-german-courts.

Notwithstanding the pre-transition work that has been achieved to date, much will remain to be done once the war is at a close, bearing in mind that wars do not necessarily end abruptly and that sporadic hostilities may continue even after 'peace' is formally declared. What can be achieved from the perspective of transitional justice will depend on the composition of the next Syrian regime and the role of Bashar al-Assad, who has become a symbol of sectarian repression and is unlikely to countenance robust justice or truth-telling processes. Whether he will be open to making a genuine commitment to reconciliation and the rehabilitation of victims remains to be seen. In any case, the most enduring legacy of the international community's pre-transition transitional justice enterprise will likely prove to be twofold. First, the international community has invested heavily in the documentation of abuses with an eye towards preserving a cache of evidence that can be tapped into as accountability processes go forward. Second is the creation of a cadre of Syrian practitioners with enhanced skills in the challenges and possibilities of transitional justice. It will be for these actors to decide what is feasible and what is desirable and whether and how to involve the international community to achieve the optimal balance between the two. With Assad still in power, there may be limited opportunities for international engagement in this regard, so Syrians across the political spectrum will have to determine for themselves whether the field of transitional justice has anything to offer as they work to rebuild their society and body politic.

12.2 The Origins and Internationalisation of the Field of Transitional Justice

The goals animating the field of transitional justice are as varied as they are ambitious. They encompass promoting accountability for gross and systematic violations of human rights, preventing a recurrence of such violations, rebuilding social cohesion, rehabilitating victims, and restoring trust in formerly abusive institutions. Transitional justice practitioners draw from a toolkit of mechanisms that respond, in various measure, to these objectives. These include trials (both civil and criminal); truth commissions, which focus on understanding the causes and consequences of violence and offering victims an opportunity to bear witness; the vetting of perpetrators from positions of trust and power (lustration); reparations devoted to the rehabilitation of victims; and the memorialisation of suffering and survival. Many transitional justice programmes will also encompass an agenda of institutional reform aimed at aligning security and justice institutions with democratic principles and human rights, while also responding to the legitimate grievances of marginalised segments of society. Collectively, these measures are meant to address the myriad impacts of authoritarianism and conflict in a way that facilitates a transition to a sustainable peace. In addition to addressing the immediate violence, modern efforts at transitional justice often focus on addressing the root causes of conflict as well, including communal grievances with respect to the perceived or actual unequal allocation of resources and other public goods.[7]

Although tracing its roots to the post–World War I and World War II periods, transitional justice emerged as a distinct field of study and policymaking in the 1980s when formerly authoritarian states began to transition to democracy and sought ways to address their lived history of human rights abuse, political repression, and mass violence.[8] While the end of the Cold War heralded a wave of transitions around the globe, the epicentre of this movement emerged in Latin America, where societies in Central and South America began to openly engage with a legacy of conflict, ethnic repression, and authoritarianism by instituting a range of transitional mechanisms, most notably amnesties and truth commissions. In Eastern Europe – where repression was less overtly violent and more bureaucratic in nature – societies experimented with lustrations and other transparency initiatives, such as opening the files of the security services.

In many of these contexts, the prosecution of those deemed responsible for the commission of international or domestic crimes was foreclosed. These impediments were both legal (the existence of an amnesty or other 'full-stop' law) and practical (because responsible individuals retained enough political or military power to jeopardise the transition if legal accountability was pursued too vigorously). As such, actors developed an array of institutional innovations – including truth and reconciliation commissions and lustration programmes – that fell short of

[7] See M. Cherif Bassiouni, *The Chicago Principles on Post-Conflict Justice* (Strasbourg: International Human Rights Institute, 2007), https://law.depaul.edu/about/centers-and-institutes/international-human-rights-law-institute/projects/Documents/chicago_principles.pdf. Principle 9 states: 'States shall engage in institutional reform to support the rule of law, restore public trust, promote fundamental rights, and support good governance.'

[8] Neil J. Kritz, 'Where We Are and How We Got Here: An Overview of Developments in the Search for Justice and Reconciliation', in *The Legacy of Abuse: Confronting the Past, Facing the Future*, ed. Alice Henkin (Washington DC: The Aspen Institute, 2002).

criminal accountability but still responded to some of the felt needs of victims for redress and reform. At the time, these measures were often seen as a second-best alternative to a more robust retributive response. Today, we recognise not only the inherent limitations of the criminal justice system when it comes to the rehabilitation of victims and the repair of societies but also that these alternative mechanisms can have value in and of themselves. So, while the transitional justice field originally developed around a menu of archetypal mechanisms that seemed to require states to choose between competing options – either amnesty or accountability; justice or peace; truth or reconciliation – today, we understand that the various interventions can be layered, coordinated, and sequenced in ways that reflect what is politically and fiscally feasible at the time to achieve the optimal mix between peace, justice, and reconciliation. In this way, the attitude of 'forgive and forget' and the demand for 'no peace without justice' are increasingly being reconciled in modern transitional justice efforts.[9]

Many transitional justice institutions have emerged from the bottom up, as victims' groups demanded some acknowledgement of their experience with violence. Others were the result of negotiations involving transitional governmental and non-governmental actors forging a grand political compromise to end hostilities and establish peace.[10] In the early days of the field, outsiders played a more limited role in helping to design and implement these measures. This is true no longer. The international community – including the UN and its many sub-components devoted to the promotion of human rights,[11] regional bodies,[12] individual donor states,[13] expert non-

[9] Mark Osiel, 'Choosing among Alternative Responses to Mass Atrocity: Between the Individual and the Collectivity', *Ethics & International Affairs*, 18 September 2015, www.ethicsandinternationalaffairs.org/2015/choosing-among-alternative-responses-mass-atrocity-individual-collectivity/.

[10] Ruti G. Teitel, *Transitional Justice* (Oxford: Oxford University Press, 2000), 213, notes that transitional justice involves 'a pragmatic balancing of ideal justice with political realism that instantiates a symbolic rule of law capable of constructing liberalizing change'.

[11] See, e.g., 'The Rule of Law and Transitional Justice in Conflict and Post-Conflict Societies', *Report of the Secretary-General*, UN Doc. S/2004/616 (23 August 2004).

[12] *See* Par Engstrom, 'Brazilian Post-Transitional Justice and the Inter-American Human Rights System', *Social Science Research Network*, 19 February 2014, https://ssrn.com/abstract=2397829, noting the role of the Inter-American human rights system in imposing transitional justice obligations on states premised on victims' rights to an effective judicial remedy and to truth.

[13] See generally Annie R. Bird, *US Foreign Policy on Transitional Justice* (Oxford: Oxford University Press, 2015), noting how transitional justice became instantiated as a core diplomatic tool of the United States.

governmental organisations,[14] and norm entrepreneurs[15] – increasingly play a role in cajoling, funding, advising, and directing states in transition to implement some form of transitional justice in order to entrench democratic values and a hard-won peace. Indeed, the international donor community is increasingly coordinated when it comes to programming and funding transitional justice priorities,[16] though it has not yet adopted the kind of synchronisation seen in sector-wide approaches (SWAps) in the public health and international development realms.

The motivation for encouraging transitional justice processes is partially inspired by a resolute belief in the deontological value of such exercises. At the same time, this international involvement also reflects a growing recognition, premised on emerging empirical research, that promoting a broad range of accountability and transitional justice measures leads to more long-term stability and democracy than leaving issues of accountability and reconciliation unaddressed.[17] Indeed, it has been demonstrated time and again that the failure to address past conflict and its underlying grievances can perpetuate cycles of violence with destabilising effects at the domestic, regional, and international levels.

Beyond these policy imperatives, other developments have contributed to the 'internationalisation' of transitional justice. For one, legalism plays a progressively important role in the field, with international law providing both a normative framework and also increasingly firm obligations governing the exercise of transitional justice. In particular, many societies have undertaken binding legal obligations by virtue of their ratification of a range of human rights and international criminal law treaties. These instruments contain express and implicit duties to prosecute breaches, provide due process and judicial protection, reject blanket amnesties,

[14] See International Center for Transitional Justice, https://www.ictj.org/.

[15] See, e.g., Special Rapporteur on the Promotion of Truth, Justice, Reparation and Guarantees of Non-Recurrence, http://www.ohchr.org/EN/Issues/TruthJusticeReparation/Pages/Index.aspx.

[16] See, e.g., UN Development Programme, 'Complementarity and Transitional Justice: Synthesis of Key Emerging Issues for Development', 16 November 2012, www.undp.org/content/dam/undp/library/Democratic%20Governance/Access%20to%20Justice%20and%20Rule%20of%20Law/Discussion%20Paper%20%E2%80%93%20Complementarity%20and%20Transitional%20Justice%20%E2%80%93%202012%20_%20EN.pdf, discussing the use of basket funds for transitional justice programming in Burundi, Guatemala, and Colombia.

[17] See Kathryn Sikkink, *The Justice Cascade: How Human Rights Prosecutions Are Changing World Politics* (New York: W. W. Norton & Company, 2011). To be sure, causal pathways in this field are complex and indeterminate. See Oskar N.T. Thoms et al., 'State-Level Effects of Transitional Justice: What Do We Know?', *International Journal of Transitional Justice* 4 (2010): 1–26.

respect and ensure the right to truth, and repair victims. As a result, confronting a legacy of past abuse is no longer something that can be fully negotiated away. In addition, certain transitional justice choices have been rendered justiciable[18] and may be invalidated through exercises of judicial review before domestic[19] or supranational courts.[20]

Second, even in highly repressive states, courageous and sophisticated civil society organisations now form part of a global epistemic community devoted to fostering human rights and accountability in the wake of abuses. These groups – with support and funding from their multinational counterparts and donor states – can make credible demands on transitioning states to translate ideals into action. They can also serve as conduits to bring new ideas and external expertise into domestic processes. At the dawn of the field, transitioning states were left to improvise, with little guidance, coordination, or outside support. Today, national actors can benefit from the lessons learned from other societies that have lived through similar experiences. There is now a growing recognition that the challenges faced by transitioning societies are not necessarily unique or without precedent, and history offers various models that can provide inspiration for local adaptation. That said (and notwithstanding these commonalities), because every post-conflict society has its own unique manifestations of violence, history of grievances, cultural traditions, and political realities, bespoke solutions are inevitable. We now recognise that different approaches might be warranted depending on whether the society is emerging from an armed conflict (international or domestic), a history of authoritarianism or repressive rule, cruelty at the hands of non-state actors, or cycles of sectarian violence. Similarly, the level of institutional and economic development will have implications for the transitional state's ability to assign legal responsibility, deliver reparations, and implement meaningful reform.[21] Finally, transitional

[18] Par Engstrom, *Transitional Justice and Ongoing Conflict*, Social Science Research Network, 1 November 2011, https://papers.ssrn.com/sol3/papers.cfm?abstract_id=2004313.

[19] For example, El Salvador's Constitutional Court ruled that the amnesty law that had been put in place at the end of the civil war was unconstitutional and in violation of international law because it infringed victims' rights to judicial protection and reparations. Naomi Roht-Arriaza, 'El Salvador's Constitutional Court Invalidates Amnesty Law', *Due Process of Law Foundation*, 22 July 2016, https://dplfblog.com/2016/07/22/el-salvadors-constitutional-court-invalidates-amnesty-law/.

[20] See, e.g., ECtHR 27 July 2004, Cases Nos. 55480/00 and 59330/00, *Sidabras and Džiautas v. Lithuania*, invalidating Lithuanian lustration laws.

[21] International Center for Transitional Justice, 'Justice in Context: Paradigms of State and Conflict', www.ictj.org/our-work/research/justice-context-paradigms-state-and-conflict.

states may also find value in welcoming, or at least accepting, international involvement in their transitional justice processes. At base, such contributions bring expertise and resources to transitional justice exercises. Such engagement can also signal legitimacy and provide assurances to vulnerable communities or groups associated with the perpetrators that they will be heard and will not be subjected to a vengeful victor's justice. At the same time, too much international engagement risks undermining local agency, generating backlash, and creating legitimacy deficits.

In Syria, in the absence of progress on negotiating an end to the conflict or implementing more robust measures within the Security Council, the international community invested in a number of pre-transition transitional justice lines of effort both unilaterally and multilaterally. Some – such as documentation and training efforts – were vigorously pursued in terms of programming and multilateral coordination. Other proposals, particularly those addressed to criminal accountability beyond the International Criminal Court, never achieved adequate momentum to generate tangible progress. Some of this engagement will likely have a lasting impact, though much depends on how the conflict gets resolved on the ground – an outcome that remains elusive at the time of this writing.

12.3 Pre-transition Lines of Effort

12.3.1 *The Imperative of Documentation*

Human rights documentation is one set of activities that has received extensive international support in the Syrian pre-transition context. Although not necessarily a transitional justice mechanism in and of itself, good documentation will undergird any number of accountability, truth-telling, and restorative mechanisms, including trials, lustrations, sanctions regimes, reparations, and other forms of social rehabilitation.[22] Many kinds of documentation can be relevant for these purposes. Disproportionate attention, however, tends to be paid to collecting potential evidence of the commission of international crimes by photographing

[22] In 2005, the International Center for Transitional Justice (ICTJ) helped develop a Documentation Affinity Group of human rights documentation centres from around the world to share information and techniques and ways to address shared challenges. Louis Bickford et al., 'Documenting Truth', https://www.ictj.org/sites/default/files/ICTJ-DAG-Global-Documenting-Truth-2009-English.pdf.

the results of attacks and collecting statements from witnesses and victims. Many documentation groups focus on gathering such crime base evidence. For example, hundreds of thousands of videos have been uploaded to YouTube purportedly showing the targeting of civilians, the execution of captured combatants, and other international offenses.[23] Such manifestations of violence play important roles in raising current awareness of atrocities and increasing the political will to take action to stop the ongoing harm. Other groups have attempted to catalogue all civilian deaths[24] or collect information about the identity and location of prisoners or clandestine detention centres.[25] However, these atrocity artefacts may not bear the indicia of authenticity or veracity to constitute formal evidence in a court of law. While compelling, an excessive focus on victims risks not only their re-traumatisation but also opening them up to impeachment challenges on cross-examination if conflicting witness statements come to light.

Beyond witness statements and other evidence attesting to the commission of international crimes, it can be equally – if not more – important to collect other forms of evidence. From a future accountability perspective, it is crucial to search for, preserve, and authenticate linkage evidence – evidence that connects the commission of a crime to a particular culprit or set of actors. These targets for prosecution will include the direct perpetrator but also his or her confederates, co-conspirators, superiors, and subordinates, who may be equally liable through doctrines of complicity, conspiracy, joint criminal enterprise, and superior responsibility. Such evidence can take the form of documents or testimony (from witnesses, insiders, or defectors) explicating the order of battle, the functioning of a regime or militia, the movement of arms, and the chain of command. Finally, although often viewed as less vital from a mandate perspective, any documentation effort should also seek to preserve public archives. These include personal records, such as birth certificates and registers indicating the ownership of land or other assets, to personnel and payroll records of key institutions. These documents can be crucial for accountability purposes (e.g. for facilitating restitution and reparations) but also in resolving disputes in the transition period,

[23] See, e.g., Exposing the Invisible, 'The Syrian Archive – Hadi Al Khatib', https://exposingtheinvisible.org/films/group/syrian-archive/; The Syrian Archive, https://syrianarchive.org/en (curating visual documentation of international crimes in Syria).

[24] See, e.g., Syrian Observatory for Human Rights, www.syriahr.com/en/.

[25] Human Rights Data Analysis Group, https://hrdag.org/syria/, collecting data on torture in prison; Syrian Network for Human Rights, http://sn4hr.org/, reporting on deaths, detentions, and disappearances.

identifying missing persons, and resettling the internally displaced and refugee populations.

This documentation work can be initiated at multiple levels, including by multilateral and regional organisations, individual states, and civil society actors with or without donor support. For example, the US State Department hosted a donors' conference that led to the establishment of the Syrian Justice and Accountability Centre (SJAC), which engages in documentation itself and has also helped to support a number of other related efforts led by Syrians.[26] By now, Syria has been the subject of dozens of fact-gathering exercises by non-governmental organisations and internationally mandated organisations; indeed, it is by now the best documented crime base in human history. And yet, these efforts are proceeding with little coordination, pursuant to different collection methodologies and evidentiary standards, without a clear sense of the end to which this information will be put or the evidentiary standards under which it will be evaluated, and – at times – at great risk to participants.[27] Besides a Commission of Inquiry devoted to Syria, the new IIIM has been mandated by the General Assembly to consolidate this information with an eye towards preparing for future criminal trials; another International Investigative Team dedicated to Iraq is focused on assisting with domestic prosecutions of ISIS.[28]

Within civil society, the Syrian conflict has prompted the emergence of a new model of privatised investigations of captured regime and ISIS documents with a focus on linking horrific crimes to specific perpetrators.[29] It remains to be seen whether these disparate documentation groups will be willing, and technologically able, to share their databases under the umbrella of the IIIM to create a truly universal

[26] See US State Department, Fact Sheet, *The Syria Justice & Accountability Center* (20 February 2013), https://2009-2017.state.gov/r/pa/prs/ps/2013/02/205031.htm.

[27] See Andras Vamos-Goldman, 'The Importance of Professional Expertise in Gathering Evidence of Mass Atrocities', *Just Security*, 27 October 2017, www.justsecurity.org/46355/rules-govern-evidence-gathering-conflict-zones/, noting that there is no single, commonly accepted set of rules of procedure and evidence governing international or domestic criminal investigations such that those undertaking this work are operating without specific guidance as to what will make their information admissible.

[28] S. C. Res. 2379, op. para 2 (21 September 2017).

[29] See Ben Taub, 'The Assad Files: Capturing Top-Secret Documents that Tie the Syrian Regime to Mass Torture and Killings', *The New Yorker*, 18 April 2016, www.newyorker.com/magazine/2016/04/18/bashar-al-assads-war-crimes-exposed, describing private criminal law investigations under way by the not-for-profit Commission on International Justice & Accountability (CIJA). The author is a member of CIJA's advisory board.

evidentiary clearinghouse. All of these efforts are prompting, and benefiting from, innovations in human rights technology around data management, secure storage, and digital forensics.

12.3.2 Training, Outreach, and Research

The imperative of Syrian ownership in determining transitional justice issues emerged as a frequent refrain in international discussions about the crisis. This language became boilerplate in multilateral resolutions.[30] Yet actors within the international community did not have a clear understanding of Syrians' preferences, needs, and capacity to undertake a fulsome process that would advance the complete range of transitional justice objectives. In particular, the potential for a transitional government to hold fair trials was unknown, given a lack of understanding about the opportunities and limitations inherent in Syrian legal framework. This is particularly so given that much of Syrian substantive and procedural law had historically been eclipsed by an Emergency Law in place since the Baathist coup of 1963 until it was rescinded in 2011 by Decree 161.

Identifying, convening, surveying, and training Syrian actors emerged as a pre-transition activity undertaken to varying degrees by the international community to prepare for an eventual transition. In the spirit of empowering Syrian ownership of transitional justice processes, the international community convened or funded various international conferences dedicated to exploring the full range of transitional justice themes. In such exercises, donor states regularly worked through civil society organisations (so-called 'implementing partners') with a mandate for promoting peace and justice to provide the necessary technical expertise. This outsourcing enables donors to catalyse the work in a way that is more cost effective, and that enjoys greater local legitimacy, than deploying government personnel directly. These conferences aimed to encourage Syrian legal experts and local leaders to identify the various lines of effort inherent to an integrated transitional justice strategy and to anticipate future legal reforms and institution-building exercises that will be

[30] See, e.g., UN Doc. A/RES/66/253, calling for 'an inclusive Syrian led political process, conducted in an environment free from violence, fear, intimidation and extremism and aimed at effectively addressing legitimate aspirations and concerns of the people of the Syrian Arab Republic'; UN Doc. S/RES/2268 (2016), www.securitycouncilreport.org/atf/cf/%7B65BFCF9B-6D27-4E9C-8CD3-CF6E4FF96FF9%7D/s_res_2268.pdf, stressing 'again that the Syrian people will decide the future of Syria'.

imperative or advisable in the transition period. Individuals were encouraged to evaluate existing transitional justice mechanisms and archetypes with an eye towards their adaptation to the Syrian context or the development of bespoke alternative models. Organisers of these events often invited civil society and governmental actors from other transitional and post-transition states in order to create opportunities for these experts to share their history of transitional justice with their Syrian counterparts.

Many of these gatherings undertook a holistic approach to transitional justice and reconciliation by advocating for transitional justice processes beyond criminal prosecutions. Indeed, coming from a repressive prosecutorial culture, Syrians often default to criminal accountability until introduced to the full suite of transitional justice tools. As such, multilateral trainings explored ways to address the root causes of the conflict; the reform of institutions; the vetting of individuals undeserving of holding positions of power and importance in the new democratic order; processes of individual and collective restitution, including the return of property and looted assets; and memorialisations. When it comes to lustration, the de-Baathification of Iraq emerged as a potent object lesson of how a process of lustration can be manipulated for political purposes and deprive a transitional state of bureaucratic expertise.[31] Because many donor states are wary of being perceived as promoting impunity, inadequate attention is often paid to ways to craft a principled, conditional, and 'legitimate' amnesty law[32] that does not necessarily entrench blanket impunity. This is unfortunate given that there will inevitably be impulses to provide amnesty as an inducement to bring leaders to the negotiating table. There are a number of ways that amnesty laws can be designed so as to contribute to, or complement, accountability mechanisms.

Two important entities emerged in this space. The first is the Syrian Expert House, an initiative implemented by the Center for Political and Strategic Studies (SCPSS) under the leadership of Radwan Ziadeh, a long-time human rights leader and member of the Syrian opposition in exile who was appointed by the interim opposition government to head the Syrian Commission on Transitional Justice. In consultation with the US

[31] Miranda Sissons and Abdulrazzaq Al-Saiedi, 'A Bitter Legacy: Lessons of De-Baathification in Iraq', *International Center for Transitional Justice*, 4 March 2013.

[32] Louise Malinder, 'Can Amnesties and International Justice Be Reconciled?', *International Journal of Transitional Justice* 1 (2007): 208, arguing that international courts should recognise amnesties enjoying some democratic approval to promote peace and reconciliation if accompanied by mechanisms to fulfil victims' rights.

State Department and funded largely by Canada, the SCPSS and the Syria Expert House hosted a conference in 2012 that brought together key Syrian opposition figures to create a Syria Transition Roadmap. This outcome document recommended a whole panoply of post-transition reforms addressed to political structures, the constitution, and the economy as well as sophisticated proposals dedicated to transitional justice. Institutionally, the Roadmap advocated the immediate creation of an Association for the Defence of the Victims of the Syrian Revolution and a National Preparatory Committee for Transitional Justice. It envisioned the eventual convening of a National Commission for Transitional Justice to manage all transitional justice activities post-transition.[33]

A second organisation that emerged to pursue this work is The Day After Project, which was first convened by the US Institute of Peace and the German Institute for International and Security Affairs in 2012 to engage in transition planning with funding from the US–Middle East Partnership Initiative (MEPI).[34] The imperative of transitional justice formed one of the pillars of its work, which envisioned the implementation of a range of retributive and more restorative measures over a notional two-year time frame post-transition. A Special Criminal Court within the Syrian judiciary to prosecute high-level figures formed a key component of its transitional justice blueprint. The report also called for conditional amnesties for lower-level figures and targeted lustrations. In its guidelines, the report advocated the inclusion of foreign expertise, 'when needed, with full respect [for] Syrian sovereignty'.[35] Although the organisers convened Syrians as part of this process, it was criticised as being too Western, which helped galvanise the SCPSS effort.

The international community also convened sessions focused more intently on advancing fair, credible, and even-handed options for criminal accountability given the pervasive wartime criminality. These included trainings devoted to a number of practical and technical topics, such as best practices for undertaking rigorous human rights and criminal law investigations; collecting and archiving potential evidence to preserve the chain of custody; and analysing documentation to prove violations of human rights and international humanitarian law and the chain of command. This work mainly engaged various networks of Syrian lawyers and judges that exist throughout Syria and in

[33] SCPSS and Syria Expert House, *Syria Transition Roadmap* 141–55 (2013), http://syrianexperthouse.org/reports/Syria_Transition_Roadmap__Full_en.pdf.

[34] USIP, The Day After Project, www.usip.org/publications/day-after-project.

[35] Ibid.

neighbouring countries with expertise on the Syrian judiciary, penal law framework, evidentiary rules, and criminal procedure. Individuals were drawn from revolutionary courts in liberated areas and alternate bar associations, such as the Free Syrian Lawyers Aggregation, the Free Syrian Lawyers Association, and the Council of the Free Syrian Judges – organisations composed mainly of judges and lawyers who defected or were operating in liberated areas.

Bringing indigenous legal expertise to bear on a future transitional justice programme enabled the candid evaluation of the state of the Syrian judicial system pre-revolution and the identification of areas in which legal reform may be advisable. Such an exercise has relevance for both ordinary and conflict-related crimes. In many transitional states, there may be a need to incorporate international or other discrete categories of crimes (such as financial crimes) and forms of responsibility into the penal code. It may also be advisable to draft provisions enabling the appointment of international personnel within the various components of the judicial branch as staff or dedicated experts; to revise certain defences or evidentiary rules; and to amend the civil code or administrative law to allow for the payment of reparations or restitution. Participants in these pre-transition gatherings can undertake drafting exercises to prepare notional decree laws (or at least the building blocks of such legislation) and even shadow indictments. Such gatherings of legal experts can also occasion a discussion about the demands of international human rights norms devoted to due process protections and the administration of the death penalty. Some of this work was undertaken in the Syrian context, but it is unclear if the right actors were engaged or if any outputs will actually be influential if there are ever openings for legislative reform.

12.3.3 Gleaning Attitudes towards Transitional Justice

In addition to these training opportunities, states and civil society organisations also commissioned studies by social scientists about Syrian attitudes towards justice and accountability. The Berkeley Human Rights Centre and other academics have undertaken a number of such population-based surveys in the past to gather empirical data on citizens' expectations and hopes around transitional justice. Many of these surveys have been administered after-the-fact to gauge a population's satisfaction with a transitional justice process already undertaken; others have been produced pre-transition or prior to a key accountability exercise.

In 2013, the Syrian Justice & Accountability Centre (SJAC) commissioned a qualitative survey of Syrians, although it only involved forty-six interviews.[36] The report found that people had high expectations for justice and fostering coexistence among Syria's various ethnic groups but low knowledge about other transitional justice options. The Day After Project conducted a larger survey in 2014 of attitudes towards transitional justice, reconciliation, and human rights involving over a thousand participants.[37] Even when aware of the range of transitional justice options, Syrians were often at odds about which mechanisms were worth prioritising.[38] The results of these inquiries remain available if Syrian policymakers are ever in a position to pursue a transitional justice programme.

12.3.4 *Promoting Psychosocial Rehabilitation*

Armed conflicts and crimes against humanity produce profound and multifaceted consequences within the societies involved. In addition to physical injury and death, individual victims, their families, and their communities may all experience multiple and debilitating forms of emotional suffering. This harm can rise to the level of diagnosable mental health illnesses, from post-traumatic stress disorder (PTSD) to anxiety to depression.[39] Co-morbidity – the simultaneous presence of two disease states in a patient – is common in victim populations.[40] Sequential traumatisation – the accumulation of traumatic events – occurs when individuals are subjected to the myriad stressors that often accompany

[36] *What Syrians Think: Views on the Conflict, Negotiations, and Transitional Justice* (January 2014), www.charneyresearch.com/resources/what-syrians-think-views-on-the-conflict-negotiations-and-transitional-justice/.

[37] The Day After, *Pilot Survey on Transitional Justice* (December 2014), http://tda-sy.org/en/publications/.

[38] The Center for Civil Society and Democracy, under the leadership of Rajaa Al-Talli, led two different surveys in 2012–2013 of Syrians inside Syria and had broad scope of participation. See www.peaceinsight.org/conflicts/syria/peacebuilding-organisations/center-for-civil-society-and-democracy-in-syria-draft/.

[39] See Beth Van Schaack, and Daryn Reicherter, eds., *Cambodia's Hidden Scars: Trauma Psychology and the Extraordinary Chambers in the Courts of Cambodia*, 2nd ed. (Phnom Penh: Documentation Center of Cambodia, 2016).

[40] See M. Creamer, P. Burgess, and A. C. McFarlane, 'Post-Traumatic Stress Disorder: Findings from the Australian National Survey of Mental Health and Well-being', *Psychological Medicine* 31, no. 7 (2001): 1237–47, finding that major depression, dysthymia (chronic but less severe depression), bipolar disorder, generalised anxiety disorder, panic disorder, agoraphobia, social phobia, and obsessive-compulsive disorder have all been linked to post-traumatic stress disorder (PTSD).

conflict, including the loss of loved ones and social networks; displacement, expulsion, and exile; poverty and economic instability; and the disintegration of a generation of life plans.[41] This psychological harm is, in turn, associated with a broad spectrum of interrelated social problems (such as substance abuse and domestic violence) and can have intergenerational effects if not appropriately addressed.[42] The impact of trauma on human psychology shows remarkable consistency across cultures.[43] Given the acute needs of victims, the World Health Organization has urged the international community to provide support for the 'implementation of programmes to repair the psychological damage of war, conflict[,] and natural disasters'.[44]

Often overlooked is the fact that participating in human rights abuses can also exert a negative psychological impact on perpetrators. The concept of moral injury describes the adverse impact on soldiers and others of undergoing a personal experience that violates core values and principles.[45] Moral injury involves a cluster of symptoms that are similar to PTSD but also has a spiritual component linked to the sanctity of life.[46] While demobilisation and reintegration programmes target former combatants, insufficient attention is paid to addressing such moral injury.

Although it will be impossible to reach all individuals in need while a conflict is ongoing, it is feasible to begin to provide some victims with appropriate psychological and psychiatric interventions in the pre-transition phase. This assistance can be provided within refugee camps, diaspora populations, and civilian safe havens (if they exist). It is also possible to work remotely with victims who remain in-country through the use of new communications platforms, such as Skype. The international community can help identify, fund, and disseminate culturally appropriate resources to provide psychosocial support services and

41 See H. Keilson, *Sequential Traumatization in Children* (Jerusalem: Magnes Press, 1992).

42 Yael Danieli, 'Assessing Trauma Across Cultures from a Multigenerational Perspective', in *Cross-Cultural Assessment of Psychological Trauma and PTSD*, eds. J. Wilson and C. Tang (New York: Springer, 2007), 65.

43 See Daryn Reicherter and Alexandra Aylward, 'The Impact of War and Genocide on Psychiatry and Social Psychology', in *Hidden Scars*, recounting comparative research in post-conflict states; Inger Agger, 'Healing the Mind: Healing after Mass Atrocity in Cambodia', *Transcultural Psychiatry* 52 (2015): 543.

44 WHO, *Resolution on Health Action in Crises and Disasters*, A58/6 (15 April 2005).

45 See R. E. Meagher and D. A. Pryer, eds., *War and Moral Injury: A Reader* (Eugene, OR: Cascade, 2018).

46 Michael D. Matthews, 'Moral Injury: Toxic Leadership, Maleficent Organizations, and Psychological Distress', *Psychology Today* (10 March 2018), www.psychologytoday.com/us/blog/head-strong/201803/moral-injury.

treatment in addition to responding to other humanitarian needs of refugees and internally displaced citizens who have had their lives destroyed. This effort can be undertaken first and foremost through a collective and community-based approach, building on local networks, indigenous leaders, victims' organisations, and families. Eventually, this work can be consolidated post-transition in collaboration with the national Ministry of Health, once it is operational. Indeed, the emergent field of 'trauma first aid' is premised on the idea that immediate psychological interventions following a traumatic event can help to forestall the development of future psychological distress and disorder while also fostering resilience and adaptive functioning.[47] Local NGOs and civil society groups can be trained in how to recognise who is suffering from extreme distress and needs further professional psychiatric and psychological treatment.

In Syria, nearly half a million individuals have died[48] and over half the population (10 million people) is internally or externally displaced.[49] Countless more have been physically maimed and psychologically traumatised. Thousands of people live in besieged areas.[50] Surveys of Syrian refugees reveal high levels of psychological distress.[51] It will be critical to address this harm in a comprehensive and culturally appropriate way once the fighting has subsided.[52] For now, the international community has provided some mental health services in refugee camps and other areas where refugees have congregated. The front-line countries in the refugee crisis, however, are overtaxed on a number of fronts and cannot

[47] See Jonathan I. Bisson and Catrin Lewis, 'Systematic Review of Psychological First Aid', www.researchgate.net/profile/Catrin_Lewis2/publication/265069490_Systematic_Review_of_Psychological_First_Aid/links/5450d15f0cf24e8f7375a73c.pdf. The concept was developed by the National Center for Post-Traumatic Stress Disorder (NC-PTSD).

[48] The Syrian Center for Policy Research put the number at 470,000 at the beginning of 2016. See Anne Barnard, 'Death Toll from War in Syria Now 470,000, Group Finds', *The New York Times*, 11 February 2016, www.nytimes.com/2016/02/12/world/middleeast/death-toll-from-war-in-syria-now-470000-group-finds.html.

[49] UN High Commissioner for Refugees, 'Syria Emergency', www.unhcr.org/en-us/syria-emergency.html. See 'Syria's Drained Population', *The Economist*, 30 September 2015, www.economist.com/blogs/graphicdetail/2015/09/daily-chart-18.

[50] Human Rights Watch, 'World Report: Syria', www.hrw.org/world-report/2018/country-chapters/syria.

[51] Khaldoun I. Marwa, 'Psychological Sequels of Syrian Conflict', *Journal of Psychiatry* 19, no. 2, 2016.

[52] See Sahr MuhammedAlly, 'Assisting Syrian War Victims', Huffington Post, www.huffingtonpost.com/sahr-muhammedally/assisting-syrian-war-victims_b_3756091.html, arguing for the creation of a Victims Assistance Program for Syria that would encompass psychosocial and medical services in addition to financial assistance to rebuild lives.

meet the acute demand, particularly given the unique needs of children or victims (both male and female) of sexual violence and the high degree of stigma associated with mental illness.[53] Moreover, the emphasis on PTSD and addressing immediate reactions to the trauma of war and displacement means that work on longer-term rehabilitation and recovery may be neglected.[54]

12.3.5 Fostering Solidarity among Victims

In the pre-transition phase, the international community can also help to catalyse the formation of victims' associations as sources of support and solidarity. Although many human rights documentation organisations regularly engage with victims, they do not necessarily represent the interests, nor respond to the innumerable needs, of all those affected by the conflict. Broadly representative victims' organisations can augment victims' political power and improve victims' ability to advocate on their own behalf with the international community around a whole range of issues, including humanitarian assistance needs, peace negotiations, transitional justice, and restitution and reparations, all in keeping with the 'nothing about us without us' theory of human rights advocacy. Membership organisations can also provide points of contact and partners for global human rights organisations, such as Human Rights Watch or Amnesty International. When it comes to designing a future transitional justice programme, victims' organisations offer a forum for victims to develop consensus positions on key decisions, articulate and advance their transitional justice interests and preferences with a more powerful and unified voice, and undertake effective diplomatic engagement with the international community and the media to ensure that victims' perspectives are a part of any multilateral conversations about political transitions and transitional justice. In the event of a consolidated transition, such organisations can play a role in advocating for victim-centred reforms to address the core grievances that motivated the uprising in the first place.

[53] Cherisse Davis and Amy Wanninger, in collaboration with International Medical Corps, 'Mental Health and Psychosocial Support Considerations for Syrian Refugees in Turkey: Sources of Distress, Coping Mechanisms, and Access to Support', January 2017, 11–12, https://internationalmedicalcorps.org/wp-content/uploads/2017/07/Mental-Health-and-Psychosocial-Support-Considerations-for-Syrian-Refugees-in-Turkey.pdf.

[54] H. Jefee-Bahloul, A. Barkil-Oteo, T. Pless-Mulloli, and F. M. Fouad, 'Mental Health in the Syrian Crisis: Beyond Immediate Relief', *Lancet* 386, no. 10,003 (2015), 1531.

The development of such an inclusive association also offers opportunities for empowering victims by connecting them to others with common experiences so they can share their stories of harm as well as strategies for survival and rehabilitation. They also create vectors to crowdsource information and facilitate mass communication among victims using traditional and social media and mobilise natural leaders within victims' communities. Associations can record and preserve victims' testimony for posterity, including for future justice, restitution/rehabilitation, and truth-telling efforts. All this work can build solidarity among victims – across genders, ethnic and religious groups, and regions – in a way that has the potential to lay the groundwork for future reconciliation and relational transformation. If a number of disparate local organisations already exist, catalysing a more broad-based coalition can also serve as a mechanism for connecting existing organisations and offering them an elevated platform for their work. If such local groups do not exist, a larger membership organisation can foster neighbourhood support groups and more community-based associations. Such organisations can also provide an immediate and long-term outlet for psychosocial and medical rehabilitation as needed, as well as the dissemination of reparations, if available.

12.3.6 Truth-Telling

Many transitional justice programmes involve a truth-telling component in the form of a truth commission (sometimes also denominated a truth and reconciliation commission, as in South Africa), a commission of inquiry, or a related body. These institutions serve multiple goals including the compilation of a definitive account of the conflict or repression, understanding the patterns and practices of violence, giving victims a forum in which to bear witness, and offering proposals for reform to ensure non-repetition. A few truth commissions have identified perpetrators by name; many have offered recommendations for reform and reparation. Given that transitional states are beset by diverging narratives of what happened and who was at fault, a truth commission staffed by experts and public figures of unimpeachable character offers a bulwark – though not an impenetrable one – against the emergence of revisionist histories of violence. They also respond to an emerging 'right to truth' enjoyed by victims.[55]

[55] See Sam Szoke-Burke, 'Searching for the Right to Truth: The Impact of International Human Rights Law on National Transitional Justice Policies', *Berkeley Journal of International Law* 33 (2015): 526.

In the past, truth commissions have always been established post-transition, often as a substitute for, or precursor to, criminal accountability. Theoretically, a truth commission could begin to function pre-transition and extraterritorially with an eye towards continuing to work in-country once conditions allow. The challenge would be to ensure that its members are broadly representative and perceived as legitimate envoys, so the commission can credibly contribute to post-conflict reconciliation processes without being perceived as a tool to condemn one side or as a civil society effort without formal sanction. Most truth commissions have operated with official approval from the state, which carries a measure of legitimacy but also a recognition that harms were done in the name of the sovereign. Although both the Syria Transition Roadmap and The Day After Project contemplated that Syrians might one day set up a truth commission, no concrete steps have been taken in this regard separate and apart from the many NGO and multilateral documentation efforts under way.

12.3.7 Proto-accountability Mechanisms Pre-transition

There is broad agreement among the international community that justice and accountability for atrocities in Syria must be an integral component of Syria's transition. Indeed, the international community deployed robust accountability messaging once the conflict in Syria broke out.[56] From the perspective of the United States, Secretary Clinton announced at an early meeting of the Friends of the Syrian People that accountability constituted a central pillar of the United States' Syria policy. The US House of Representatives overwhelmingly passed a resolution calling for the United Nations to establish a tribunal dedicated to the crimes committed by all sides in Syria.[57] Other states followed suit with similar demands.

[56] See, e.g., UN Doc. A/PRST/2011/16, 3 August 2011, 'those responsible for the violence should be held accountable'.

[57] See H.Con.Res.121, www.congress.gov/bill/114th-congress/house-concurrent-resolution/00121, asking the president to direct his ambassador at the United Nations to promote the establishment of a war crimes tribunal in the Security Council where the war crimes and crimes against humanity being committed could be addressed. Rep. Chris Smith (R-NJ) authored the resolution. Jeff Sagnip, 'Syrian War Crimes Tribunal Bill Taken Up by Key House Committee' (2 March 2016), https://chrissmith.house.gov/news/documentsingle.aspx?DocumentID=398749. The resolution did not account for the fact that Russia was unlikely to support any such initiative.

In the absence of a tangible threat of actual prosecutions, however, such messaging exerted a limited rhetorical effect. Views continued to differ on the best means to advance these ends and how criminal accountability would fit into a larger transitional justice strategy. Many states remained fixated on calling for the Security Council to undertake an ICC referral despite the obvious and unyielding obstacles to such an endeavour.[58] This singular focus on the ICC eclipsed other worthy avenues for accountability that might have been pursued. There are a number of diplomatic, operational, and technical activities that were, or could have been, undertaken mid-conflict by the international community to lay the groundwork for future criminal prosecutions of crimes committed by all sides during the Syrian conflict, even in the absence of an ICC referral, multilateral consensus within the Council, or Syrian consent.

Other available modalities include action at the General Assembly; an international or hybrid tribunal created by way of an international agreement among interested states; domestic trials before specialised chambers in liberated areas in Syria with varying degrees of international involvement; trials in specially affected states under various principles of extraterritorial jurisdiction; building a shell of a special chamber that could be eventually inserted into the Syrian judicial system post-transition; and opportunistic trials in any states with jurisdiction over perpetrators. These proposals could have resulted in the establishment of a fully functioning and stand-alone tribunal or a skeletal legal framework for an eventual tribunal of which Syrian constituencies would ultimately take ownership and in which they would play central roles. In all cases, the substantive law to be applied could be international criminal law, domestic criminal law, or a combination of the two. Any mechanism would have to be created and operate consistently with international law and norms. Although a number of innovative proposals were floated, no tangible progress was made on the multilateral level until late 2016 when the General Assembly authorised the creation of the IIIM, which remains primarily an investigative body without prosecutorial powers.[59]

It is worth pausing to consider the propriety and feasibility of trying to jumpstart an accountability process mid-conflict. Even while atrocities were ongoing, the Syrian government was unlikely to cooperate in any

[58] See UN Doc. S/2014/348 (22 May 2014), draft resolution referring the situation in Syria to the ICC, www.securitycouncilreport.org/atf/cf/%7B65BFCF9B-6D27-4E9C-8CD3-CF6E4FF96FF9%7D/s_2014_348.pdf.

[59] G. A. Res. 71/248 (21 December 2016).

prosecutorial effort, and the full panoply of perpetrators could not likely be apprehended.[60] Ratcheting up the perceived prosecutorial threat for perpetrators on all sides of the conflict would have lent strength to the international community's accountability messaging while also demonstrating, and solidifying, international resolve to ultimately hold perpetrators accountable. Furthermore, it is always hoped that the promise of individual accountability will deter future abuses or at least bring about a new range of incentives for the parties to change their behaviour. At a minimum, it might contribute to the decision-making calculus of would-be defectors and deserters and inspire overt and covert acts of resistance to unlawful orders. Signalling that accountability will be forthcoming can also prevent the emergence of a climate of collective/sectarian vigilantism motivated by a quest for private vengeance. It might also build confidence in future justice institutions. Diplomatic and operational efforts around accountability may have helped ultimately to cohere a Syrian constituency around principles of justice and accountability in a way that would enhance transition planning and support for a unified opposition. A process of building an accountability mechanism pre-transition would also contribute to capacity building within the Syrian legal community to hold fair and effective trials as well as the inculcation of rule-of-law principles in keeping with the principle of positive complementarity.

12.4 Post-transition

The situation in Syria demonstrates that, to a point, there is a range of initiatives that members of the international community can undertake – multilaterally and individually – to prepare for, and potentially even hasten, an eventual transition. Although many worthy proposals were not pursued, these various lines of effort have laid some groundwork for the instantiation of a transitional justice programme in the post-transition period. In the immediate transition phase, and assuming Assad remains in power in some capacity, it is likely that violence will be ongoing and that the government in place may lack legitimacy or nationwide control. There may be limited possibilities for the international community to engage on transitional justice issues with emergent

[60] See Beth Van Schaack and Ryan Goodman, 'What Is To Be Gained by Pursuing Accountability Now in Syria', Just Security (2 June 2014), www.justsecurity.org/11057/gained-pursuing-accountability-syria/, articulating some of these arguments.

governmental structures, given the long-standing hostility towards Assad and the lack of effective levers with his regime. This will necessitate a focus on civil society and local actors at first. It is hoped that these interlocutors will have the knowledge and expertise to begin a public dialogue about a range of accountability and transitional justice options. These may exert short-term effects of deterring violence – and especially acts of retribution – and medium-term objectives of conceptualising and implementing systematic justice processes. These would include truth-telling and memorialisation, at the national and community levels, through formal and informal mechanisms. Psychosocial rehabilitative work – to include services to victims of torture as well as support for refugees and the internally displaced – should be initiated as soon as possible. Likewise, the international community can deploy forensic assistance to preserve and exhume mass graves in what will likely be a chaotic post-war environment.

If prosecutions are ever undertaken, the international community should help establish standards and guidelines so that relevant authorities will be prepared to review the files of current detainees and order the release of political prisoners, rebels who did nothing more than fight, protesters, and other individuals unfairly arrested by the Assad regime. It may also be possible to help shape an appropriate amnesty strategy in keeping with international humanitarian law for members of the Free Syrian Army and other rebels, with a view towards creating incentives for combatants who are not associated with abuses to disarm and return to civilian life. At the same time, the international community will need to stand ready to recommend against granting amnesty for those who have committed international crimes, and the idea of any amnesty for residual ISIS fighters will not be well received. To the extent that a partial or conditional amnesty is being considered, the international community can help to identify clear criteria for eligibility. In addition, international experts can convey lessons learned and technical assistance on developing processes for vetting members of the transitional and new regional governmental bodies, emerging police forces and militias, and the 'rump' security sector.

In order to address the root causes of the conflict, it will be necessary to focus on the reform of institutions. The international community should thus support long-term policies and programmes that address systemic inequity and injustice in addition to the most immediate violence. The international community should also be prepared to provide support to appropriate Syrian civil society and media organisations to manage the expectations of the public in terms of what various transitional justice mechanisms can achieve, including the limitations of formal judicial redress and reparations. Proceeding without managing these expectations could undermine the credibility of the new justice system and create dissatisfaction, which may lead to renewed violence. Moreover, if Assad remains in power, all of this work may have been for naught, unless he can be convinced of the need to undertake a genuine process of reckoning with the past in order to instantiate a more peaceful and inclusive future.

13

Syrian Kurds

Rising from the Ashes of Persecution

SIRWAN KAJJO

13.1 Introduction

The Kurds in Syria, numbering roughly 3 million before the Syrian uprising, were the forgotten minority – the smallest of the Kurdish populations of the Middle East. That changed, however, as the Syrian war expanded northward and particularly as the Kurds of Iraq tried and failed in their quest for independence. The rapidly changing dynamics of the war have placed the Syrian Kurds in the spotlight as both Kurds and Syrians now try to piece together a future.

Syrian Kurdish politics have never been local. In fact, Kurdish politics in Syria have largely been driven and inspired by other Kurdish movements – notably in Iraq and Turkey. In addition to ideological support, Syrian Kurdish parties have traditionally relied on regional benefactors for long-term survival. In the past, this meant protection against government oppression. In the present crisis in Syria, it furthers their fragmentation.

Since the founding of the modern Syrian state in 1946, and even earlier during the short-lived Kingdom of Syria in 1918, Syrian Kurds were marginalised by successive governments. Their cultural and political rights were denied, and their relatively resource-rich areas were left neglected for decades.[1]

Syria's civil war, and later the rise of ISIS in early 2014, left Syrian Kurds with an unprecedented opportunity to control their areas in the north and north-eastern part of the war-torn country. As Kurdish-led forces showed their effectiveness in fighting ISIS, international support

[1] Michael M. Gunter, *Out of Nowhere: The Kurds of Syria in Peace and War* (Oxford: Oxford University Press, 2014), 2, 32.

for their effort in combatting terrorism grew, particularly from the United States. The Kurds quietly expanded their territory and took control of non-Kurdish areas, retaking much of what was once considered to be the heartland of ISIS's self-proclaimed caliphate in northwest Syria. By 2017, Kurdish-led groups controlled more than one-quarter of Syria's territory, the second-largest region after the government-controlled areas of Syria.

Emerging as a local actor, the once-marginalised Syrian Kurds have been striving to become a more powerful player in the country's increasingly complex military and political arena. Officially seizing control of their traditional regions in 2012, Syrian Kurds have set up local councils responsible for running local affairs. They have also proposed a federated system to replace the current centralised governing system in the Arab-majority country.

Deemed one of the most organised groups in Syria, Kurds have been positioned to push for more recognition in terms of local governance and self-rule. However, the ultimate desire of the Syrian Kurds is to be a model for other parts of the country. This self-rule proposal, they argue in their federalism manifesto, is a guarantee of stability and democracy in post-war Syria.[2] However, political fragmentation within the Syrian Kurdish community and their respective regional and political patrons may undermine their chance for autonomy. This chapter examines the state of the Kurds in Syria while providing a historical perspective and an assessment of possible post-war scenarios.

13.2 The Kurds in Syria: Historical Background

The history of Syrian Kurds, similar to that of Kurds in the rest of the Middle East, is one of exclusion. The end of World War I resulted in a series of agreements that divided the Ottoman territories between the main stakeholders, namely the British and the French. It also resulted in the establishment of the short-lived Syrian Arab Kingdom, an unrecognised state that existed for little over four months, from 8 March to 24 July 1920, until it surrendered to French forces. King Faisal bin Hussein, who led the Syrian Arab Kingdom, implemented a set of policies that asserted the Arab identity of the country, even including the word 'Arab' in the kingdom's official name. Thus, Kurds and other ethnic

[2] The Charter of Social Contract [in Rojava]. Qamishli, 29 January 2014. Founding Conference, https://peaceinkurdistancampaign.com/charter-of-the-social-contract/.

minorities were excluded from national politics, and their local leaders were not made a part of the new authority. No mention of Kurdish rights was made in the constitution of Faisal's cabinet. The only official language in the new kingdom was Arabic.[3]

The first time Kurds officially entered Syrian national politics was 1928, when five Kurdish members of the French-controlled Syrian parliament submitted a petition that included a set of demands on behalf of the Kurdish community. The Kurdish members asked the authorities to provide adequate services in the Kurdish regions and acknowledge the Kurds – and their language and culture – in the constitution. These demands were ignored by the parliament.[4]

Although the French-sponsored constitution of 1928 didn't mention the Kurds by name, it did refer to the fact that all Syrians were equal before the law and enjoyed the same political and civic rights regardless of their religious, ethnic, or linguistic backgrounds. Article 8 of the same constitution stipulated that different elements of the society could teach their respective languages.[5]

In 1927, a group of intellectuals, most of whom were exiled Kurds from Turkey, founded the first political organisation among Kurds in Syria: Khoyboun (Xoybûn; 'independence' in Kurdish). It was established on the premise of supporting the Kurdish cause in Turkey following the failed rebellion of Sheikh Saeed Piran in 1925 against the Turks, the first large-scale nationalist Kurdish rebellion.[6] In the early years of its activism, the secular Xoybûn advocated for Kurdish nationalism in Turkey. The fact that most of its founders were Kurds from Turkey (who were exiled because of their anti-Kemalist activities) did contribute to the political orientation of the organisation, which focused on fundraising and campaigning for a Kurdish revolt in Turkey. Those Syrian Kurds who were involved in Xoybûn's activities did not hesitate to support their fellow Kurds across the border. At the time, the French-controlled Syria was a safe haven for many Kurdish intellectuals and revolutionaries.[7]

3 Jordi Tejel, *Syria's Kurds: History, Politics, and Society* (New York: Routledge, 2009), 8.

4 Khaled Issa, 'Dirasa Tarikhiya – al-Akrad That al-Intidab al-Faransi', *Gilgamish Center for Kurdish Studies and Research*, 1 September 2008, http://www.gilgamish.org/2008/09/01/12118.html.

5 Jan Habash, 'An Examination of the Syrian Constitution', *Damascus Center for Theoretical Studies and Civic Rights*, www.hem.bredband.net/cdpps/repdcc.jan.htm.

6 Robert O. Olson, *The Emergence of Kurdish Nationalism and the Sheikh Said Rebellion, 1880–1925* (Austin: University of Texas Press, 1989), 30.

7 Ali Mirani, *Al-Hayat al-Hizbiya al-Sirriya Fi Kurdistan – Suriya 1898–2008* (Duhok: Duhok University Press, 2009), 31.

After nearly two decades of political activism, Xoybûn began to limit itself to cultural and social activities. Diverging political views and the focus on the Kurdish cause in Turkey led many Syrian Kurds to leave the group. By November 1946, Xoybûn was formally dissolved.[8] The remnants of Xoybûn remained for nearly two more years, focusing on preserving the Kurdish language and culture.[9]

13.3 Kurdish Political Institutions

13.3.1 The Kurdistan Democratic Party of Syria: First Kurdish Political Party

The Kurdistan Democratic Party of Syria (KDP-S) is the oldest political party in Syria, established in 1957. Syrian Kurdish nationalism was inspired by the 1945 declaration of the Republic of Mahabad by Qazi Mohammad, a renowned Iranian Kurdish leader. This short-lived republic brought to life the first Kurdish political party, the Kurdistan Democratic Party (KDP). One year later, Kurdish General Mullah Mustafa Barzani – who served as commander-in-chief for Mahabad's army – founded the Kurdistan Democratic Party in Iraq. Urgency to develop sophisticated nationalist platforms in Syria and Turkey led to the formation of sister parties in both countries. Mustafa Barzani's popularity with Kurds across the Middle East spiked during his revolt against the Iraqi monarchy from 1943 to 1945, which helped him spread his party's ideas throughout Kurdish communities in Syria and Turkey.[10]

During the 1940s and 1950s, the Kurds in Syria were inspired by the civic and cultural legacies of Xoybûn. In the relatively free atmosphere, the idea of establishing a Syrian Kurdish political movement began to crystallise. Discussions among the intellectual elite became more visible. Kurdish intellectuals began to congregate in Damascus and Beirut with the hope of receiving a better understanding of what the Kurdish population in Syria was demanding.

At that time, Kurdish leaders such as Osman Sabri, Nureddine Zana, and Nuri Dersimi began to weigh the prospects of founding a Kurdish political party in Syria. The men came from different economic

[8] Ahmed Mulla Mohammed, *Khoybun: The Kurdish Independence Association 1927–1946 and Kurdish-Armenian Relations* (Beirut: Kawa Cultural League, 2000), 142.
[9] Kerim Yildiz, *Kurds in Syria* (London: Pluto Press, 2005), 48.
[10] Tejel, 48.

backgrounds, but they were all considered a part of the intellectual elite among the Kurdish community.[11]

The KDP-S was founded in Damascus on 14 June 1957.[12] Its single objective was to liberate and unify Kurdistan. This meant that the main duty of the party was to mobilise and organise the Kurdish community in Syria to work for the creation of Greater Kurdistan. The founding members of the party came from different political and ideological backgrounds. This included leftists, nationalists, and conservatives. Despite being a *Syrian* Kurdish party, the leadership of the KDP-S was almost entirely made of those who had Kurdish-Turkish background.[13]

This newly established party in Syria won widespread early support thanks to its affiliation with Barzani's KDP in Iraq. However, that support dwindled over the years as the party began to splinter and factions emerged affiliated with particular leaders, geographic interests, and political philosophies. Despite a long period of fractures and breakaways, the KDP-S remains strong in Syria, drawing on its historical roots and close affiliation with the KDP party that controls the Kurdistan Regional Government (KRG) of Iraq.[14]

13.3.2 PUK and PDK

Jalal Talabani (1933–2017), the late Iraqi Kurdish leader and first democratically elected president of Iraq, founded the Patriotic Union of Kurdistan (PUK) in 1975 while in exile in Damascus. During his stay, Talabani – who served as the emissary of Mustafa Barzani – established close relations with important Syrian Kurds, with whom he found a common language speaking about the future of the Kurdish nation. Those relations assisted Talabani in the establishment of the PUK, a new party aimed at developing a Syrian Kurdish leadership connected to the broader Kurdish alliance in the region. Having developed a loyal core leadership, Talabani, along with some Syrian Kurds like Hamid Haji Darwish and Nureddine Zana, made a strong push to win support among Syrian Kurds. Members of KDP-S, who agreed with the leftist-

11 Kurd Zana, *Al-Aqaliya al-Kurdiya fi Suriya wa Tabi'atoha al-Ithniya wa Haqouha fi Taqreer al-Maseer* (Sulaimaniyah: Ashti Center for Studies and Research, 2013), 18.

12 Christian Sinclair and Sirwan Kajjo, 'The Evolution of Kurdish Politics in Syria', *MERIP*, 31 August 2011, http://www.merip.org/mero/mero083111.

13 Abdulhamid Darwish, *Adhwa' 'Ala al-Harakah al-Siyasiyeh al-Kurdiya fi Suriya* (Damascus: Private Publisher, 1993), 83.

14 Abdulbaset Seida, *Al-Mas'alah al-Kurdiya Fi Suriya* (Uppsala: Nina Tryckeri, 2003).

progressivist platform of the PUK, defected and formed a group that pledged absolute loyalty to Talabani and his newly established PUK. In Syria, this became the Kurdish Progressive Democratic Party in Syria (PDKS).[15] The PDKS had close ties with the Iraqi PUK, but both viewed themselves as secular leftists dissimilar to Barzani and his traditional conservative ideology.

The PDKS, led by long-time General Secretary Hamid Haji Darwish, presented a cautious approach towards the Kurdish demands in Syria. This was predominantly determined by historical ties between Talabani's PUK and the Assad government, which had granted Talabani amnesty in exchange for some degree of political control in Syria. This, in addition to the PUK's historical connections to Iran, meant that the PDKS often favoured compromise with Damascus over confrontation. As a result, the Syrian government often went after leaders and members of other Kurdish parties such as the KDP-S and smaller parties that had no regional patronage. The PDKS continued this relationship after Hafez al-Assad died in 2000 and his son, Bashar, became president.[16]

13.3.3 PKK, PYD, and YPG

In the late 1980s, the Turkey-based Kurdistan Workers' Party (PKK) infiltrated the Syrian Kurdish society. Building on their reputation as a Kurdish nationalist resistance movement, the PKK developed a set of tempting slogans to liberate and unify Greater Kurdistan (parts of Turkey, Iraq, Syria, and Iran). The presence in Syria of now-jailed, then-exiled Turkish PKK leader Abdullah Ocalan accelerated this recruitment effort. The PKK developed a mutually beneficial relationship with the Syrian government: they were given a safe space to influence the Syrian Kurdish population so long as their activities matched the government's policies towards neighbouring countries and the domestic Kurdish population.[17]

The PKK pumped fresh blood into the arteries of the political life of Syrian Kurds. Its energetic recruitment efforts, based on the allure of a transnational Kurdish resistance movement and organisational discipline, seduced many Kurds, particularly the youth. In the 1980s and

15 Mirani, 103.

16 Abdulhamid Darwish, *Lamhah Tarikhiya ʿAn Akrad al-Jazirah* (Damascus: Private Publisher, 1996), 39.

17 Dimitar Bechev, 'Syria: The Kurdish View', *European Council on Foreign Relation*, 23 June 2013, www.ecfr.eu/article/commentary_syria_the_kurdish_view142.

1990s, many were recruited and dispatched to the Qandil Mountains for training to fight the Turkish government. But the PKK's tough policies towards political rivals, combined with its conspicuous alignment with the Syrian government, meant they quickly lost support among the Syrian Kurdish population. By the late 1990s, outspoken critics began to question the relationship between the PKK and the Syrian government. When the Syrian government gave up PKK leader Abdullah Ocalan to Turkey, the party lost even greater support among Syrian Kurds.[18] Subsequently, the once-strong relationship between the PKK and the Syrian government dramatically deteriorated. Many PKK leaders and cadres based in Syria were now arrested and given long prison sentences.

Once in prison, Ocalan adopted new ideas of nationalism that morphed into a form of egalitarian socialism.[19] Thus, the idea of liberating and unifying Greater Kurdistan, on which the PKK had relied for years to mobilise Kurds and recruit fighters, was now abandoned. Following Ocalan's instructions, the PKK leadership convened with delegates from Syria, Turkey, Iraq, and Iran to discuss the prospects of establishing local parties in each of these countries. The objective was to launch political parties and social groupings that didn't overtly pledge allegiance to the PKK. There were two reasons behind this objective: first, to avoid persecution by ruling governments for associating with the PKK; and second, to put Ocalan's new political theories into practice.

In October 2003, the Democratic Union Party (PYD) was established as the Syrian branch of the PKK. PYD's founding congress was held in Iraqi Kurdistan, with all its newly elected leaders coming from Syrian origins. They were the same individuals who had previously held high-ranking positions within the PKK leadership. One year later, the PYD – under the PKK command – established a military wing for Syrian Kurds called the People's Protection Units (YPG), which remained inactive until early 2012 when the waves of change began to hit the Kurdish region in Syria.[20] From 2003 to 2012, PYD leaders and members continued to resist a fierce Syrian government crackdown as part of the

[18] Tejel, 76.

[19] Abdullah Ocalan, *The Political Thought of Abdullah Ocalan: Kurdistan, Woman's Revolution and Democratic Confederalism* (London: Pluto Press, 2017), 22, 29, 31, 45.

[20] Rodi Hevian, 'The Main Kurdish Political Parties in Iran, Iraq, Syria, and Turkey: A Research Guide', *Rubin Center*, 19 August 2013, www.rubincenter.org/2013/08/the-main-kurdish-political-parties-in-iran-iraq-syria-and-turkey-a-research-guide/.

agreement between Damascus and Ankara that was put in place with the arrest of Ocalan.[21]

13.3.4 *Independents*

By the 1990s, former PKK members and other activists who had broken away from KDP-S started to form their own parties, believing there was a need for independent voices in Syrian Kurdish politics. They mainly believed the Kurdish question needed to be resolved within the boundaries of Syria. Thanks to grassroots recruiting efforts that included protest wall decals and leaflet distribution demanding Kurdish rights, several independent groups took root among Syrian Kurds and garnered a more prominent role on the Kurdish street. These groups included Yekiti (Unity), Azadi (Freedom), and the Kurdish Future Movement. They promoted the concept of Syrian Kurdistan but with key constraints. Civil disobedience and regular protests in Damascus and Qamishli became a pivotal part of their strategy in calling for Kurdish rights and dealing with the Syrian regime. Though initially successful, they were heavily repressed: hundreds were subject to long-term prison sentences, and leading members were threatened, kidnapped, and often arrested.[22]

The popularity of independent parties reached its zenith during a 2004 uprising sparked by the massacre of dozens of Kurds after a soccer match in Qamishli.[23] These independent parties organised massive demonstrations across the country. They also played an important role in organising protests in 2005 after the assassination of Sheikh Mashuq Khaznawi, a popular, open-minded Kurdish cleric. In the early days of the protests, these independent groups were able to take the lead in the agitated streets. Their popularity, however, significantly declined in the wake of a major Syrian government crackdown. Due to their lack of regional benefactors, the independent political parties were the most vulnerable to Syrian government repression.

In October 2011, a well-known Kurdish politician, Michel Tammo, leader of the Kurdish Future Movement, was assassinated inside his Qamishli apartment. Kurdish activists accused the government of

[21] Soner Cagaptay, 'Syria and Turkey: The PKK Dimension', *The Washington Institute for Near East Policy*, 5 April 2012, www.washingtoninstitute.org/policy-analysis/view/syria-and-turkey-the-pkk-dimension.

[22] Sinclair and Kajjo, 2011.

[23] Abdulbaqi Youssef, *Al-Infijar al-Suri* (Sulaimaniyeh: Dar Azzaman for Publishing, 2017), 92, 93.

Tammo's assassination, as he actively demanded regime collapse in Syria and supported the Turkey-based national opposition. As many independent activists were rounded up or fled the country, the reins of power in the Syrian Kurdish community fell into the hands of their competitors, who received increased support from regional benefactors.[24]

13.3.5 The Kurdish Political Spectrum in Syria since the Beginning of the Syrian Uprising

The Syrian uprising threatening to topple Bashar al-Assad's government necessitated the PDKS's change of its compromising position. The move started in early 2011, when party leadership came out with an unprecedented statement condemning the use of violence by the Syrian government against civilian protesters elsewhere in the country. This generated a new policy for the PDK, which had been less critical of the Syrian government during previous crackdowns, such as those following the 2004 Qamishli riots.

In September 2011, the PDKS played a crucial role in helping the KDP-S form the Kurdish National Council (KNC), a quasi-united body consisting of fourteen parties,[25] women's organisations, and youth coordination committees. The PDKS, most popular among Kurdish Syrian urban bourgeoisie, positioned itself as the party of reconciliation during the Syrian civil war. It is also sponsored by the PUK in Iraq, which allows the party to absorb smaller parties that have split from it over the years. Additionally, this move aimed to provide a balance against the growing influence of PKK-supported groups and Barzani-supported groups. Despite this support, the PDKS is not as powerful as the KDP-S, but may gain a significant role in the future should the international community push for negotiations with the Syrian regime.

The KDP-S leads the effort to unify the disparate political parties representing Syrian Kurds. One major example of these efforts is the agreement of most Kurdish political parties to establish the KNC, mentioned in the previous paragraph. The KDP-S has established representative offices in predominantly Kurdish-populated areas in Qamishli,

[24] Zana, 39, 41.

[25] Some of these are: Kurdistan Democratic Party in Syria (KDPS); Kurdish Yekiti Party in Syria; Kurdish Azadi Party in Syria; The Kurdish Reform Movement in Syria; and The Kurdish Future Movement in Syria.

Afrin, and elsewhere and has sponsored several women's, cultural, and youth organisations.[26]

The KNC promises to develop a strong, unified platform for Syria's Kurds and is an advocate for a peaceful resolution to the conflict. The future political success of the KDP-S in Syria will depend on whether its leadership can adapt to rapid changes in the country's political dynamics and respond to the daily needs of Syrian Kurds.

As for the PKK/PYD, the Syrian conflict has presented an enormous opportunity for reacquiring the power it once enjoyed in the 1980s. The well-organised and trained guerrilla resistance movement has taken advantage of the fighting to seize control of major Syrian Kurdish towns and key strategic resources. When Syrian military and security forces voluntarily withdrew from most of the Kurdish areas in July 2012, well-trained fighters affiliated with the PYD took control and became the de facto rulers.

The PYD (and, consequently, the YPG) are widely known as an offshoot of the PKK, even to many Syrian Kurds. They retain their own power base outside the KNC structure set up by Erbil (capital of Iraqi Kurdistan) and oppose the fact that the KNC is heavily influenced by the Kurdistan Regional Government of Iraq (KRG). The PYD stands for a federal state in Syria where Kurds and other ethnic groups enjoy their democratic rights, but it has no problem using historical ties to the Syrian government to strike bargains when convenient.

The PYD has been deeply influenced by the writings of Murray Bookchin, a Marxist-inspired theorist who called for a radical form of grassroots democracy.[27] Bookchin's self-described socialist ideology is taught today in Kurdish classrooms and indoctrinated into YPG recruits.[28]

Although militarily powerful, the PYD struggles to win the hearts and minds of the Kurdish population in Syria. They have tried to provide services to vulnerable Kurdish residents, such as distributing gas tanks and heating oil, but their repressive policies towards independent activists and those affiliated with opposing political parties have resulted in a huge

[26] 'The Kurdish National Council in Syria', Carnegie Endowment for International Peace, http://carnegie-mec.org/syriaincrisis/?fa=48502.

[27] Murray Bookchin, *The Ecology of Freedom* (Palo Alto: Cheshire Books, 1982).

[28] Liz Sly, 'US Military Aid Is Fueling Big Ambitions for Syria's Leftist Kurdish Militia', *The Washington Post*, 7 January 2017, www.washingtonpost.com/world/middle_east/us-military-aid-is-fueling-big-ambitions-for-syrias-leftist-kurdish-militia/2017/01/07/6e457866-c79f-11e6-acda-59924caa2450_story.html?utm_term=.44ac0033a558.

rift between them and the populace. In early July 2013 in the northeastern town of Amude, PYD security forces fired on a demonstration demanding the release of local activists, killing six civilians. This killing escalated the tensions between the PYD and other political parties.[29] The PYD's striving for popular support has waned with their oppressive behaviour; however, defending Kurdish-populated areas such as Ras al-Ayn and Tal Abyad, Kobani, and other areas against extremist groups such as the al-Nusra Front and ISIS means that sympathy from residents persists. Though popular in wartime, the PYD has not developed enough infrastructure as yet to extend its political relevancy in the post-conflict period.

Independent parties in Syria's Kurdish community continue to struggle to retain popularity, particularly without regional political and financial support. Some have resorted to a self-reliance strategy, basing themselves on local capacity and funding. Others have been following a pre-emptive policy of appeasement of both major political poles – the KRG-supported KNC and the PKK-supported PYD/YPG – in order to guarantee their survival. Additionally, independent parties derive most of their support from younger Syrian Kurds who respect their independence and steadfast advocacy for Kurdish aspirations of equality and self-determination.

As a result of these dynamics, two main Syrian Kurdish groups compete for popular support: the KNC and the Democratic Society Movement (TEV-DEM), an alliance that consists of pro-PYD parties.[30] Some parties of the KNC, under pressure from their supporters, created armed wings in early 2012 in order to keep the balance of power in the face of the PYD and its YPG armed wing. Anticipating a possible outbreak of intra-Kurdish violence in July 2012, the Kurdistan Regional Government of Iraq called both groups for an urgent meeting in Erbil. The meeting resulted in the establishment of the Supreme Kurdish Commission, an umbrella for all Kurdish political forces in Syria. Though ambitious, this unification has not met the demands of most mainstream Syrian Kurds. The main reason for this is the rivalry between the PYD and the KNC, which continues to plague the Supreme Kurdish Commission.

[29] 'Under Kurdish Rule: Abuses in PYD-run Enclaves of Syria', *Human Rights Watch*, 19 June 2014, www.hrw.org/report/2014/06/19/under-kurdish-rule/abuses-pyd-run-enclaves-syria.

[30] These parties are: Democratic Union Party (PYD); Kurdish Left Party in Syria; The Kurdistan Green Party; The Democratic Peace Party of Kurdistan; The Star Union.

This imbalance between intended political power-sharing and the fact that the PYD is dominating the political sphere makes it easier for regional powers to derail any attempts at Syrian Kurdish unification. In January 2014, the PYD and its alliance declared a self-rule administration in three Kurdish cantons: Jazira, Kobani, and Afrin.[31] These cantons are run by Ocalan's socialist principles which are inspired by Bookchin's ecological democratic philosophy. The KNC is not part of the canton system and does not recognise its authority. With the YPG's military advances across the region against ISIS militants, the KNC has become increasingly irrelevant on regional and international scales, whereas the PYD has gained more recognition from the West and its US-led coalition against extremist groups in Syria and Iraq.

13.4 Anti-Kurdish Policies by Successive Syrian Governments

In contrast to the flourishing of Kurdish nationalism, successive Syrian governments consistently carried out anti-Kurdish policies. These policies, Kurdish groups argue, were aimed at changing the demography of the Kurdish region, weakening Kurdish nationalism, and assimilating ethnic Kurds into the larger Arab-centric Syria.

13.4.1 Mohammed Talab Hilal's Study

Mohammed Talab Hilal, the Damascus-appointed head of the Political Division in the province of Hasaka and an Arab nationalist, prepared a study for officials in the Damascus government in November 1962 proposing a demographic change in Kurdish-majority Hasaka. Living in the Kurdish heartland for many years, Hilal realised the danger of the growing sense of Kurdish nationalism. The study suggested certain measures which would take effect over a long period of time. These included a displacement campaign in the Kurdish region by which 'dangerous individuals' were to be moved to non-Kurdish cities; the prevention of the establishment of colleges and scientific institutions in the Kurdish region; and stripping citizenship from those carrying

[31] Erika Solomon, 'Amid Syria's Violence, Kurds Carve out Autonomy', *Reuters*, 22 January 2014, www.reuters.com/article/us-syria-kurdistan-specialreport/special-report-amid-syrias-violence-kurds-carve-out-autonomy-idUSBREA0L17320140122.

Turkish citizenship – nearly 100,000 Kurds.[32] The policy recommendation also sought to nationalise Kurdish-owned lands, initiate a large anti-Kurdish propaganda campaign, and institute measures aimed at weakening Kurdish politics and preventing Kurdish political sentiments.[33]

Another important policy recommendation, which was implemented in part, was to place Arab families in Kurdish regions to increase monitoring abilities by the regime and prevent Kurdish expansionist moves. The report suggested to turn the northern border in the Jazira region into a military zone in order to allow further displacement of Kurds.[34]

13.4.2 The Exceptional Census

In 1962, an exceptional census stripped an estimated 120,000 Syrian Kurds – roughly 20 per cent of the Syrian Kurdish population – of their Syrian citizenship. Decree No. 93, signed in August 1962 by then-President of the Republic Nazim al-Qudsi, ordered that a special census be conducted in Hasaka province in north-eastern Syria.[35] The law went into effect, and the census began on 5 October 1962.[36] The exceptional decree included only Kurdish residents in order to amend the civic records, as proposed by Hilal's study. Kurds were the only ethnic group targeted by this census. Consequently, Syria's Kurds were divided into three categories: Kurds who enjoyed Syrian citizenship; Kurds who were stripped of their citizenship and registered in civic records as aliens – commonly known as *Ajaneb* (Arabic for aliens); and Kurds who were stripped of their citizenship and not registered in civic records – called *Maktoumeen*, or hidden. These Kurds had no papers to prove their existence. Technically, they didn't exist.

The exceptional census occurred before the Baath party came to power, at the time of the unity government with Egypt. However, it was perpetuated as the Baathists consolidated their reign in Syria. The Baathists didn't address this issue as a national problem. Instead, they continued treating the Kurds as if they were foreigners. The implementation of the census took only a few months. There are no official figures

[32] Mohammed Talab Hilal, 'Dirasa 'An Muhafazat al-Jazira Min al-Nawahi al-Qawmiya al-Ijtimahiya wa al-Siyasiya', Amude.net, www.amude.net/erebi/mihemed/taleb-hilal-lekolin.pdf (accessed 10 December 2017).

[33] Ibid.

[34] Ibid.

[35] 'Syria – The Silenced Kurds', *Human Rights Watch/Middle East* 8, no. 4 (E) (October 1996): 13, www.hrw.org/sites/default/files/reports/SYRIA96.pdf.

[36] Tejel, 50–1.

detailing how many Kurds live with no citizenship due to this law; however, Kurdish political parties assess there are roughly 300,000 such Kurds. They also estimate that roughly 120,000 Kurds were originally stripped of their citizenship in 1962.[37]

13.4.3 *The Arab Belt*

The Arab Belt was devised by the Baath authority along the border with Turkey in the hopes of changing the demography of the region and creating a buffer between Kurds in Syria and Turkey. The project, planned in 1973, was executed along an area 350 kilometres long and 10–15 kilometres deep. The region of this belt is considered one of the most fertile agricultural lands in Syria.[38]

Law No. 521 was issued by the Syrian branch leadership of the Baath Party on 24 June 1974. Two members of the leadership were appointed to oversee the execution of the law. Members of the Baath branch in Hasaka province, the provincial governor, and police and security forces were also notified.

The process started with confiscating lands from Kurdish landowners and granting them to Arab families who had come from Raqqa and Aleppo provinces. By the end of the process, forty-one Arab settlements were built in the Kurdish region, and 233,000 hectares[39] were given to Arab families at the expense of the Kurds. The government's excuse was that those Arab families needed to be temporarily resettled in the Jazira region because their houses were destroyed as a result of a flood of the Euphrates River.[40]

13.5 Regional and International Stakeholders

Syrian Kurds remained suppressed and marginalised by the Assad regime up until the early weeks of the uprising in 2011. Realising their significant weight in political activism, the regime attempted to placate the Kurds and keep them neutral in the civil war by granting citizenship to some of the thousands of local Kurds whose citizenship had been stripped due to the exceptional census.[41] The Syrian regime also began offering other

[37] Ibid., 53.
[38] Mirani, 209.
[39] Ibid.
[40] Ibid.
[41] 'Syria's Assad Grants Nationality to Hasaka Kurds', *BBC*, 7 April 2018, www.bbc.com/news/world-middle-east-12995174.

incentives, such as a meeting between the Kurdish political leaders and Bashar al-Assad, an offer that was rejected by the Kurds.[42] By doing so, Assad also hoped to keep in check any potential rise of Kurdish nationalism given the anticipated turmoil in the country. The regime indeed succeeded with this until 2014 and the swift rise of ISIS, which brought the Kurds to the attention of the international community.[43]

In September 2014, ISIS launched a major onslaught on the Syrian Kurdish city of Kobani, located on the border with Turkey. YPG fighters, who had been in control of the town, were swiftly overrun by ISIS's offensive. However, they were able to fight back in two remaining districts of the city. The continued resistance of the local Kurdish fighters, coupled with pleas to the international community to intervene to save the city, was one of the reasons that prompted the US-led anti-ISIS coalition to launch an air strike campaign against ISIS in Kobani. In January 2015, Kobani was completely freed from ISIS. From that point on, Kurdish YPG fighters gained the full support of the United States and other allies in their fight against ISIS, particularly in eastern Syria.[44]

The rise of ISIS changed US priorities in Syria, with the United States now considering the elimination of the terror group its main objective. The unlikely alliance between the USA and the YPG paved the way for new dynamics in the war-torn country. For instance, the United States built several military bases in the Kurdish-held north to help its advisers and local Kurdish partners continue their successful campaign against ISIS.[45]

As the war on ISIS dragged on, the partnership between the USA and Syrian Kurds grew, although it has largely remained confined to military cooperation. Kurdish forces continued to press the USA to turn the successful partnership into political recognition, through which they could push for local autonomy. However, the United States has not done so, cautious to not further infuriate its NATO ally, Turkey.

[42] Hamza Hamki, 'Why Kurdish Parties Refused to Meet Assad in 2011: Answering to the Public or Due to Pressure from the Security Apparatus?', *Rok Online*, 8 February 2017, www.rok-online.com/?p=7173.

[43] Katarina Montgomery, 'Kobani Marks the Rising Profile, Prominence and Power of Syria's Kurds', *News Deeply – Syria Deeply*, 22 October 2014, www.newsdeeply.com/syria/articles/2014/10/22/kobani-marks-the-rising-profile-prominence-and-power-of-syrias-kurds.

[44] Susanna Capelouto, 'ISIS Pushed Back With Help of US Airstrikes in Kobani', *CNN Online*, 17 October 2014, www.cnn.com/2014/10/16/world/meast/isis-threat/index.html.

[45] 'US Plans Open-Ended Military Presence in Syria', *BBC*, 18 January 2018, www.bbc.com/news/world-middle-east-42731222.

13.5.1 *Turkey's Lookout*

Turkey opposed the increased American support of the YPG. Ankara views the YPG/PYD as an extension of the PKK and considers it a terrorist organisation. Moreover, Ankara has been frightened by the rise of Kurdish nationalism in the region. While the Kurds controlled much of the Syria–Turkey border, Turkey would continue opposing the establishment of a Kurdish entity in northern Syria, whether it was run by a PKK affiliate or any other Kurdish group. Aimed at mitigating Turkish objections to arming the YPG, the USA helped form a new military entity: the Syrian Democratic Forces (SDF). The SDF, largely dominated by the YPG, was founded in October 2015 and included Arab and Assyrian/Syrian fighters.[46]

The establishment of the SDF was an attempt to rebrand the YPG. Making massive advances against ISIS, the SDF continued to garner more support from their American allies. The longer the war on ISIS dragged on, the more military support the Kurdish-led SDF gained.

Turkey sharply objected to the US bid to arm the SDF offensive on the Sunni Arab–majority Raqqa, ISIS's self-proclaimed capital. Despite the objections, the United States went ahead with its plan, and Raqqa was liberated from ISIS in October 2017. For the first time in Syria's history, Kurdish forces were able to expand their control into non-Kurdish territories.

Ankara is well aware of the changing map of the Middle East. With greater power granted from autonomy in Iraq and de facto freedom in Syria, Kurds are better equipped than ever to tip long-prevailing regional alliances. Yet Turkey is also confident that this would not be possible without Turkish approval or support. In Iraq, Turkey initially opposed the very idea of an autonomous Kurdish entity. However, as Turkey's relationship with Baghdad deteriorated, Erdogan's government proactively sought a more constructive approach with Erbil, the capital of the autonomous Iraqi Kurdistan. Turkey and Iraqi Kurdistan have developed a strong relationship based on mutual economic interests, and the KRG will soon replace Germany as Turkey's most lucrative trading partner. Despite its fierce opposition to the independence referendum that was held by the KRG on 25 September 2017, Turkey maintained ties with Erbil. The Ibrahim Khalil border crossing between Turkey and the KRG

[46] Aron Lund, 'Origins of Syrian Democratic Forces: A Primer', *News Deeply – Syria Deeply*, 22 January 2016, https://www.newsdeeply.com/syria/articles/2016/01/22/origins-of-the-syrian-democratic-forces-a-primer.

was the only outlet that remained open at the height of tensions between Erbil and Baghdad in the aftermath of the controversial vote for Iraqi Kurdish independence.

If the KRG–Turkey scenario is replicated in the case of Syrian Kurds, Turkey will stand to gain in the post-conflict rebuilding process. Yet, Turkey is hedging its bets by building relationships with Islamists and Arab nationalists in Syria as well. These proxies have been active, especially in northern areas where the PYD has strong control. Ankara's leaders have also resorted to diplomacy with KRG leader Massoud Barzani to contain the political rise of Syrian Kurds. Amid deteriorating relations between Ankara and its counterparts in Damascus and Tehran, Barzani and the KRG have emerged as an essential partner for Turkey. What Turkey initially wanted from Barzani was simple: mediate between the PYD and the KNC, and empower those parties deemed moderate by Turkey to take the lead in Syrian Kurdish politics. Yet Barzani did not succeed in keeping this pledge. He could not keep pace with accelerating developments taking place among Syrian Kurds, which helped the Turkish claim that further action will be needed from the outside. Realising this, the Turks are relying on the surrounding Arab perimeter to contain the Syrian Kurds. In addition to Islamist and Arab nationalist rivals to Syrian Kurds, the Turks have employed Arab tribes, who until not long ago were strongly aligned with the Syrian government. Now more closely associating with Turkey, some of these tribes have been used against the Kurds in an attempt to undermine Kurdish ambitions, particularly the PYD.

Realising how difficult it is to use diplomacy to convince the United States and other Western powers to stop supporting the PYD and the YPG, on 20 January 2018 Turkey launched a full-scale offensive against the Kurdish enclave of Afrin in north-western Syria. Using Islamist rebel groups that already have anti-Kurdish sentiments, the Turkish army invaded the Kurdish enclave, hoping to dislodge the PYD/YPG from the region. By doing so, Turkey would finally achieve its goal in separating Afrin from the other two Kurdish enclaves in northern Syria, Kobani and Jazira, and thus dispel the Kurdish dream of creating a contiguous entity in Syria's north.

13.5.2 The Iran Factor

Though vigorously supportive of the Syrian government, Iran hedges its bets on Syrian Kurdistan. Iran is exploring two trajectories to build support among the Syrian Kurdish community. First, through the PKK, Iran is playing on the frustration among commanders with the Ocalan-led peace process in Turkey. Second, Iran is working to ensure the long-term national political viability of the Iraqi Kurdish PUK party, which relies on the Iraqi Shiʾa in Baghdad.

Iran's interests overlap with the PUK in Syria, which sees itself as a revolutionary party. The PUK, based in eastern Iraqi Kurdistan and led by Hero Talabani, the powerful widow of former Iraqi President Jalal Talabani, has long maintained historical ties with Tehran. These ties, reinforced by cross-border trade, have grown as a result of the Barzani–Turkey partnership.

In the Syrian context, the PUK believes Barzani and his party monopolise Kurdish politics under the cover of the KRG. The PUK would like to have a role in the future of Syria and have been working on re-empowering its traditional allies in Syria. For example, during clashes in 2013 near the oil-rich towns of Rumeilan and Ras al-Ayn, a small group of armed PYD men fought side by side with the PDKS against Islamists. Prior to this, the two parties did not have normalised relations. This suggests a growing rapprochement between the PUK and the PKK as a counterweight to the strong Barzani–Turkey alliance in Syria. As much as the PDKS's involvement in those clashes were viewed as symbolic of Kurdish solidarity against Islamists, the PUK continues to favour a PYD dominance in Kurdish politics in Syria, which would ultimately serve as a political victory against its home rival – the KDP-I. However, given the PUK's internal problems, its regional ambitions have naturally weakened. Thus, instead of supporting its traditional ally, the Progressive Party, the PUK has been hedging its bets on continued dominance of the PYD in Syrian Kurdistan.

13.6 Post-War Scenarios

Though the outcome of Syria's conflict is not yet clear, one thing is certain: Syrian Kurds, supported by the transnational networks discussed in this chapter, have an unprecedented opportunity to establish political autonomy. However, regional interests will determine the fate of Syria's Kurdish question. Syrian Kurds are an important constituency in the conflict. A decision on their behalf regarding whether they should support the government or the opposition may determine the fate of the war. Yet, like other opposition groups, Kurdish factions are controlled by competing regional powers.

Geography, political philosophy, and regional patronage have divided Syrian Kurdish politics between those communities based in Erbil and those around Qandil, the stronghold of the PKK. Though the rivalries between these two factions run deep, neither believes the Kurdish community should fully assimilate into a larger Syria. Syrian Kurdish independents championed this position, but they have been marginalised by the armed conflict. At this point, only a small proportion of Syrian Kurds have agendas independent of Erbil and Qandil.

The Syrian Kurds hope that the military gains made by the YPG would translate into international support. This international support, they argue, would help them continue shaping their political autonomy from Damascus. However, once the war on ISIS is over, local Kurds fear that the US support may stop and thus their ongoing project of a federal region in Kurdish-majority areas in north and northeastern Syria may fail.

Regardless of how things unfold in the broader region, Syrian Kurds will continue to play a vital role in shaping the future of Syria. Their strong military presence and nationalist ambitions mean they will continue to be relevant even after the present conflict. Whether Assad's government remains in power or not, Kurds – with their military and political gains accumulated in years of revolution – would have leverage in any future talks on Syria's fate. Their current autonomy may be tentative in a war-ravaged country, but their status as an emerging domestic powerhouse is likely to continue to rise.

14

Epilogue

The Future of Syria and the Middle East

DR KAMAL ALLABWANI, MD

I will never forget the day I decided to devote my life to creating a democratic Syria. In 1976, while studying medicine at Damascus University, I became active in the National Democratic Assembly opposition groups – a forbidden activity at the time. In 1981, at the age of twenty-four, I graduated as an MD, and shortly after I began my mandatory national service as a military physician. At the time, Hama, along with many other Syrian cities, was in turmoil as a result of the conflict between the Baathist regime and the Muslim Brotherhood, which had been leading attacks and protests against the regime. The Syrian army besieged the town for twenty-seven days, continually attacking through bombings and air strikes until the town fell. Roughly 200 residents of Hama were members of the Muslim Brotherhood. Out of 500,000 residents of Hama, 40,000 were killed during the siege. Men between the ages of sixteen and sixty were detained and investigated. It was a massacre and a serious wound to Syrian society.

One month after the massacre I was sent to Hama as a young military physician. My job was supposed to be simple: pass through twenty checkpoints to arrive at the military headquarters in Hama and offer medical care to the Syrian army. My commander once asked me to treat a prisoner who needed care for his bad back. The prison was a converted elementary school building. A hundred people were crammed into what used to be a classroom. Most had signs of torture on their bodies – bruises and cuts. Each person was very sick and needed immediate treatment, but I could only help one person at a time. As each walked towards me, clutching a stomach or an arm, begging for help, I could not bear meeting their eyes.

The once-vibrant city of Hama was razed, reduced to a few lone buildings and structures, its streets now desolate. Walking down empty roads, I saw collapsing structures that were once homes. I saw cafes where men used to drink coffee and play backgammon, now deserted and gutted. I saw playgrounds where children had played, now abandoned due to fear of attack. But mostly I saw the cruelty and brutality of a regime that would stop at nothing to remain in power. These events were the catalyst for my realisation that, without democratic reform, Syria would soon face a civil war.

Following my military service, I became increasingly involved in opposing the Baathist government. I knew I would never feel safe in a country whose government is willing to torture its own people. I recognised that the status quo of fear and violence could not be tolerated any longer. For fifteen years, Syria endured terrible repression, fanaticism, and sectarian hatred. I saw the government destroy civilian life and political activity. Although the world began to change and the Soviet Union came to its end, the Stalinist-style regime in Syria was not affected, even when – for a brief moment – Syria joined the Americans in the Gulf War with the goal of liberating Kuwait.

***

Upon President Hafez al-Assad's death, his son Bashar succeeded him as leader with promises of reform. Along with a group of activists, I established a movement which called for political reforms, as well as the strengthening of civil society and institutions. I played a significant role in what later became known as the 'Damascus Spring' events of 2000–2001.

With Bashar al-Assad's rise to power, many in Syria were hopeful that crucial reforms and steps towards democracy would be enacted. We arranged meetings in our homes where we would discuss a more promising future for Syria. I was arrested for those actions and was first sentenced to three years in prison by the Supreme State Security Court. For the entirety of my sentence, between 2001 and 2004, I was held in solitary confinement.

My time in prison did not hamper my fervour to promote change in Syria. Upon my release, I reached out to Western embassies in Damascus, as I believed foreign aid was necessary to create reform. Encouraged by the Western occupation of Iraq, I founded the Syrian Liberal Democratic Union, which opposed the Assad government and called for democracy and liberalism in Syria. From my experience living and working in Syria, I was certain that the country was barrelling towards a civil war. Fanaticism and sectarianism were increasing, the economic gap between the regime (most of whom were ʾAlawites) and everyone else widened, and corruption became widespread. In 2005, I visited the EU headquarters, England, France, Germany, and the United States. In the USA I was hosted by the International Visitors Program, which provided the opportunity for official meetings in the State Department, Congress, the Pentagon, the National Security Council, and the White House. My goal was to warn the US government that a major conflict was imminent in Syria. I informed them that the issues in Syria could only be solved by dismantling the Assad regime.

The White House, perhaps partially due to my persuasion, declared its support for democratic reform in Syria. I returned to Syria on 7 November 2005 and was promptly arrested in the airport. This time I was sentenced to twelve years in prison by a criminal court and three additional years by a military court. I stayed in prison as a civilian political activist while the situation outside deteriorated, culminating in the street demonstrations of 2011, also called the 'Syrian Spring'. Seven months after the revolution began I was released from prison – a gesture on the part of the regime aimed at pacifying the protesters. However, this has not changed my strong belief that nothing can be accomplished without deposing the regime.

Following demonstrations in Tunisia, Egypt, Libya, and Yemen, the Syrian demonstrations began on 18 March 2011 in Daraa. From there it spread to Homs, Banias, and Deir ez-Zur. It is important to remember that these were peaceful demonstrations, led by advocates for democracy, who had for decades been struggling against the totalitarian rule. Initially, the authorities reacted violently, just as they had in the past. As the security forces and army used increasingly violent methods against the demonstrations, the protesters began to defend themselves using simple weapons. By mid-2011, they were aided by the newly formed Free Syrian Army (FSA) led by defecting officers of the Syrian army. At first, the FSA successfully freed many cities and defeated the Syrian army. The FSA – which was really a collection of local resistance groups – was initially successful not because of particularly good leadership or weaponry but rather due to strong support from the Syrian people. Indeed, the FSA's success changed to failure once the regime altered its strategy, waging war against the Syrian people. Foreign militias and forces and mainly forces supported by Iran and Hezbollah were welcomed into the country. Chemical weapons and other arms were used, and countless innocent civilians were detained, imprisoned, and executed. The terror that was shown by government and pro-government forces prompted massive displacement and immigration.

Local rebels began to lose traction due to weapons shortages and waning social support. For some, their last remaining means of sustaining the fight was to unite themselves under the Islamist groups who were able to gain some support from their own proxy funders. This, however, had further propelled the chaos as the battle became crueller, with both sides, the regime and the rebels, more powerful than before. The different groups began to pit themselves against each other, with the bleeding and suffering civilians caught in the middle, neglected by the belligerents. International powers regarded the situation in Syria solely as an issue of security, while struggling with the humanitarian crisis unfolding which was sending floods of refugees to neighbouring countries and to the EU.

During this period, those international leaders who were politically aligned with Syria preferred to believe the regime's claims that it was 'fighting terrorism' and not its own people. Moreover, terrorist organisations pose a threat to other countries. Therefore, other countries were more inclined to intervene in the fight against the terrorist elements, namely ISIS. However, for those of us who supported the push for democratic reform in Syria, it appeared that these terrorists, namely ISIS and the al-Nusra Front, were colluding with the Syrian government and Iran or at least providing another reason for Assad and his allies to continue the fight against his own people.

Upon my release from prison at the end of 2011, I realised that Syria needed support from Western countries to prevent a full-blown civil war from breaking out. This realisation led me to flee Syria, and I was granted political asylum in Sweden. As a member of the Syrian National Council, and later the coalition, I attempted to dissuade the opposing organisations from their Islamic affiliation. However, this proved to be difficult, since their support came from the Muslim Brotherhood and particularly the Gulf states and Turkey. I also tried, and failed, to convince Western ambassadors to revise their approach to the conflict and heed my warning of terrorism. Aside from diplomatic rhetoric, we saw no international intervention in 2013. This was a lost opportunity as thereafter the situation became too complicated to manage. I resigned from all opposition councils when I believed we were losing everything in the beginning of 2014.

Currently, the regime is stronger than ever, to the point where it may seem as though we have entered a never-ending, intractable conflict. Unfortunately, Assad's sweeping victories could have been obstructed. The United States chose to concentrate on stopping the spread of ISIS and, by doing so, provided indirect support to the regime rather than fighting Assad's brutality. The fear of attacks by ISIS and the wave of terrorism which overtook Europe made it easy to ignore the well-documented human rights abuses of the Assad regime, focusing solely on combating terrorism. Russia has always been a loyal ally of the Syrian regime and certainly when the Syrian war became more complicated. Russia was invited to further intervene under the guise of fighting the Russian-speaking ISIS members, but it in fact desired to bolster the Assad regime and increase its own influence in the Middle East. Iran, another loyal ally, joined the fray to support Assad and counter the Sunni majority with a motivation of increasing Shiʾa influence and solidifying its presence in the area and in proximity to the Israeli border. In response to this development, I visited Israel to hear the Israeli perspective on Syria, as we have similar concerns about the behaviour of Assad and Iran.

I regret to conclude that the revolution, at least for now, has failed. The Syrian people were defeated and the war was won for the Assad regime with the help of Russia and Iran. This victory strengthens the dictatorial axis in the Middle East and a radical agenda that seeks to further destroy the allies of Western civilisation.

***

My vision for Syria is one I have fought for, been imprisoned for, and for which I have been exiled. It is of a democratic Syria, one with equal rights for all citizens, one where the government has checks on its power – one where Syria gains its economic independence and sees the return of its people, who had to flee during this time of war. This vision may appear a dream at the moment – a moment when the uprising is practically defeated – but visions begin as dreams and dreams can live even when reality does not match them.

Syria presently is a failed state plagued by economic, societal, and political collapse. It must be rebuilt promptly to maintain regional security. However, the new Syria cannot simply be a facsimile of the old state, with the same leaders and societal structures; it must have a new economy, a more open culture, and a liberal democracy.

Syria is not an isolated entity in the Middle East; its neighbouring countries are involved in and affected by its actions. Syria is crucial to peace in the region. Despite the obvious difficulties involved in its restoration, I sought to see Syria as a pilot model for its neighbours. It could set a positive example for the tumultuous region.

For the past several decades, the Middle East has been afflicted by wars and terrorism, with cities and towns decimated and depopulated.

A strategy such as the US Marshall Plan for Europe – financing Europe with $13 billion after World War II – is most advisable in the Middle East to increase economic opportunities, starting with Syria as a model. The money must be transferred directly to civilians as opposed to being allocated through the government, which would probably misuse it. Although this plan requires a major upfront investment, like all foreign aid it will ultimately pay for itself. Think of Japan and Germany: after US capital flooded their countries, they became two of the biggest trading partners for the United States.

Syria already has natural resources, such as oil, that can be utilised by foreign investors and companies. This, under a different trajectory of events, could have jumpstarted Syria's economic growth. But Syria does not only need cash and investments; it needs ideas and technology. Assistance from Israel, for example, could be crucial in spurring innovation in Syria. Despite its shortage of natural resources, Israel has managed to build an economy based on technology. In the new, globalised economy, ideas will be more important than resources. Imagine if Israeli innovators could bring their technology to Syria and mentor young Syrians in developing new ideas. This could help Syria adapt to the new world economy and ensure cooperation and peace between the two countries and the region at large.

A strengthened economy would not only contribute to regional stability but also help with some of Syria's cultural issues. For example, it will alleviate the refugee crisis. Many have fled the Middle East in search of economic opportunities in Europe. If the Middle East can become an economic powerhouse, many economic refugees will want to return to their homes and reap the benefits, which will in turn expedite Syria's recovery. Additionally, a 'Marshall Plan' would combat extremism. Many disaffected youths turn to terrorism and extremism in reaction to stagnation and lack of opportunities. By ensuring that all citizens have the ability to make a living wage, we can vastly limit the spread and appeal of terrorism.

Many of the refugees who will return to Syria will have now lived abroad for almost five years. In refugee camps, some came in contact with extremists, those calling for a radical interpretation of Islam and for the death of the West. However, they will also have seen life in Europe: the egalitarianism, equality, and secularism. We must rebuild Syria's culture to adapt to the needs of returning refugees.

Another critical component is a movement within Syria to reform Islam. Radical and absolutist conceptions of Islam played a major part in this war, both in Syria and, later, beyond, as refugees had taken some of these influences with them to Europe. We need to encourage the reading of the Quran through a literary rather than scientific lens, by reading the parables as allegory rather than indisputable fact. We need to connect with the core of Islam – a religion which preaches compassion, charity, and kindness.

To ensure that hard-line Islamist thought does not pervade the new Syrian republic, we must carefully monitor mosques to prevent potential funding by outside groups promoting radical agendas. We must be well acquainted with what mosques are preaching in order to combat negative teachings. Mosques need to be directed by moderates to spread moderate ideas and concepts. To counteract the funding of extremist mosques and imams, religious leaders who understand the true nature of Islam, a religion of peace and tolerance, should receive funding so they can hold talks and release books with their interpretations of the Quran. They will be prepared to answer hard questions about Islam. This funding of moderates will create an attractive alternative to hardliners and extremists.

In keeping with this, Syria's re-creation must include a liberal and open culture with freedom of thought and ideas. The Syrians who are returning home will have seen this model in the West and will be anxious to implement it in their new country. However, we cannot ask people to abandon their religion and morals in favour of total liberalism. We need to provide Syrians with the tools to have a freer culture, one that has been reconciled with the collective cultural morals and ethics of Islam.

Implementation of international law is fundamental to Syria's rebirth. If major powers such as Russia and Iran – powers who support the regime and its proxies – continue to handicap Syria's freedoms, Syria will continue to be a source of violence and war. Under the rule of Assad and the Syrian/Iranian reinforcement, it is clear that voices of reform and change will not be allowed to operate. We cannot overcome the negative influence of such countries without the support of responsible democracies such as the United States and the EU. A coalition of these powers, aimed at defeating terrorist organisations such as ISIS and Hezbollah, can help Syrian civilians regain their homeland. Syrians themselves are essential in countering terrorism and foreign armies to attain peace.

The aforementioned potential international coalition would need to create a transition period, during which Syria can put an end to violence and start rebuilding civil society. Syria's new government must be democratic to limit conflict and guarantee equal representation of all citizens, including the many minorities who reside within its borders. Additionally, many Syrians returning from the European Union will be expecting a democratic government, having been accustomed to such in Europe. A strong Syrian identity, based on positive sentiments towards the state rather than rooted in sectarianism or tribalism, will assure a cohesive government. We must capitalise on the shared excitement felt during the uprising's early days, when Syrians were united in hope of a better future.

Syria cannot be a nation state that is based on an old, irrelevant revolution; Syria must be a constitutional state, its identity connected to the land and its people with both minority and majority ethnic groups in positions of power. Prior to the conflict, the vast majority of military positions and political positions were held by ʾAlawites. This led to a widespread feeling of disenfranchisement, as well as a disdain for ʾAlawites. Careful steps must be taken to ensure that the division of positions of power between the different sects in Syria better reflect its diverse demographics. Accordingly, Sunni Muslims, who constitute a majority within Syria, must be represented accordingly. The most effective way to guarantee all voices are heard is to institute a full democratic federal system. This way, all people will be able to choose leaders that most accurately represent them and their views.

This vision appears distant at present and perhaps lost at this phase of the war. In fact, much of what I wrote here – consistent with what I had called for since the beginning of the war – has not materialised. The trajectory of events could have been different if the West were to assume responsibility and offer a different degree of intervention, enabling a progress that would have been welcomed by the majority of Syrian people. Unfortunately, at the moment, we will likely not see the birth of a more democratic Syria. Rather, we are witnessing an end for much of the hope that still remains amongst those who marched in the Arab Spring of 2011. This hope had died with the Syrian war, expelled from the country and left with few friends in world. Nevertheless, I am a believer in my country and people, and I believe in hope which one day might be reignited.

15

Conclusion

HILLY MOODRICK-EVEN KHEN, NIR T. BOMS, AND SARETA ASHRAPH

As of this writing, the political reality of a post-conflict Syria is beginning to take shape. The nearing end of the conflict is defining winners and losers as well as an 'emerging endgame' capable of maintaining a degree of stability in a war-torn country. However, justice for the Syrian people who have borne the brunt of the war remains, for now, out of reach.

It is always a risky exercise to summarise chapters in history, especially in the absence of historical perspective. Nevertheless, this recent long and bloody conflict provides insights not only into the Syrian machine and mosaic but also into the nature of war in the twenty-first century, the politics of nations, and the role and limitations of the international system as it struggles to exercise its responsibility to protect and bring to justice those accountable for crimes which are a shock to the human conscience.

This book analysed some of the key dimensions of the Syrian conflict. It classified the belligerents and their associated camps and defined their legal responsibilities; it provided analysis of both the Syrian government's responsibility for some of the key violations committed within the conflict and other warring parties' liability for those crimes, including foreign and proxy stakeholders who became an integral part of this conflict.

The interdisciplinary approach pursued in this book provided us with various perceptions of the conflict and its implications. It is the combination of scholars and practitioners of different academic disciplines, working in different parts of the world, that facilitated and enriched the answers to the questions we posited in the beginning of the research; in addition, this interdisciplinary scholarship offered a broader perspective on issues that are often controversial and, at times, ideological or political.

Part I of the volume, which introduced the factual and legal framework of the conflict, directed us through the conflict's evolution, its changing, multifaceted character, and its growing number of belligerents and their supporters. It also provided clearer understandings of the scale of atrocities, the seeming inability of the international community to prevent or punish them, and the reasons for the conflict's deterioration and aggravation. This section also addressed the lacuna in the current legal and political framework in overcoming the bloodshed and laying responsibility upon those accountable for core international crimes.

As we widened our field of view outside Syria and towards its neighbours in Part II, we focused on the grave implications and spillover of the conflict. The Syrian war generated shockwaves of influence in the region, most notably in the form of an enormous number of refugees and IDPs (estimated to comprise half of Syria's pre-conflict population). The refugees fled into neighbouring states and beyond, mainly into Europe. Yet most of the states that accepted them were largely unprepared to address their plight. The analysis of the Syrian neighbourhood also examined the interests and actions of some adjacent stakeholders – mainly Iran, Hezbollah, Israel, and Jordan – and their role in influencing the direction of the conflict. Clarifying the multiple agendas and motivations of these different actors shed additional light on the development of the Syrian war. It also emphasised how the Syrian people fell victim to a proxy war and an expanding conflict which focused on the pre-conflict power structure in Syria and caused much of its frailty.

In Part III we looked beyond the events of the conflict to address some questions regarding its aftermath. As the conflict has not yet been fully resolved, questions of justice and accountability remain open. Although trajectories for processes of transitional justice and reconciliation were explored in this section, it appears that the key stakeholders are far from adopting such frameworks at the present.

The frictions between the different groups composing Syrian society – the Alawite minority versus the Sunni majority; Islamists against secularists; and tensions between and among other minority and religious groups – have deepened the Syrian crisis and redefined power relations within it. The post-war reality paints Syria in different colours in terms of its political structure, demography, and foreign influences. In this context we focused on the Kurdish case which, unlike other minority groups, emerged from the conflict somewhat victorious, asserting features of independence and demonstrating successes in keeping communal cohesion. The Kurdish gain, however, remains precarious since, like other groups in Syria, the Kurds are also subjected to the power-structure dynamics and to stakeholders who seek to weaken their gains.

As the analysis of the conflict was completed for the scope of this volume, many indeterminacies remained. They include, among others, the shape and form of the emerging political structure of Syria – that is, how independent its government will be and whether any degree of autonomy will be given to the various groups composing the state, how the refugee crisis will be resolved, and whether international justice could be achieved. Yet the conclusions of the volume portray guidelines for political or legal attempts that will be made to resolve those indeterminacies. It is the mapping and analysis of how the fundamental norms of the international community were brutally violated and the difficulties of restoring justice at the moment, while also elaborating on the developments within the political arena in which all of these events take place, that provide keys for coping with the challenges that both Syria and the international community are and will be facing.

The emerging post-war reality in Syria emphasises the victors' role in shaping Syria's future. However, while the Syrian government seems to have formally won the war, the real victory – however temporary or indecisive it may be – belongs to those who facilitated it, mainly Russia and Iran and, to a lesser extent, Turkey: all of these states now share de facto control of the Syrian state. It appears that these victors will likewise play a major role in shaping the new Syrian reality and in the efforts for reconstructing the devastated country. Other stakeholders, including the United States, the Western alliance, and the United Nations, will likely have a much smaller influence, despite the efforts they invested in changing the course of the war.

Talks regarding the future of Syria were held throughout the years of the conflict, including different states and the international community and taking place in various locations including Turkey, Jorden, Geneva, Cairo, and elsewhere in the West. Yet only the talks in Astana, Kazakhstan, which began in 2017, and the talks in Sochi, held in May 2018, have resulted in some practical suggestions for the future of Syria. These talks have likewise highlighted that Russia is the most influential factor in determining future developments in Syria and the reconstruction of the state's political mechanisms and administration.

In May 2018, President Putin met with President al-Assad and presented a framework for Syria's future: the Syrian constitution will be amended so as to confer more rights upon the different sects in Syria (Russian jurists will be sent to assist the Syrian government with adding these amendments); Russia should attain more franchises for Russian corporations and companies (at the expense of Iranian companies) that will be involved in the reconstruction of Syria; and lastly, Russia demanded that Iran will limit its military involvement in Syria, a positive development for Israel, the neighbour and foe whose interests and involvement in the conflict have been discussed in this volume.

While Russia's suggested trajectory for restructuring Syria allegedly leads Syria in a more pluralistic direction, it is clear, as concluded in Dr. Kamal Allabwani's epilogue, that the opposition groups and those who began the rebellion against the Syrian government are far from interested in adopting this imposed foreign framework, as are most of the other factions of Syrian society. For these objectors, the nature of the despotic regime has only been strengthened by its new allies. More so, the post-war reality further weakens Syrian society and renders Syria much more of a proxy state than it was before the war began.

While it appears that Syria has survived the war as a consolidated state and that it will not be divided or dissolved into several entities, it is still too early to predict whether the current emerging political framework for Syria will survive in the long term. As we write these lines, the Syrian government does not effectively control all of Syrian territory, which renders the situation in Syria fragile and unstable. Foreign forces – Russians, Iranians, Americans, and Turkish – as well as a plethora of foreign militias are still present in the country and have influence on some key territories. Some of these forces, mainly those pro-Iranian, were even integrated into the Syrian security apparatus, which strengthened their influence over the Syrian government and diluted the government's control over them.

As we begin to conclude this grave tragedy – and, in many ways, the most tragic episode in the modern history of the Middle East – we have seen another international failure to prevent a mass calamity and to protect those millions of innocent civilians who fell victim to a web of cynical and political interests of the leading world powers and other stakeholders. Unfortunately, it appears that the international community has, so far, been unable to deliver post-conflict justice. Despite the establishment of the UN International, Impartial and Independent Mechanism to assist in the investigation of international crimes in Syria, criminal or other processes of defining accountability for the crimes committed in the conflict have not been exerted. Irrespective of the developments within Syria, it is already clear that the implications of this conflict will accompany us for years to come, and it is not unthinkable that a new chapter of this war will be ignited again in the future.

INDEX